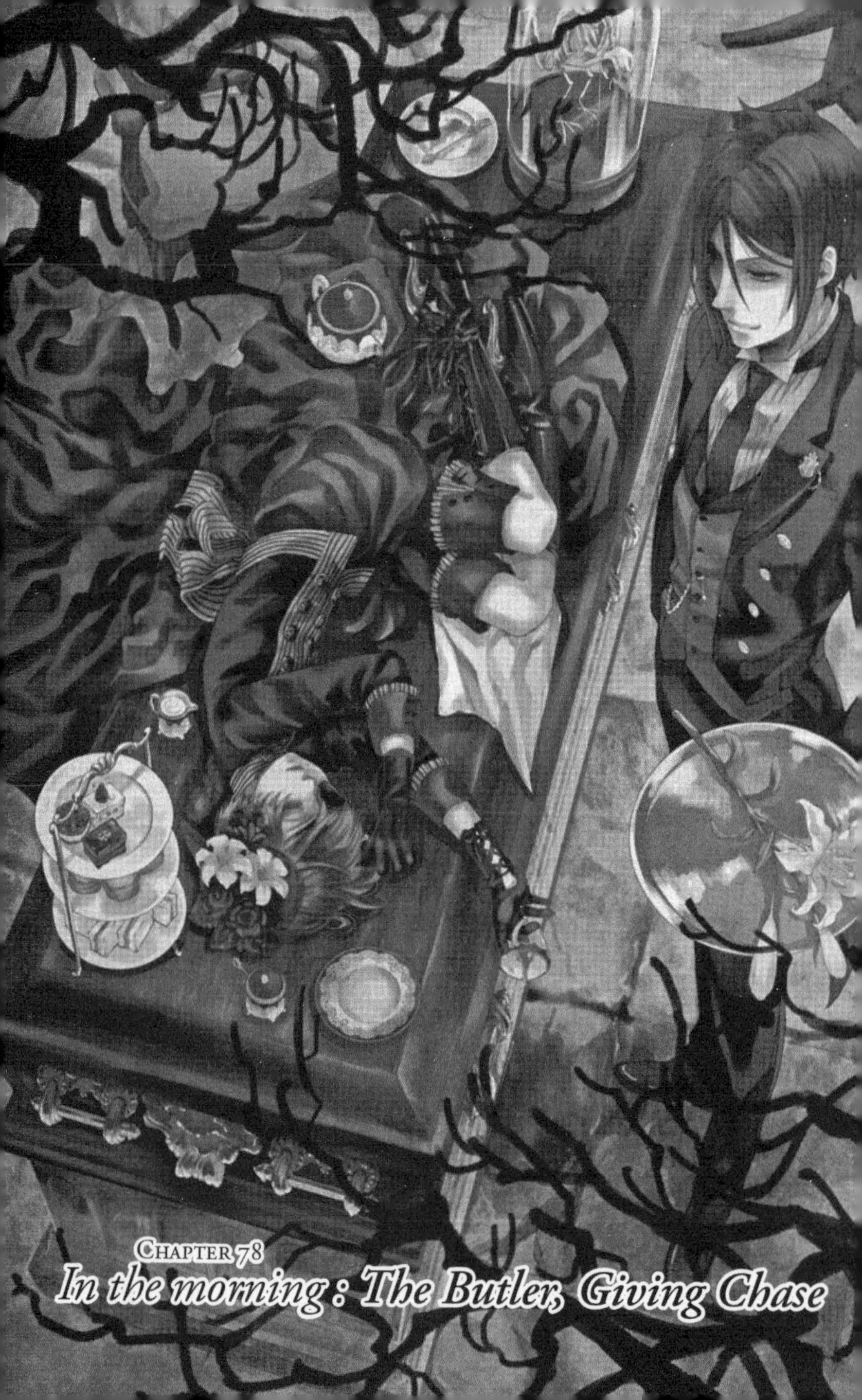

Chapter 78
In the morning : The Butler, Giving Chase

Black Butler

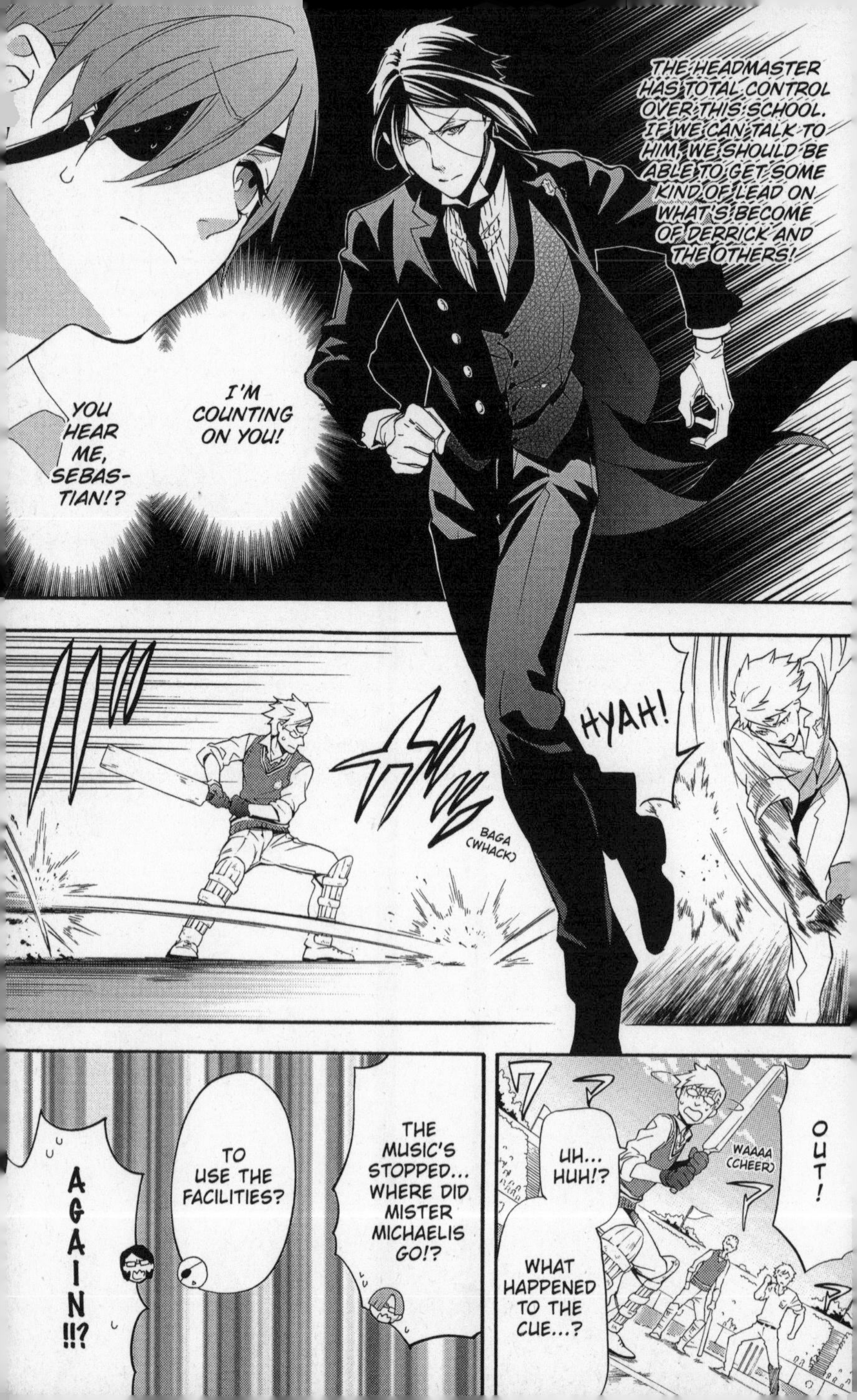
THE HEADMASTER HAS TOTAL CONTROL OVER THIS SCHOOL. IF WE CAN TALK TO HIM, WE SHOULD BE ABLE TO GET SOME KIND OF LEAD ON WHAT'S BECOME OF DERRICK AND THE OTHERS!
I'M COUNTING ON YOU!
YOU HEAR ME, SEBAS-TIAN!?
HYAH!
BAGA (WHACK)
OUT!
WAAAA (CHEER)
UH... HUH!?
WHAT HAPPENED TO THE CUE...?
THE MUSIC'S STOPPED... WHERE DID MISTER MICHAELIS GO!?
TO USE THE FACILITIES?
AGAIN!!?

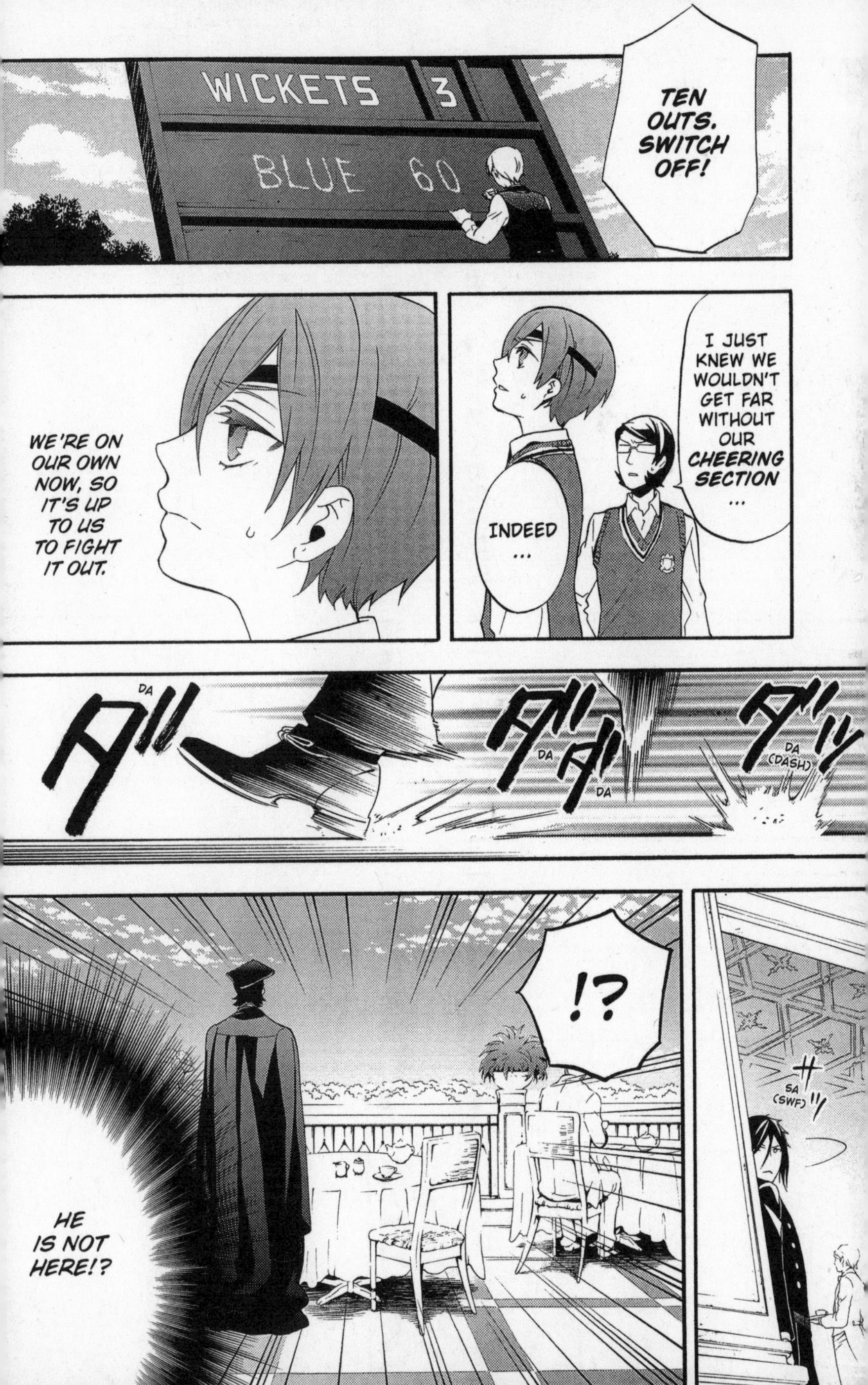
TEN OUTS. SWITCH OFF!
WICKETS 3
BLUE 60
I JUST KNEW WE WOULDN'T GET FAR WITHOUT OUR CHEERING SECTION ...
INDEED ...
WE'RE ON OUR OWN NOW, SO IT'S UP TO US TO FIGHT IT OUT.
DA (DASH)
DA
DA
DA
SA (SWF)
!?
HE IS NOT HERE!?

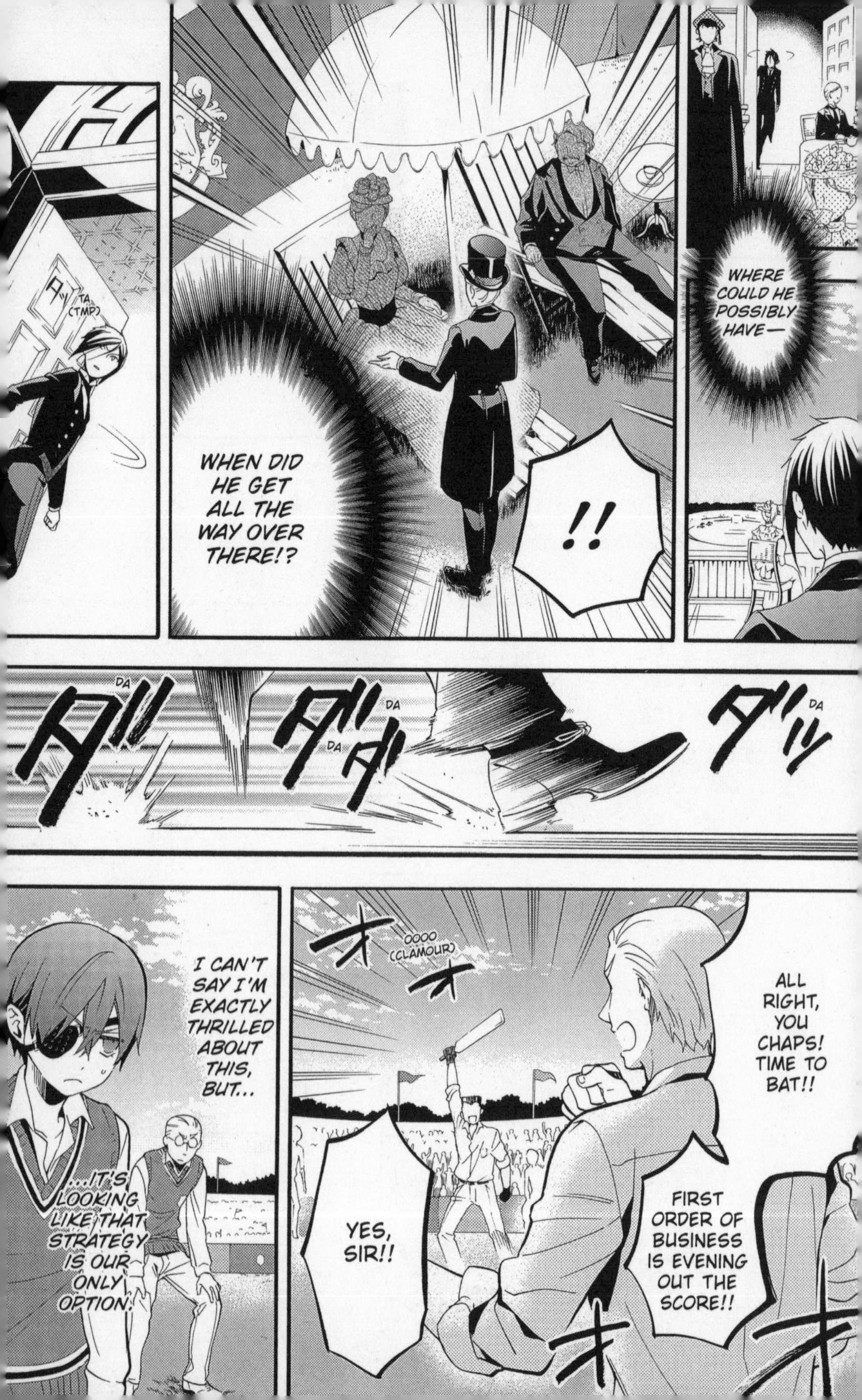
WHERE COULD HE POSSIBLY HAVE—
!!
WHEN DID HE GET ALL THE WAY OVER THERE!?
TA (TMP)
DA
DA
DA
DA
ALL RIGHT, YOU CHAPS! TIME TO BAT!!
OOOO (CLAMOUR)
FIRST ORDER OF BUSINESS IS EVENING OUT THE SCORE!!
YES, SIR!!
I CAN'T SAY I'M EXACTLY THRILLED ABOUT THIS, BUT...
...IT'S LOOKING LIKE THAT STRATEGY IS OUR ONLY OPTION.

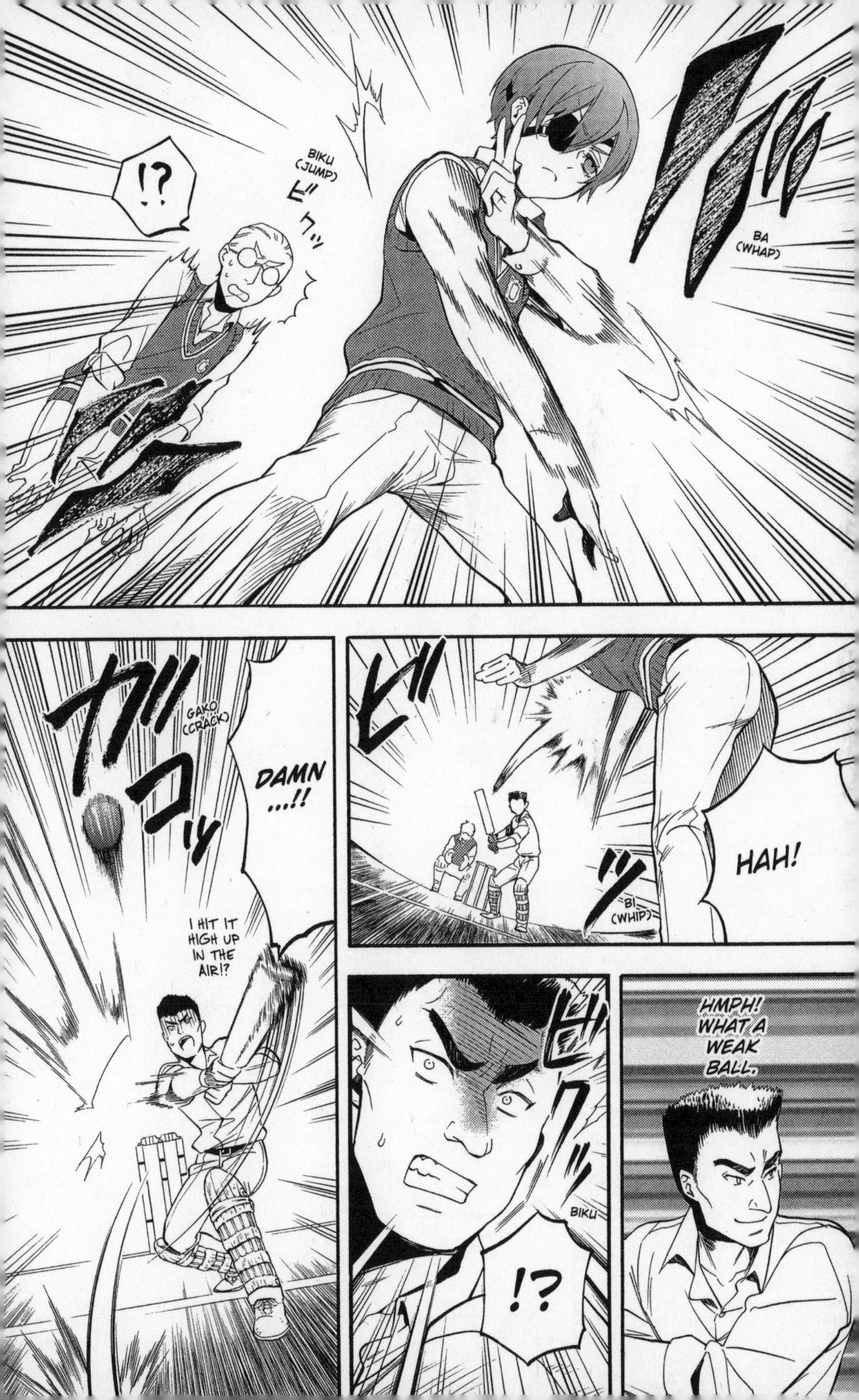

BA (WHAP)
BIKU (JUMP)
!?
HAH!
BI (WHIP)
HMPH! WHAT A WEAK BALL.
BIKU
!?
GAKO (CRACK)
DAMN ...!!
I HIT IT HIGH UP IN THE AIR!?

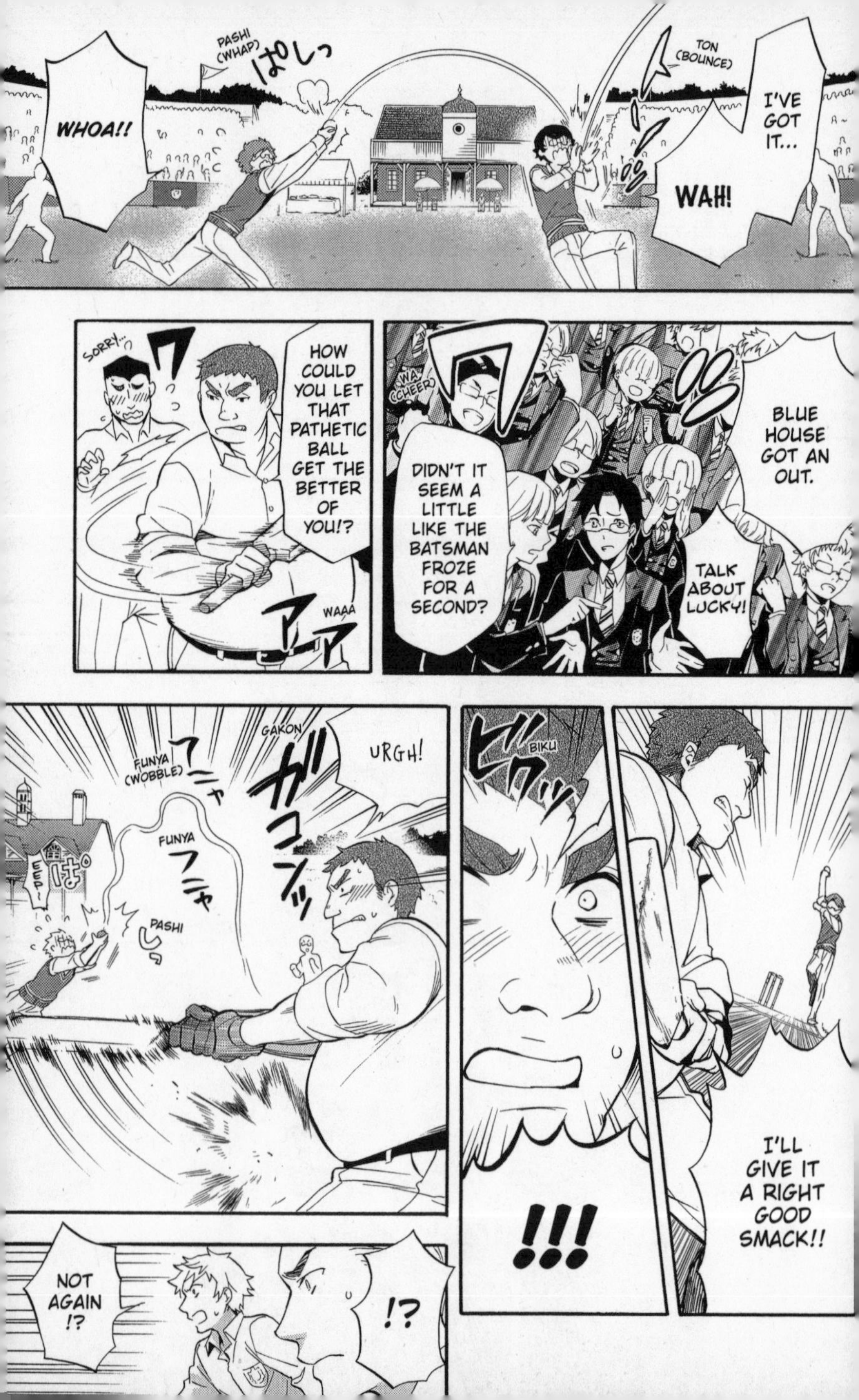
TON (BOUNCE)
I'VE GOT IT...
WAH!
PASHI (WHAP)
WHOA!!
BLUE HOUSE GOT AN OUT.
WA (CHEER)
DIDN'T IT SEEM A LITTLE LIKE THE BATSMAN FROZE FOR A SECOND?
TALK ABOUT LUCKY!
HOW COULD YOU LET THAT PATHETIC BALL GET THE BETTER OF YOU!?
SORRY...
WAAA
I'LL GIVE IT A RIGHT GOOD SMACK!!
BIKU
!!!
URGH!
GAKON
FUNYA (WOBBLE)
FUNYA
PASHI
EEP!
!?
NOT AGAIN !?

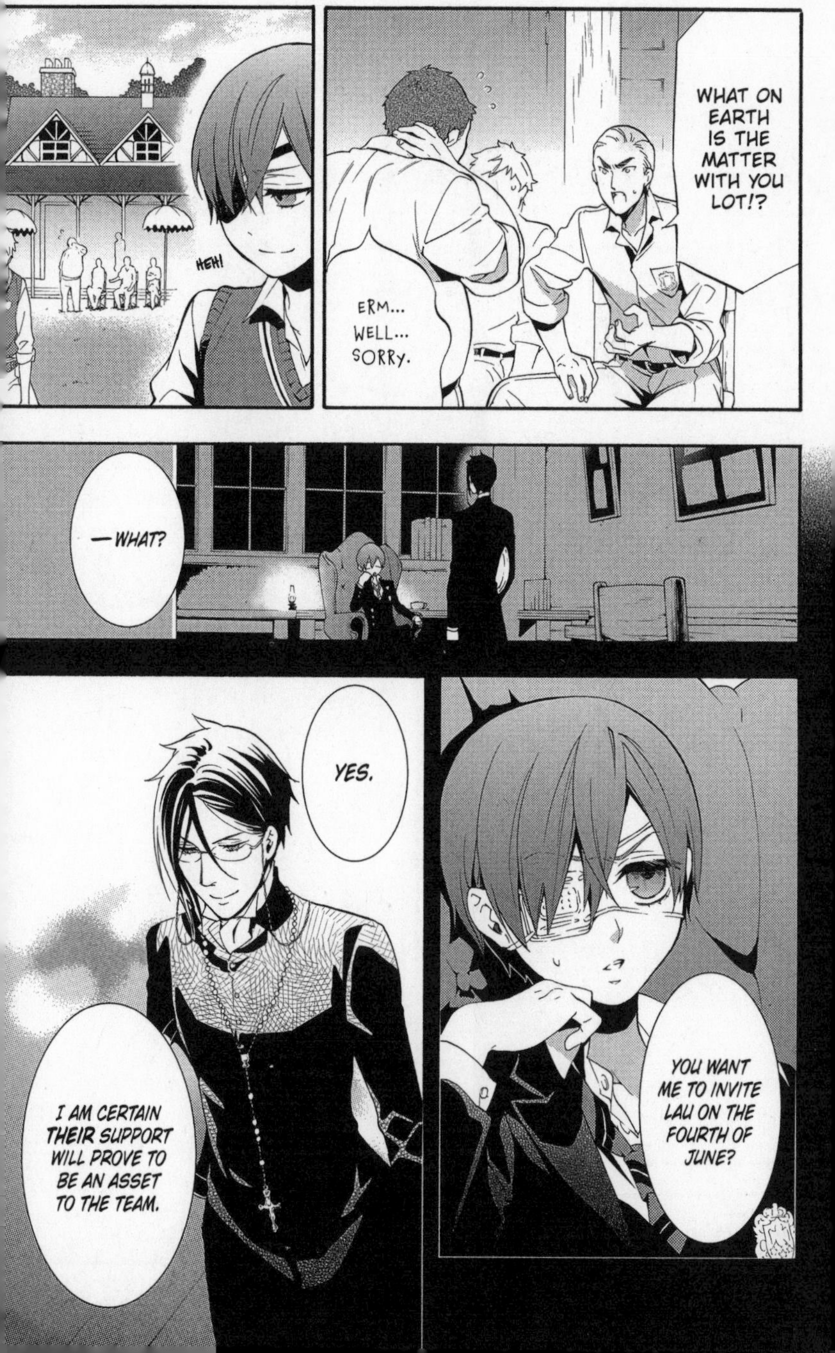
WHAT ON EARTH IS THE MATTER WITH YOU LOT!?
ERM... WELL... SORRY.
HEH!
—WHAT?
YOU WANT ME TO INVITE LAU ON THE FOURTH OF JUNE?
YES.
I AM CERTAIN THEIR SUPPORT WILL PROVE TO BE AN ASSET TO THE TEAM.

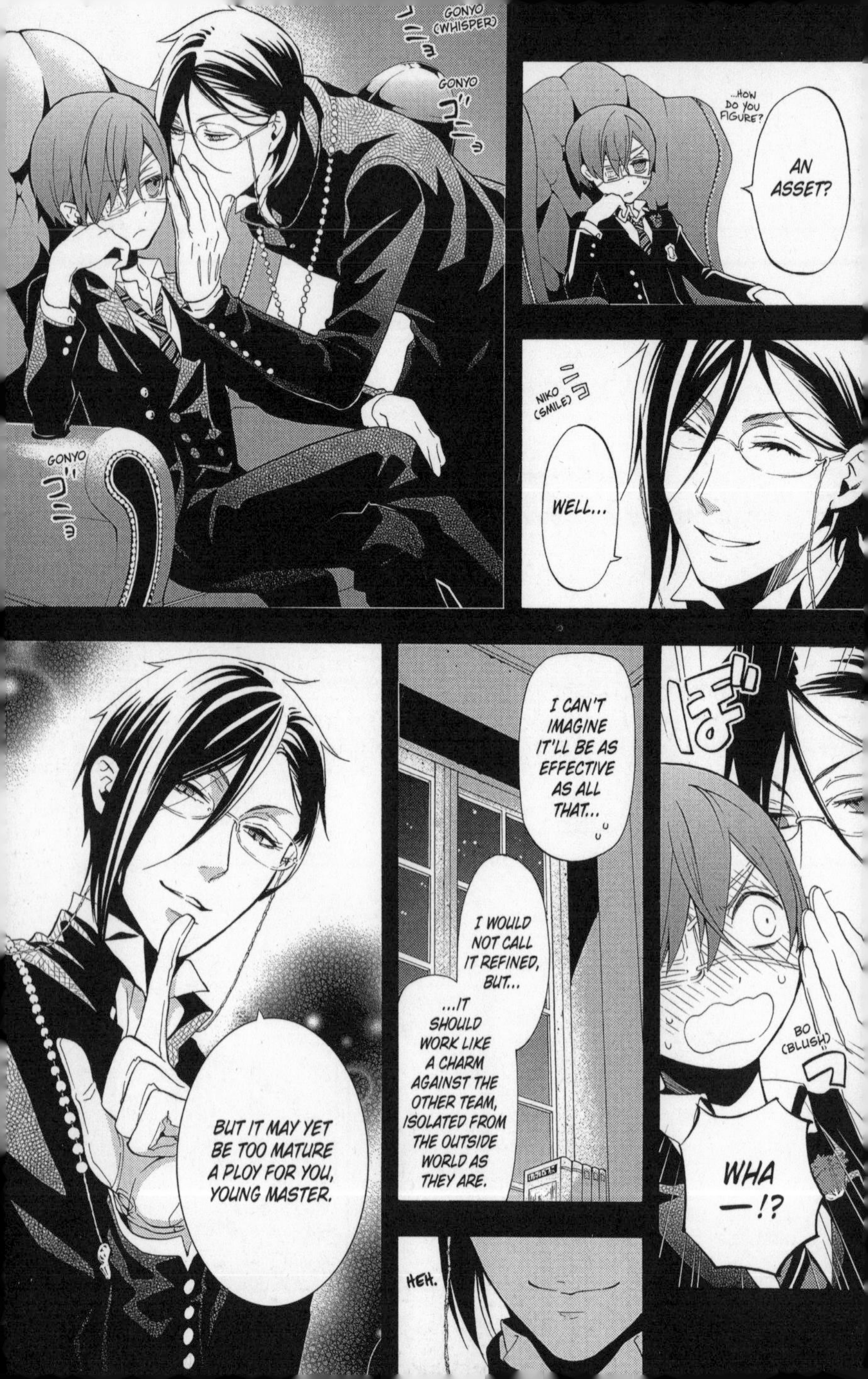
...HOW DO YOU FIGURE?
AN ASSET?
ニコ
NIKO (SMILE)
WELL...
ゴニョ
GONYO (WHISPER)
ゴニョ
GONYO
ゴニョ
GONYO
ぼっ
BO (BLUSH)
WHA—!?
I CAN'T IMAGINE IT'LL BE AS EFFECTIVE AS ALL THAT...
I WOULD NOT CALL IT REFINED, BUT...
...IT SHOULD WORK LIKE A CHARM AGAINST THE OTHER TEAM, ISOLATED FROM THE OUTSIDE WORLD AS THEY ARE.
HEH.
BUT IT MAY YET BE TOO MATURE A PLOY FOR YOU, YOUNG MASTER.

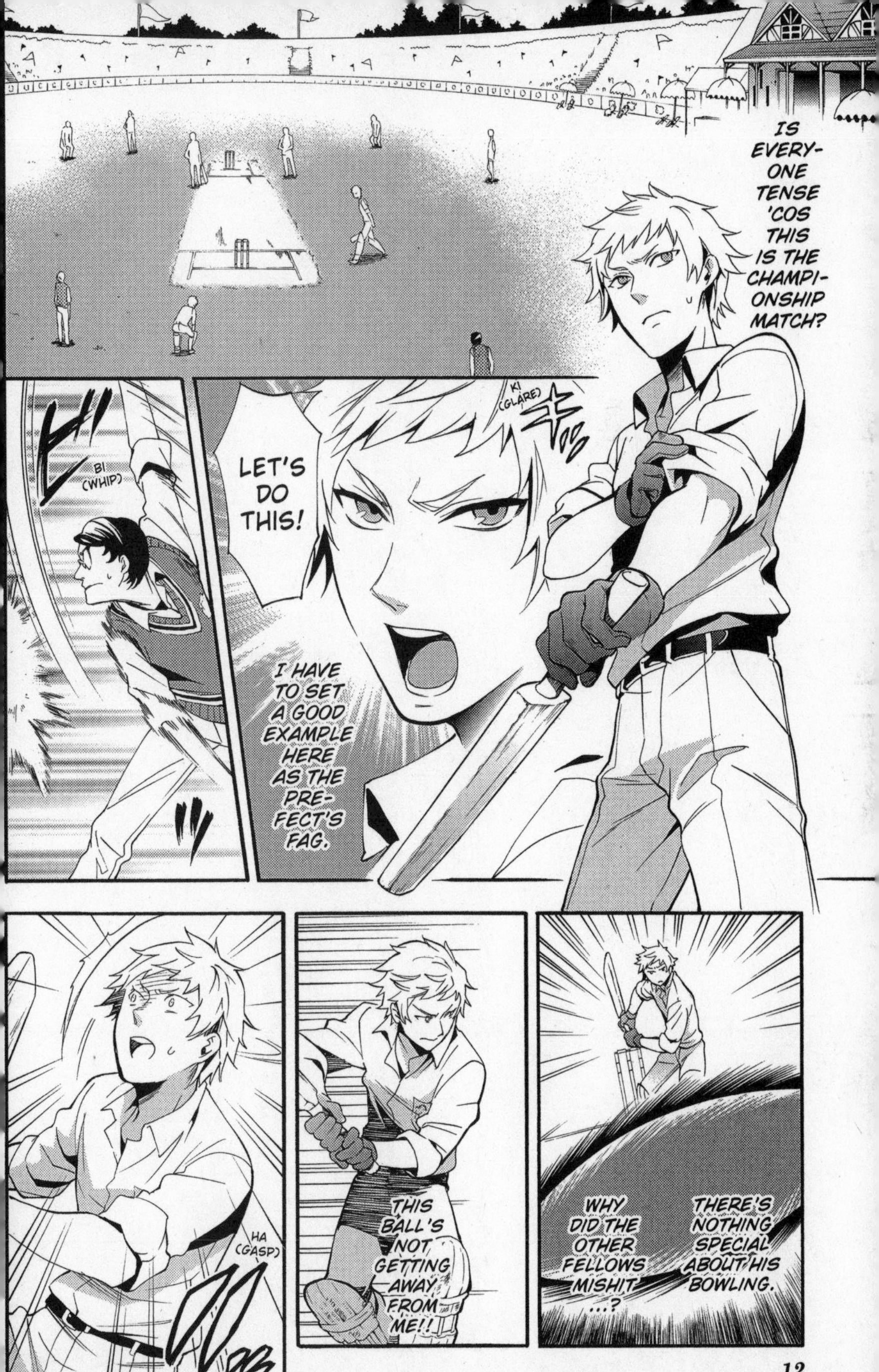
IS EVERYONE TENSE 'COS THIS IS THE CHAMPIONSHIP MATCH?
KI (GLARE)
LET'S DO THIS!
I HAVE TO SET A GOOD EXAMPLE HERE AS THE PREFECT'S FAG.
BI (WHIP)
THERE'S NOTHING SPECIAL ABOUT HIS BOWLING.
WHY DID THE OTHER FELLOWS MISHIT ...?
THIS BALL'S NOT GETTING AWAY FROM ME!!
HA (GASP)

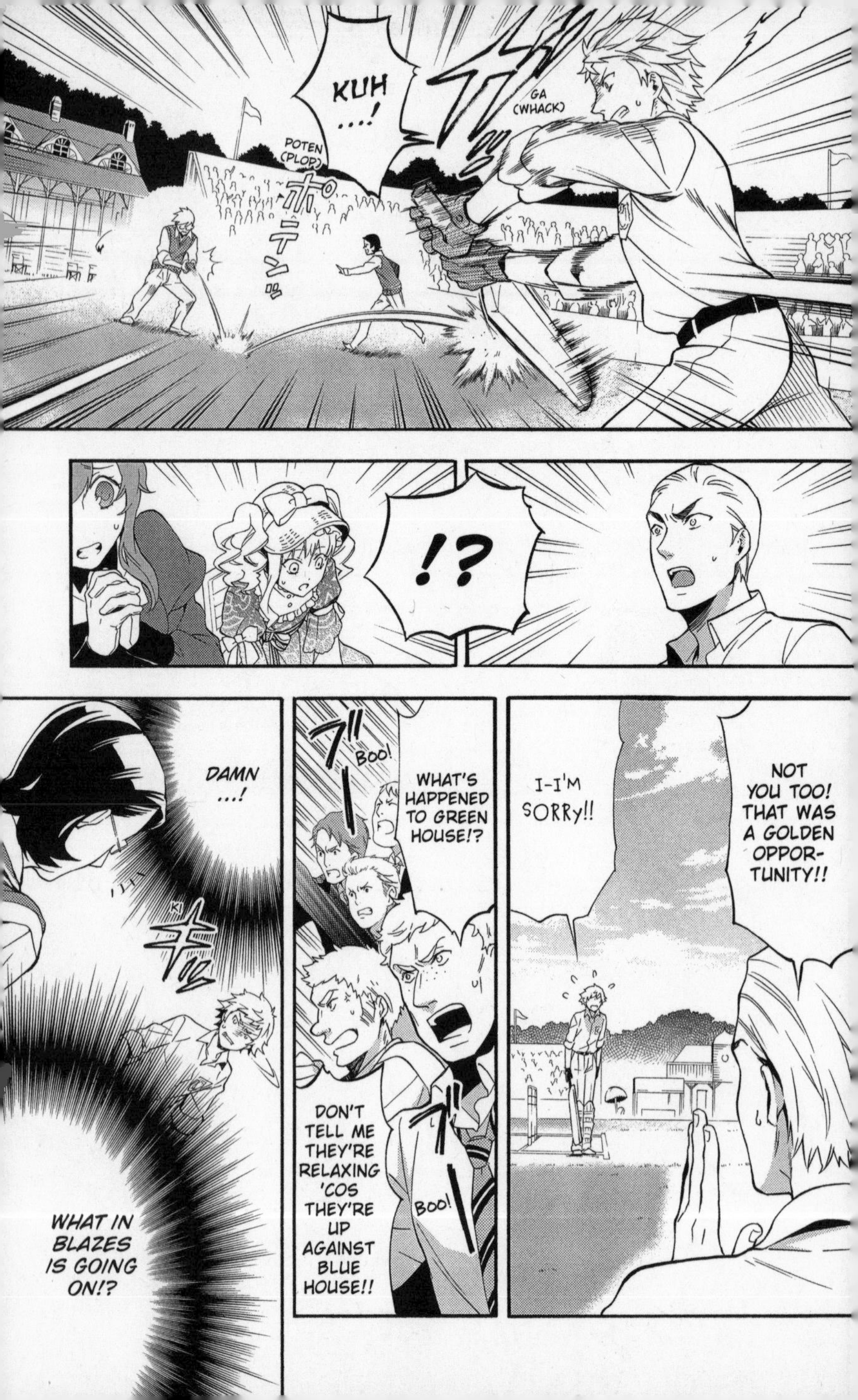
GA (WHACK)
KUH ...!
POTEN (PLOP)
ポテン
!?
NOT YOU TOO! THAT WAS A GOLDEN OPPORTUNITY!!
I-I'M SORRY!!
BOO!
WHAT'S HAPPENED TO GREEN HOUSE!?
DON'T TELL ME THEY'RE RELAXING 'COS THEY'RE UP AGAINST BLUE HOUSE!!
BOO!
DAMN ...!
KI
WHAT IN BLAZES IS GOING ON!?

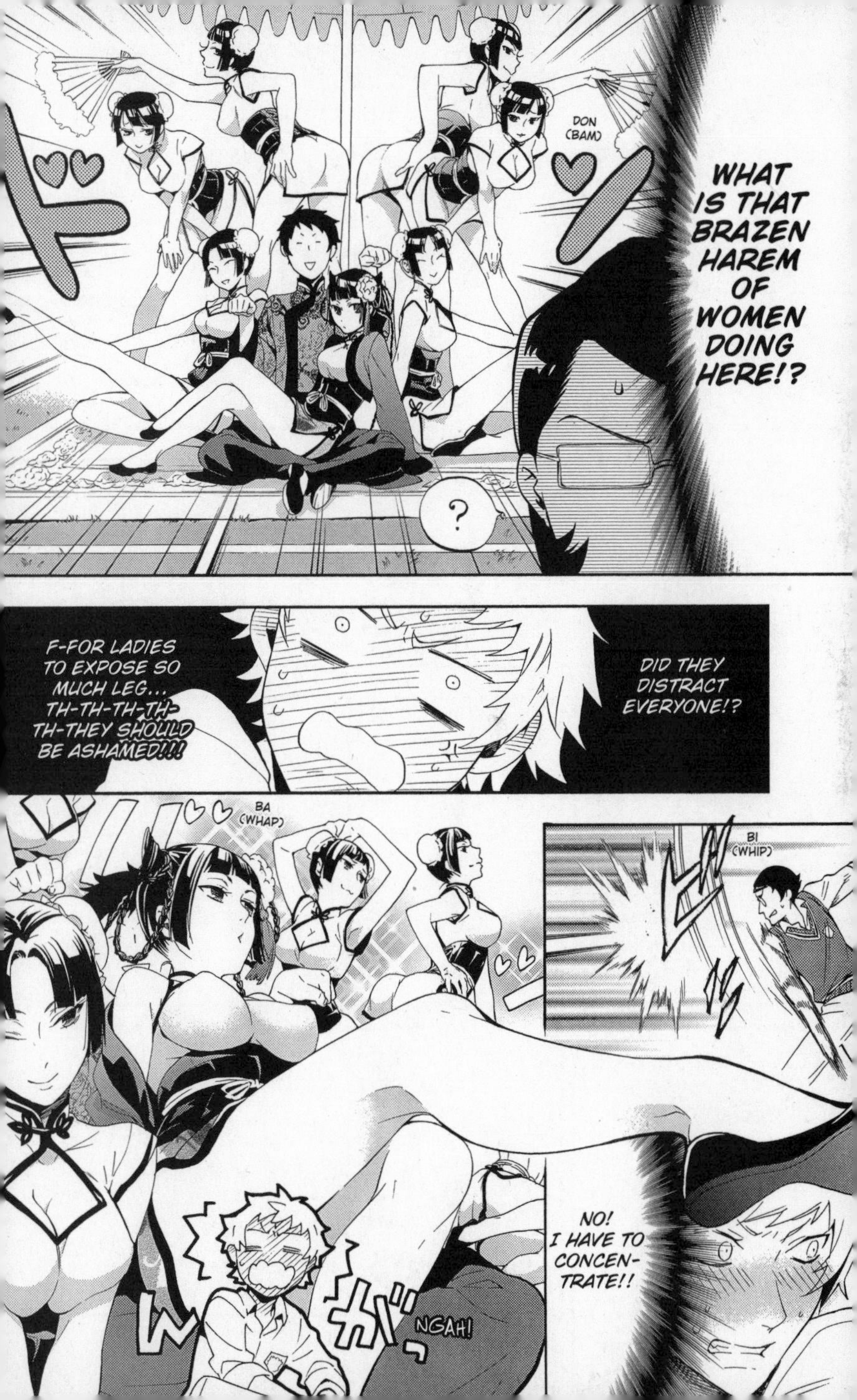
WHAT IS THAT BRAZEN HAREM OF WOMEN DOING HERE!?
DON (BAM)
?
DID THEY DISTRACT EVERYONE!?
F-FOR LADIES TO EXPOSE SO MUCH LEG... TH-TH-TH-TH-TH-THEY SHOULD BE ASHAMED!!!
BI (WHIP)
NO! I HAVE TO CONCEN-TRATE!!
BA (WHAP)
NGAH!

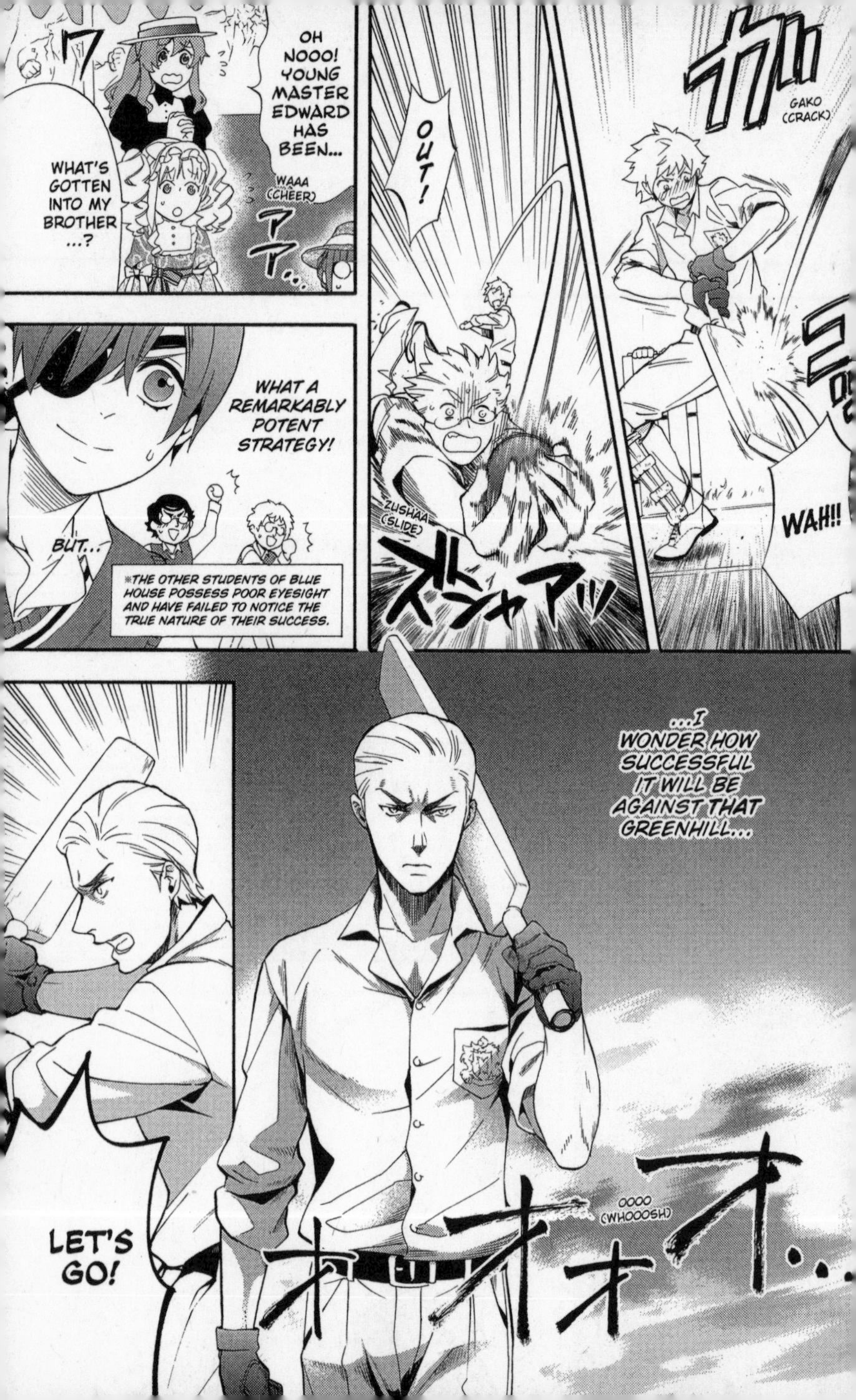
GAKO (CRACK)
OUT!
WAH!!
ZUSHAA (SLIDE)
OH NOOO! YOUNG MASTER EDWARD HAS BEEN...
WAAA (CHEER)
WHAT'S GOTTEN INTO MY BROTHER ...?
WHAT A REMARKABLY POTENT STRATEGY!
BUT...
※THE OTHER STUDENTS OF BLUE HOUSE POSSESS POOR EYESIGHT AND HAVE FAILED TO NOTICE THE TRUE NATURE OF THEIR SUCCESS.
...I WONDER HOW SUCCESSFUL IT WILL BE AGAINST THAT GREENHILL...
OOOO (WHOOOSH)
LET'S GO!

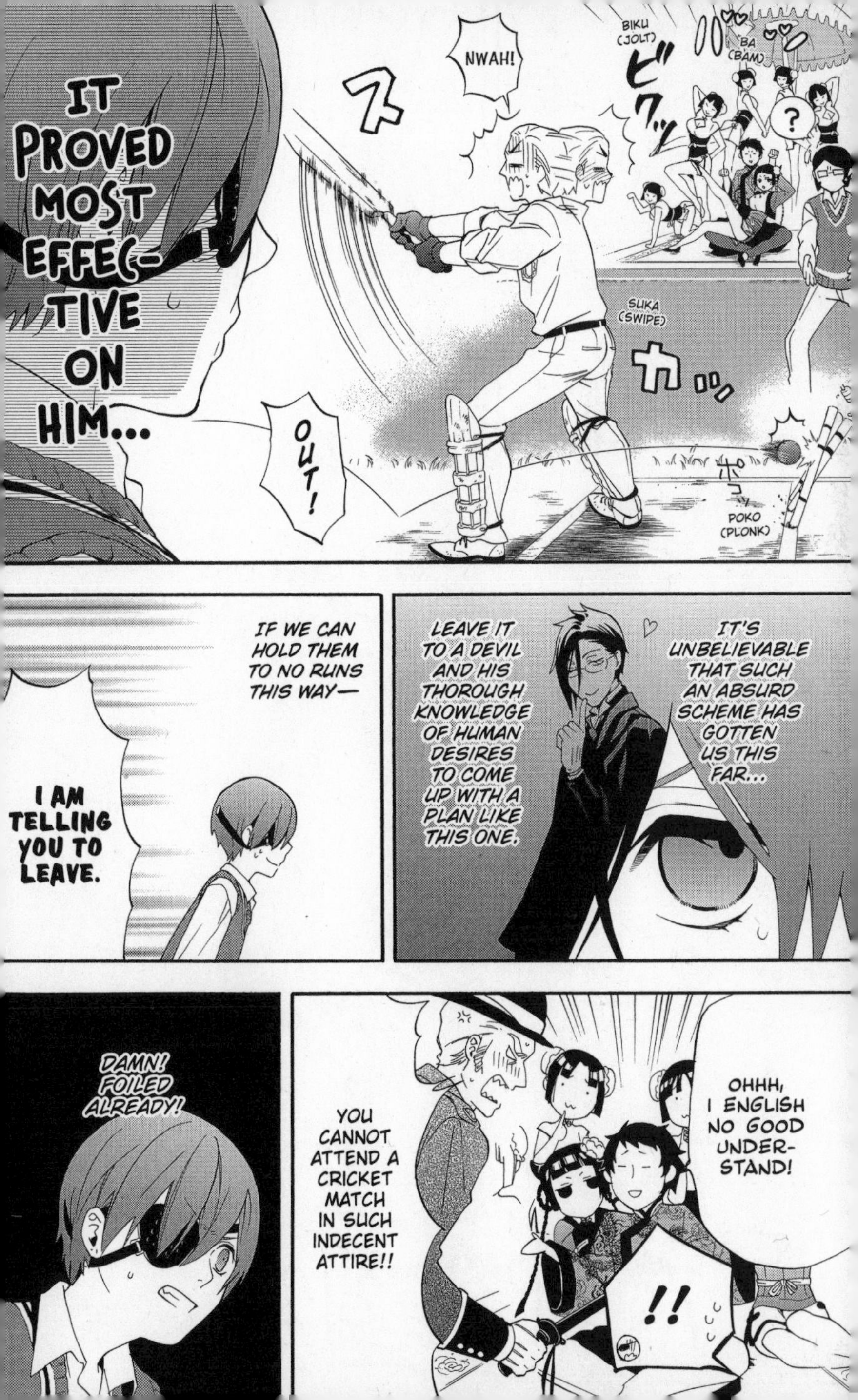
BIKU (JOLT)
BA (BAM)
?
NWAH!
SUKA (SWIPE)
POKO (PLONK)
OUT!
IT PROVED MOST EFFEC-TIVE ON HIM...
IT'S UNBELIEVABLE THAT SUCH AN ABSURD SCHEME HAS GOTTEN US THIS FAR...
LEAVE IT TO A DEVIL AND HIS THOROUGH KNOWLEDGE OF HUMAN DESIRES TO COME UP WITH A PLAN LIKE THIS ONE.
IF WE CAN HOLD THEM TO NO RUNS THIS WAY—
I AM TELLING YOU TO LEAVE.
OHHH, I ENGLISH NO GOOD UNDER-STAND!
YOU CANNOT ATTEND A CRICKET MATCH IN SUCH INDECENT ATTIRE!!
!!
DAMN! FOILED ALREADY!

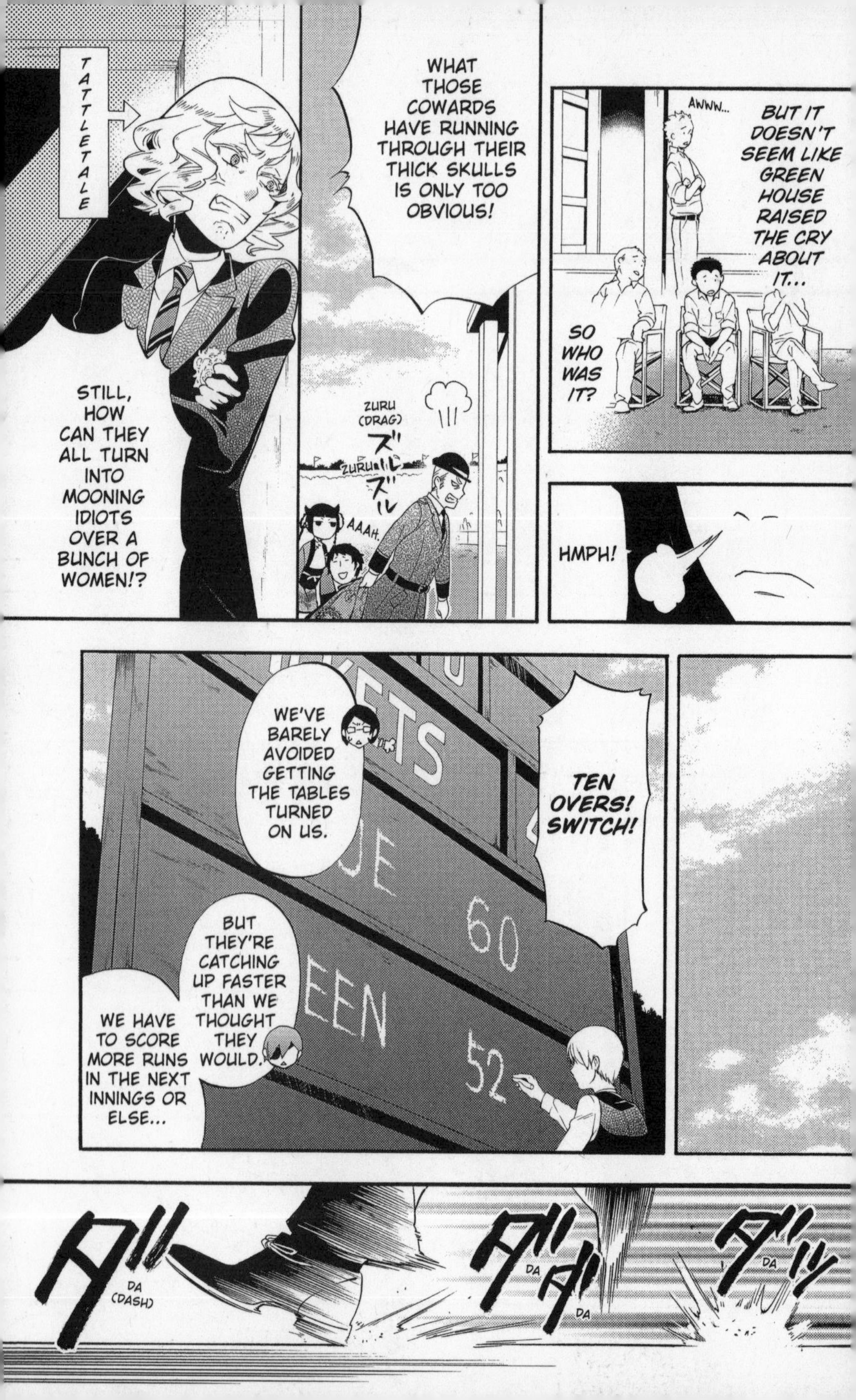
AWWW...
BUT IT DOESN'T SEEM LIKE GREEN HOUSE RAISED THE CRY ABOUT IT...
SO WHO WAS IT?
HMPH!
WHAT THOSE COWARDS HAVE RUNNING THROUGH THEIR THICK SKULLS IS ONLY TOO OBVIOUS!
ZURU (DRAG)
ズルズル
ZURU
AAAH.
TATTLETALE
STILL, HOW CAN THEY ALL TURN INTO MOONING IDIOTS OVER A BUNCH OF WOMEN!?
TEN OVERS! SWITCH!
WE'VE BARELY AVOIDED GETTING THE TABLES TURNED ON US.
BUT THEY'RE CATCHING UP FASTER THAN WE THOUGHT THEY WOULD.
WE HAVE TO SCORE MORE RUNS IN THE NEXT INNINGS OR ELSE...
60
52
ダッ
DA
ダダ
DA
DA
ダッ
DA (DASH)

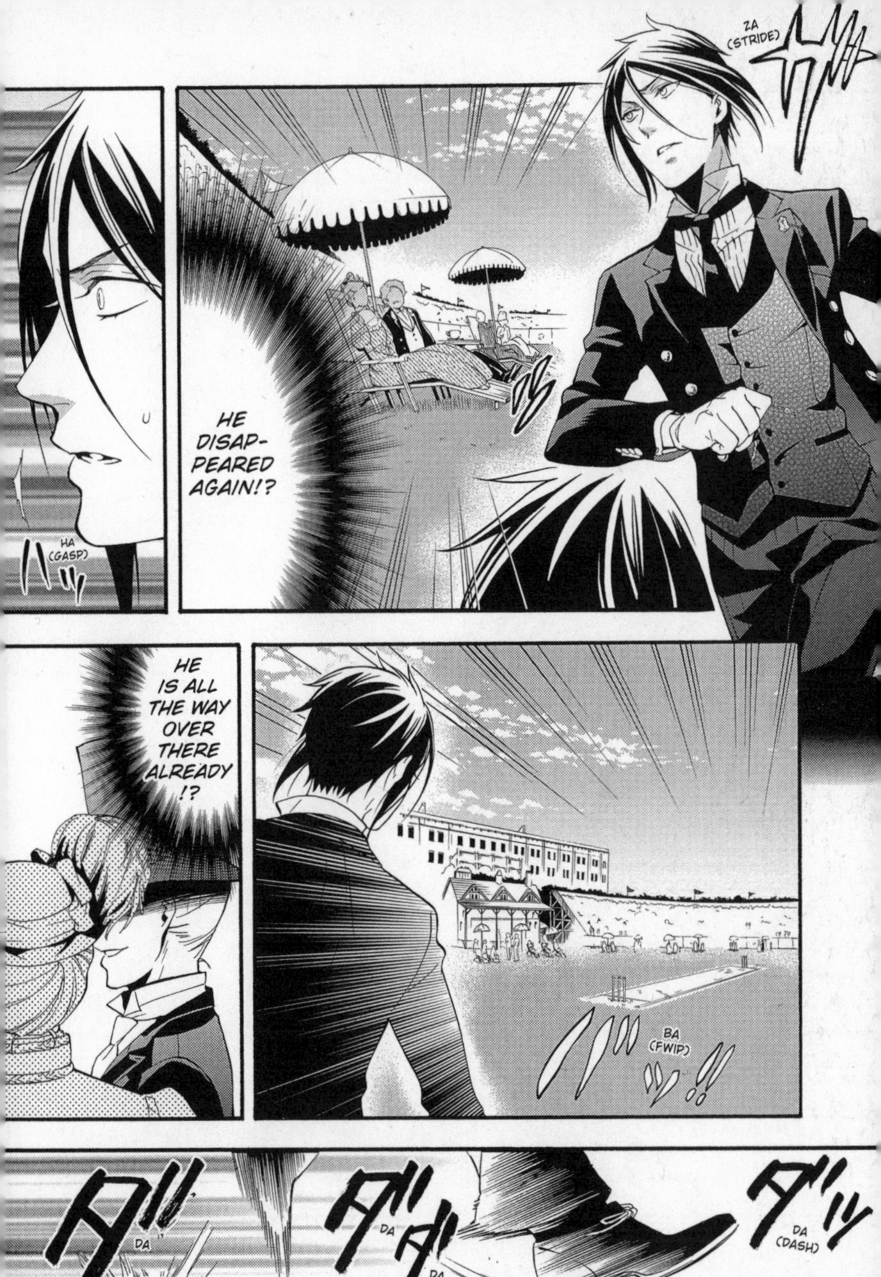
ZA (STRIDE)
HE DISAPPEARED AGAIN!?
HA (GASP)
BA (FWIP)
HE IS ALL THE WAY OVER THERE ALREADY!?
DA (DASH)
DA
DA
DA

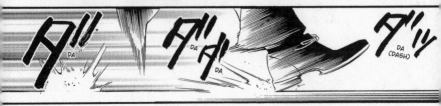

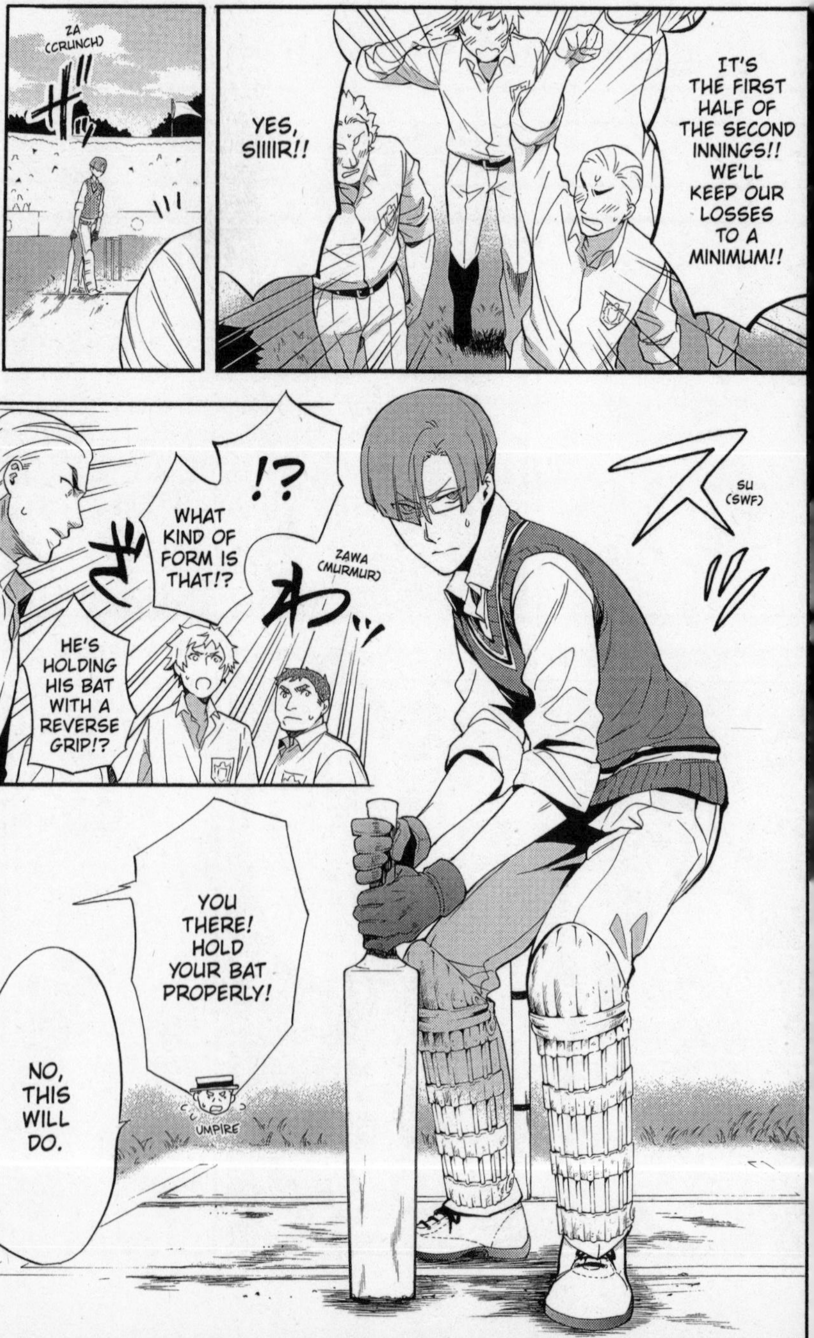
IT'S THE FIRST HALF OF THE SECOND INNINGS!! WE'LL KEEP OUR LOSSES TO A MINIMUM!!
YES, SIIIIR!!
ZA (CRUNCH)
SU (SWF)
!?
WHAT KIND OF FORM IS THAT!?
ZAWA (MURMUR)
HE'S HOLDING HIS BAT WITH A REVERSE GRIP!?
YOU THERE! HOLD YOUR BAT PROPERLY!
UMPIRE
NO, THIS WILL DO.

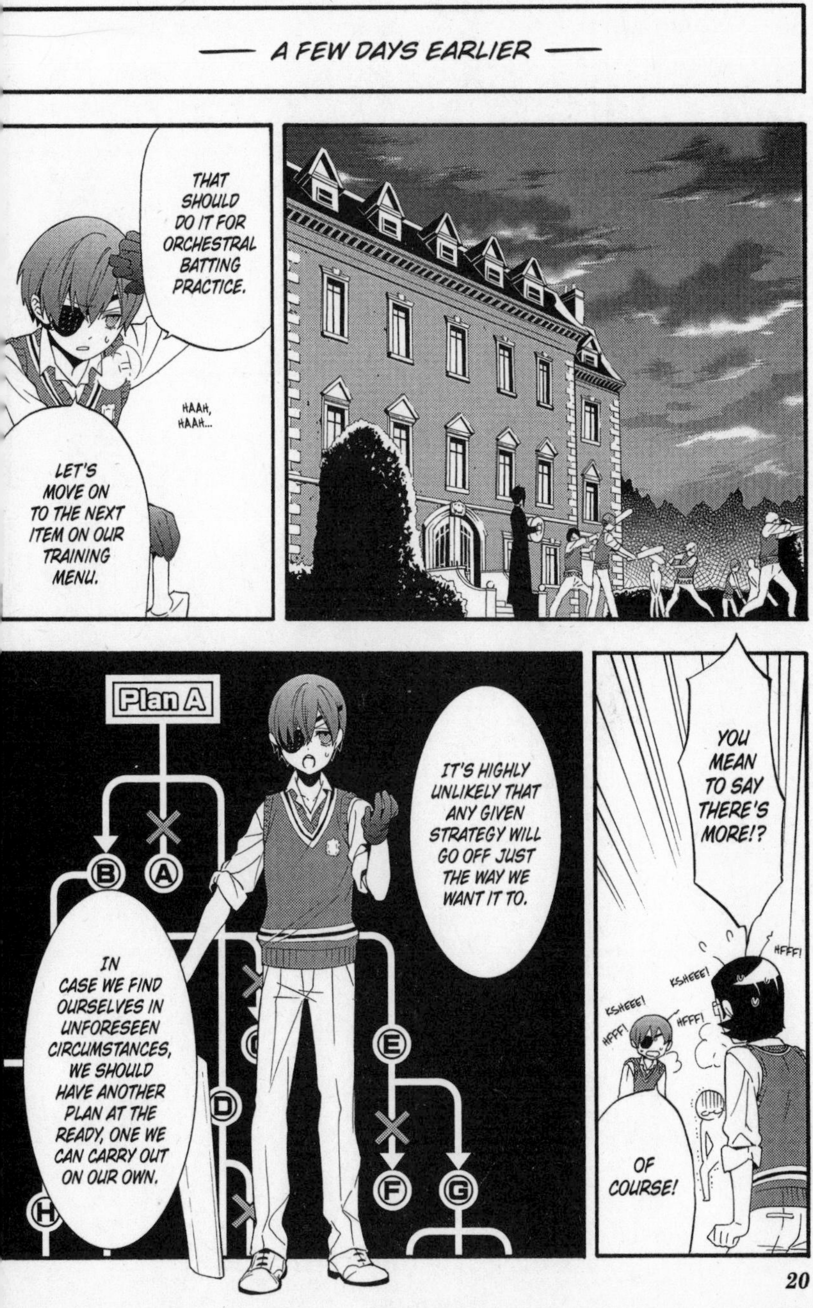
— A FEW DAYS EARLIER —
THAT SHOULD DO IT FOR ORCHESTRAL BATTING PRACTICE.
HAAH, HAAH...
LET'S MOVE ON TO THE NEXT ITEM ON OUR TRAINING MENU.
YOU MEAN TO SAY THERE'S MORE!?
HFFF!
KSHEEE!
HFFF!
KSHEEE!
HFFF!
OF COURSE!
Plan A
IT'S HIGHLY UNLIKELY THAT ANY GIVEN STRATEGY WILL GO OFF JUST THE WAY WE WANT IT TO.
IN CASE WE FIND OURSELVES IN UNFORESEEN CIRCUMSTANCES, WE SHOULD HAVE ANOTHER PLAN AT THE READY, ONE WE CAN CARRY OUT ON OUR OWN.

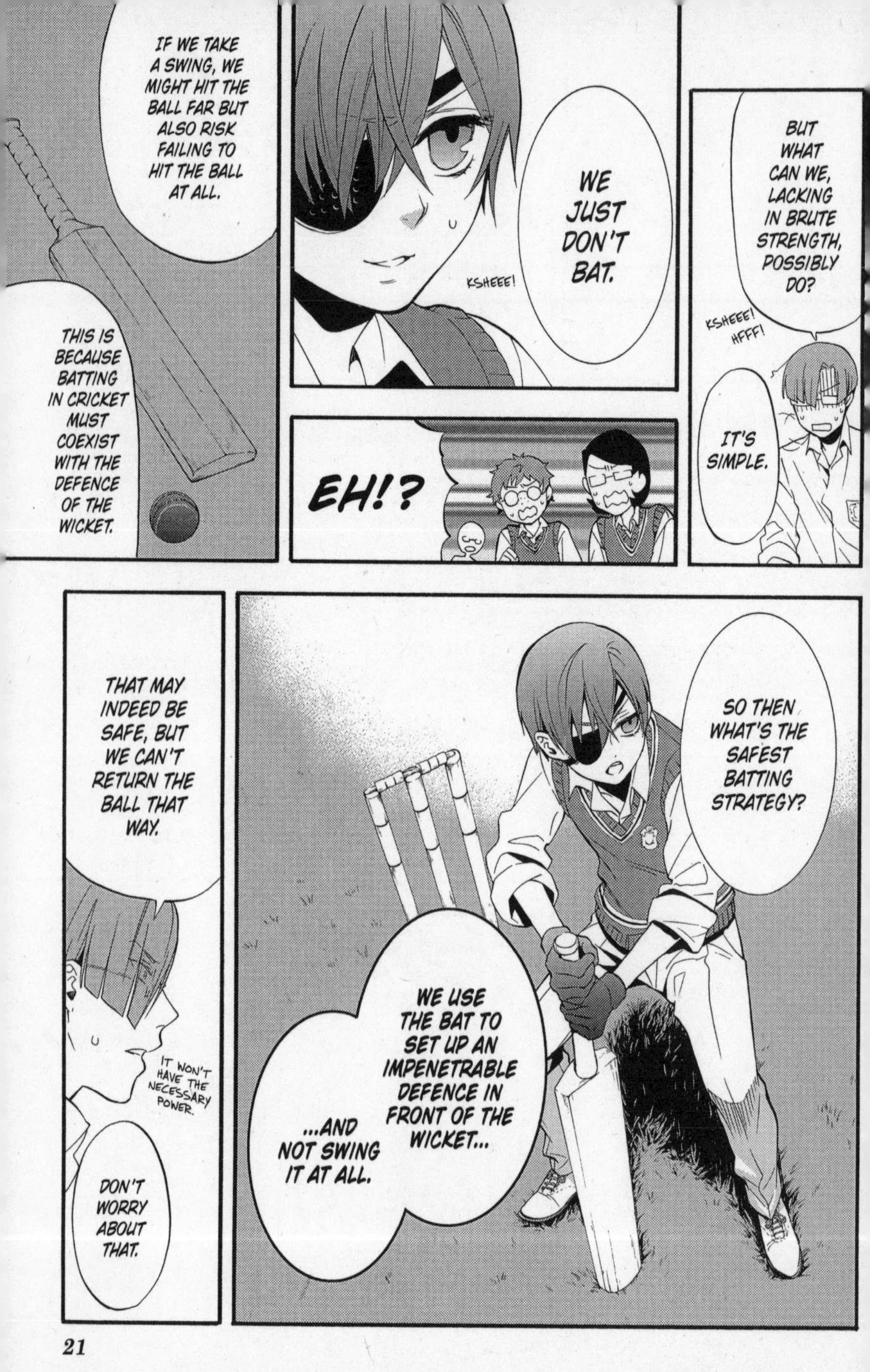
BUT WHAT CAN WE, LACKING IN BRUTE STRENGTH, POSSIBLY DO?
KSHEEE! HFFF!
IT'S SIMPLE.
WE JUST DON'T BAT.
KSHEEE!
EH!?
IF WE TAKE A SWING, WE MIGHT HIT THE BALL FAR BUT ALSO RISK FAILING TO HIT THE BALL AT ALL.
THIS IS BECAUSE BATTING IN CRICKET MUST COEXIST WITH THE DEFENCE OF THE WICKET.
SO THEN WHAT'S THE SAFEST BATTING STRATEGY?
WE USE THE BAT TO SET UP AN IMPENETRABLE DEFENCE IN FRONT OF THE WICKET...
...AND NOT SWING IT AT ALL.
THAT MAY INDEED BE SAFE, BUT WE CAN'T RETURN THE BALL THAT WAY.
IT WON'T HAVE THE NECESSARY POWER.
DON'T WORRY ABOUT THAT.

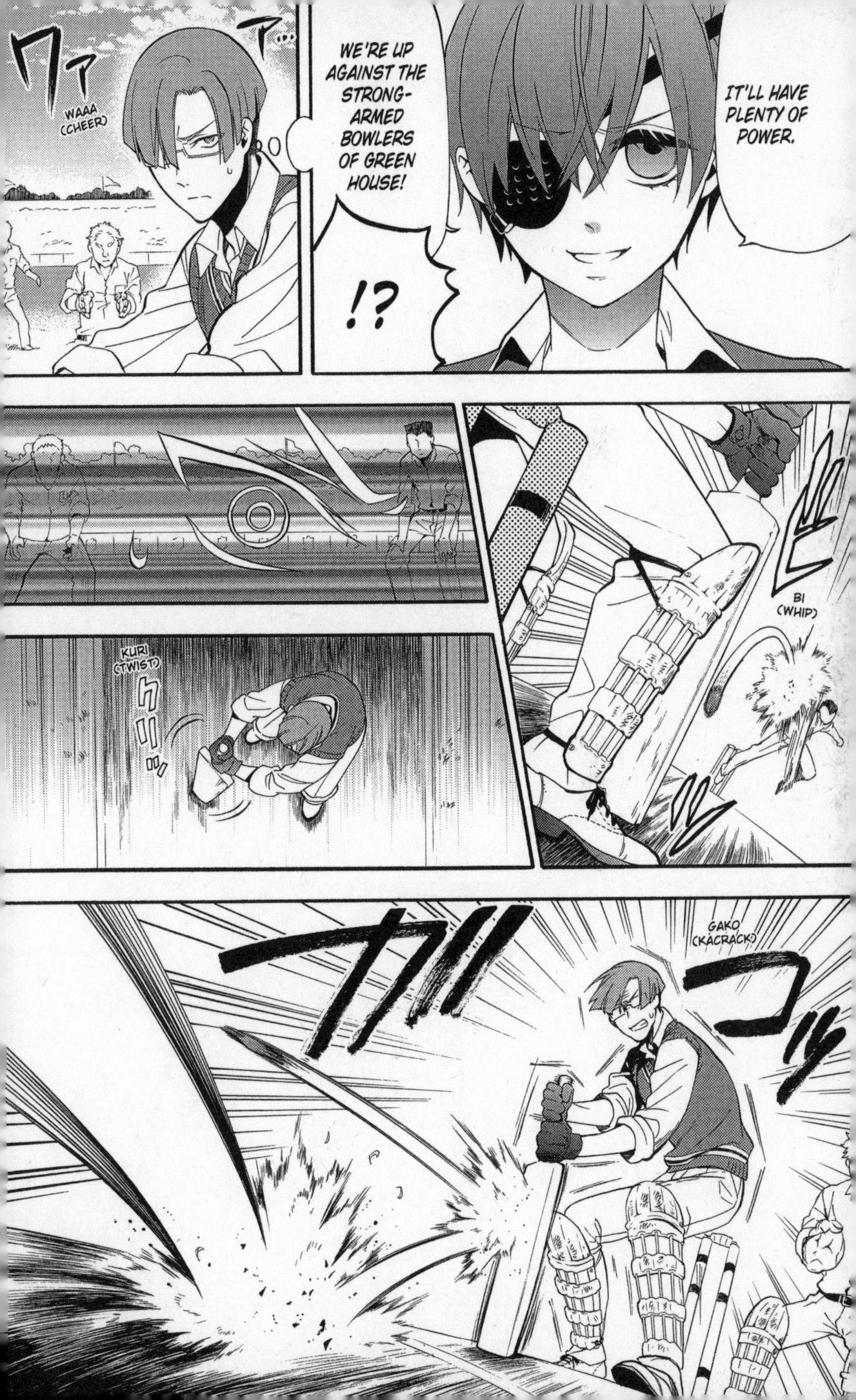

IT'LL HAVE PLENTY OF POWER.
WE'RE UP AGAINST THE STRONG-ARMED BOWLERS OF GREEN HOUSE!
!?
ワァ ア…
WAAA (CHEER)
BI (WHIP)
KURI (TWIST)
GAKO (KACRACK)

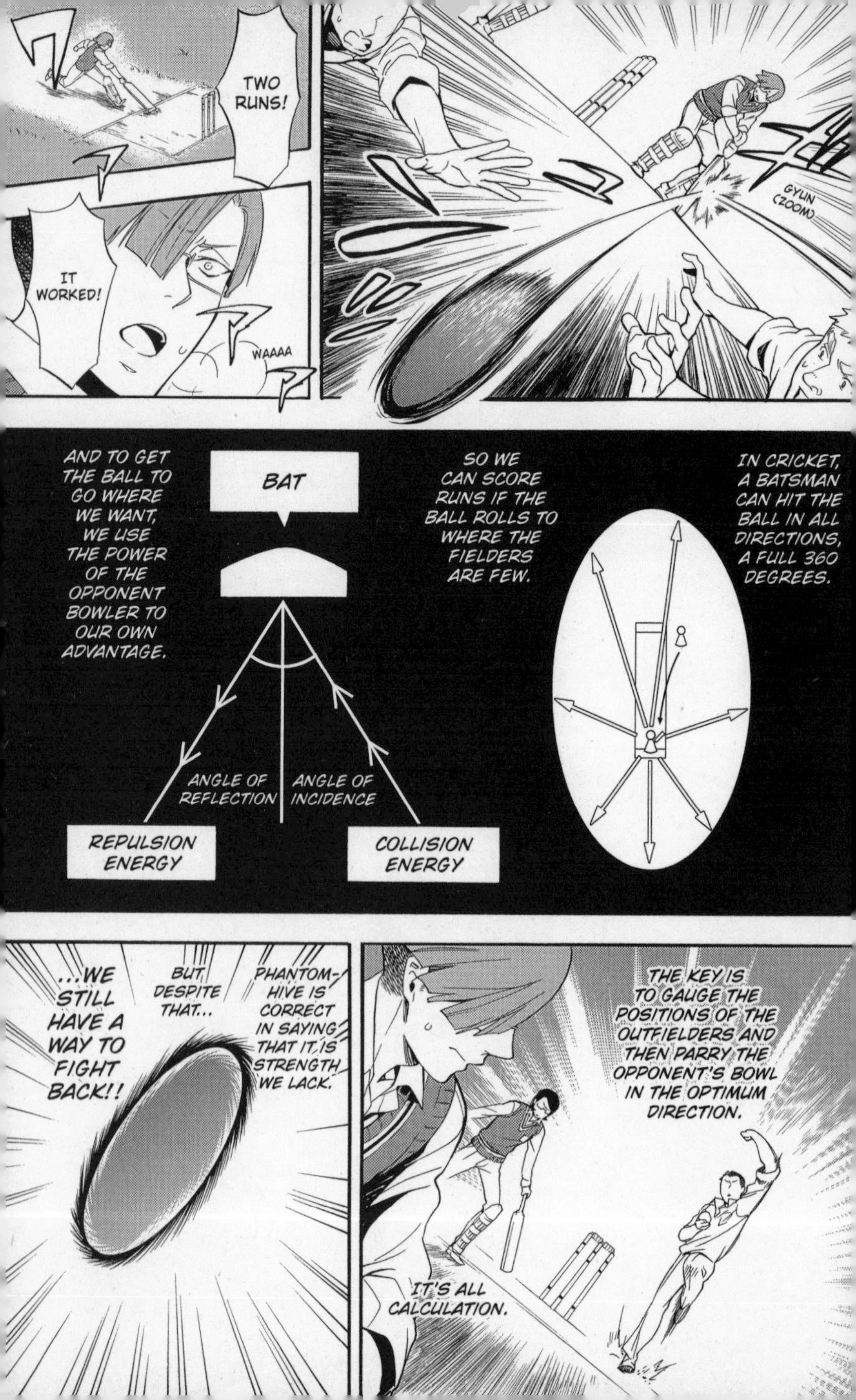
GYUN (ZOOM)
TWO RUNS!
IT WORKED!
WAAAA
IN CRICKET, A BATSMAN CAN HIT THE BALL IN ALL DIRECTIONS, A FULL 360 DEGREES.
SO WE CAN SCORE RUNS IF THE BALL ROLLS TO WHERE THE FIELDERS ARE FEW.
AND TO GET THE BALL TO GO WHERE WE WANT, WE USE THE POWER OF THE OPPONENT BOWLER TO OUR OWN ADVANTAGE.
BAT
ANGLE OF INCIDENCE
ANGLE OF REFLECTION
COLLISION ENERGY
REPULSION ENERGY
THE KEY IS TO GAUGE THE POSITIONS OF THE OUTFIELDERS AND THEN PARRY THE OPPONENT'S BOWL IN THE OPTIMUM DIRECTION.
IT'S ALL CALCULATION.
PHANTOM-HIVE IS CORRECT IN SAYING THAT IT IS STRENGTH WE LACK.
BUT DESPITE THAT...
...WE STILL HAVE A WAY TO FIGHT BACK!!

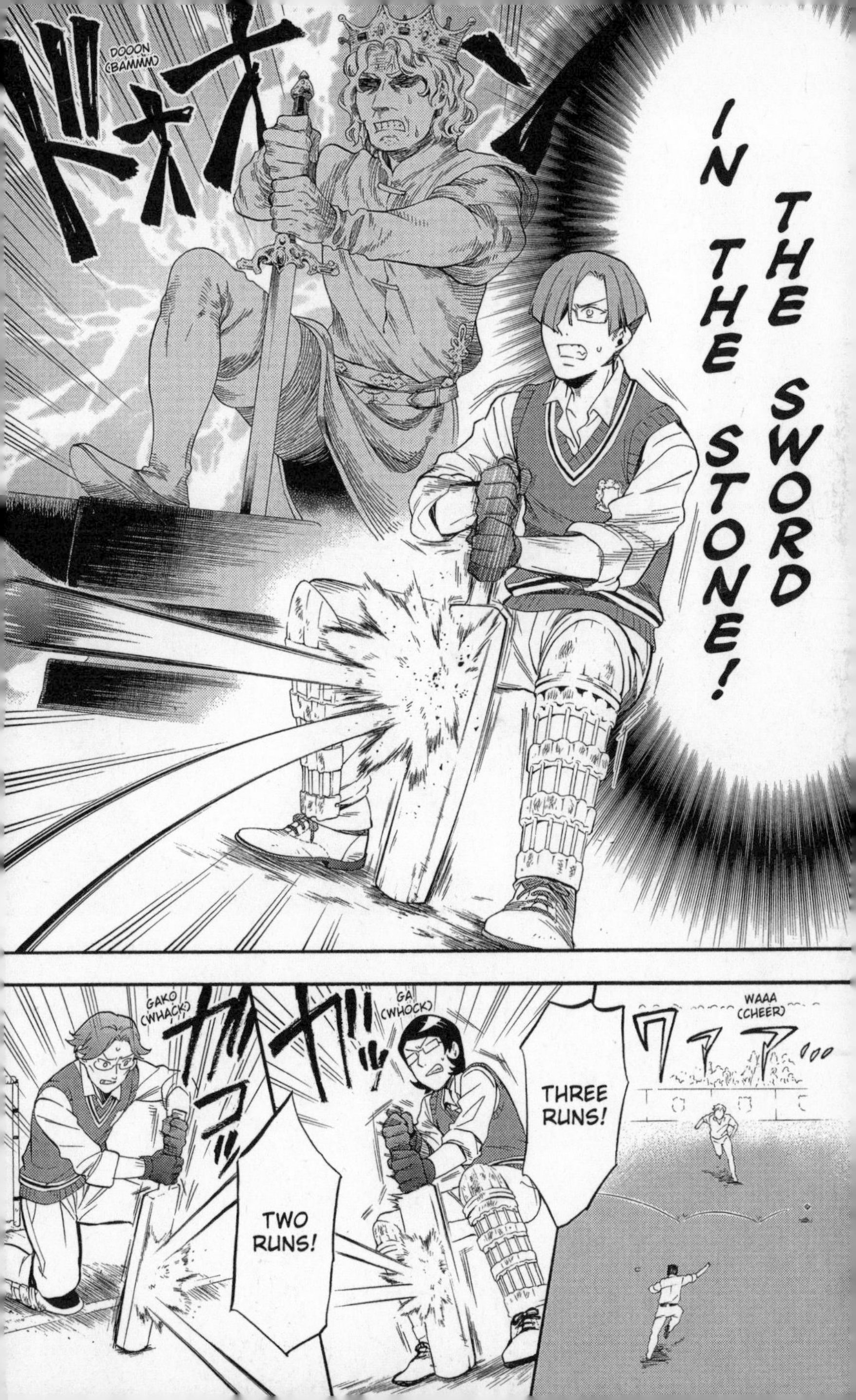
THE SWORD IN THE STONE!
DOOON (BAMMM)
WAAA (CHEER)
THREE RUNS!
GA (WHOCK)
TWO RUNS!
GAKO (WHACK)

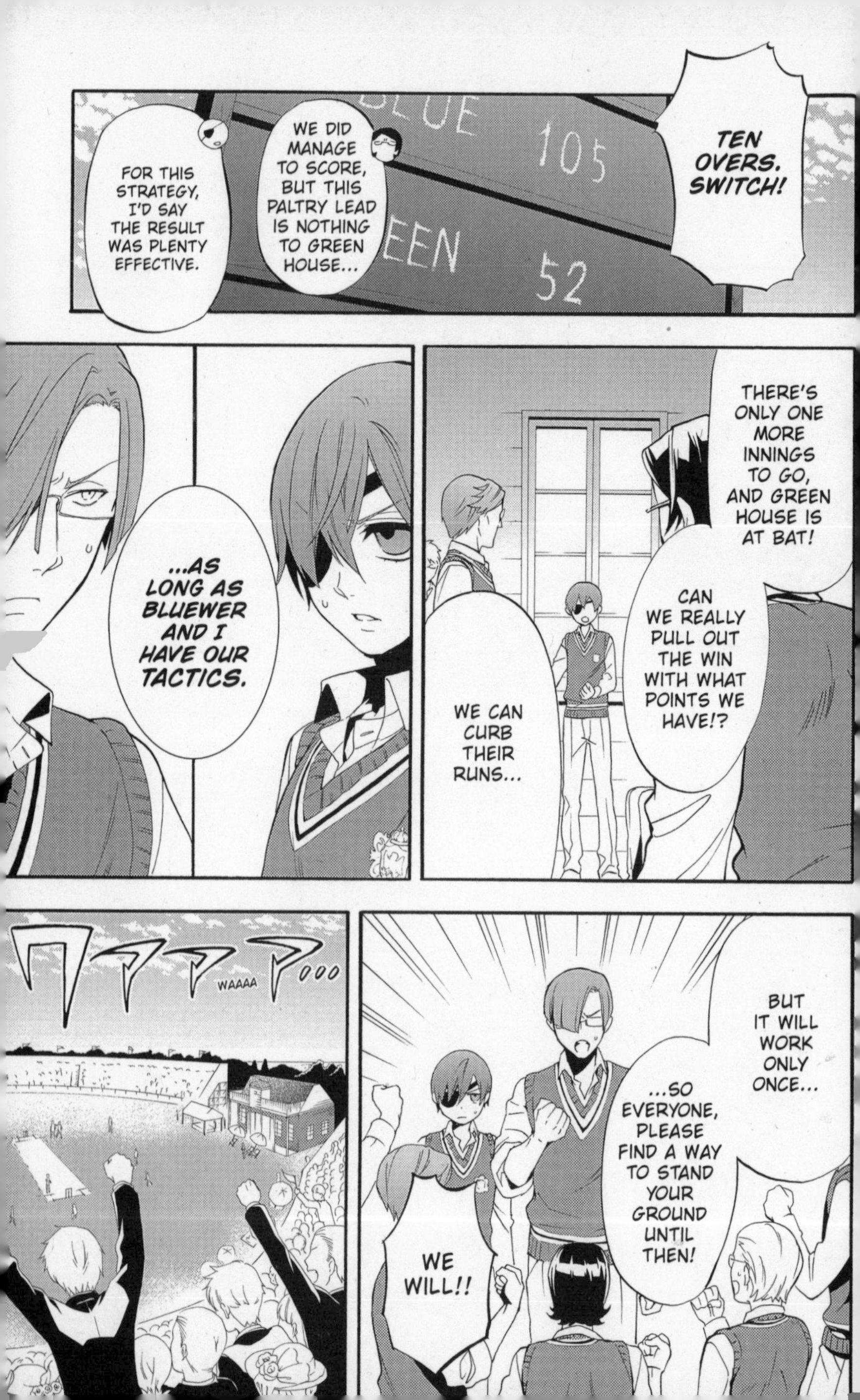
TEN OVERS. SWITCH!
WE DID MANAGE TO SCORE, BUT THIS PALTRY LEAD IS NOTHING TO GREEN HOUSE...
FOR THIS STRATEGY, I'D SAY THE RESULT WAS PLENTY EFFECTIVE.
BLUE 105
EEN 52
THERE'S ONLY ONE MORE INNINGS TO GO, AND GREEN HOUSE IS AT BAT!
CAN WE REALLY PULL OUT THE WIN WITH WHAT POINTS WE HAVE!?
WE CAN CURB THEIR RUNS...
...AS LONG AS BLUEWER AND I HAVE OUR TACTICS.
BUT IT WILL WORK ONLY ONCE...
...SO EVERYONE, PLEASE FIND A WAY TO STAND YOUR GROUND UNTIL THEN!
WE WILL!!
WAAAA

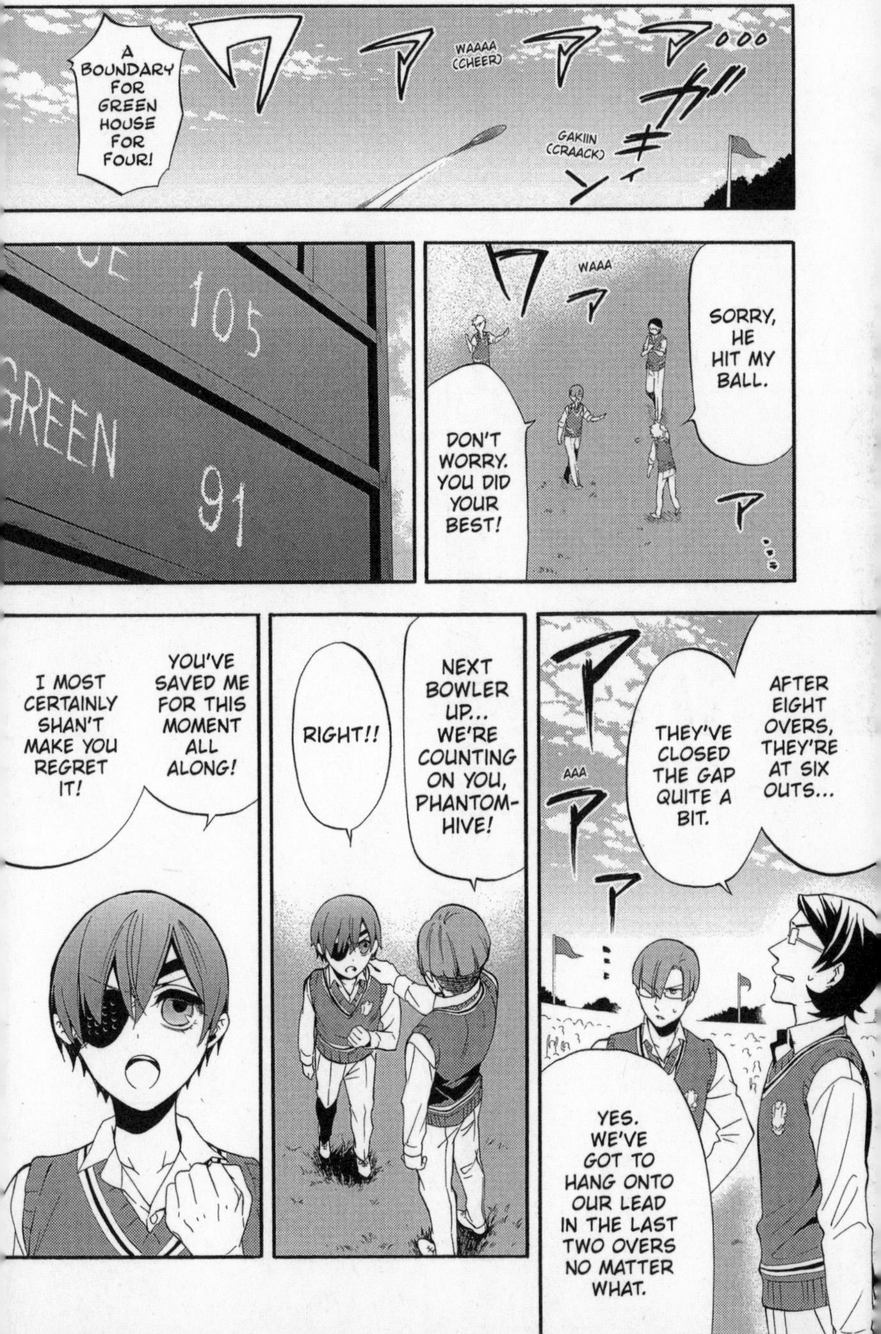
WAAAA (CHEER)
GAKIIN (CRAACK)
A BOUNDARY FOR GREEN HOUSE FOR FOUR!
WAAA
SORRY, HE HIT MY BALL.
DON'T WORRY. YOU DID YOUR BEST!
105
GREEN
91
AFTER EIGHT OVERS, THEY'RE AT SIX OUTS...
THEY'VE CLOSED THE GAP QUITE A BIT.
AAA
YES. WE'VE GOT TO HANG ONTO OUR LEAD IN THE LAST TWO OVERS NO MATTER WHAT.
NEXT BOWLER UP... WE'RE COUNTING ON YOU, PHANTOM-HIVE!
RIGHT!!
YOU'VE SAVED ME FOR THIS MOMENT ALL ALONG!
I MOST CERTAINLY SHAN'T MAKE YOU REGRET IT!

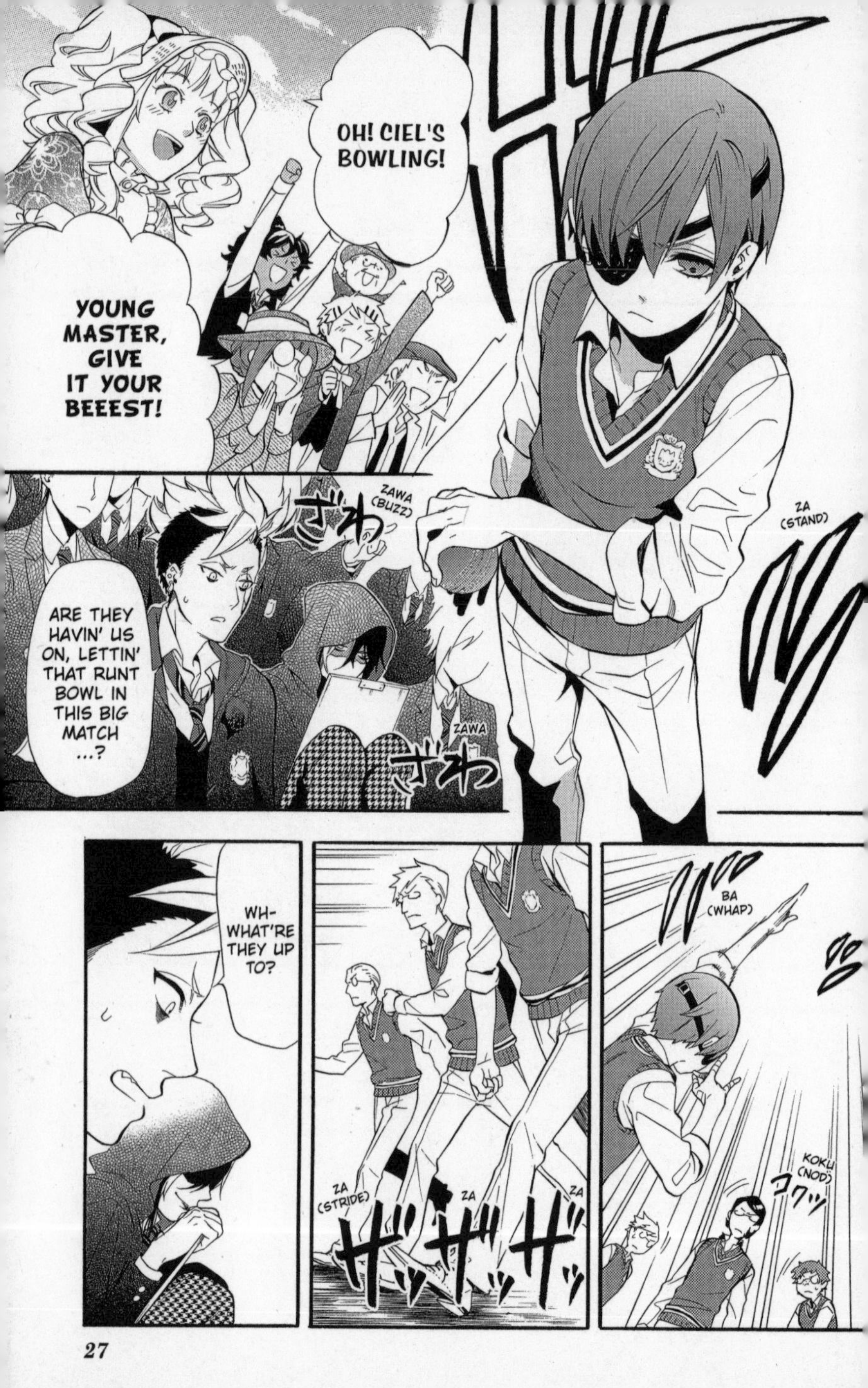
ZA (STAND)
OH! CIEL'S BOWLING!
YOUNG MASTER, GIVE IT YOUR BEEEST!
ZAWA (BUZZ)
ZAWA
ARE THEY HAVIN' US ON, LETTIN' THAT RUNT BOWL IN THIS BIG MATCH ...?
BA (WHAP)
KOKU (NOD)
ZA (STRIDE)
ZA
ZA
WH-WHAT'RE THEY UP TO?

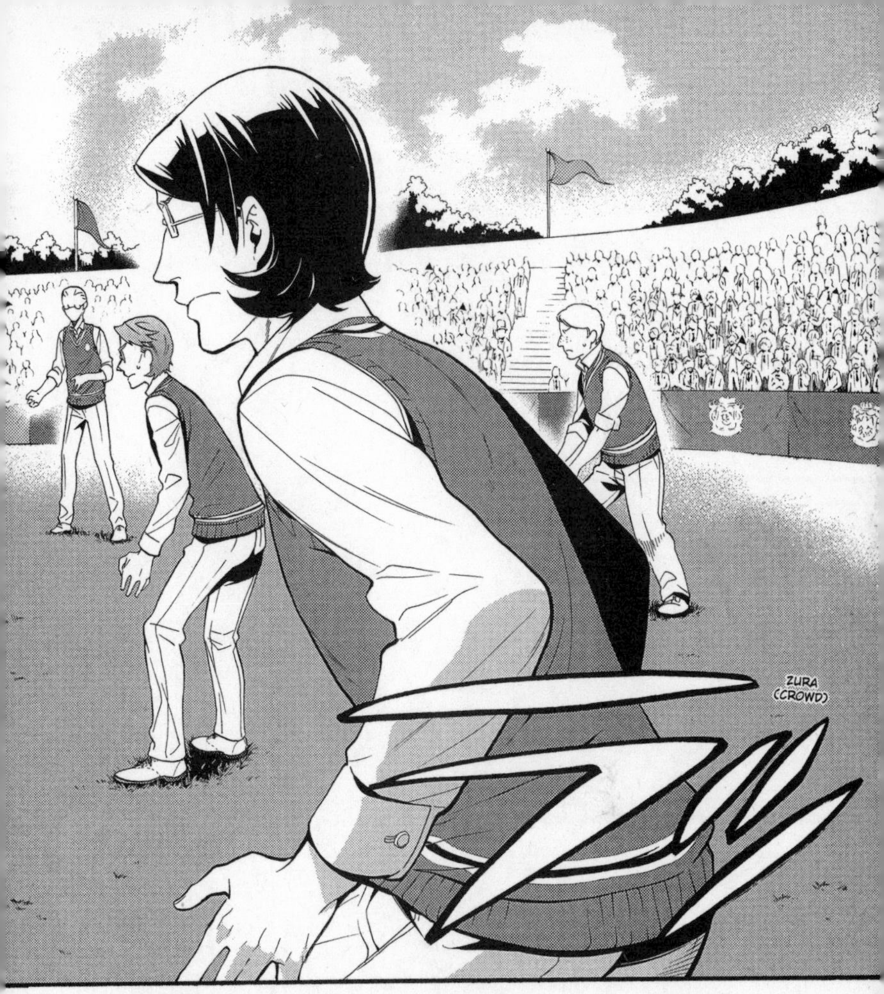
ZURA (CROWD)
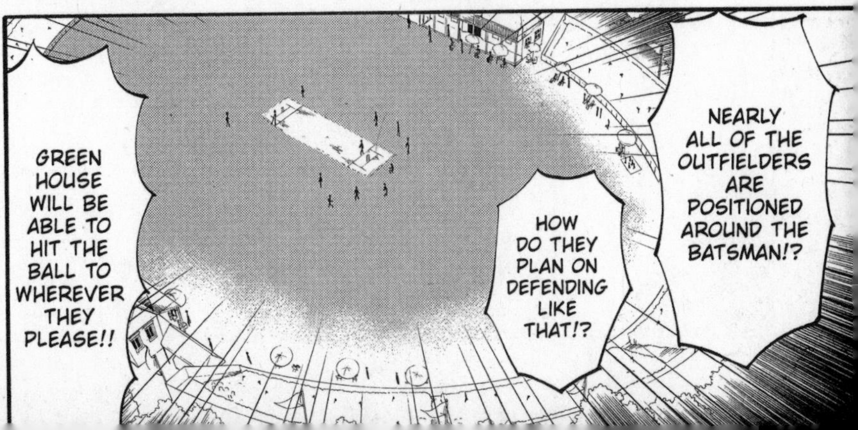
NEARLY ALL OF THE OUTFIELDERS ARE POSITIONED AROUND THE BATSMAN!?
HOW DO THEY PLAN ON DEFENDING LIKE THAT!?
GREEN HOUSE WILL BE ABLE TO HIT THE BALL TO WHEREVER THEY PLEASE!!

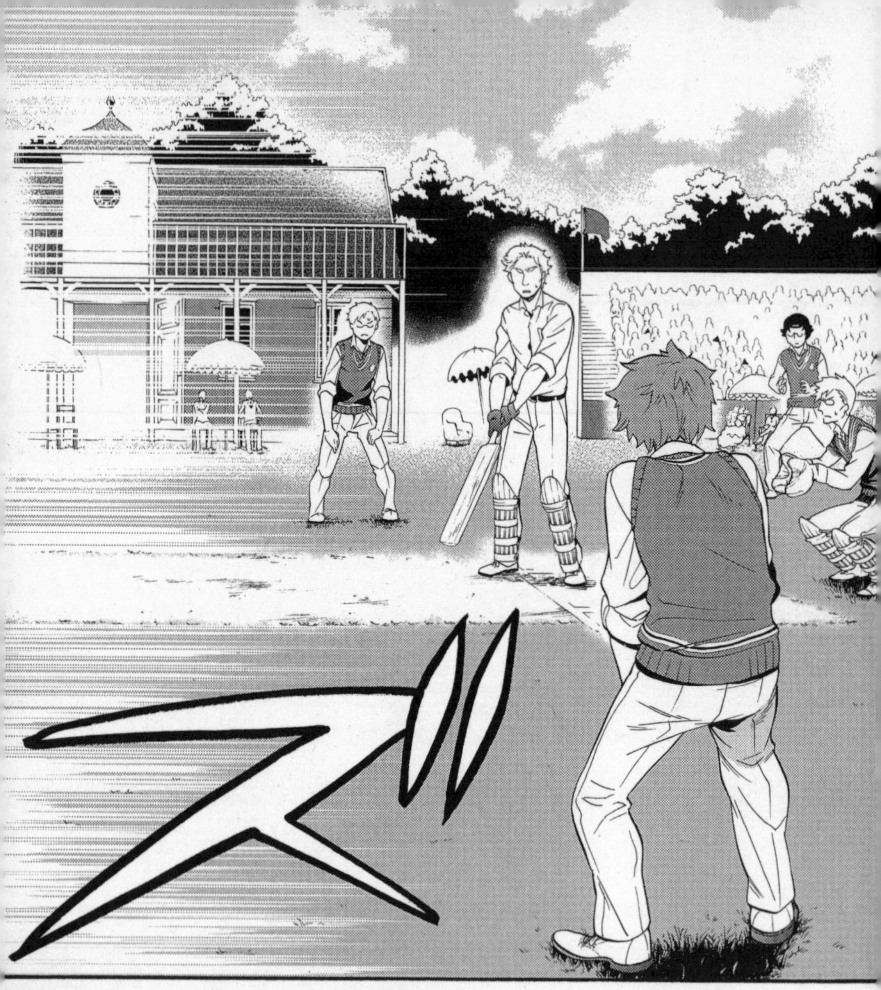

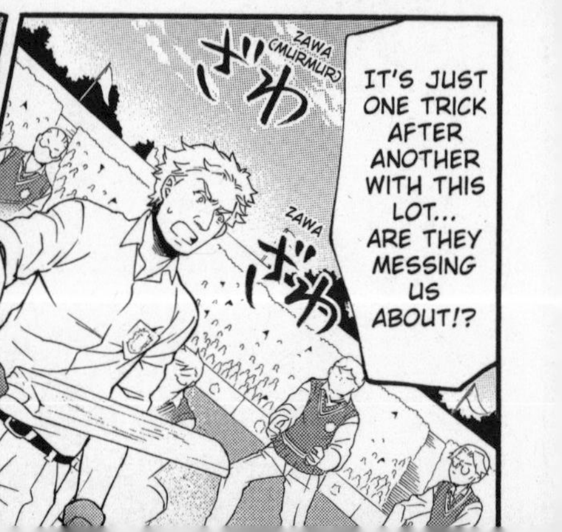
ZAWA (MURMUR)
ざわ
IT'S JUST ONE TRICK AFTER ANOTHER WITH THIS LOT... ARE THEY MESSING US ABOUT!?
ZAWA
ざわ

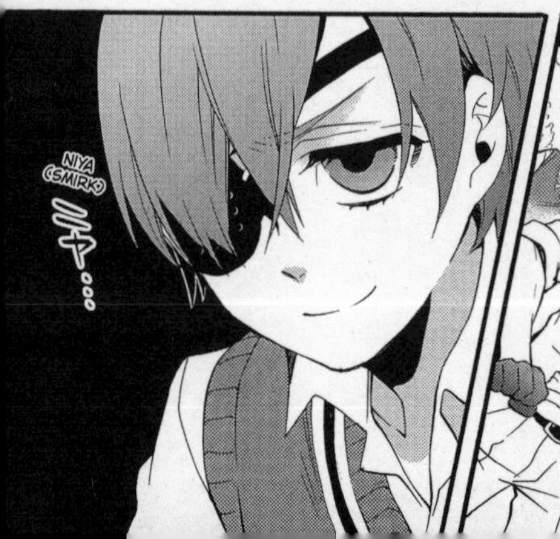
NIYA (SMIRK)
ニヤ…

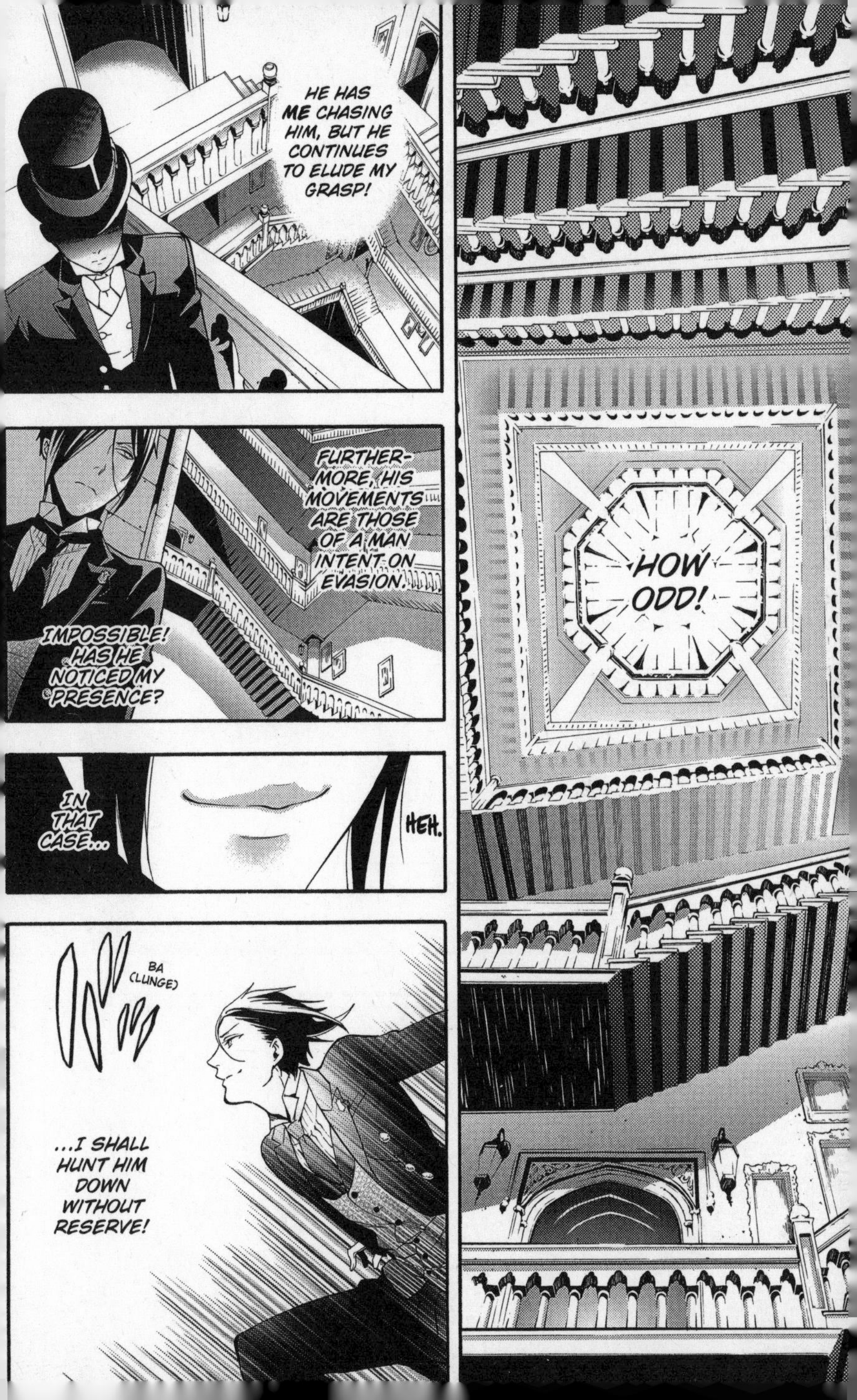
HOW ODD!
HE HAS ME CHASING HIM, BUT HE CONTINUES TO ELUDE MY GRASP!
FURTHERMORE, HIS MOVEMENTS ARE THOSE OF A MAN INTENT ON EVASION.
IMPOSSIBLE! HAS HE NOTICED MY PRESENCE?
HEH.
IN THAT CASE...
BA (LUNGE)
...I SHALL HUNT HIM DOWN WITHOUT RESERVE!

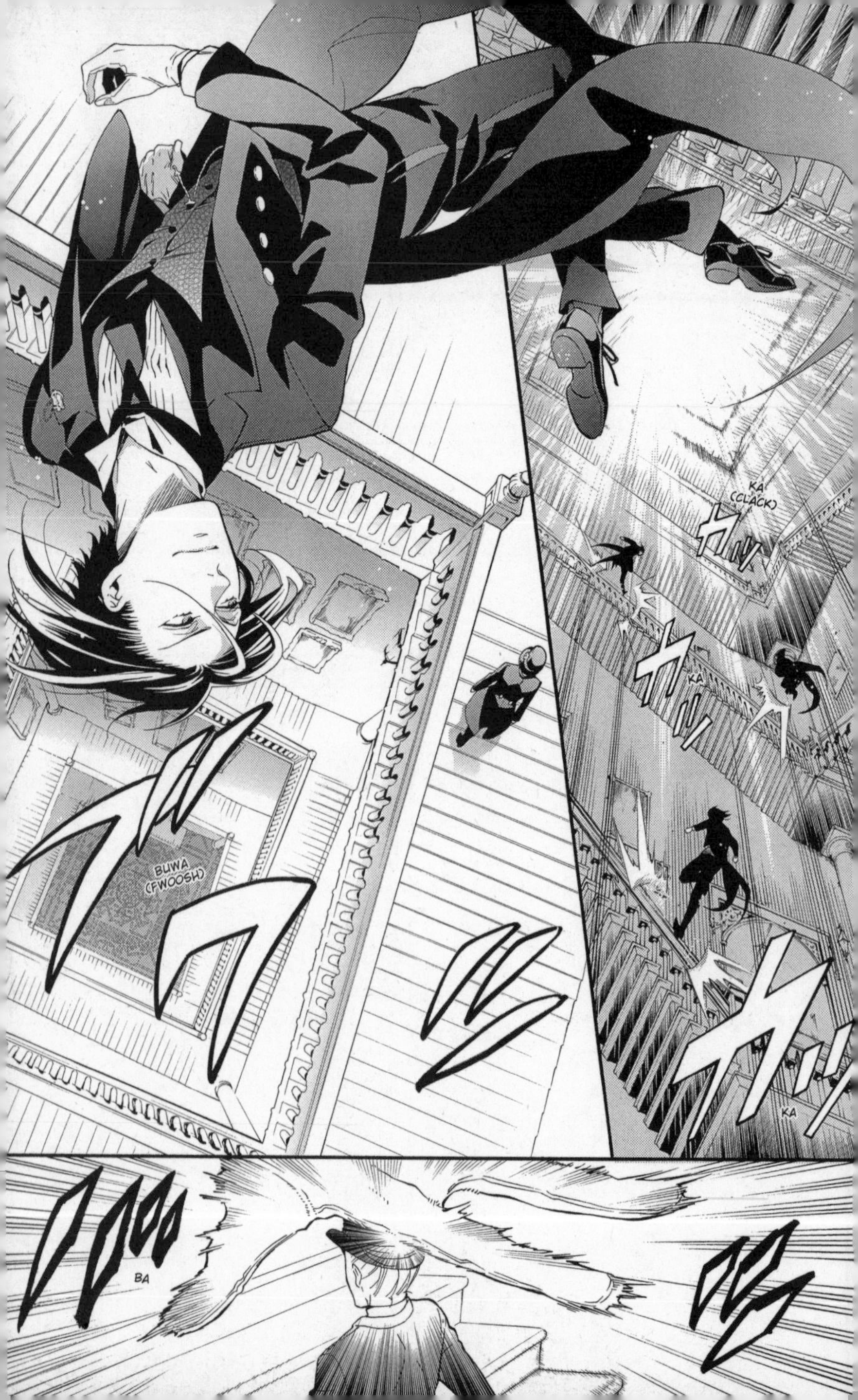
KA
(CLACK)
KA
KA
BUWA
(FWOOSH)
BA

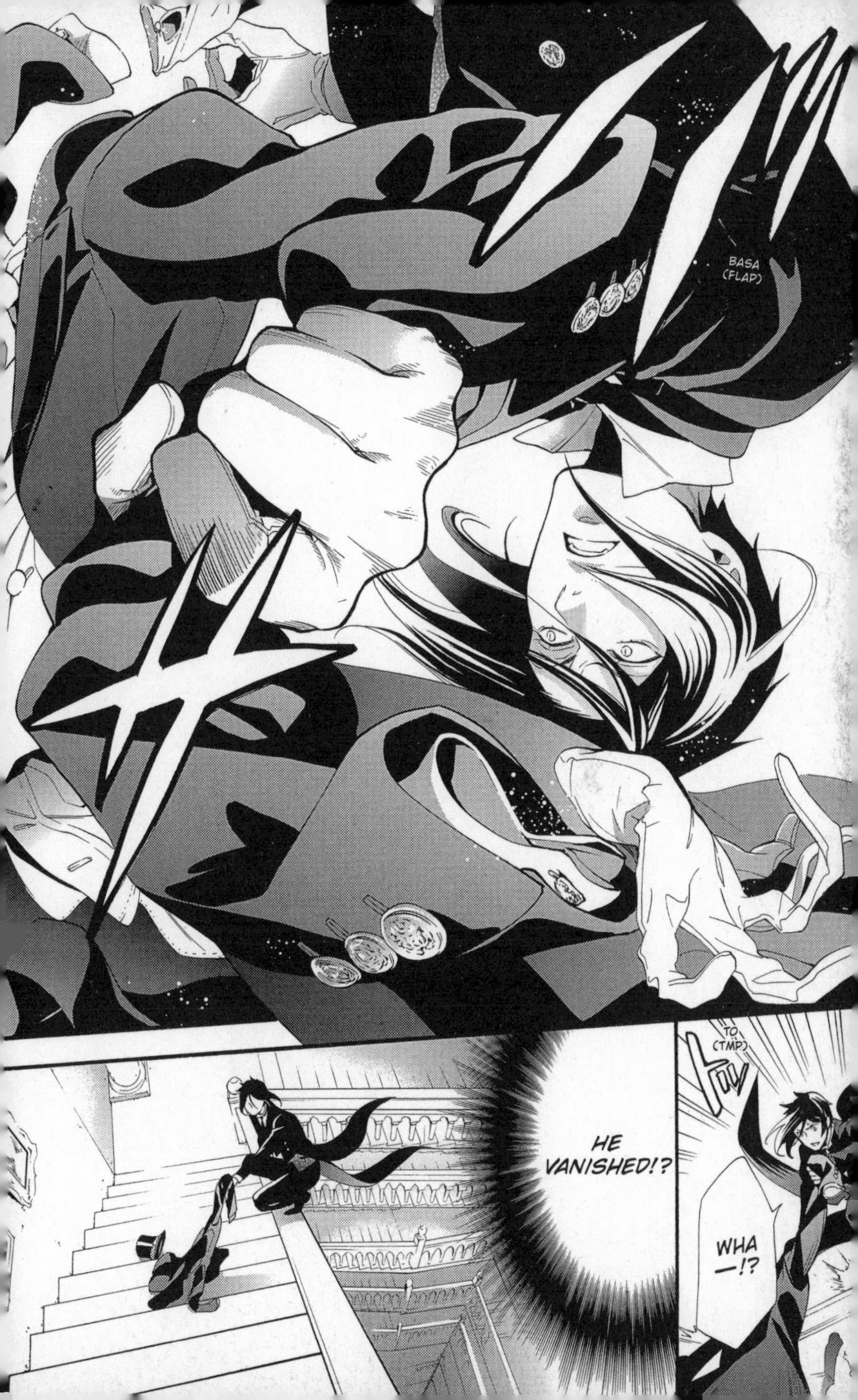
BASA
(FLAP)
TO
(TMP)
WHA
—!?
HE
VANISHED!?

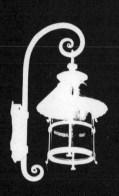

Black Butler

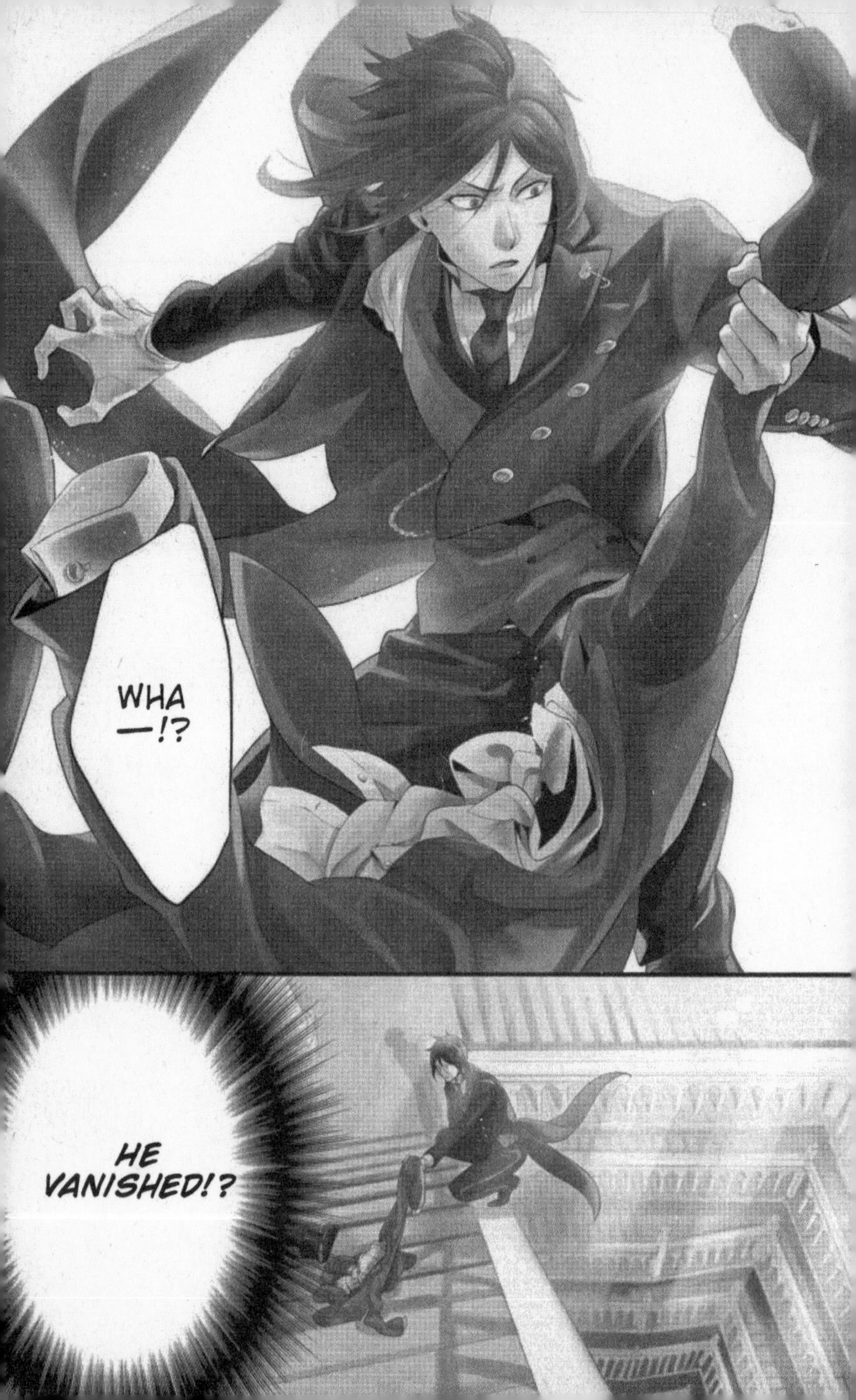
WHA—!?
HE VANISHED!?

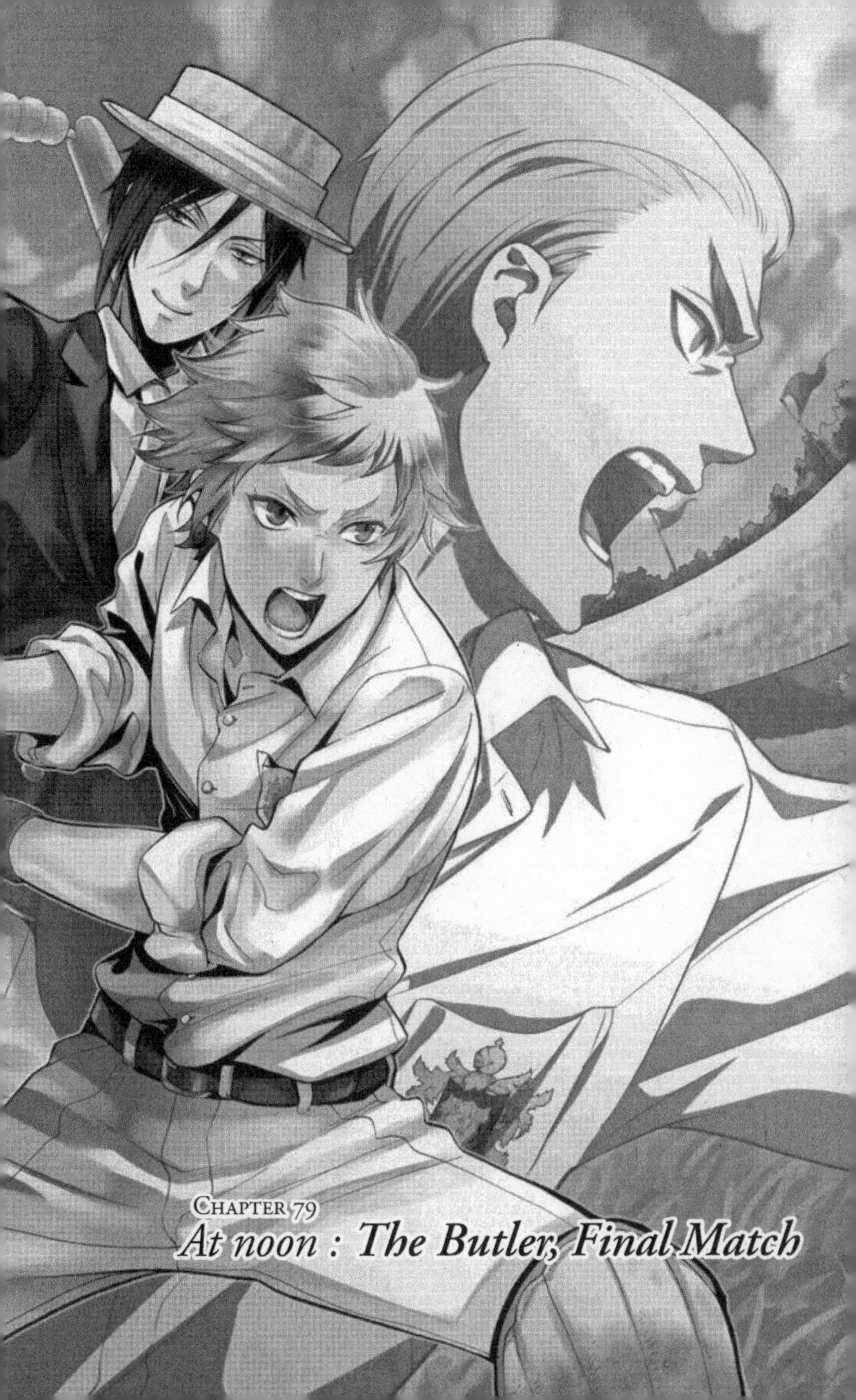
CHAPTER 79
At noon : The Butler, Final Match

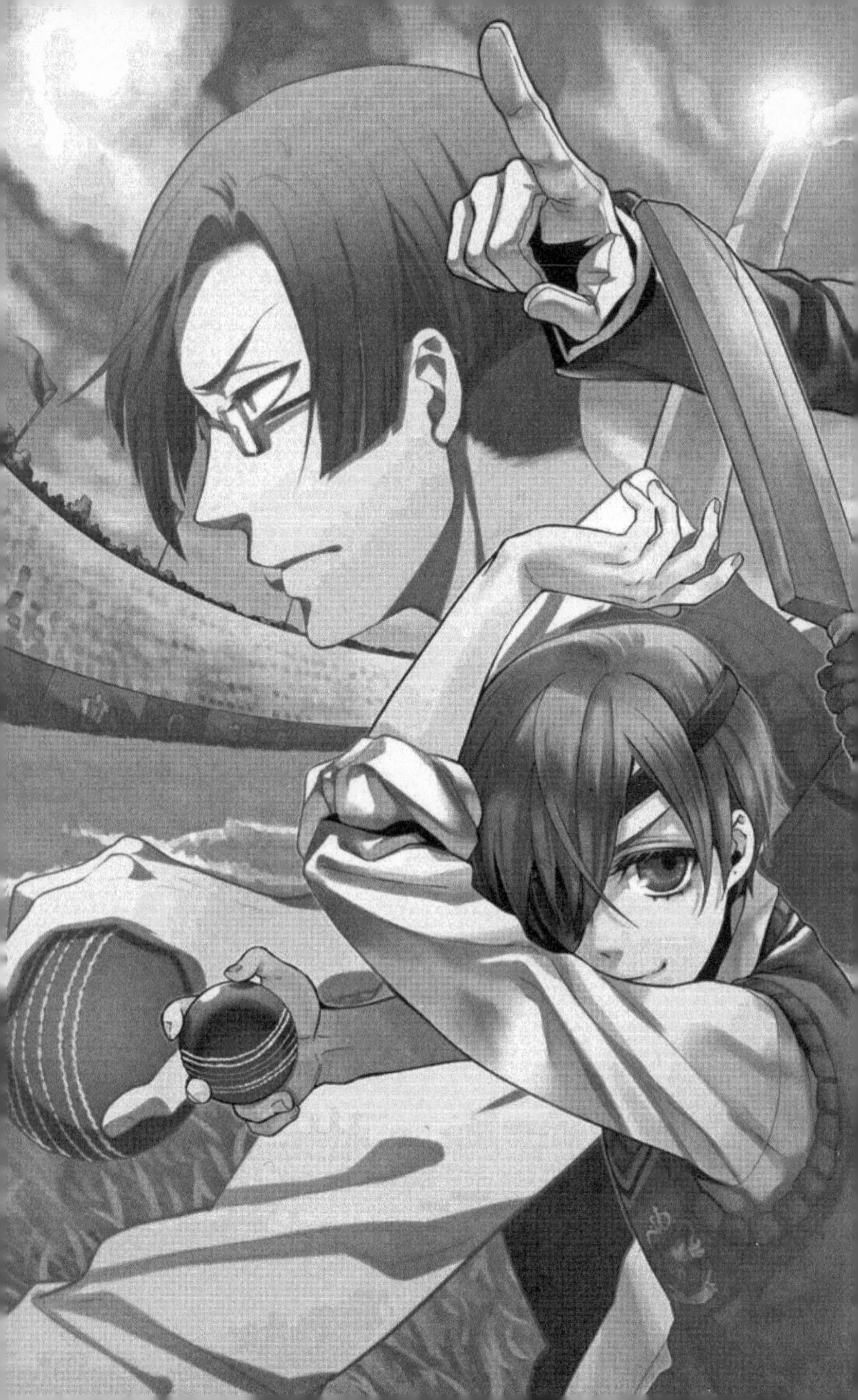

Black Butler

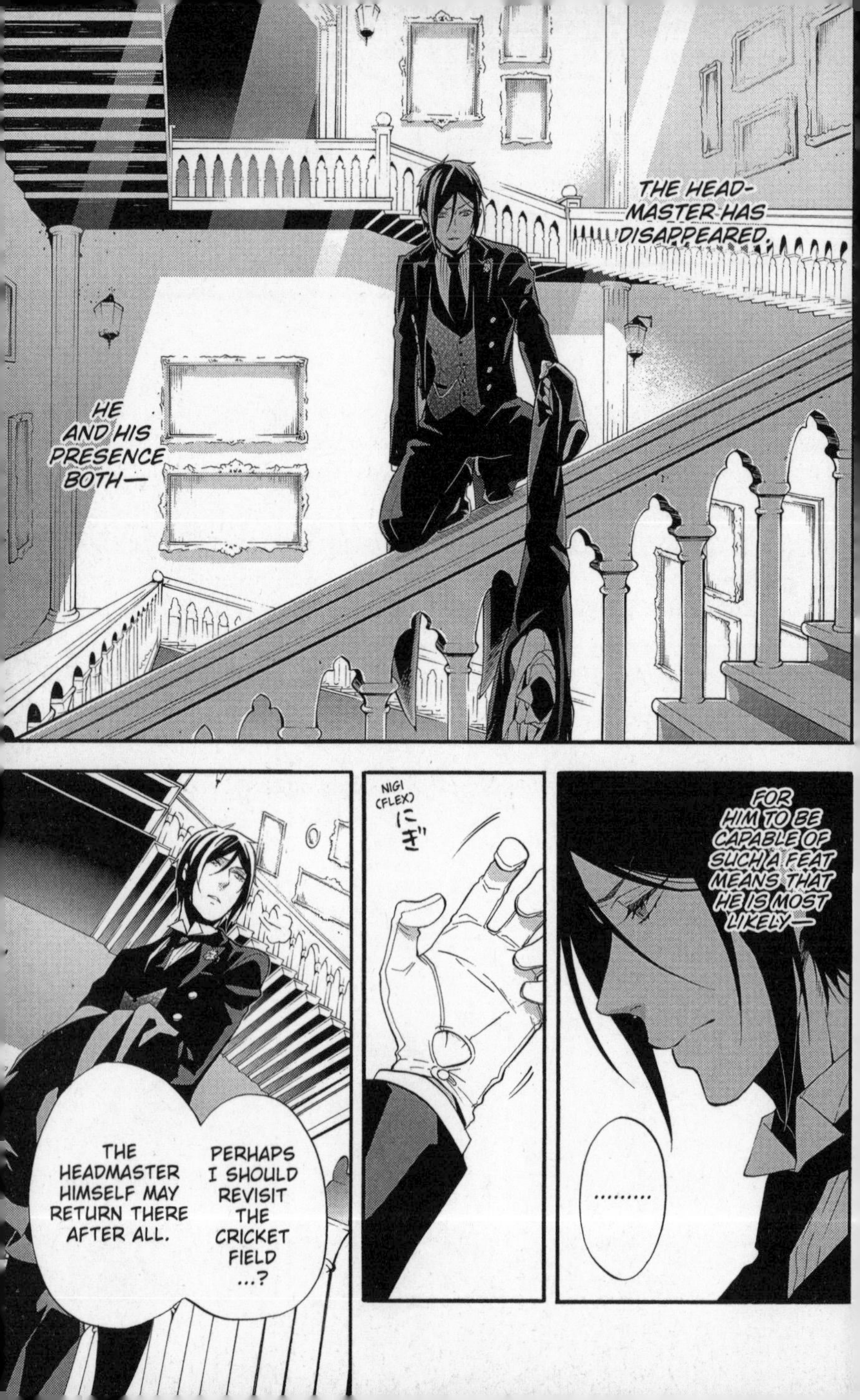
THE HEAD-MASTER HAS DISAPPEARED.
HE AND HIS PRESENCE BOTH—
FOR HIM TO BE CAPABLE OF SUCH A FEAT MEANS THAT HE IS MOST LIKELY—
....
NIGI (FLEX)
にぎ
PERHAPS I SHOULD REVISIT THE CRICKET FIELD ...?
THE HEADMASTER HIMSELF MAY RETURN THERE AFTER ALL.

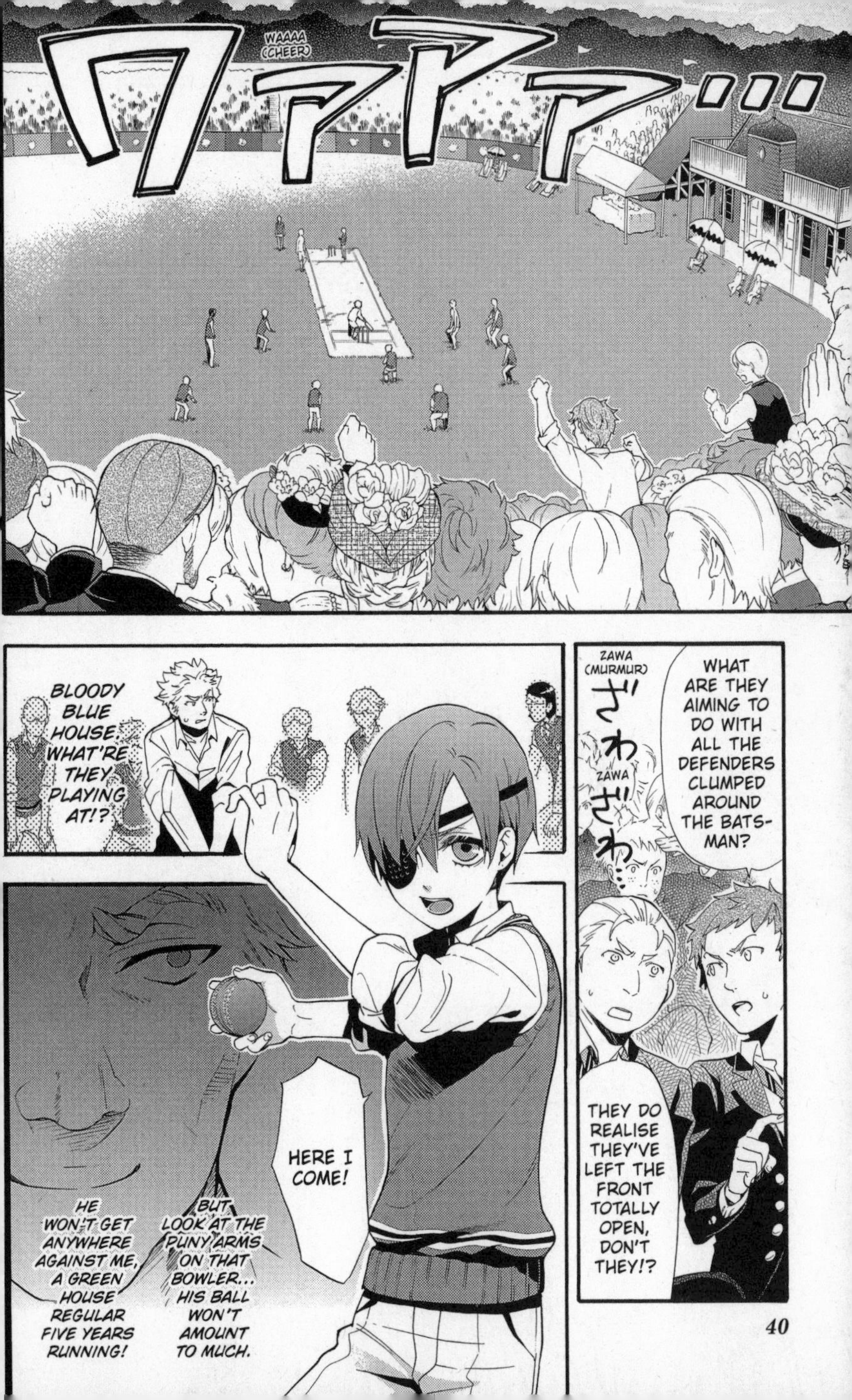
ワァアア…
WAAAA (CHEER)
ZAWA (MURMUR) ざわ ZAWA ざわ
WHAT ARE THEY AIMING TO DO WITH ALL THE DEFENDERS CLUMPED AROUND THE BATSMAN?
THEY DO REALISE THEY'VE LEFT THE FRONT TOTALLY OPEN, DON'T THEY!?
BLOODY BLUE HOUSE. WHAT'RE THEY PLAYING AT!?
HERE I COME!
BUT LOOK AT THE PUNY ARMS ON THAT BOWLER... HIS BALL WON'T AMOUNT TO MUCH.
HE WON'T GET ANYWHERE AGAINST ME, A GREEN HOUSE REGULAR FIVE YEARS RUNNING!

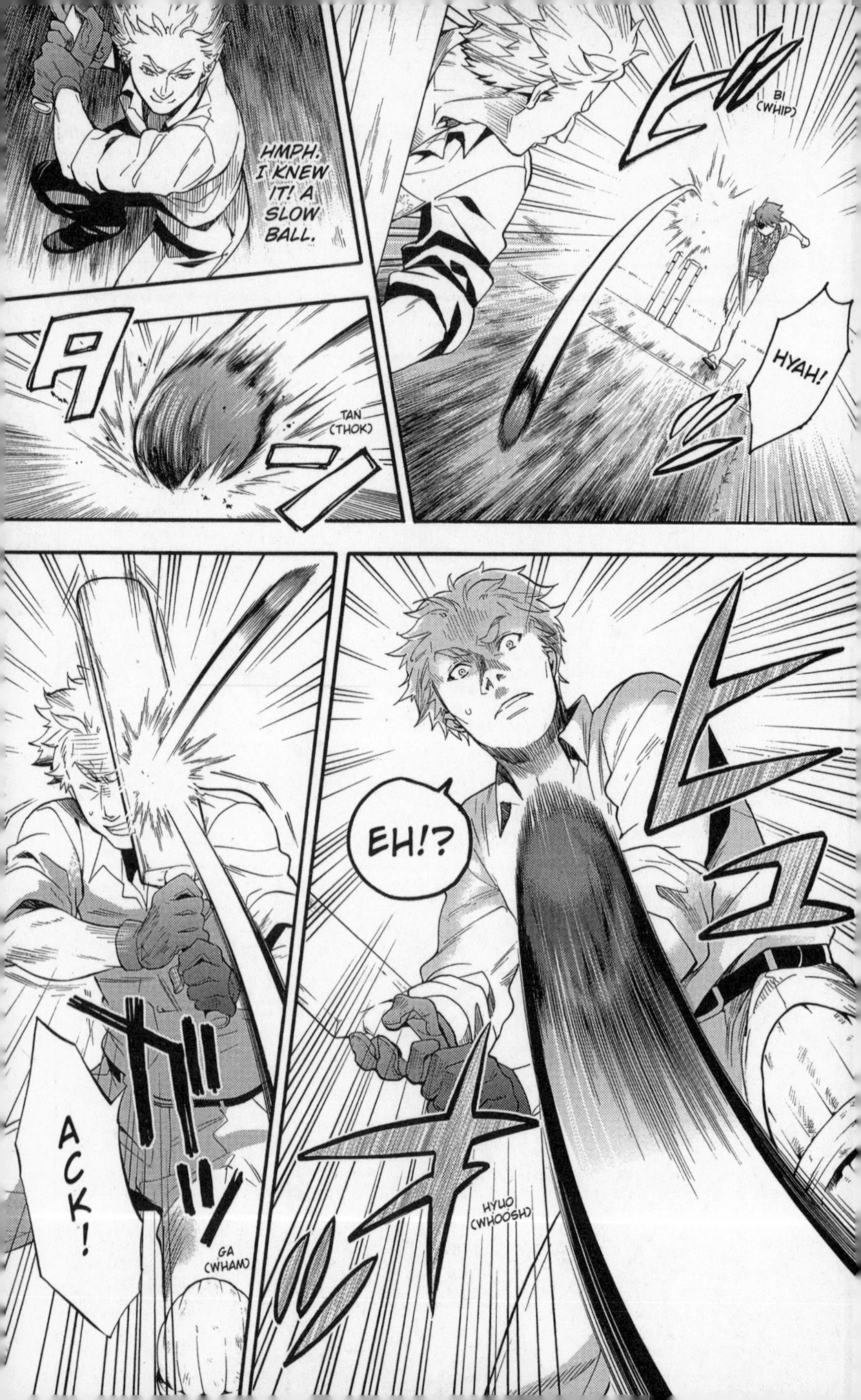
BI (WHIP)
HYAH!
HMPH. I KNEW IT! A SLOW BALL.
TAN (THOK)
EH!?
HYUO (WHOOSH)
GA (WHAM)
ACK!

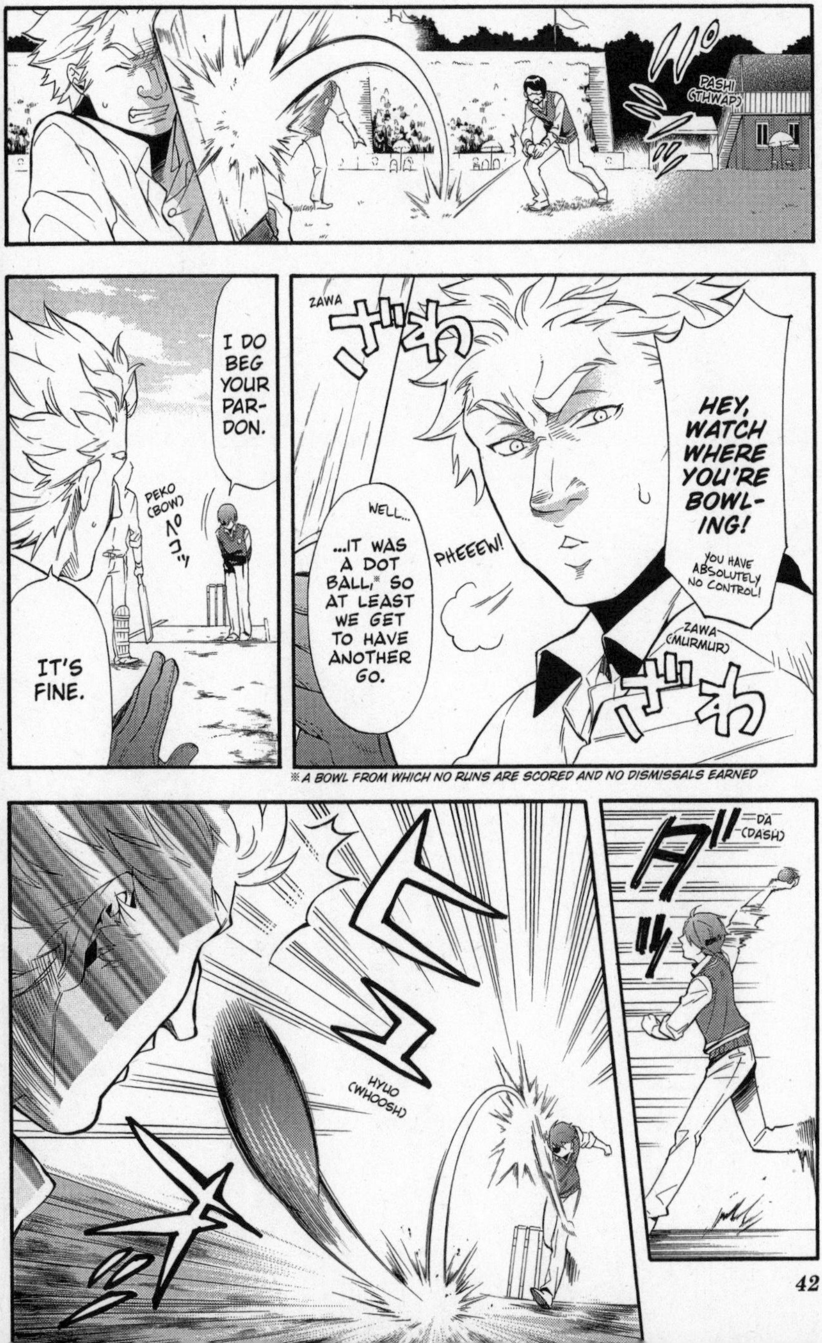
PASHI (THWAP)
ZAWA
HEY, WATCH WHERE YOU'RE BOWL-ING!
YOU HAVE ABSOLUTELY NO CONTROL!
ZAWA (MURMUR)
PHEEEW!
WELL...
...IT WAS A DOT BALL,※ SO AT LEAST WE GET TO HAVE ANOTHER GO.
I DO BEG YOUR PAR-DON.
PEKO (BOW)
IT'S FINE.
※A BOWL FROM WHICH NO RUNS ARE SCORED AND NO DISMISSALS EARNED
DA (DASH)
HYUO (WHOOSH)

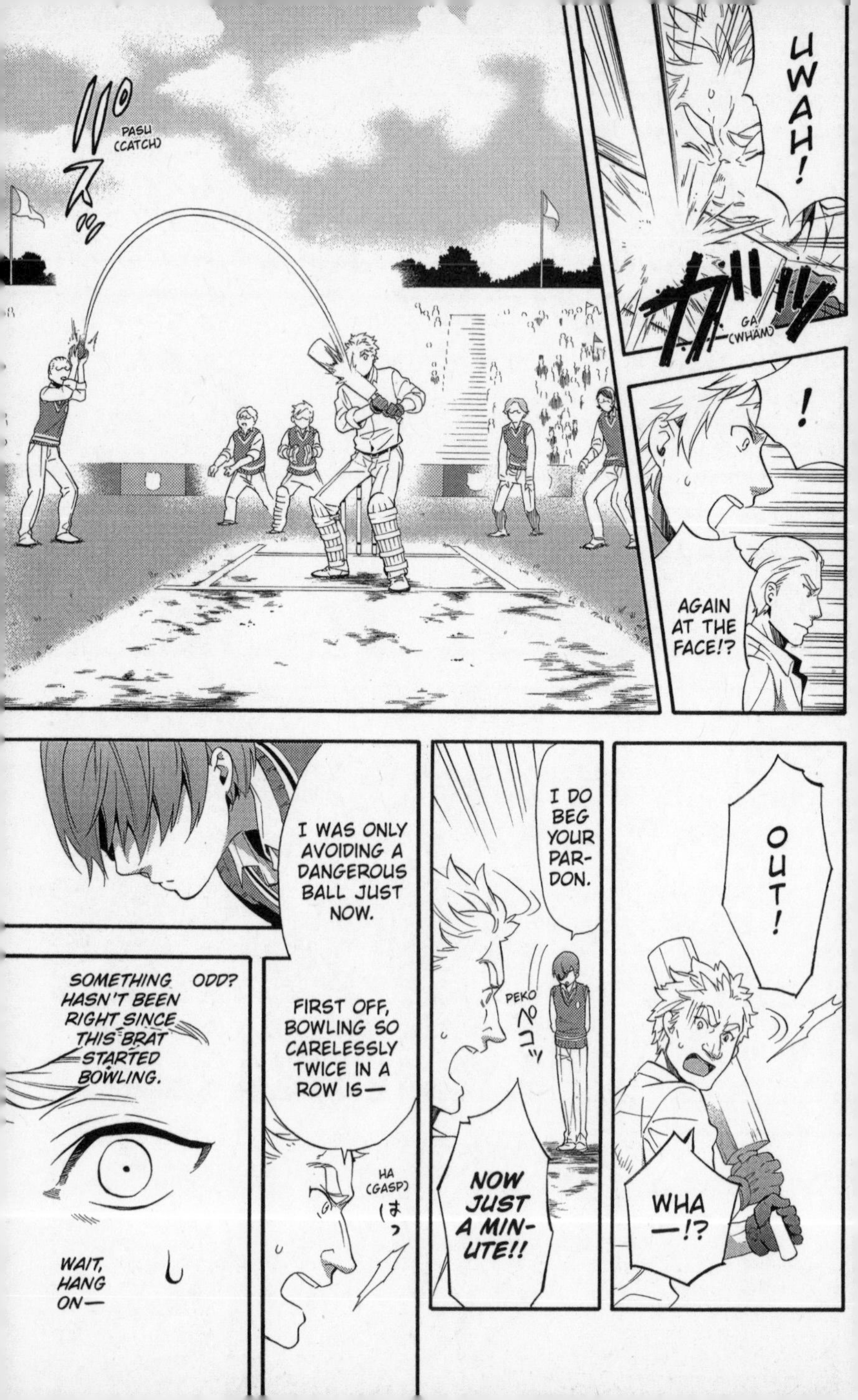
UWAH!
GA (WHAM)
!
AGAIN AT THE FACE!?
PASU (CATCH)
OUT!
WHA—!?
I DO BEG YOUR PARDON.
PEKO
NOW JUST A MINUTE!!
I WAS ONLY AVOIDING A DANGEROUS BALL JUST NOW.
FIRST OFF, BOWLING SO CARELESSLY TWICE IN A ROW IS—
HA (GASP)
SOMETHING ODD? HASN'T BEEN RIGHT SINCE THIS BRAT STARTED BOWLING.
WAIT, HANG ON—

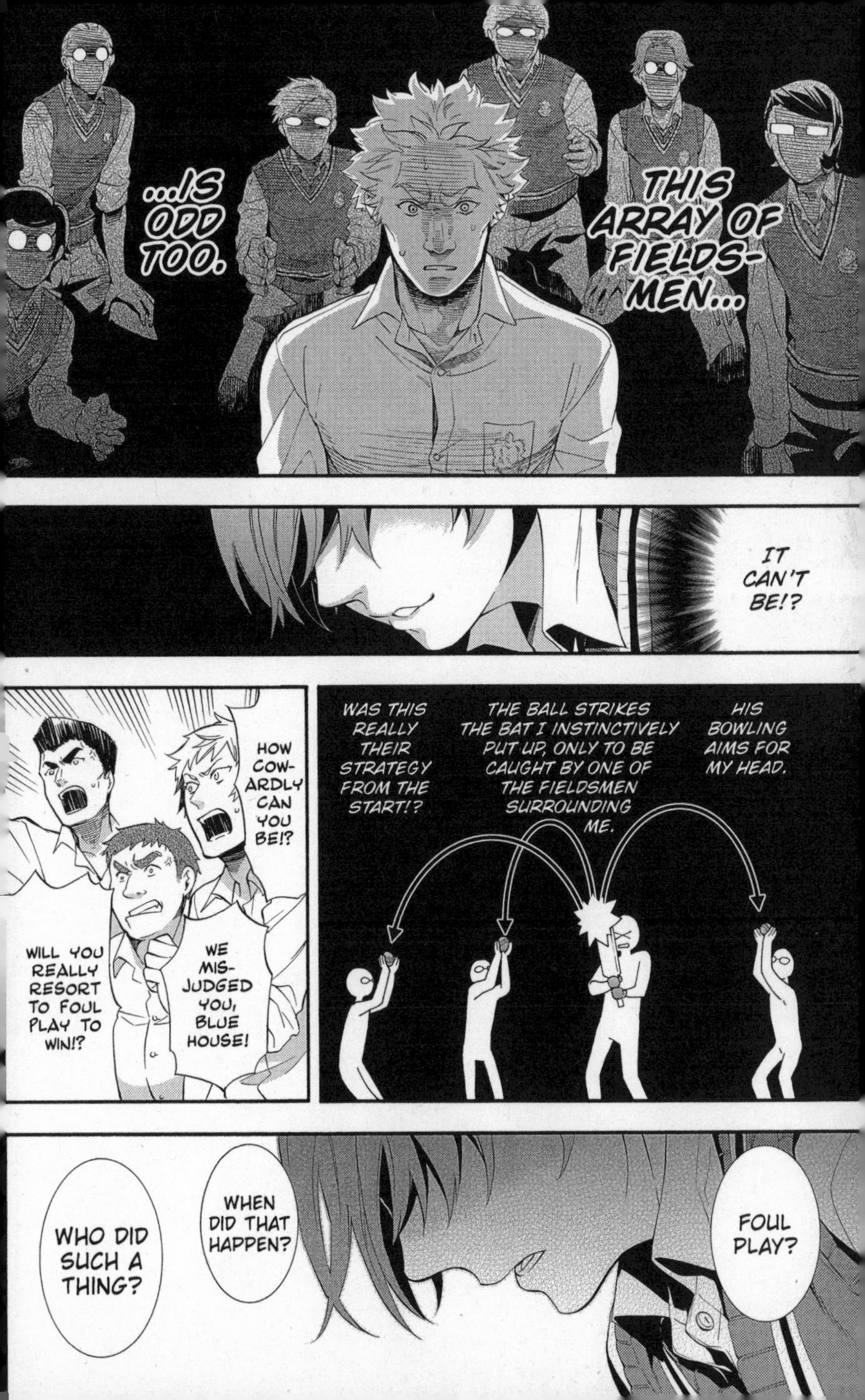
THIS ARRAY OF FIELDS-MEN...
...IS ODD TOO.
IT CAN'T BE!?
HIS BOWLING AIMS FOR MY HEAD.
THE BALL STRIKES THE BAT I INSTINCTIVELY PUT UP, ONLY TO BE CAUGHT BY ONE OF THE FIELDSMEN SURROUNDING ME.
WAS THIS REALLY THEIR STRATEGY FROM THE START!?
HOW COWARDLY CAN YOU BE!?
WE MISJUDGED YOU, BLUE HOUSE!
WILL YOU REALLY RESORT TO FOUL PLAY TO WIN!?
FOUL PLAY?
WHEN DID THAT HAPPEN?
WHO DID SUCH A THING?

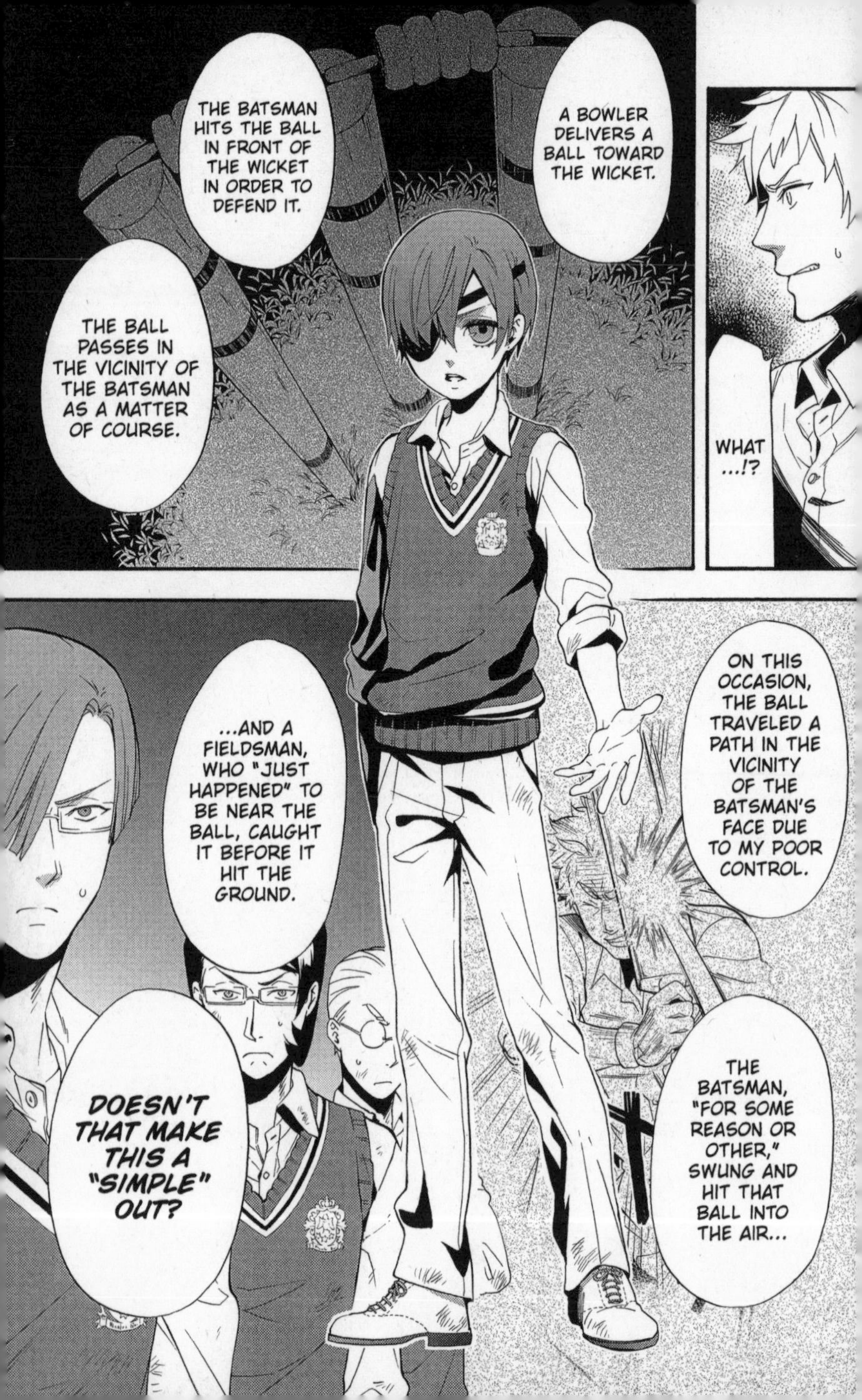
WHAT ...!?
A BOWLER DELIVERS A BALL TOWARD THE WICKET.
THE BATSMAN HITS THE BALL IN FRONT OF THE WICKET IN ORDER TO DEFEND IT.
THE BALL PASSES IN THE VICINITY OF THE BATSMAN AS A MATTER OF COURSE.
ON THIS OCCASION, THE BALL TRAVELED A PATH IN THE VICINITY OF THE BATSMAN'S FACE DUE TO MY POOR CONTROL.
THE BATSMAN, "FOR SOME REASON OR OTHER," SWUNG AND HIT THAT BALL INTO THE AIR...
...AND A FIELDSMAN, WHO "JUST HAPPENED" TO BE NEAR THE BALL, CAUGHT IT BEFORE IT HIT THE GROUND.
DOESN'T THAT MAKE THIS A "SIMPLE" OUT?

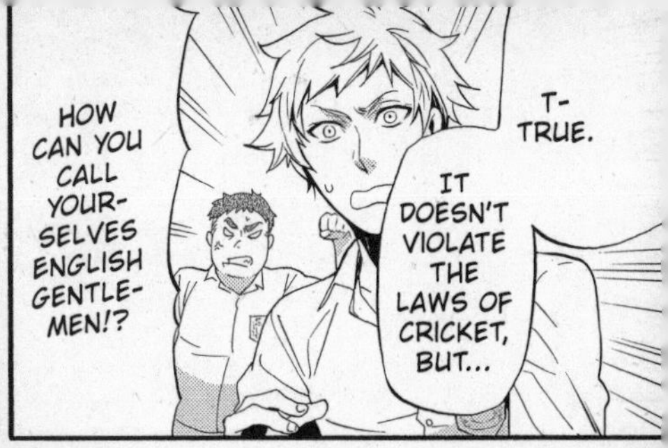
T-TRUE.
IT DOESN'T VIOLATE THE LAWS OF CRICKET, BUT...
HOW CAN YOU CALL YOURSELVES ENGLISH GENTLEMEN!?

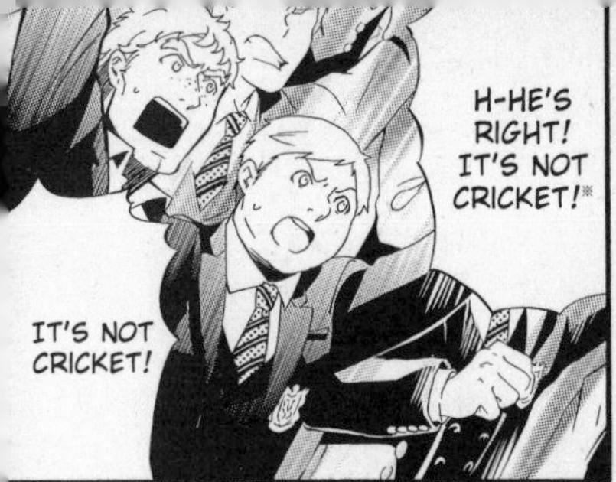
H-HE'S RIGHT! IT'S NOT CRICKET!※
IT'S NOT CRICKET!

※ THIS EXPRESSION IS USED TO MEAN, "IT'S NOT FAIR," AS THE SPIRIT OF CRICKET PUTS GREAT VALUE ON FAIR PLAY.

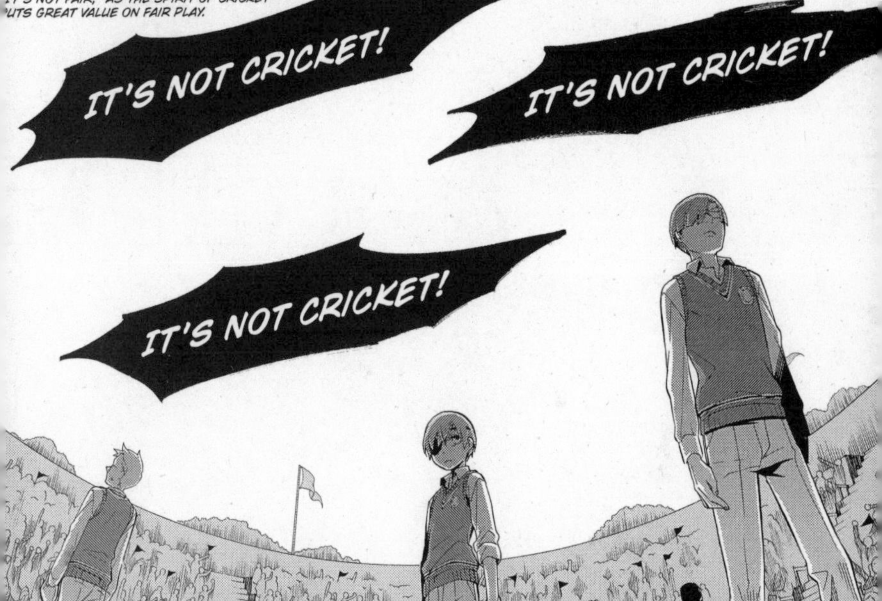
IT'S NOT CRICKET!
IT'S NOT CRICKET!
IT'S NOT CRICKET!

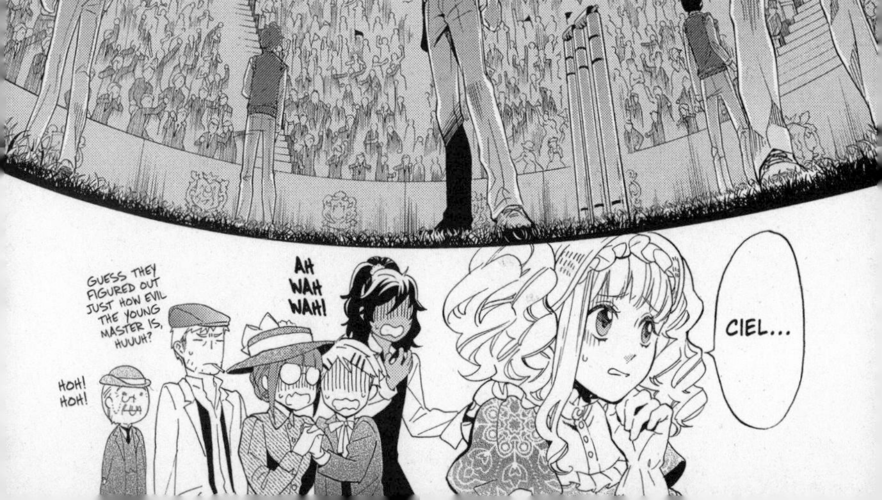
CIEL...
AH WAH WAH!
GUESS THEY FIGURED OUT JUST HOW EVIL THE YOUNG MASTER IS, HUUUH?
HOH! HOH!

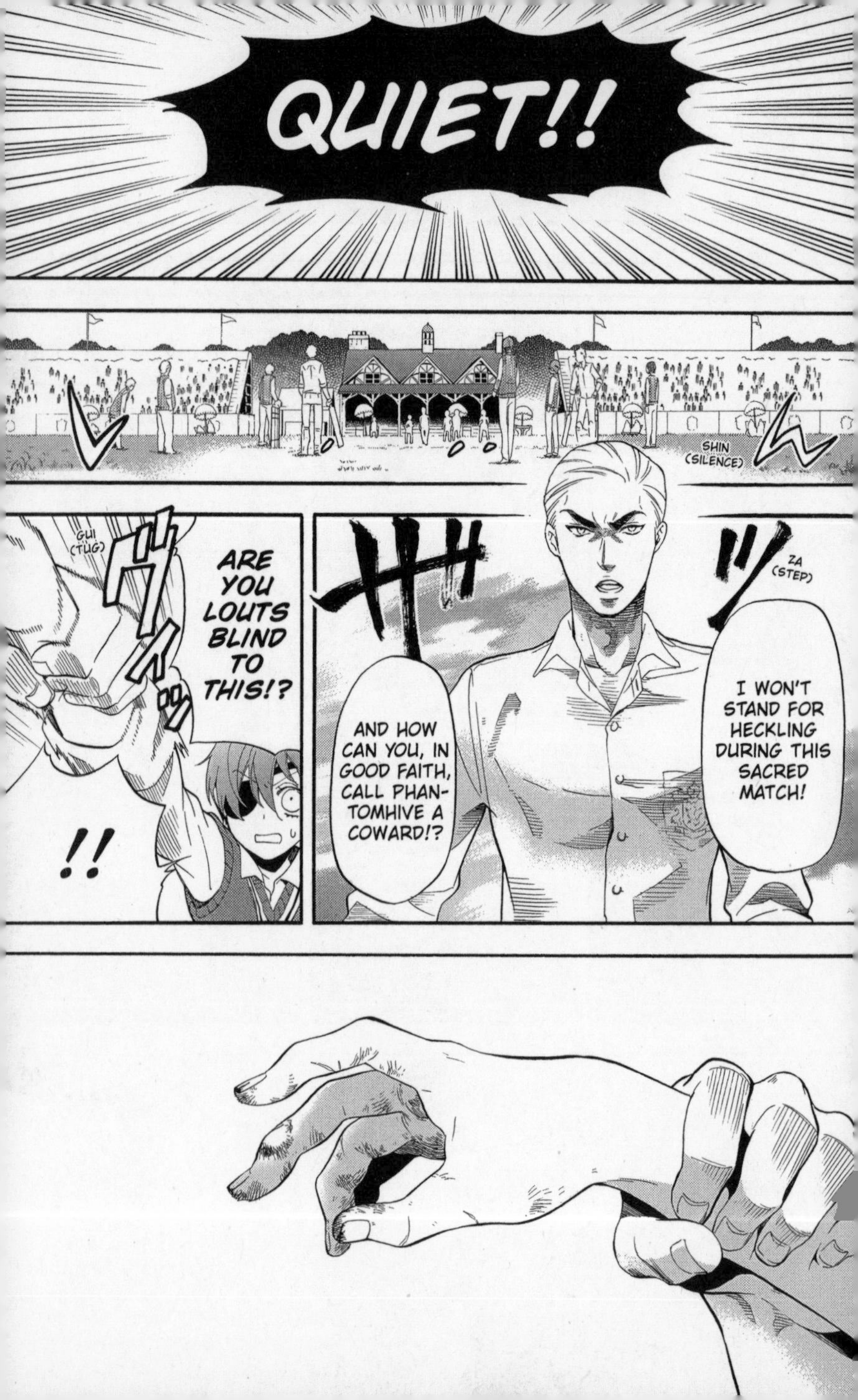
QUIET!!
SHIN (SILENCE)
ZA (STEP)
I WON'T STAND FOR HECKLING DURING THIS SACRED MATCH!
AND HOW CAN YOU, IN GOOD FAITH, CALL PHANTOMHIVE A COWARD!?
GUI (TUG)
ARE YOU LOUTS BLIND TO THIS!?
!!

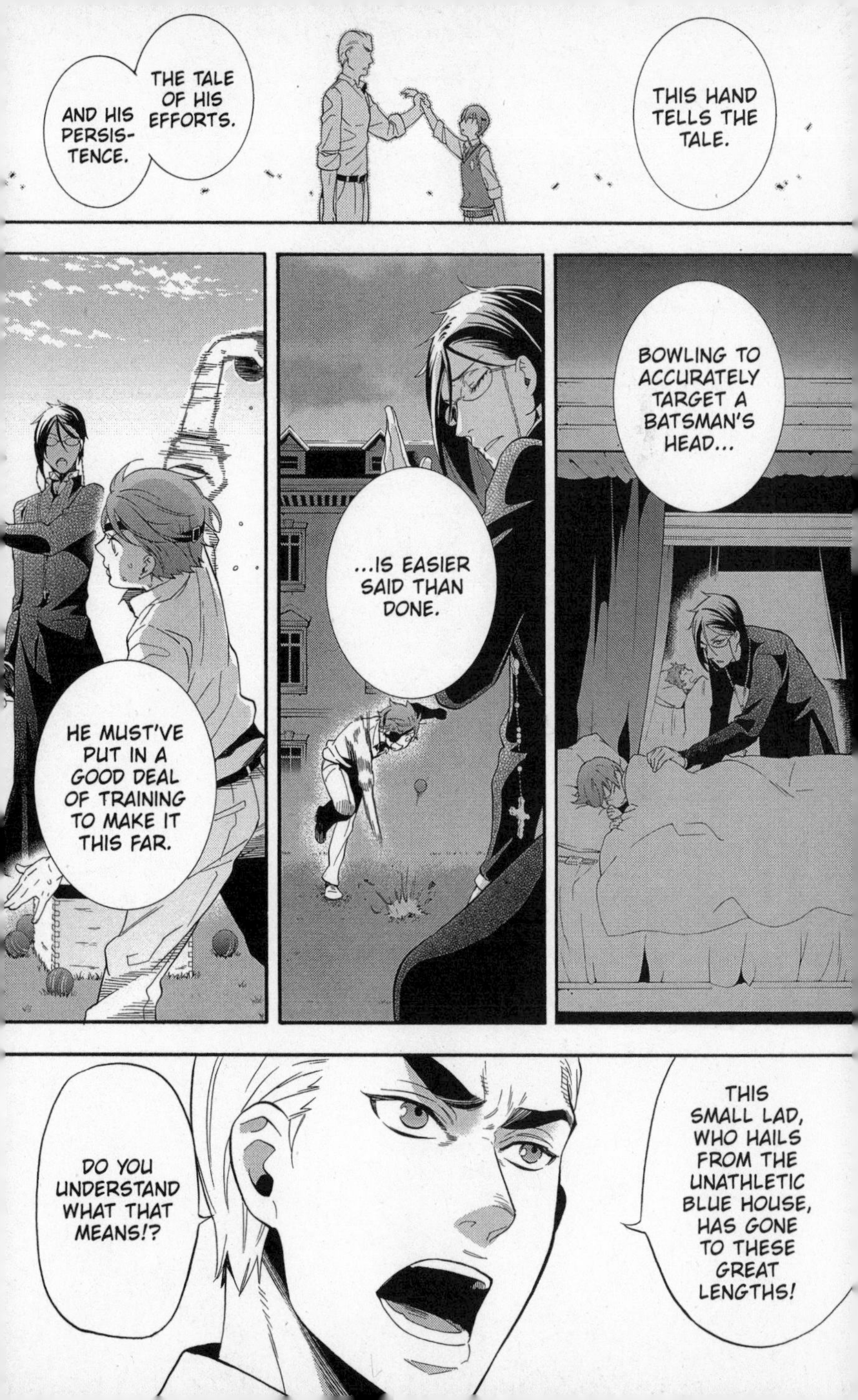
THIS HAND TELLS THE TALE.
THE TALE OF HIS EFFORTS.
AND HIS PERSIS-TENCE.
BOWLING TO ACCURATELY TARGET A BATSMAN'S HEAD...
...IS EASIER SAID THAN DONE.
HE MUST'VE PUT IN A GOOD DEAL OF TRAINING TO MAKE IT THIS FAR.
THIS SMALL LAD, WHO HAILS FROM THE UNATHLETIC BLUE HOUSE, HAS GONE TO THESE GREAT LENGTHS!
DO YOU UNDERSTAND WHAT THAT MEANS!?

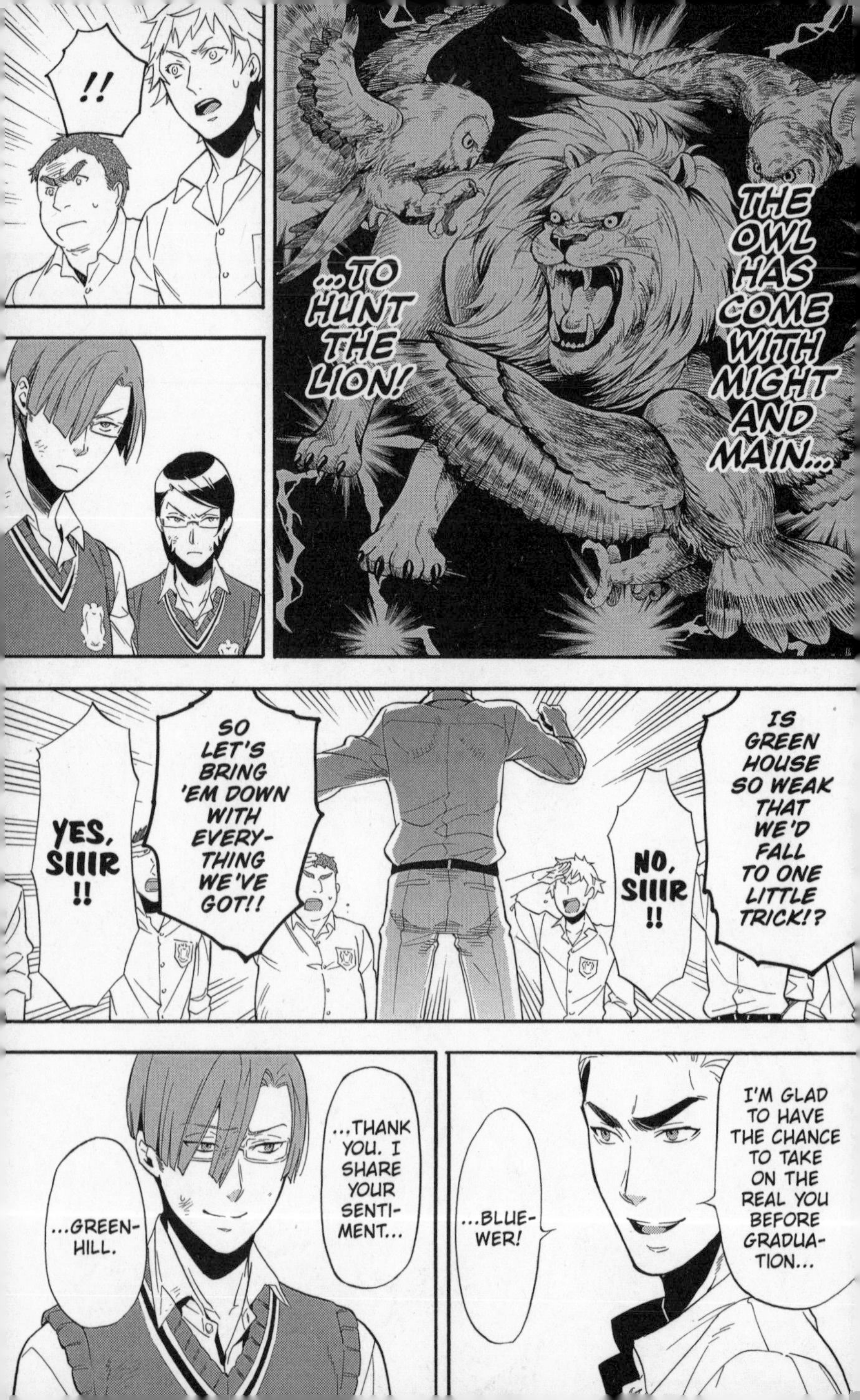
THE OWL HAS COME WITH MIGHT AND MAIN...
...TO HUNT THE LION!
!!
IS GREEN HOUSE SO WEAK THAT WE'D FALL TO ONE LITTLE TRICK!?
NO, SIIIR!!
SO LET'S BRING 'EM DOWN WITH EVERYTHING WE'VE GOT!!
YES, SIIIR!!
I'M GLAD TO HAVE THE CHANCE TO TAKE ON THE REAL YOU BEFORE GRADUATION...
...BLUEWER!
...THANK YOU. I SHARE YOUR SENTIMENT...
...GREENHILL.

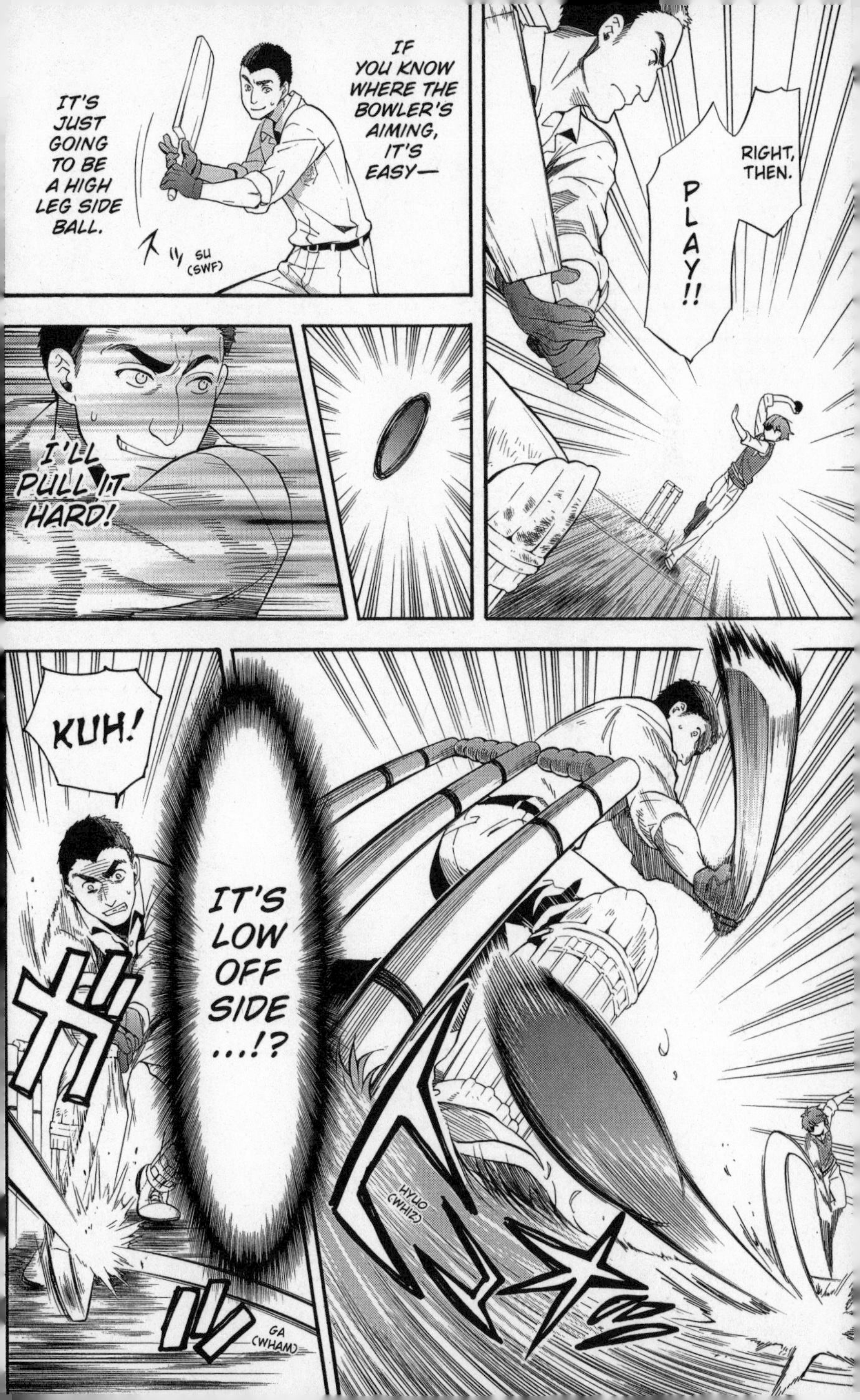
RIGHT, THEN.
PLAY!!
IF YOU KNOW WHERE THE BOWLER'S AIMING, IT'S EASY—
IT'S JUST GOING TO BE A HIGH LEG SIDE BALL.
SU (SWF)
I'LL PULL IT HARD!
KUH!
IT'S LOW OFF SIDE...!?
HYUO (WHIZ)
GA (WHAM)

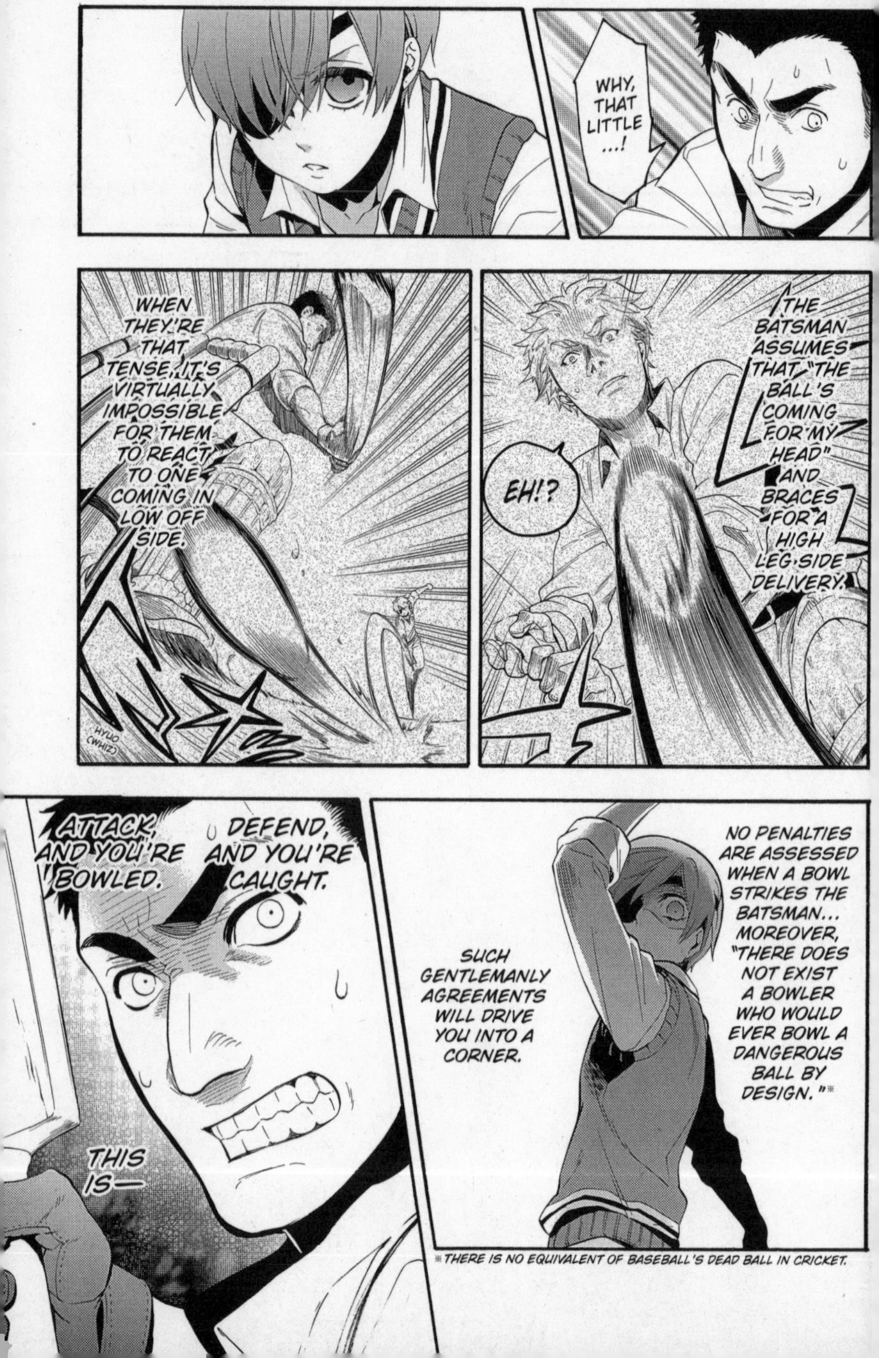
WHY, THAT LITTLE ...!
THE BATSMAN ASSUMES THAT "THE BALL'S COMING FOR MY HEAD" AND BRACES FOR A HIGH LEG-SIDE DELIVERY.
EH!?
WHEN THEY'RE THAT TENSE, IT'S VIRTUALLY IMPOSSIBLE FOR THEM TO REACT TO ONE COMING IN LOW OFF SIDE.
HYUO (WHIZ)
NO PENALTIES ARE ASSESSED WHEN A BOWL STRIKES THE BATSMAN... MOREOVER, "THERE DOES NOT EXIST A BOWLER WHO WOULD EVER BOWL A DANGEROUS BALL BY DESIGN."※
SUCH GENTLEMANLY AGREEMENTS WILL DRIVE YOU INTO A CORNER.
ATTACK, AND YOU'RE BOWLED.
DEFEND, AND YOU'RE CAUGHT.
THIS IS—

※THERE IS NO EQUIVALENT OF BASEBALL'S DEAD BALL IN CRICKET.

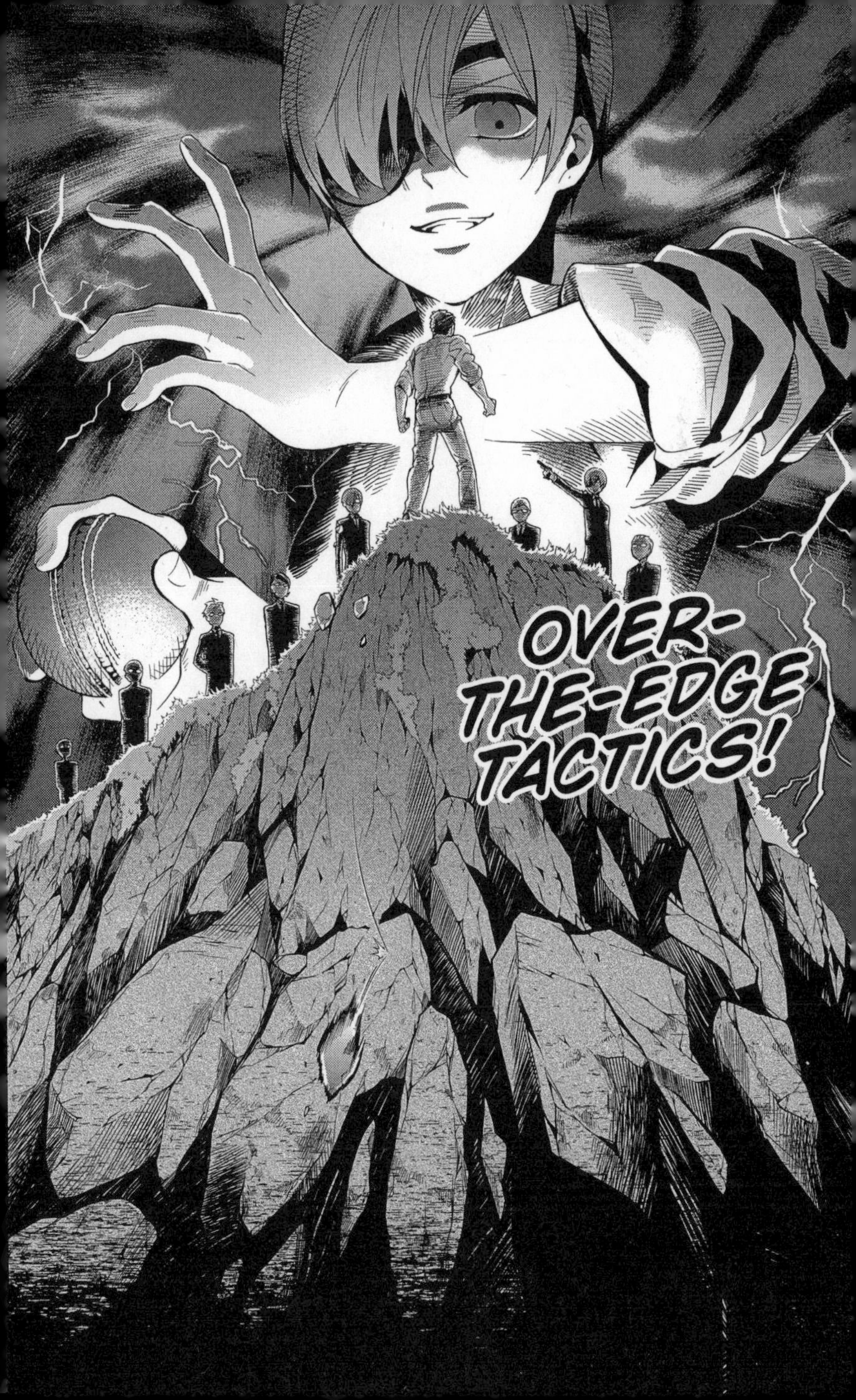
OVER-THE-EDGE TACTICS!

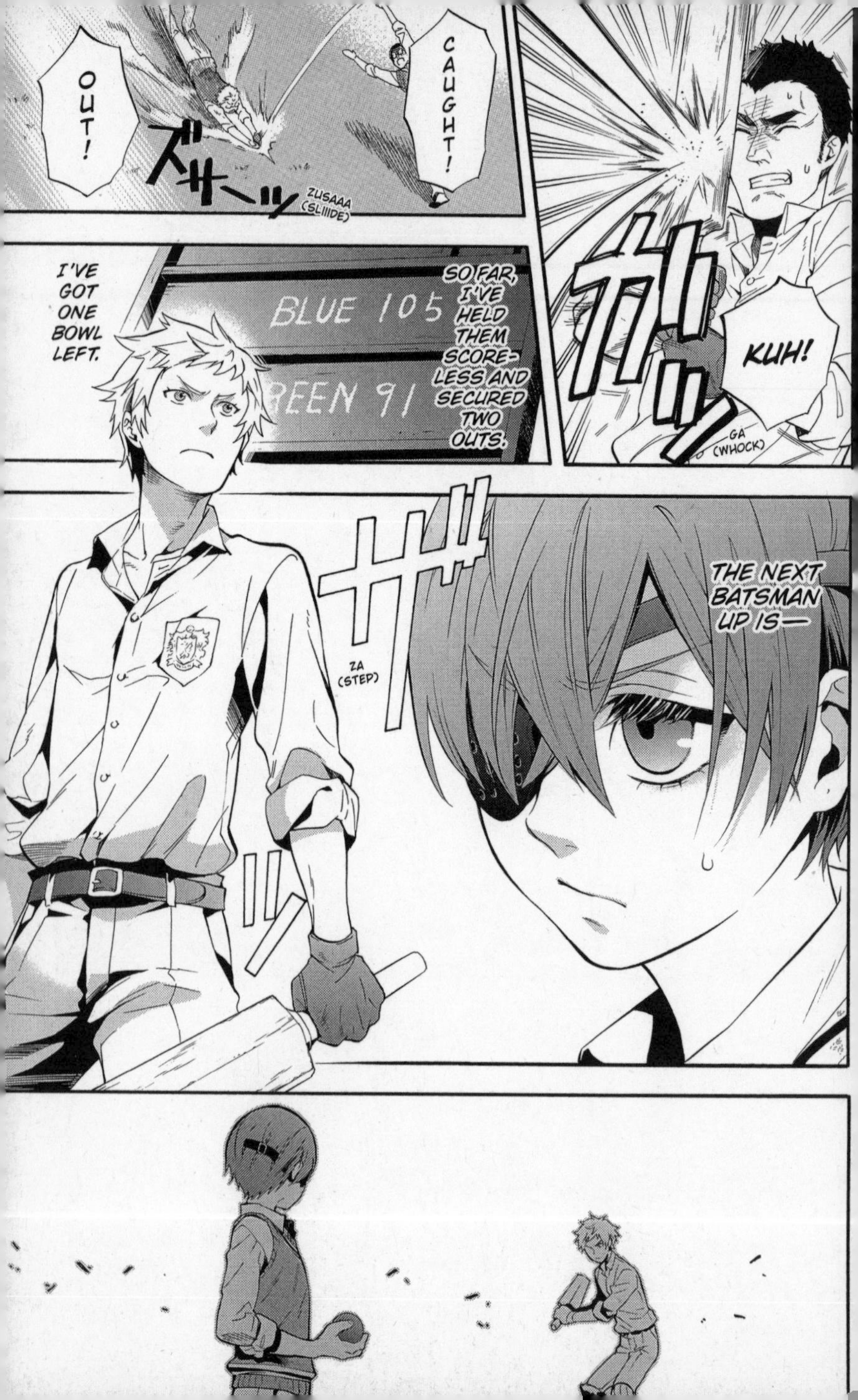
KUH!
GA (WHOCK)
CAUGHT!
OUT!
ZUSAAA (SLIIIDE)
SO FAR, I'VE HELD THEM SCORELESS AND SECURED TWO OUTS.
BLUE 105
REEN 91
I'VE GOT ONE BOWL LEFT.
THE NEXT BATSMAN UP IS—
ZA (STEP)

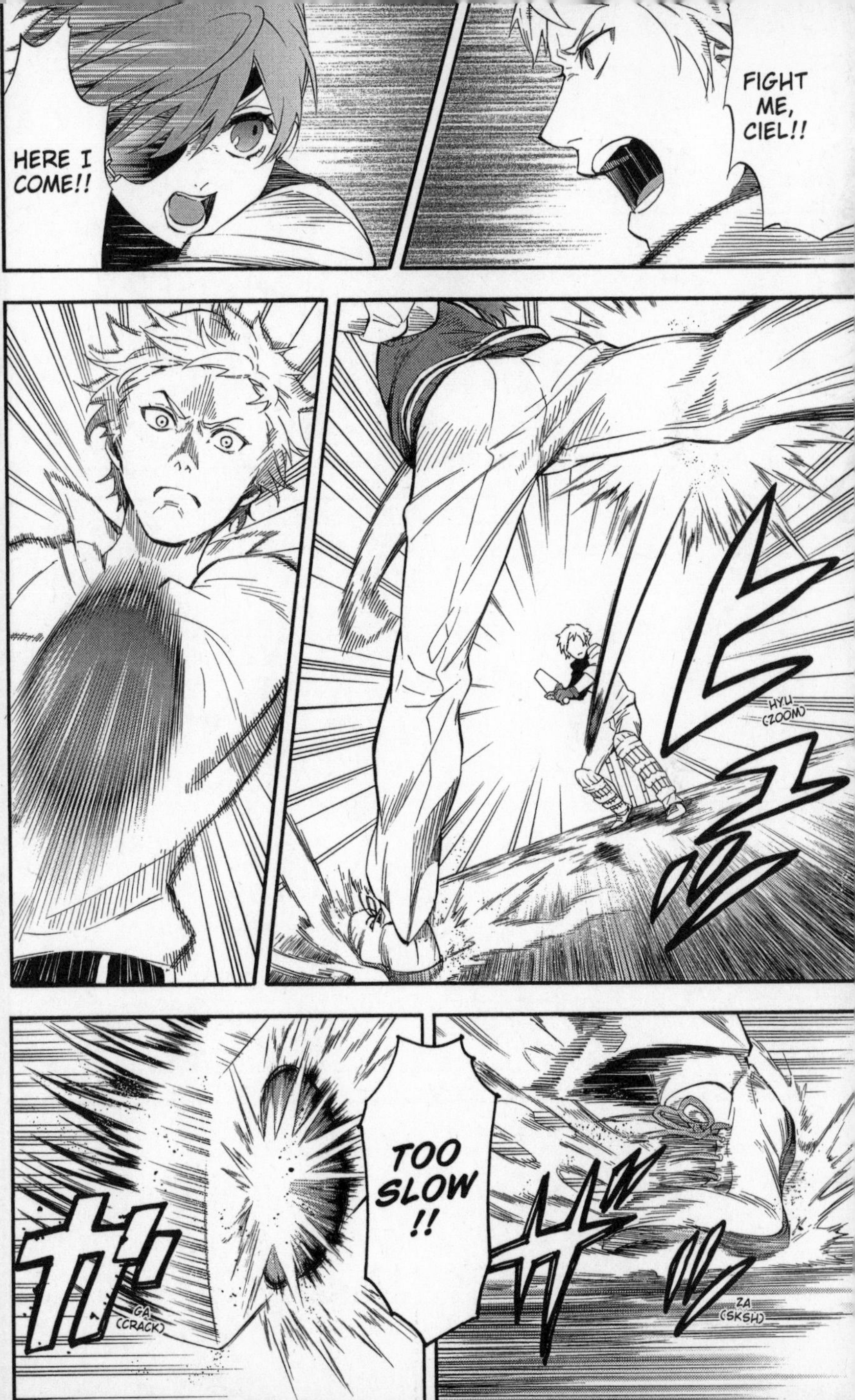
FIGHT ME, CIEL!!
HERE I COME!!
HYU (ZOOM)
ZA (SKSH)
TOO SLOW!!
GA (CRACK)

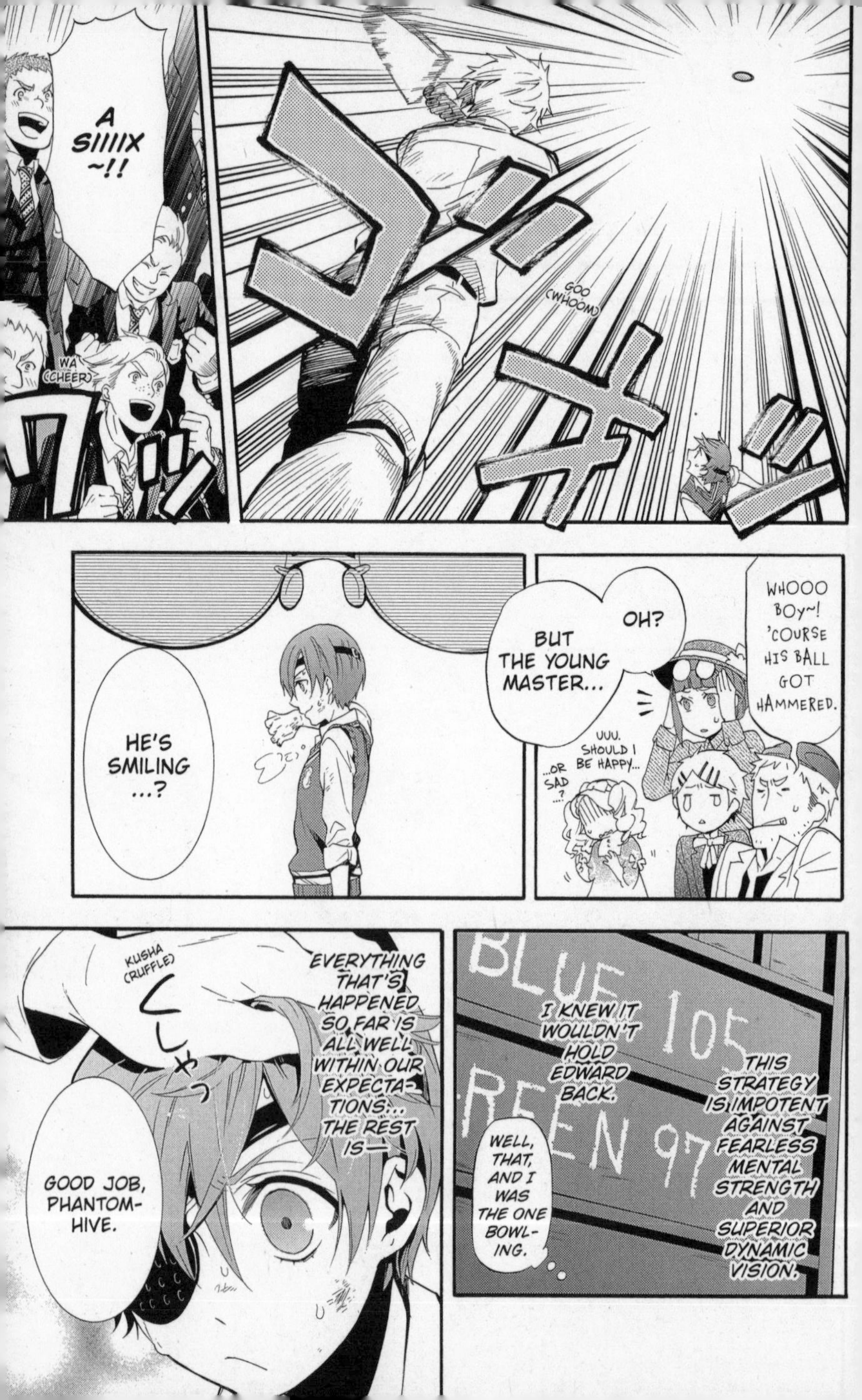
GOO (WHOOM)
A SIIIIX ~!!
WA (CHEER)
WHOOO BOy~! 'COURSE HIS BALL GOT HAMMERED.
OH? BUT THE YOUNG MASTER...
UUU. SHOULD I BE HAPPY...
...OR SAD ...?
HE'S SMILING ...?
BLUE 105
REEN 97
THIS STRATEGY IS IMPOTENT AGAINST FEARLESS MENTAL STRENGTH AND SUPERIOR DYNAMIC VISION.
I KNEW IT WOULDN'T HOLD EDWARD BACK.
WELL, THAT, AND I WAS THE ONE BOWLING.
KUSHA (RUFFLE)
EVERYTHING THAT'S HAPPENED SO FAR IS ALL WELL WITHIN OUR EXPECTATIONS... THE REST IS—
GOOD JOB, PHANTOMHIVE.

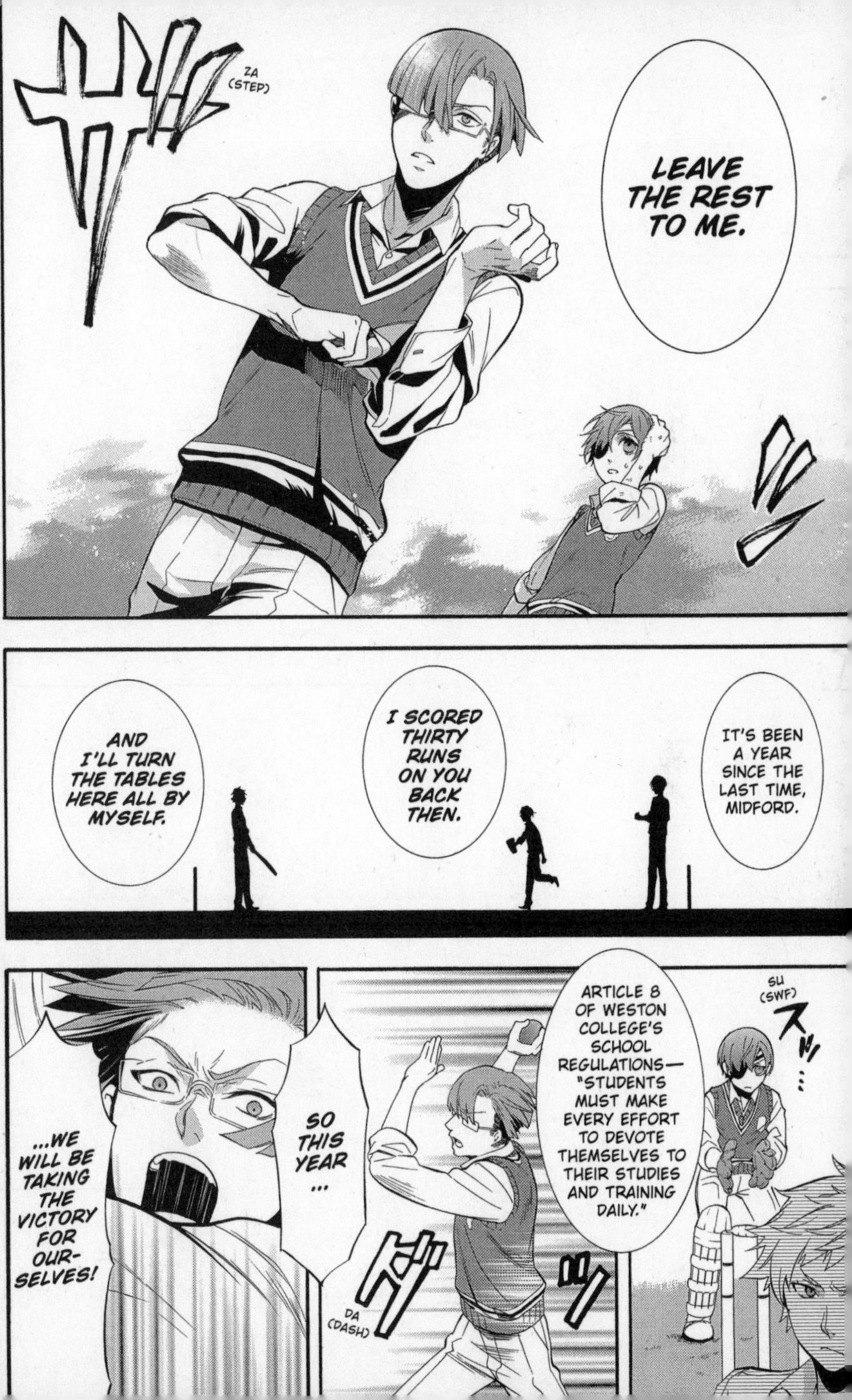
LEAVE THE REST TO ME.
ZA (STEP)
IT'S BEEN A YEAR SINCE THE LAST TIME, MIDFORD.
I SCORED THIRTY RUNS ON YOU BACK THEN.
AND I'LL TURN THE TABLES HERE ALL BY MYSELF.
SU (SWF)
ARTICLE 8 OF WESTON COLLEGE'S SCHOOL REGULATIONS— "STUDENTS MUST MAKE EVERY EFFORT TO DEVOTE THEMSELVES TO THEIR STUDIES AND TRAINING DAILY."
DA (DASH)
SO THIS YEAR...
...WE WILL BE TAKING THE VICTORY FOR OURSELVES!

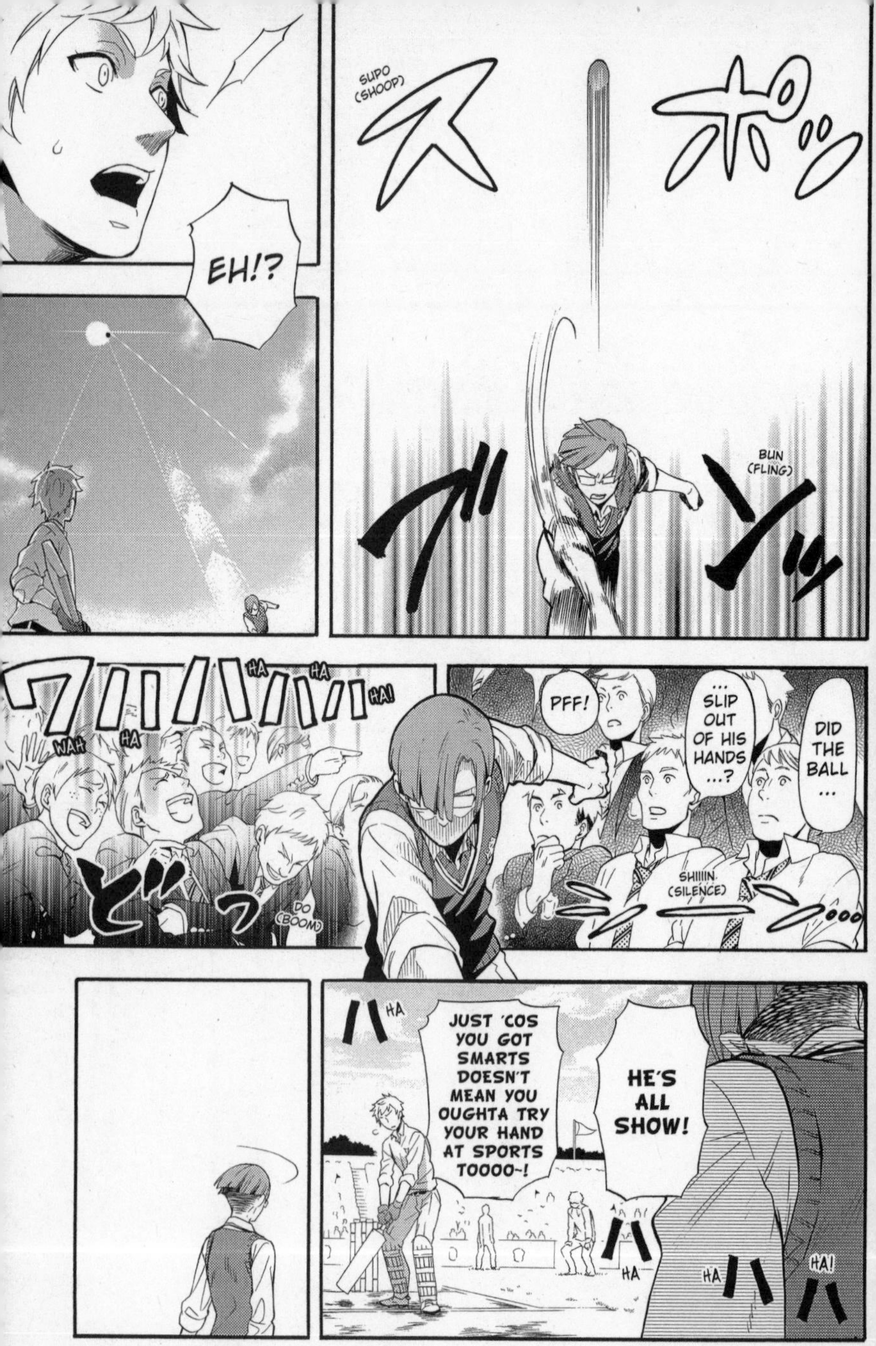
SUPO (SHOOP)
BUN (FLING)
EH!?
DID THE BALL ...
... SLIP OUT OF HIS HANDS ...?
PFF!
SHIIIN (SILENCE)
HA
HA
HA!
WAH
HA
DO (BOOM)
HE'S ALL SHOW!
JUST 'COS YOU GOT SMARTS DOESN'T MEAN YOU OUGHTA TRY YOUR HAND AT SPORTS TOOOO~!
HA
HA
HA
HA!
HA

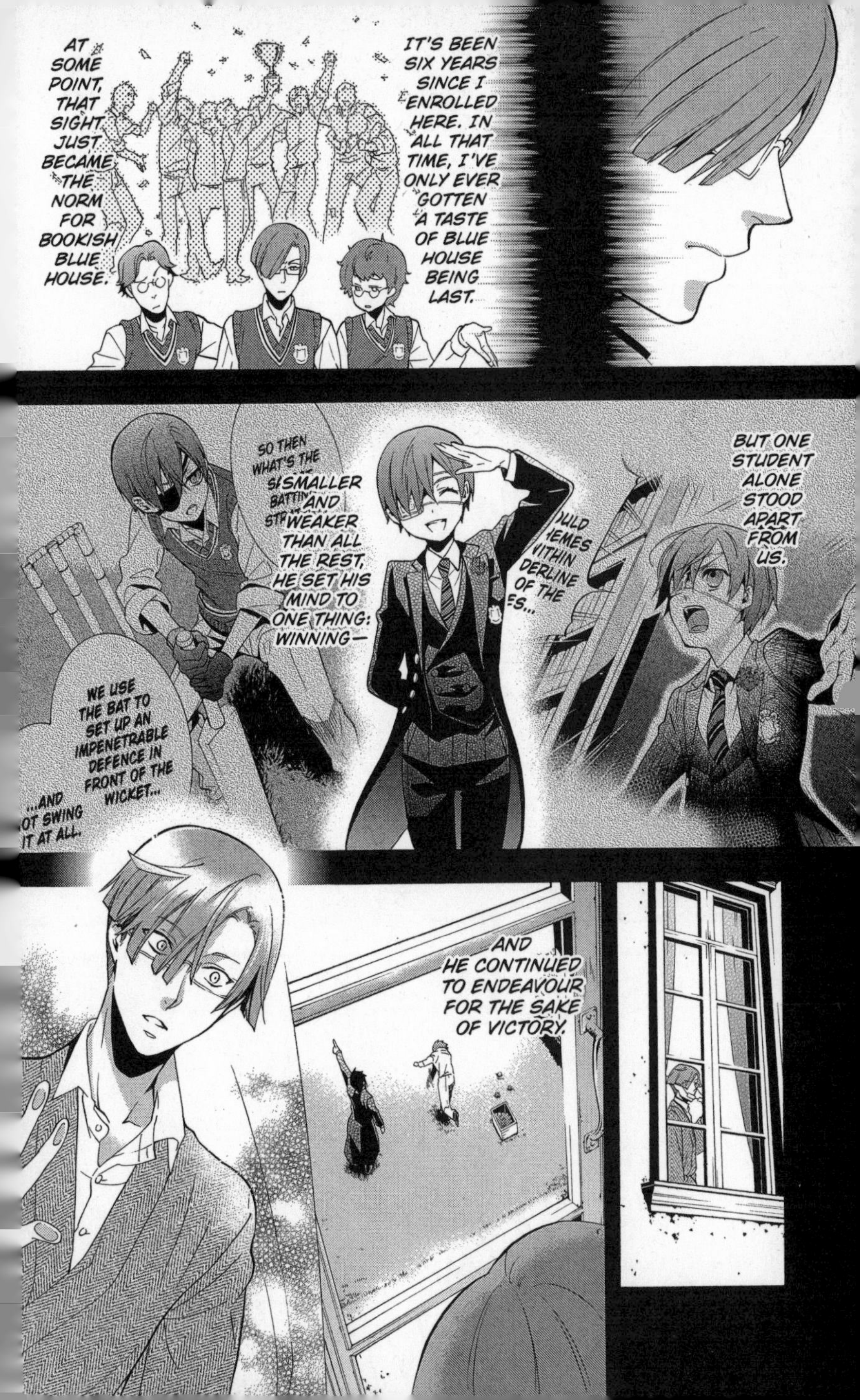
IT'S BEEN SIX YEARS SINCE I ENROLLED HERE. IN ALL THAT TIME, I'VE ONLY EVER GOTTEN A TASTE OF BLUE HOUSE BEING LAST.
AT SOME POINT, THAT SIGHT JUST BECAME THE NORM FOR BOOKISH BLUE HOUSE.
BUT ONE STUDENT ALONE STOOD APART FROM US.
SMALLER AND WEAKER THAN ALL THE REST, HE SET HIS MIND TO ONE THING: WINNING—
SO THEN WHAT'S THE
WE USE THE BAT TO SET UP AN IMPENETRABLE DEFENCE IN FRONT OF THE WICKET...
...AND
IT AT ALL.
AND HE CONTINUED TO ENDEAVOUR FOR THE SAKE OF VICTORY.

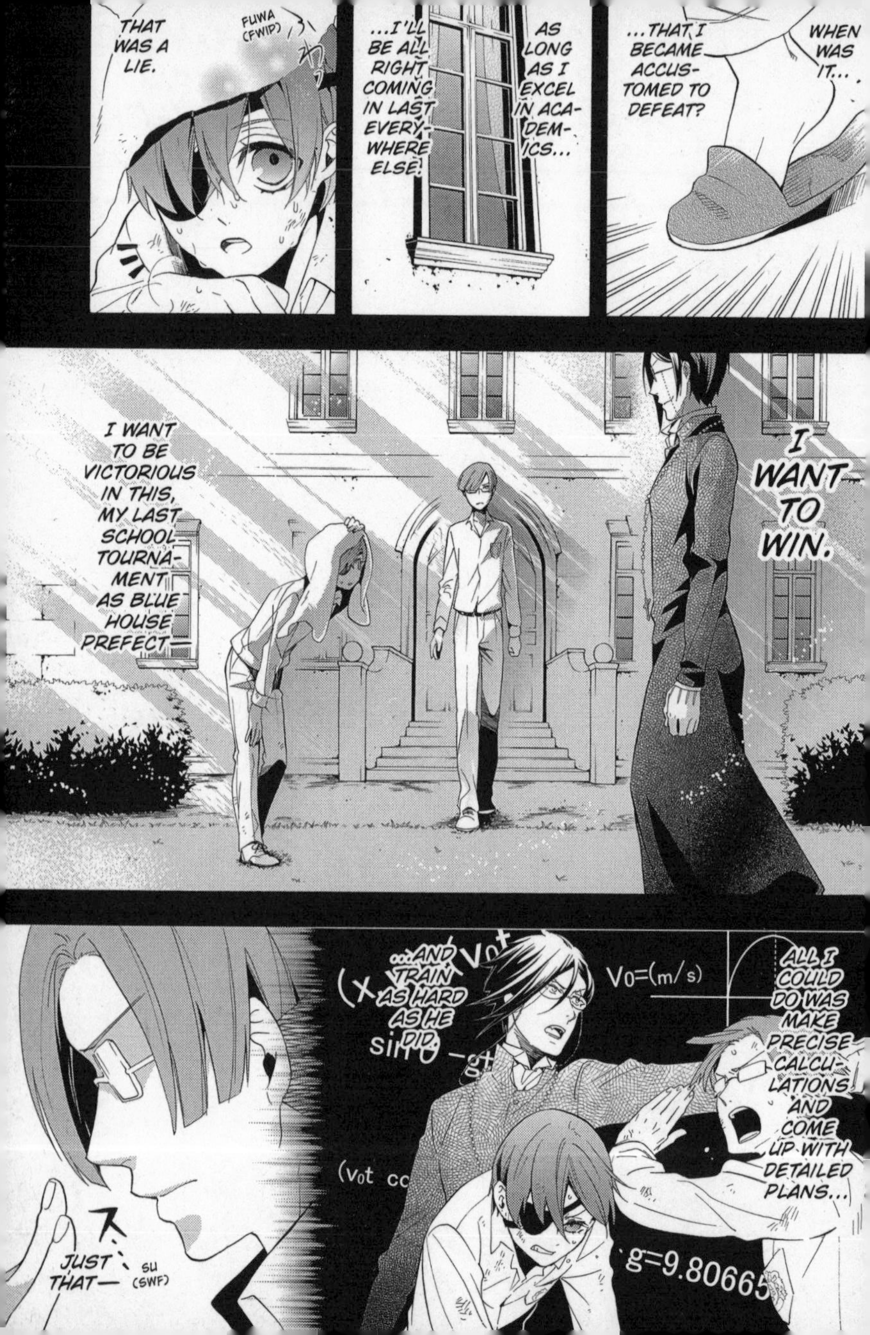
WHEN WAS IT...
...THAT I BECAME ACCUSTOMED TO DEFEAT?
AS LONG AS I EXCEL IN ACADEMICS...
...I'LL BE ALL RIGHT COMING IN LAST EVERYWHERE ELSE.
FUWA (FWIP)
THAT WAS A LIE.
I WANT TO BE VICTORIOUS IN THIS, MY LAST SCHOOL TOURNAMENT AS BLUE HOUSE PREFECT—
I WANT TO WIN.
ALL I COULD DO WAS MAKE PRECISE CALCULATIONS AND COME UP WITH DETAILED PLANS...
V0=(m/s)
...AND TRAIN AS HARD AS HE DID.
g=9.80665
SU (SWF)
JUST THAT—

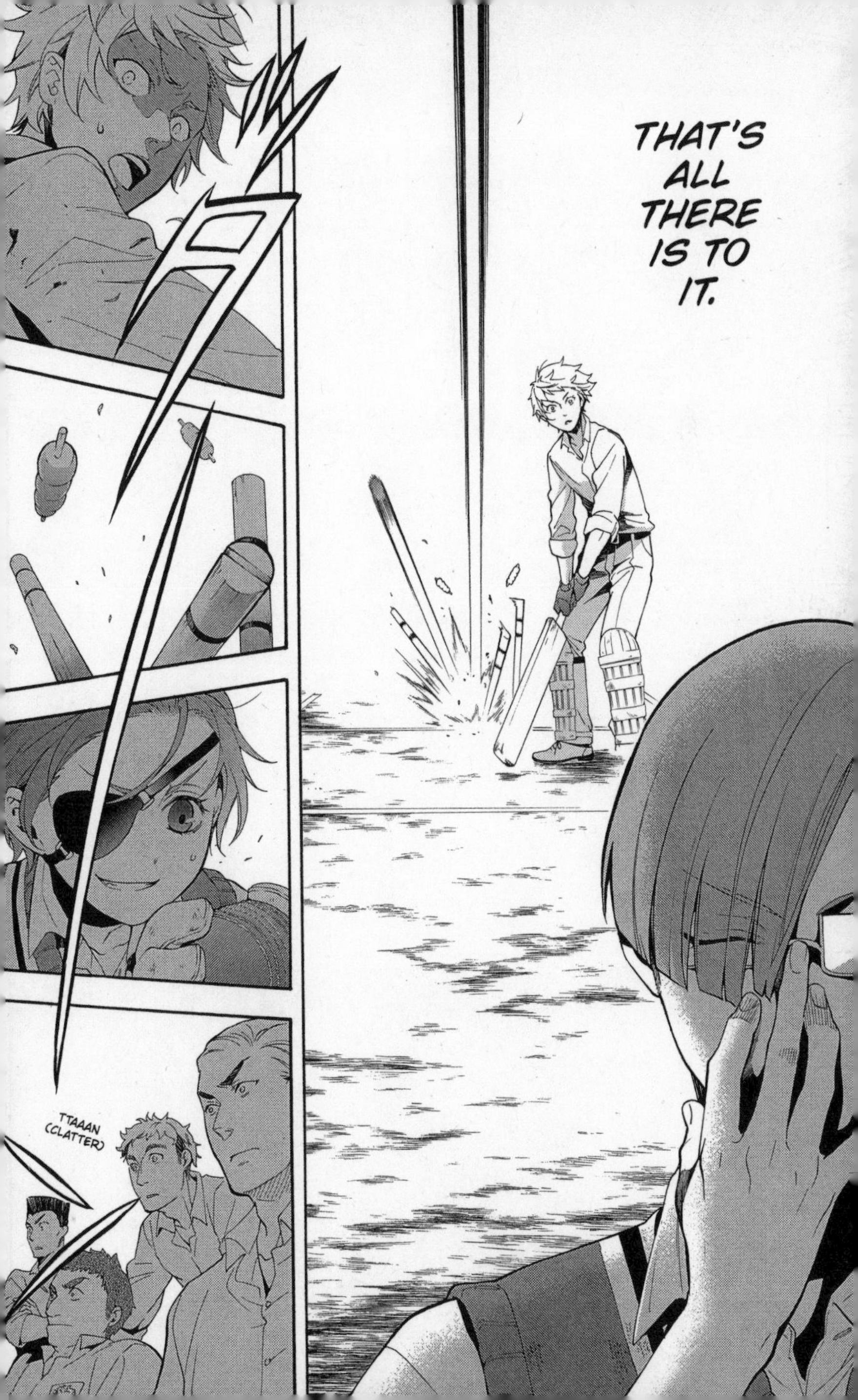
THAT'S ALL THERE IS TO IT.
TTAAAN (CLATTER)

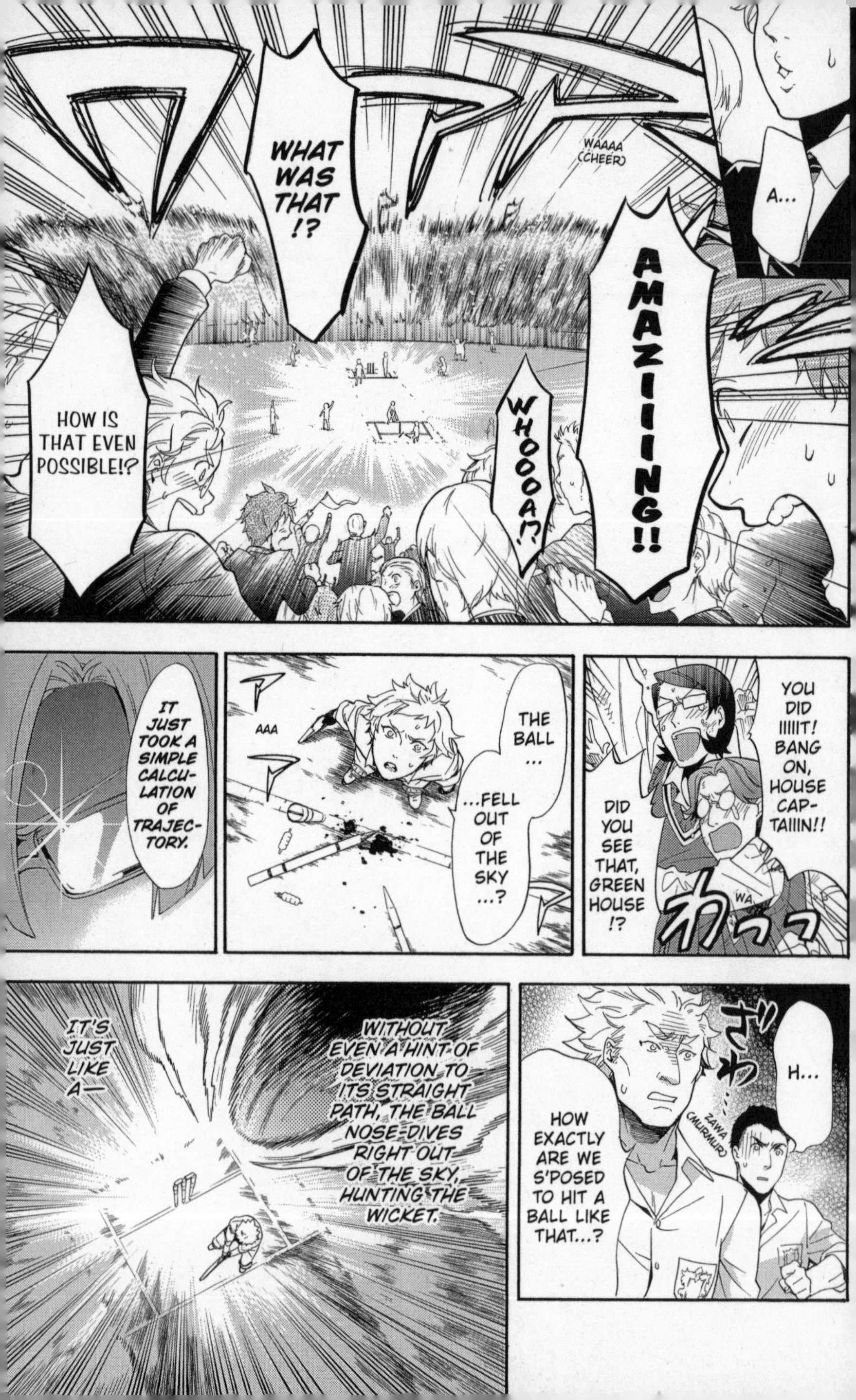
A...
WAAAA (CHEER)
AMAZIIIING!!
WHAT WAS THAT!?
WHOOOA!?
HOW IS THAT EVEN POSSIBLE!?
YOU DID IIIIIT! BANG ON, HOUSE CAPTAIIIN!!
DID YOU SEE THAT, GREEN HOUSE!?
WA
THE BALL...
...FELL OUT OF THE SKY...?
AAA
IT JUST TOOK A SIMPLE CALCULATION OF TRAJECTORY.
H...
ZAWA (MURMUR)
HOW EXACTLY ARE WE S'POSED TO HIT A BALL LIKE THAT...?
WITHOUT EVEN A HINT OF DEVIATION TO ITS STRAIGHT PATH, THE BALL NOSE-DIVES RIGHT OUT OF THE SKY, HUNTING THE WICKET.
IT'S JUST LIKE A—

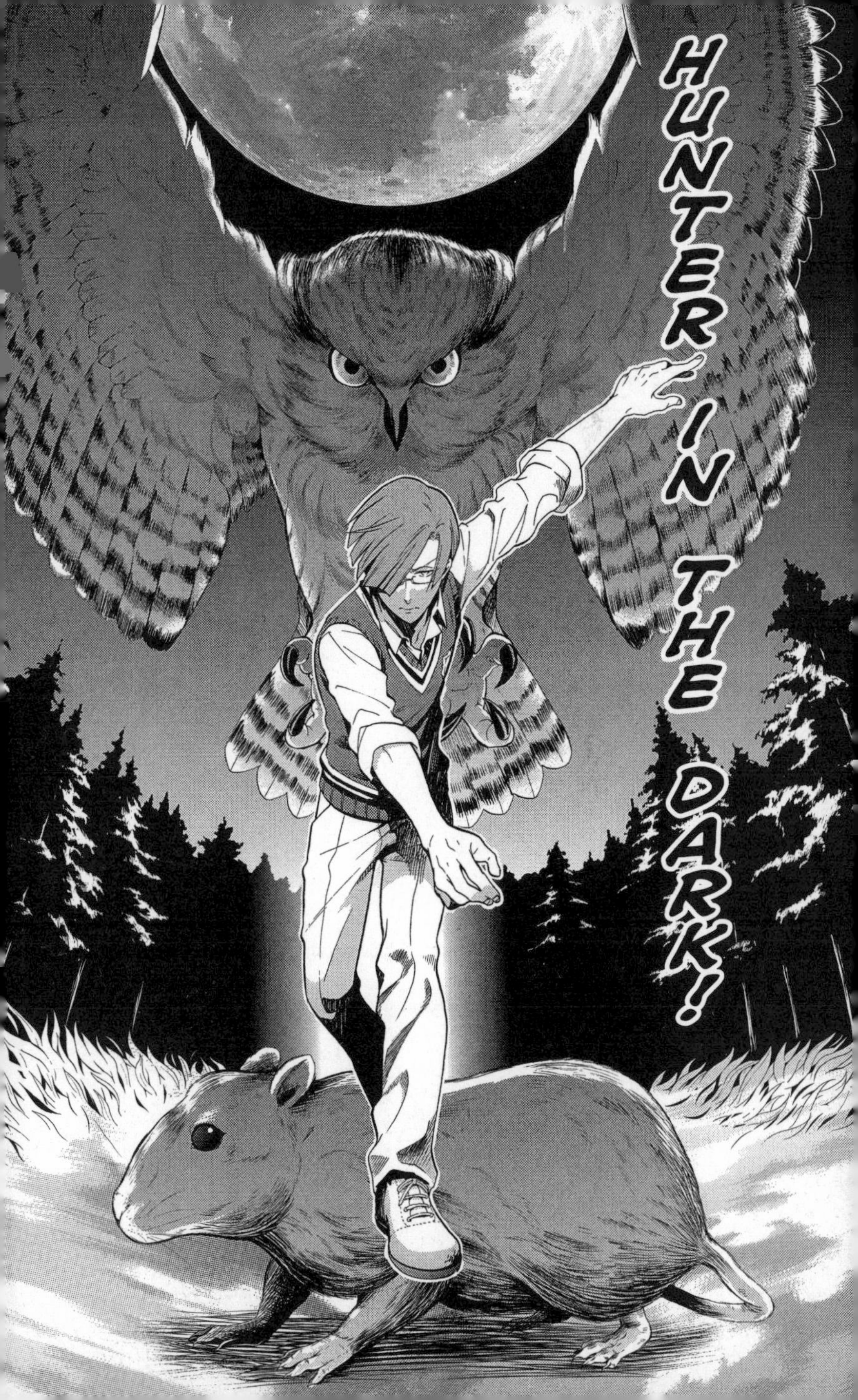
HUNTER IN THE DARK!

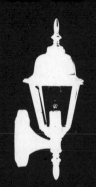

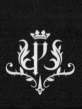

Black Butler

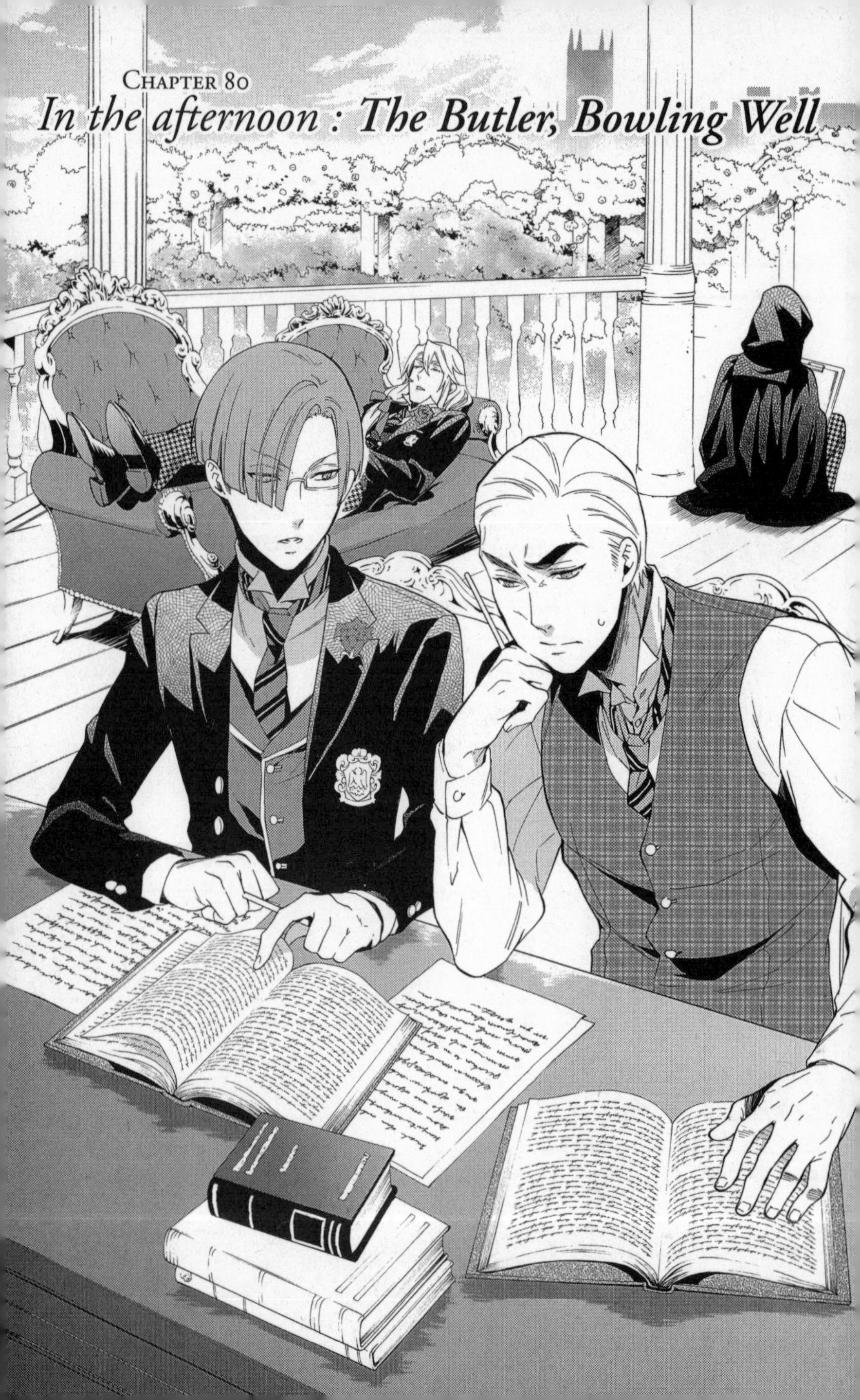
CHAPTER 80
In the afternoon : The Butler, Bowling Well

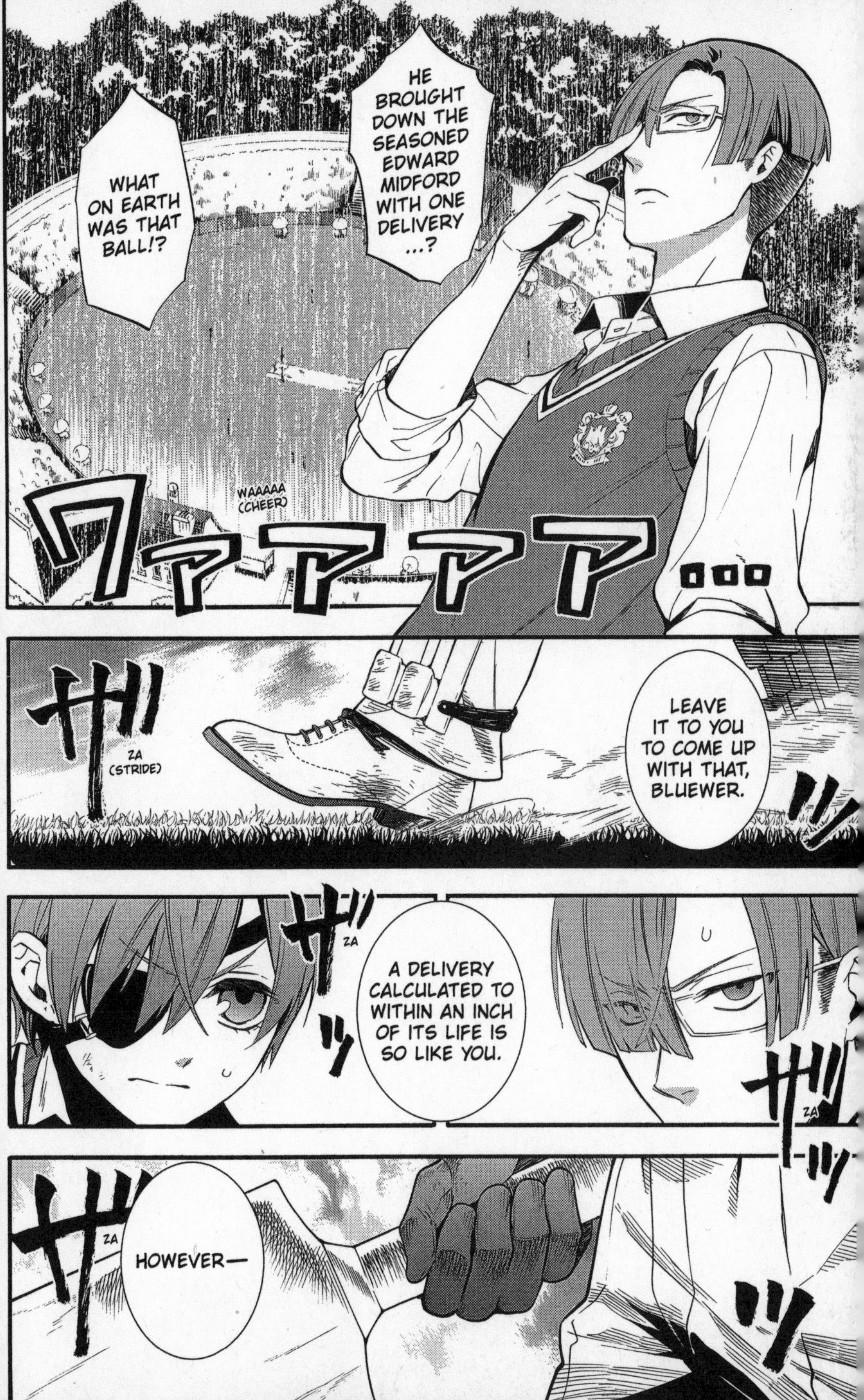
HE BROUGHT DOWN THE SEASONED EDWARD MIDFORD WITH ONE DELIVERY ...?
WHAT ON EARTH WAS THAT BALL!?
WAAAAA (CHEER)
LEAVE IT TO YOU TO COME UP WITH THAT, BLUEWER.
ZA (STRIDE)
ZA
A DELIVERY CALCULATED TO WITHIN AN INCH OF ITS LIFE IS SO LIKE YOU.
ZA
HOWEVER—
ZA

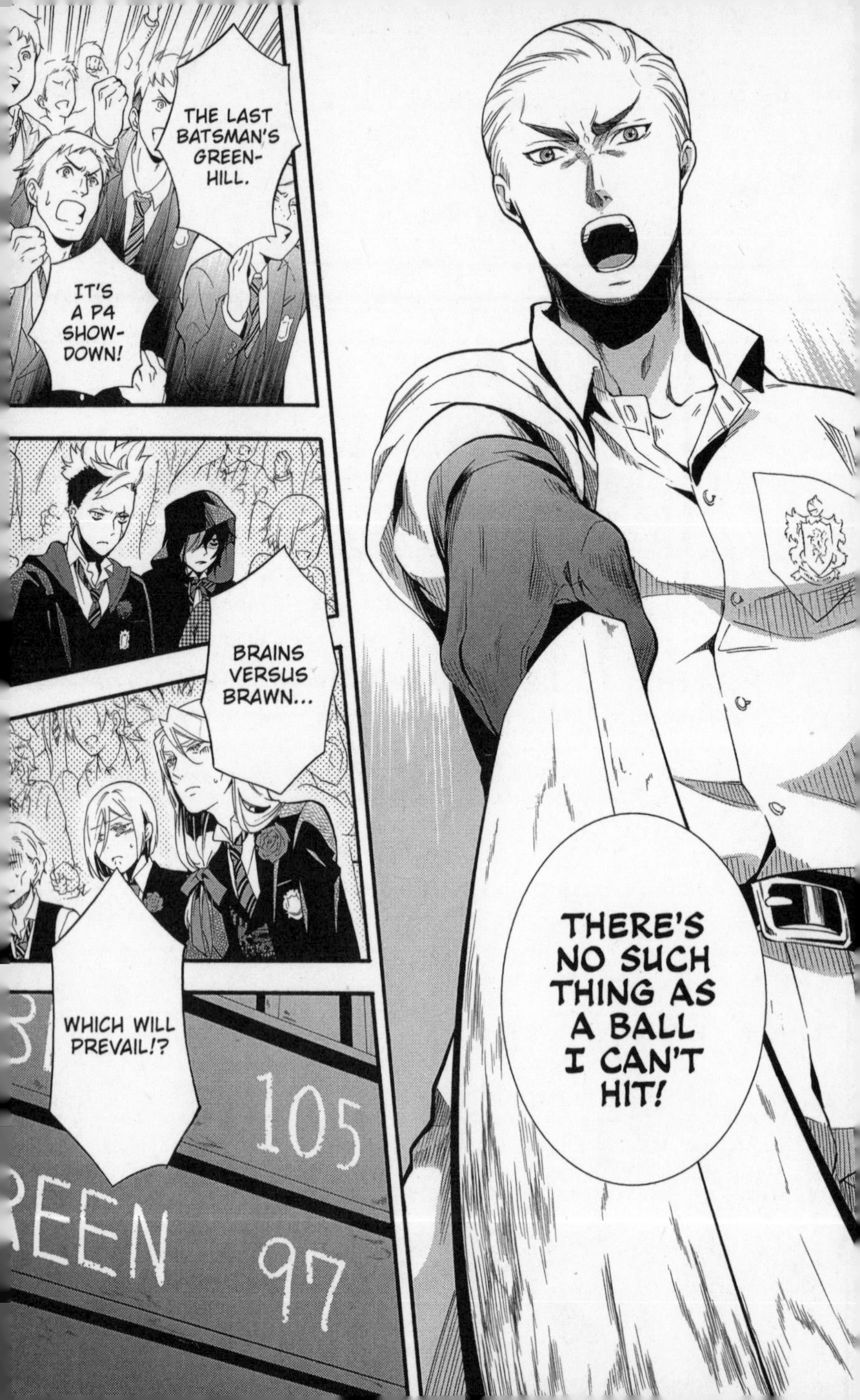
THERE'S NO SUCH THING AS A BALL I CAN'T HIT!
THE LAST BATSMAN'S GREEN-HILL.
IT'S A P4 SHOW-DOWN!
BRAINS VERSUS BRAWN...
WHICH WILL PREVAIL!?
105
97

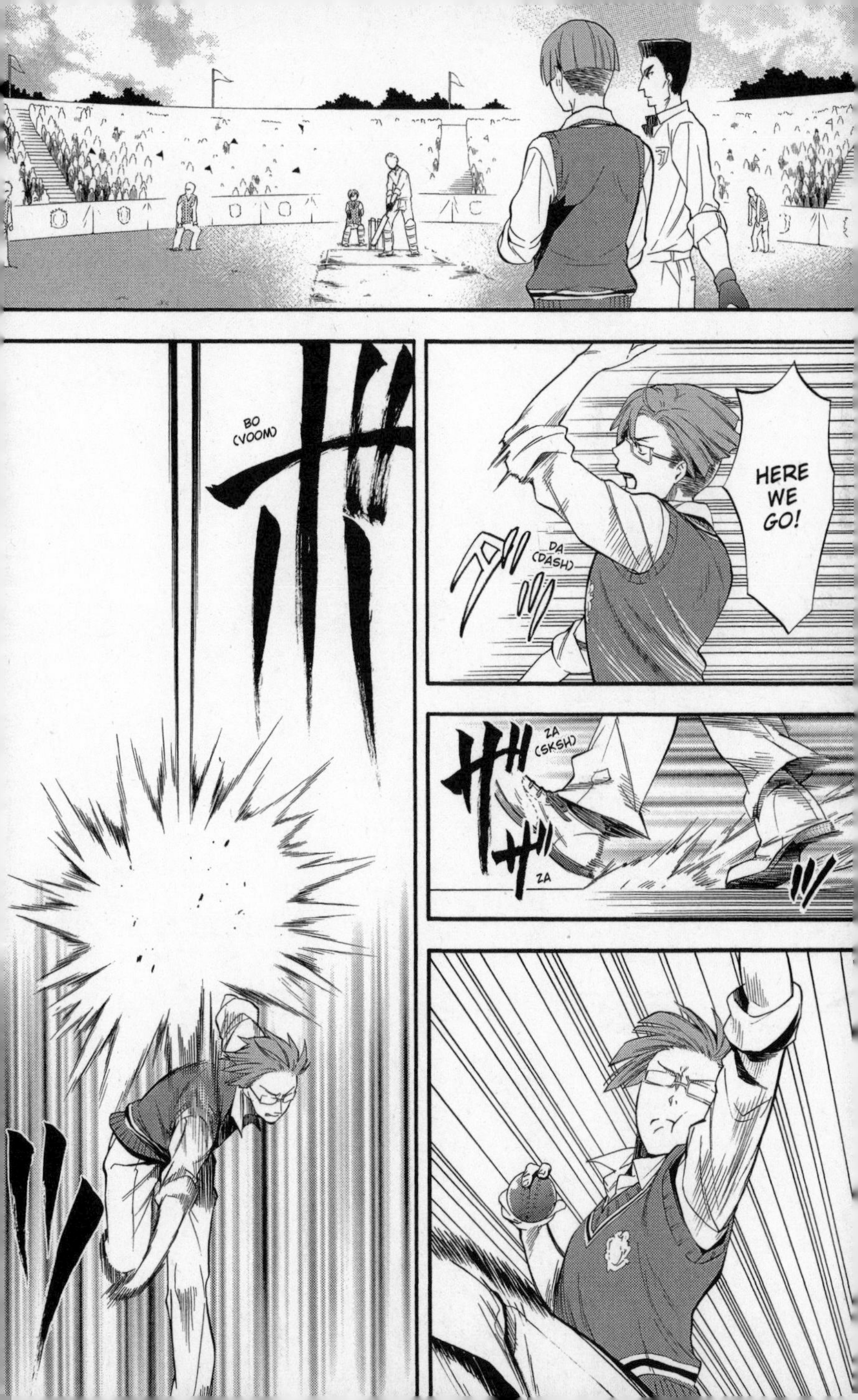
HERE WE GO!
DA (DASH)
ZA (SKSH)
ZA
BO (VOOM)

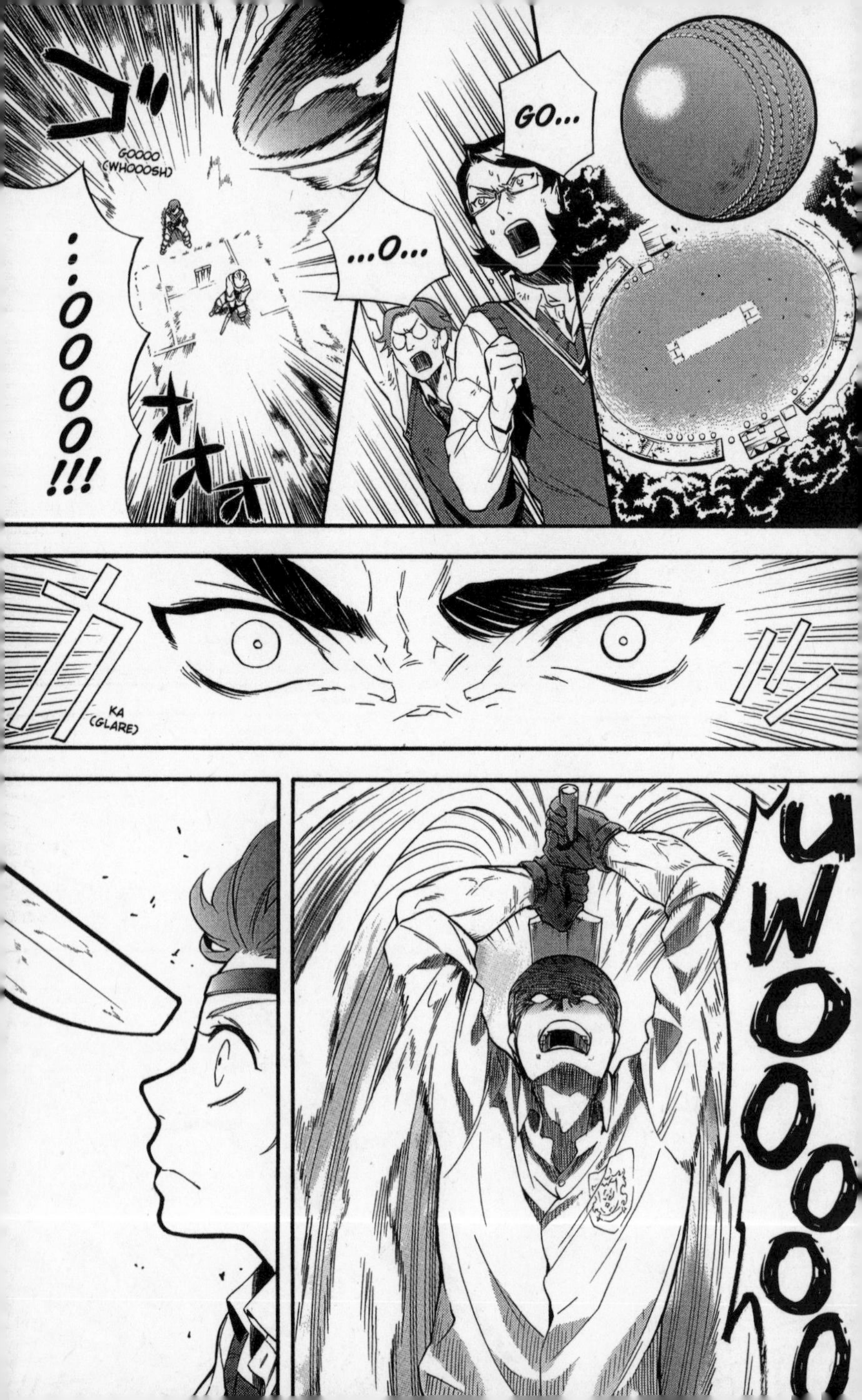
GO...
...O...
...OOOOOO!!!
GOOOO (WHOOOSH)
KA (GLARE)
UWOOOOOO

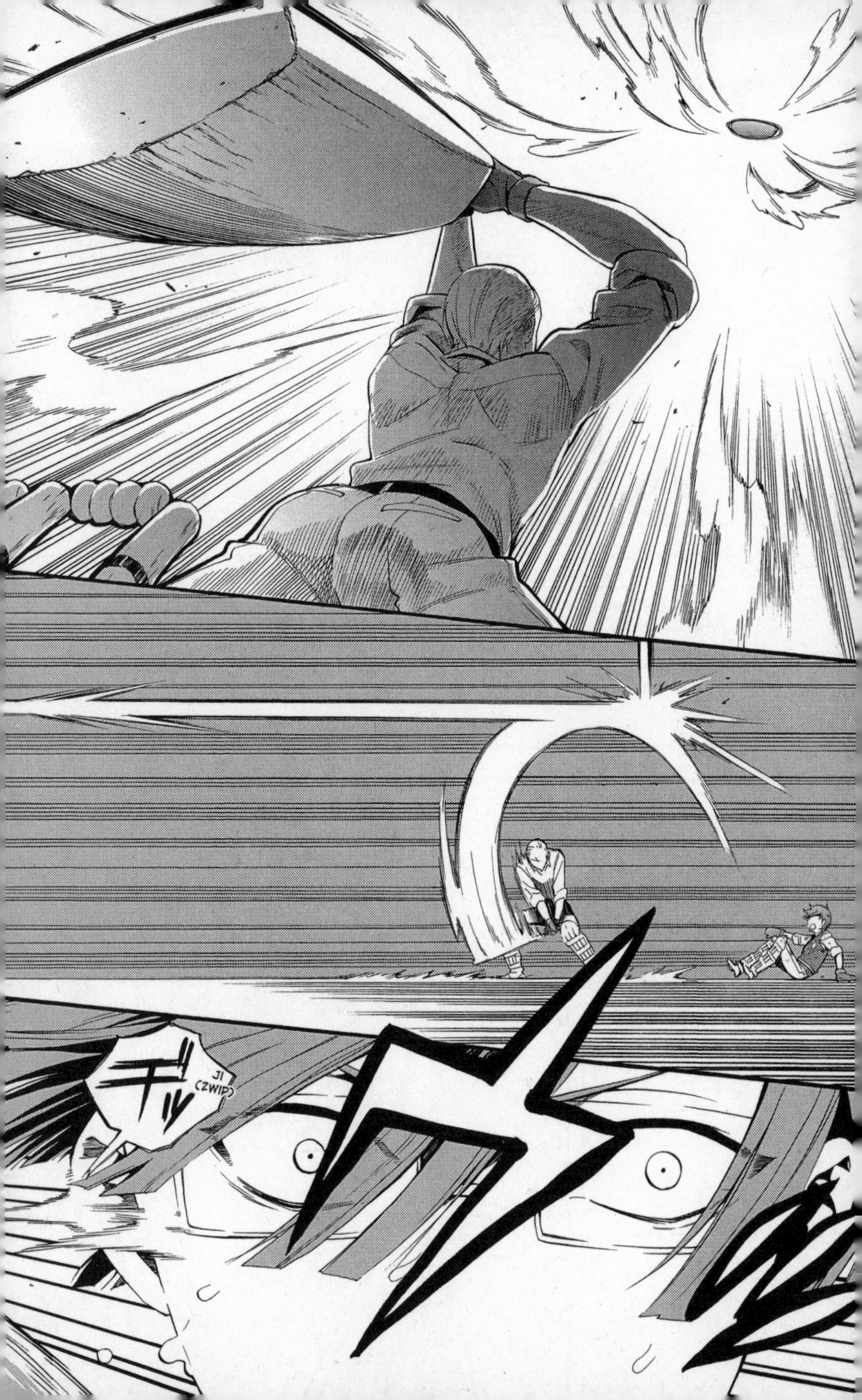
ギッ
JI
(ZWIP)

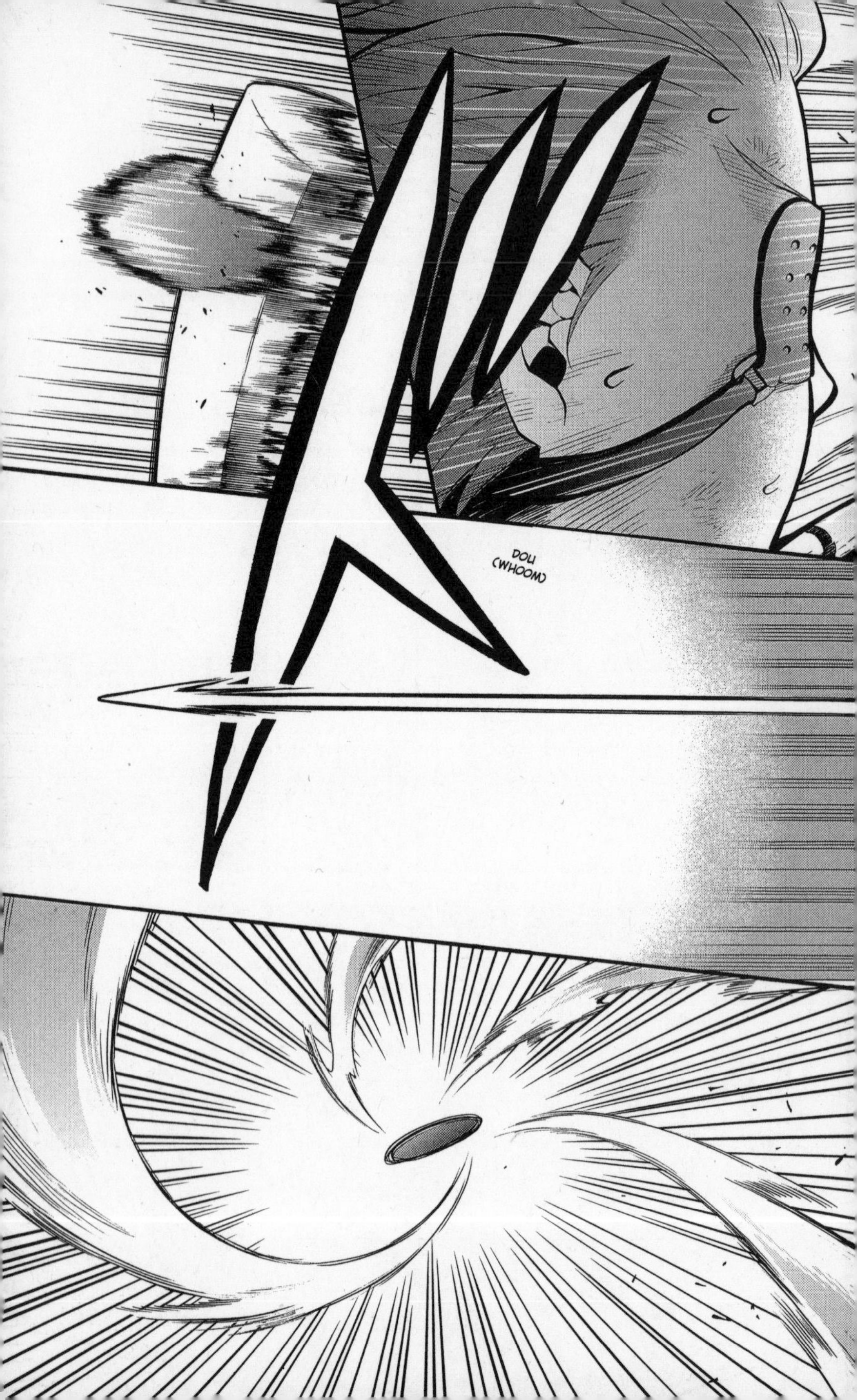
DOU
(WHOOM)

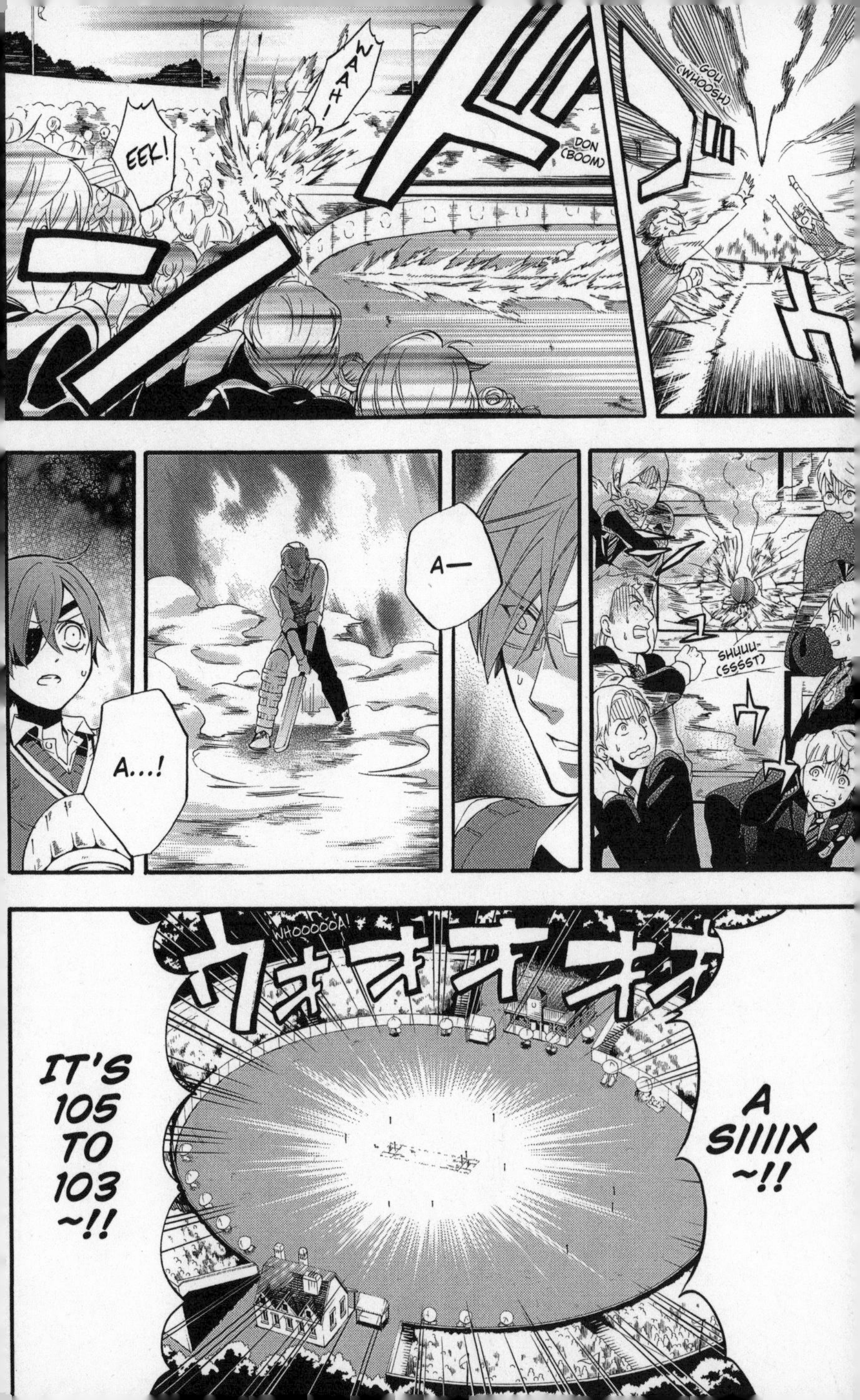
GOU (WHOOSH)
DON (BOOM)
WAAH!
EEK!
SHUUU- (SSSST)
A—
A...!
A SIIIIX ~!!
WHOOOOOA!
IT'S 105 TO 103 ~!!

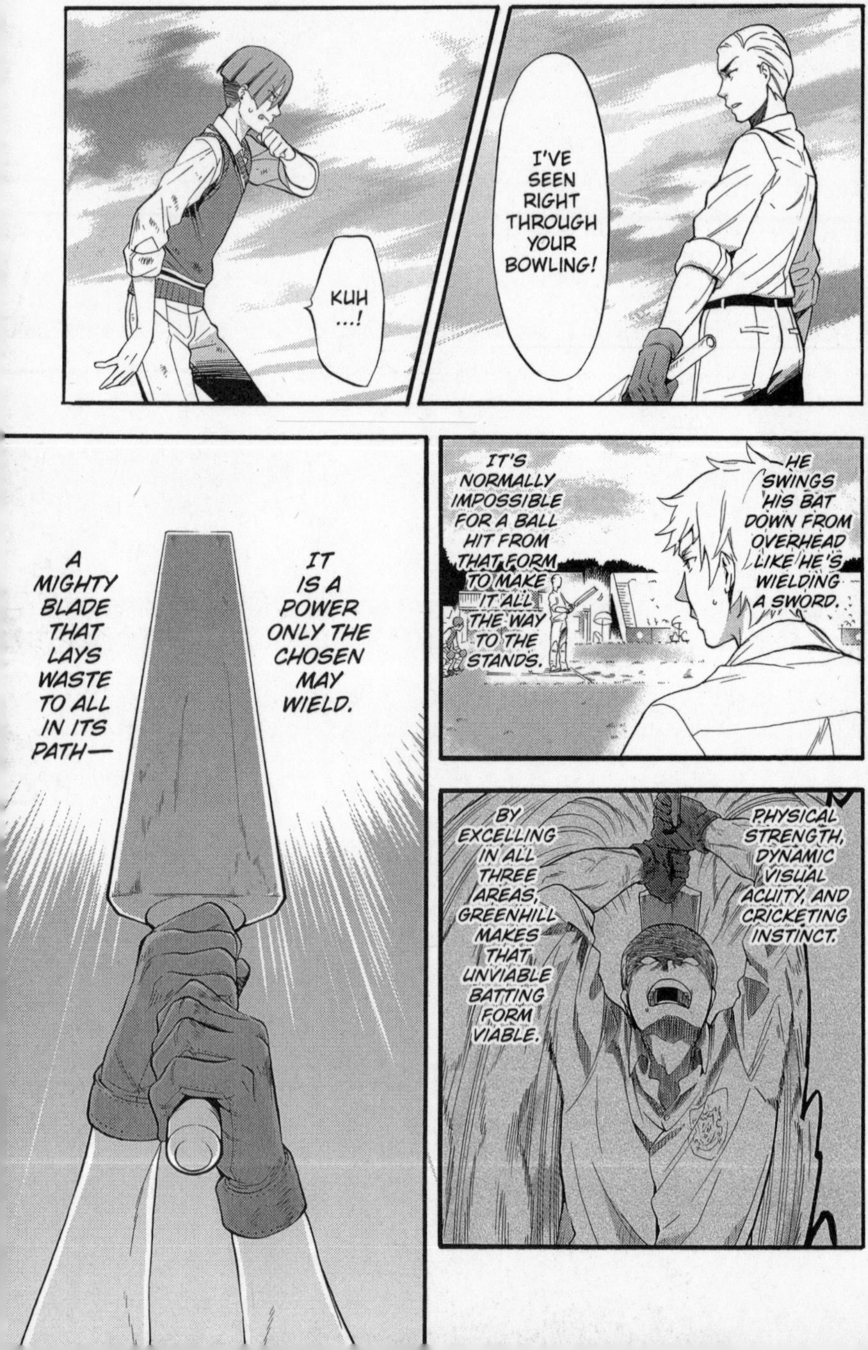
I'VE SEEN RIGHT THROUGH YOUR BOWLING!
KUH ...!
HE SWINGS HIS BAT DOWN FROM OVERHEAD LIKE HE'S WIELDING A SWORD.
IT'S NORMALLY IMPOSSIBLE FOR A BALL HIT FROM THAT FORM TO MAKE IT ALL THE WAY TO THE STANDS.
PHYSICAL STRENGTH, DYNAMIC VISUAL ACUITY, AND CRICKETING INSTINCT.
BY EXCELLING IN ALL THREE AREAS, GREENHILL MAKES THAT UNVIABLE BATTING FORM VIABLE.
IT IS A POWER ONLY THE CHOSEN MAY WIELD.
A MIGHTY BLADE THAT LAYS WASTE TO ALL IN ITS PATH—

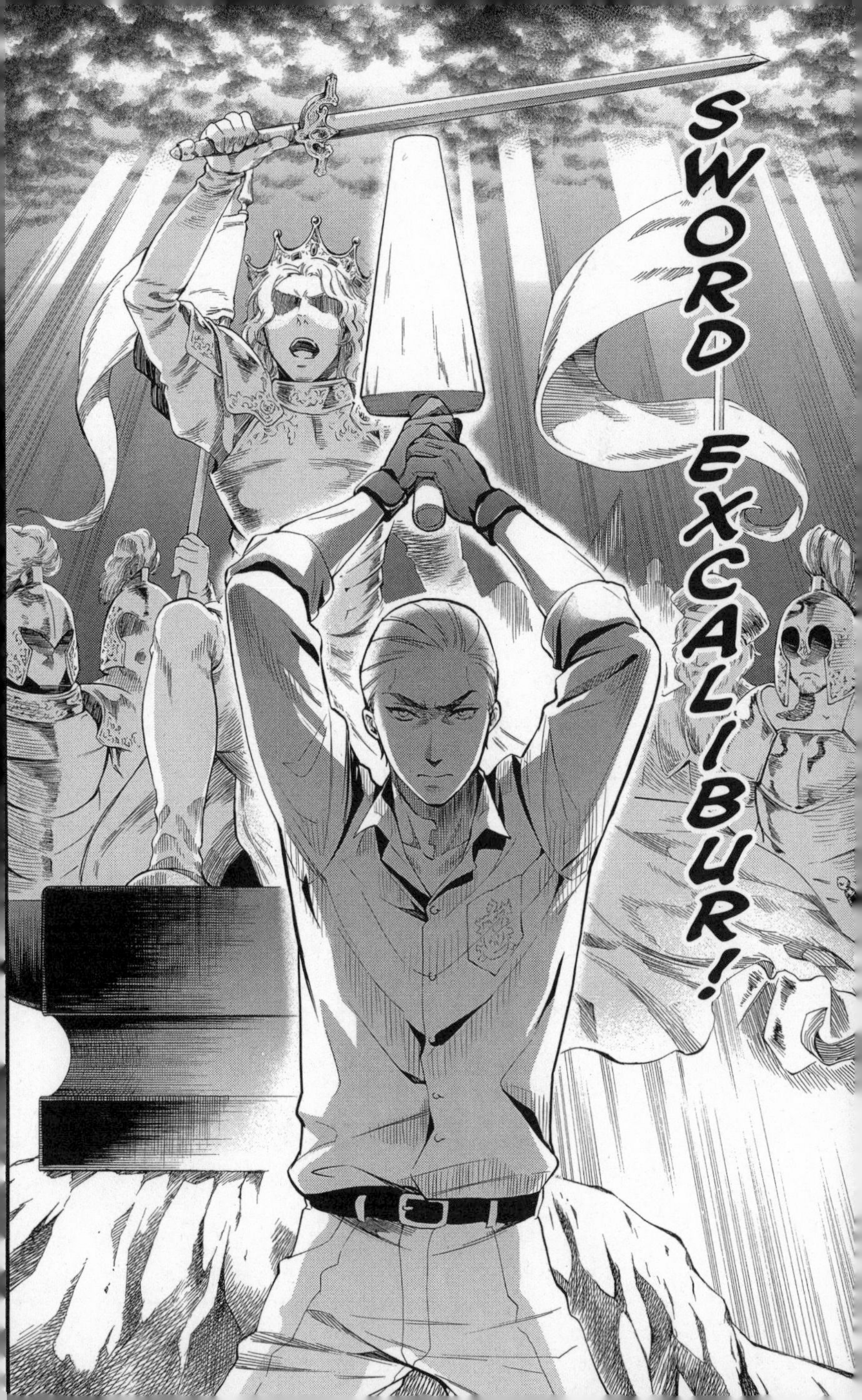
SWORD EXCALIBUR!

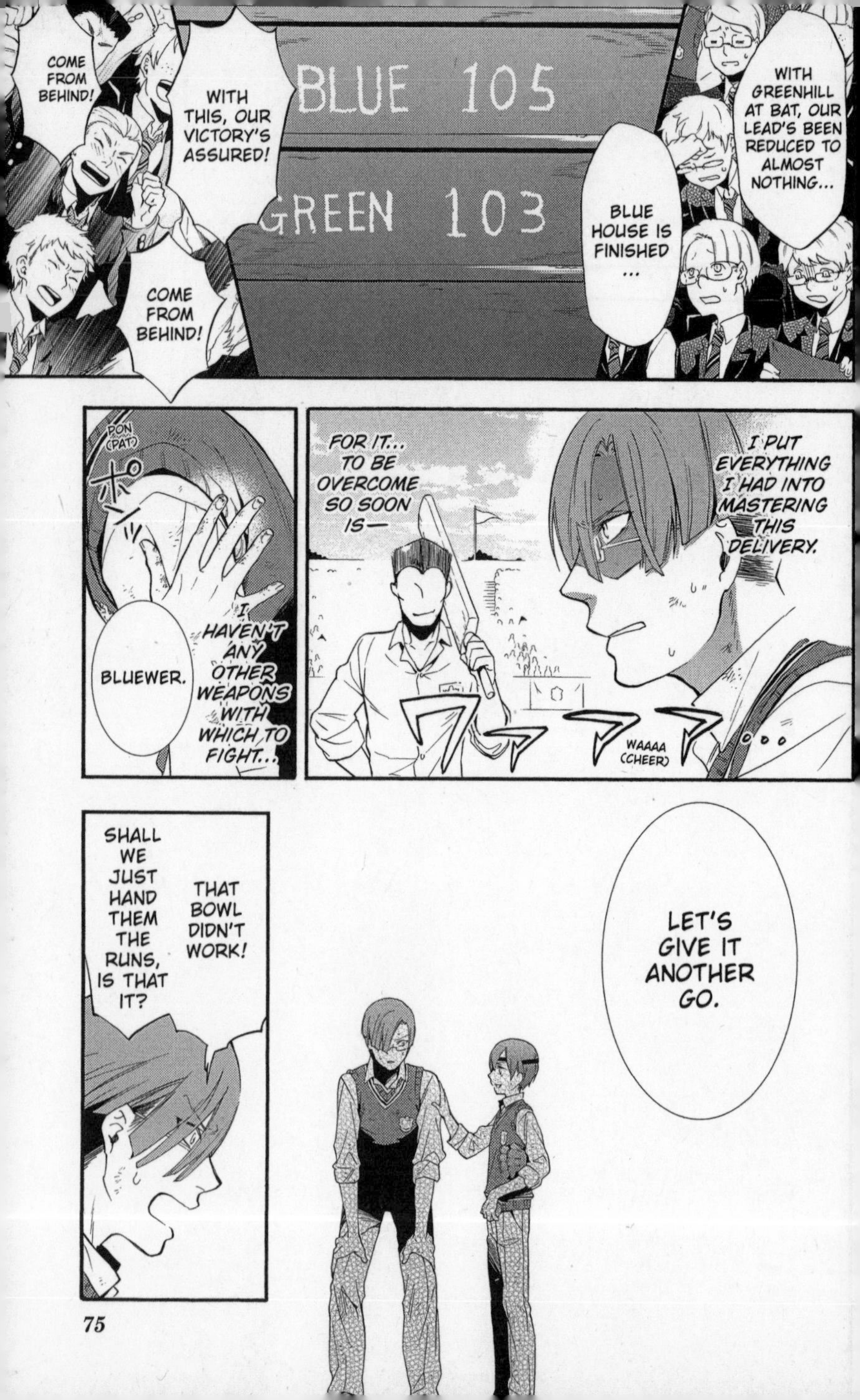
WITH GREENHILL AT BAT, OUR LEAD'S BEEN REDUCED TO ALMOST NOTHING...
BLUE HOUSE IS FINISHED ...
BLUE 105
GREEN 103
WITH THIS, OUR VICTORY'S ASSURED!
COME FROM BEHIND!
COME FROM BEHIND!
I PUT EVERYTHING I HAD INTO MASTERING THIS DELIVERY.
FOR IT... TO BE OVERCOME SO SOON IS—
WAAAA (CHEER)
PON (PAT)
I HAVEN'T ANY OTHER WEAPONS WITH WHICH TO FIGHT...
BLUEWER.
LET'S GIVE IT ANOTHER GO.
THAT BOWL DIDN'T WORK!
SHALL WE JUST HAND THEM THE RUNS, IS THAT IT?

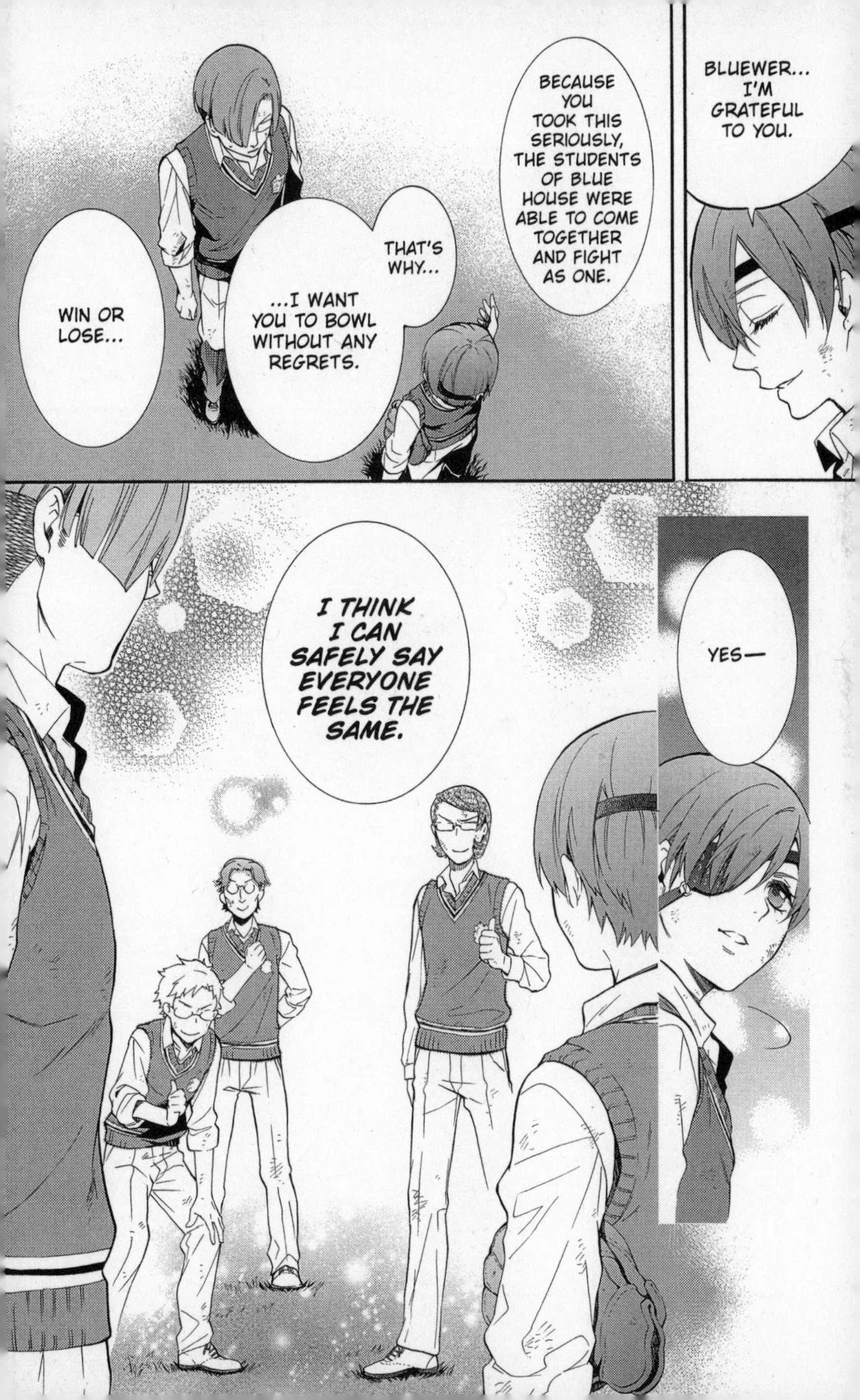
BLUEWER... I'M GRATEFUL TO YOU.
BECAUSE YOU TOOK THIS SERIOUSLY, THE STUDENTS OF BLUE HOUSE WERE ABLE TO COME TOGETHER AND FIGHT AS ONE.
THAT'S WHY...
...I WANT YOU TO BOWL WITHOUT ANY REGRETS.
WIN OR LOSE...
YES—
I THINK I CAN SAFELY SAY EVERYONE FEELS THE SAME.

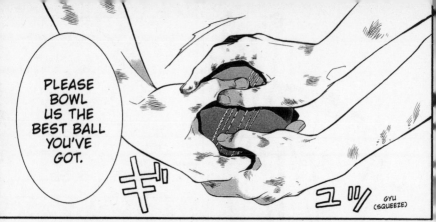

PLEASE BOWL US THE BEST BALL YOU'VE GOT.

ギ

ユ ッ GYU (SQUEEZE)

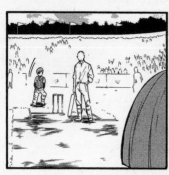

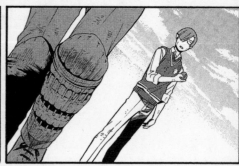

THIS DELIVERY WILL DECIDE IT ALL.

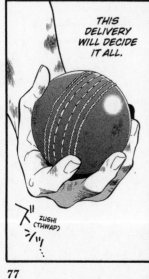

ズ ッ ZUSHI (THWAP)
ッ ッ

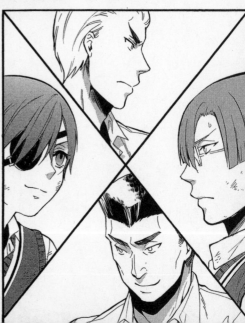

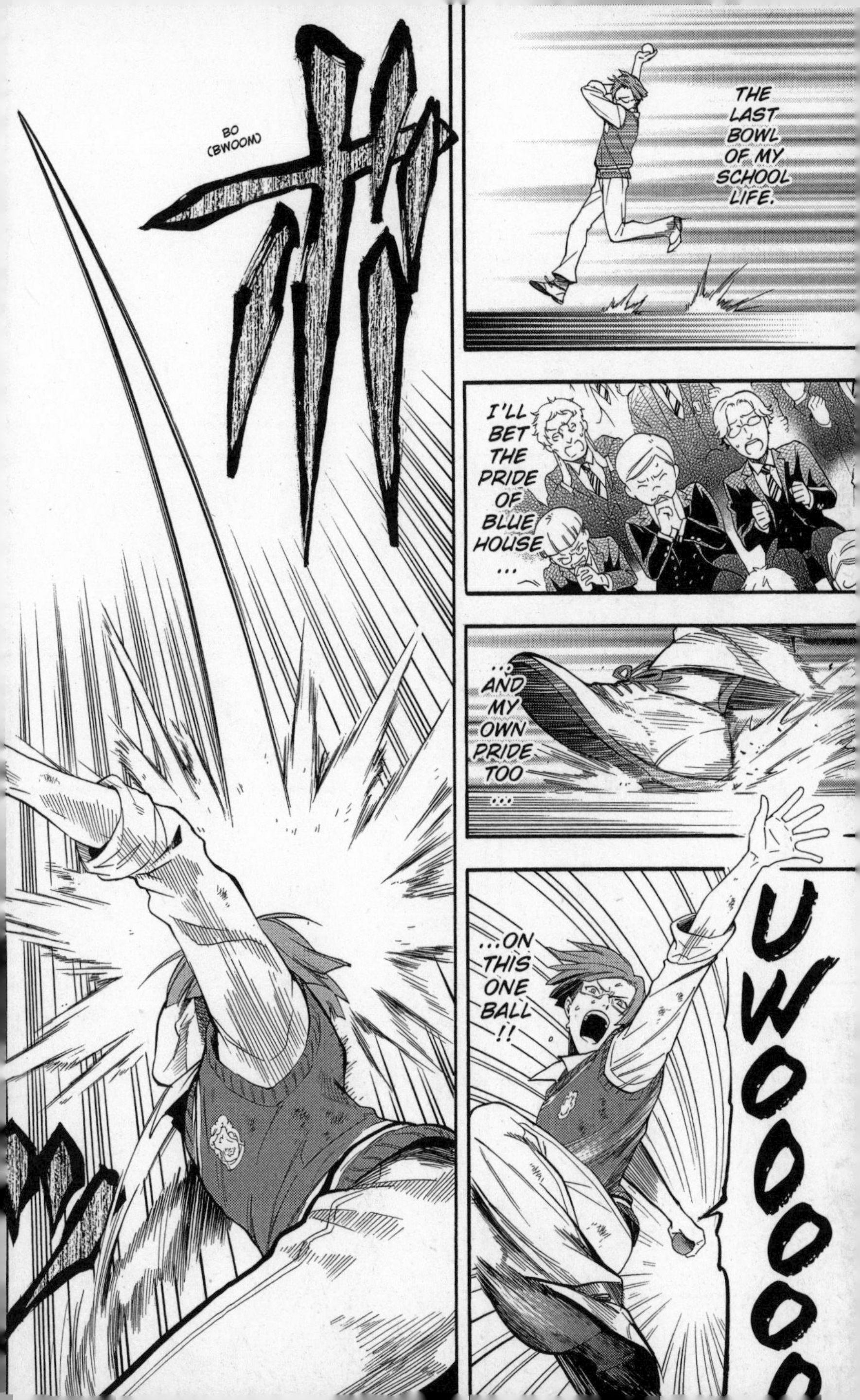

THE LAST BOWL OF MY SCHOOL LIFE.
I'LL BET THE PRIDE OF BLUE HOUSE...
...AND MY OWN PRIDE TOO...
...ON THIS ONE BALL!!
UWOOOOO
BO (BWOOM)

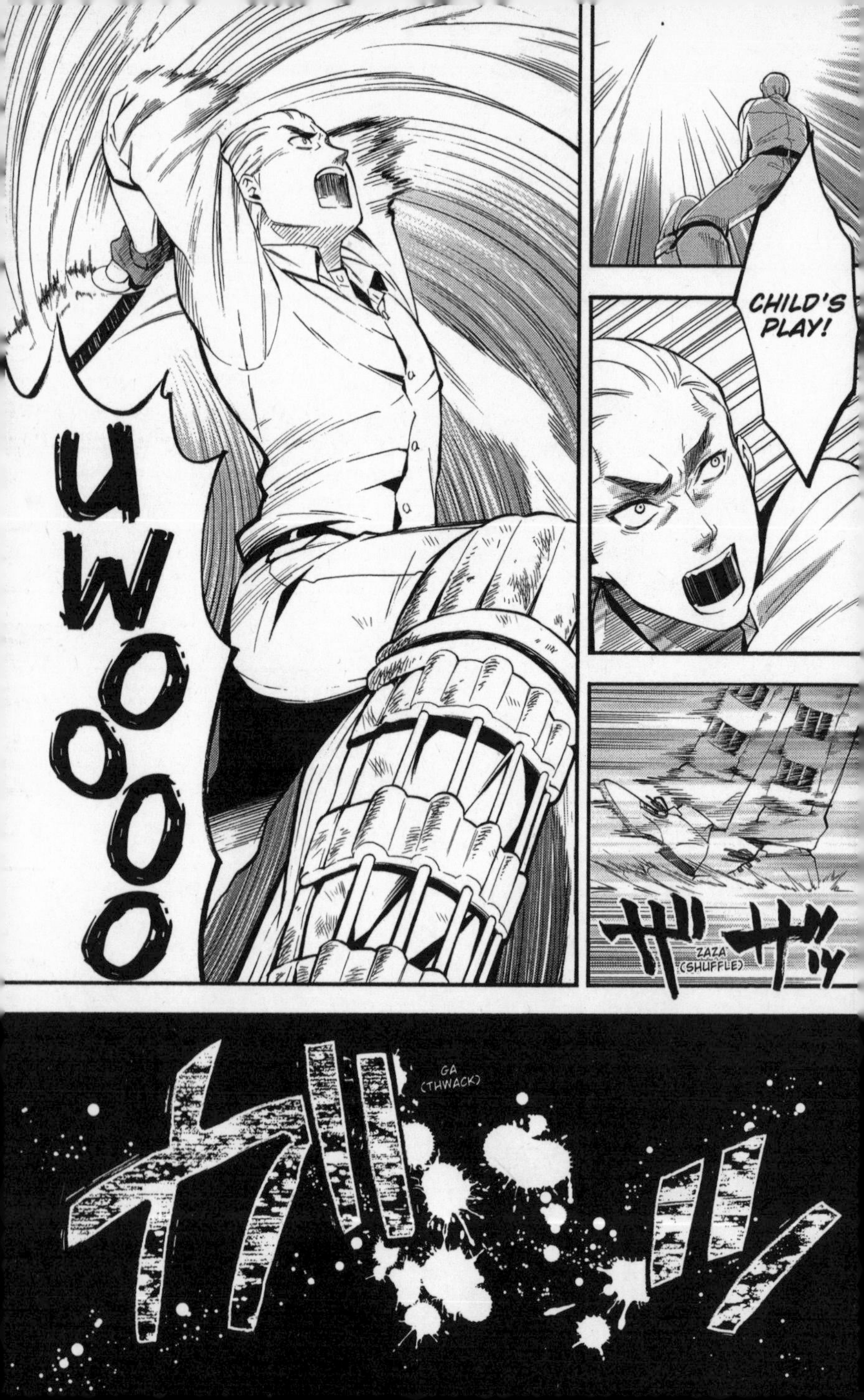
CHILD'S PLAY!
ZAZA (SHUFFLE)
UWOOO
GA (THWACK)

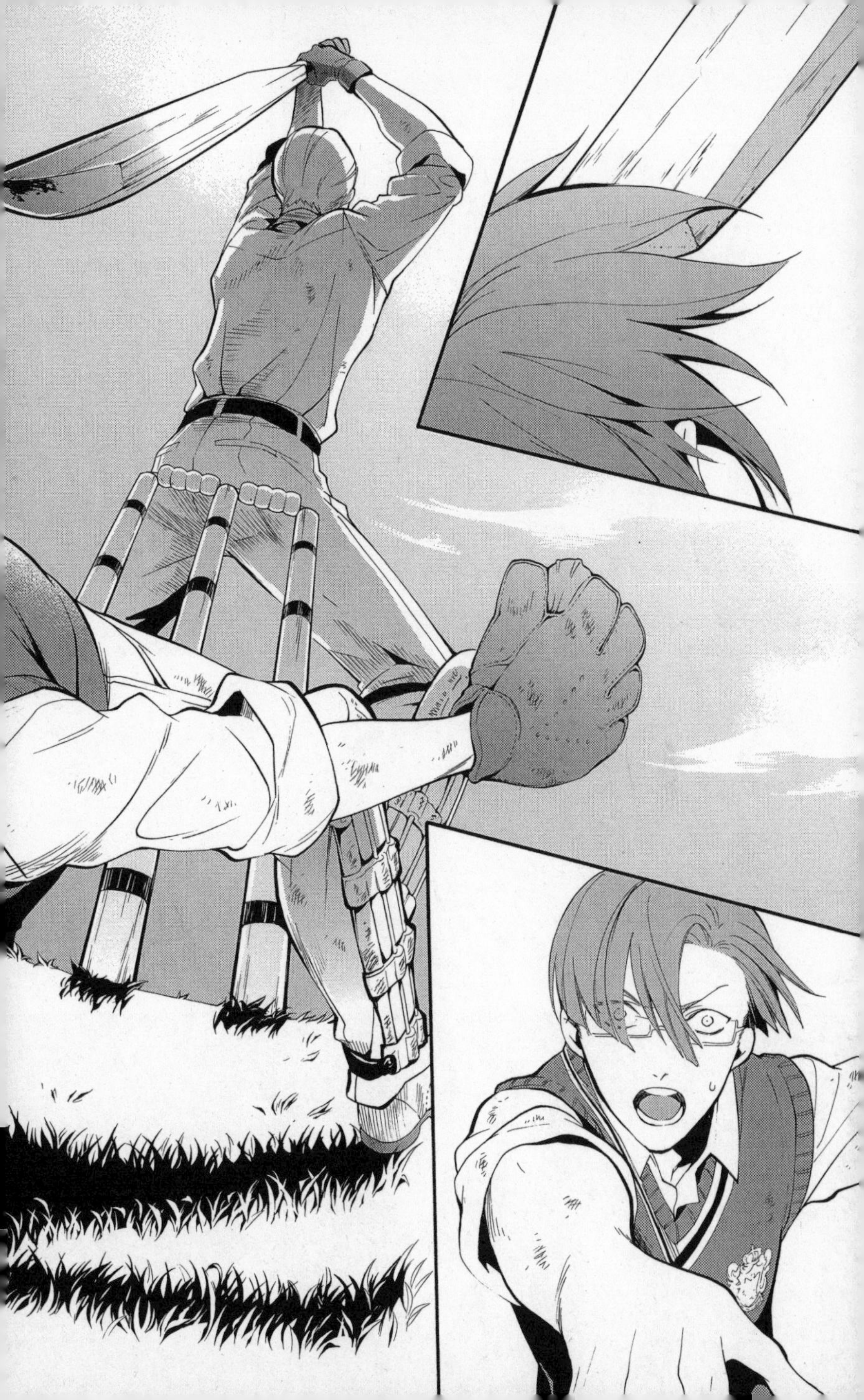

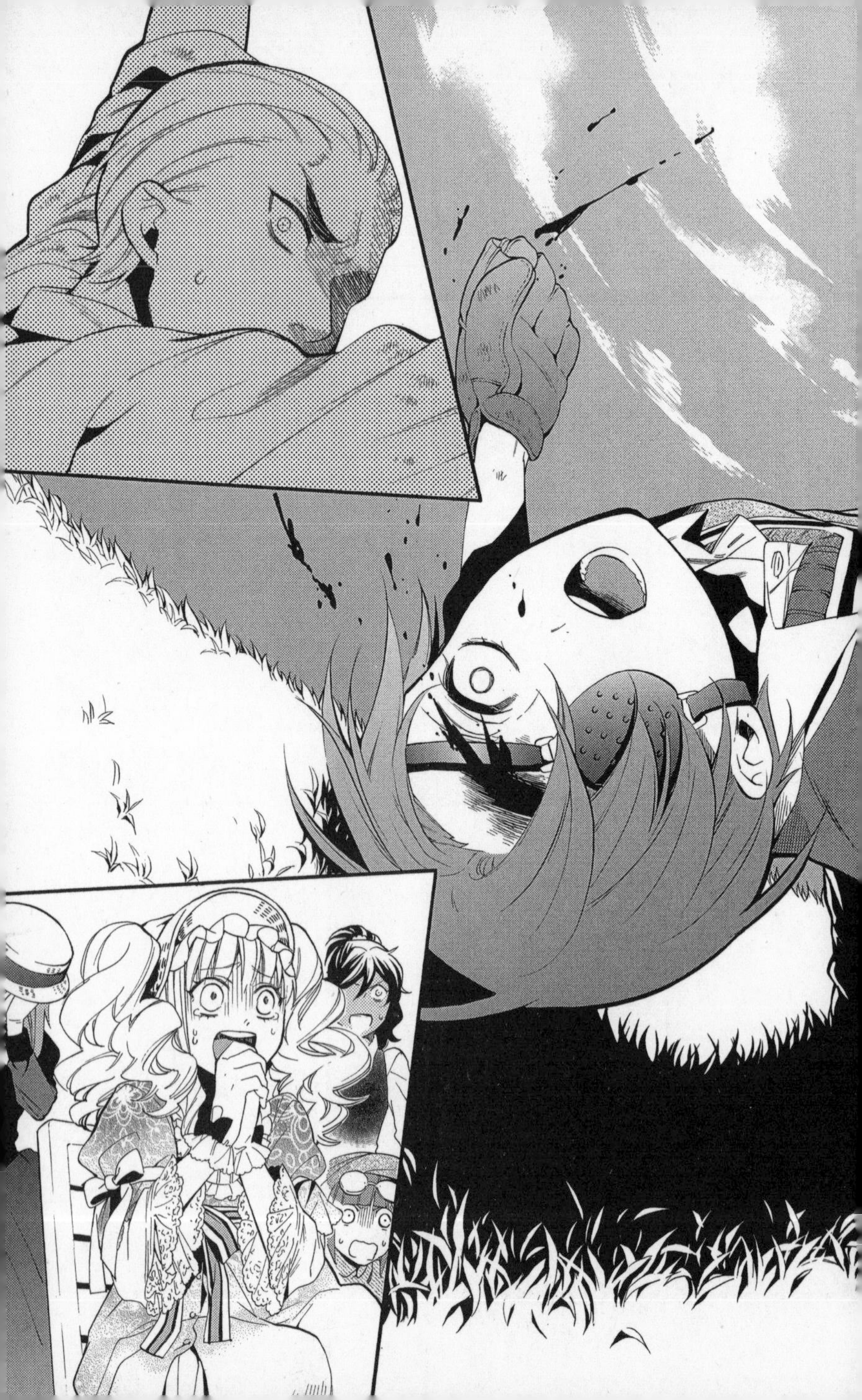

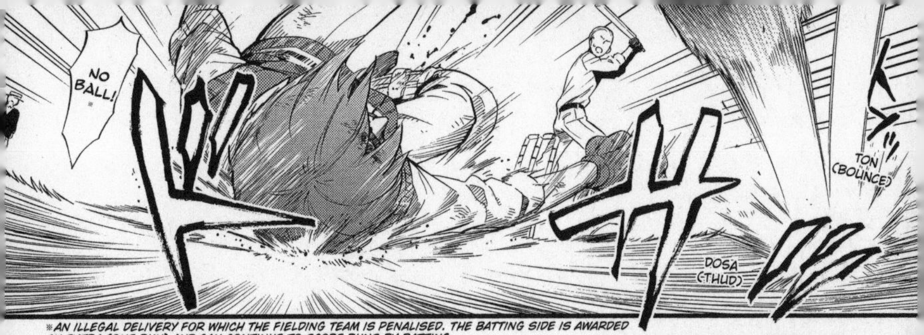
TON (BOUNCE)
DOSA (THUD)
NO BALL! ※

※AN ILLEGAL DELIVERY FOR WHICH THE FIELDING TEAM IS PENALISED. THE BATTING SIDE IS AWARDED AN EXTRA (ONE RUN) AND CAN CONTINUE TO SCORE RUNS BY BATTING.

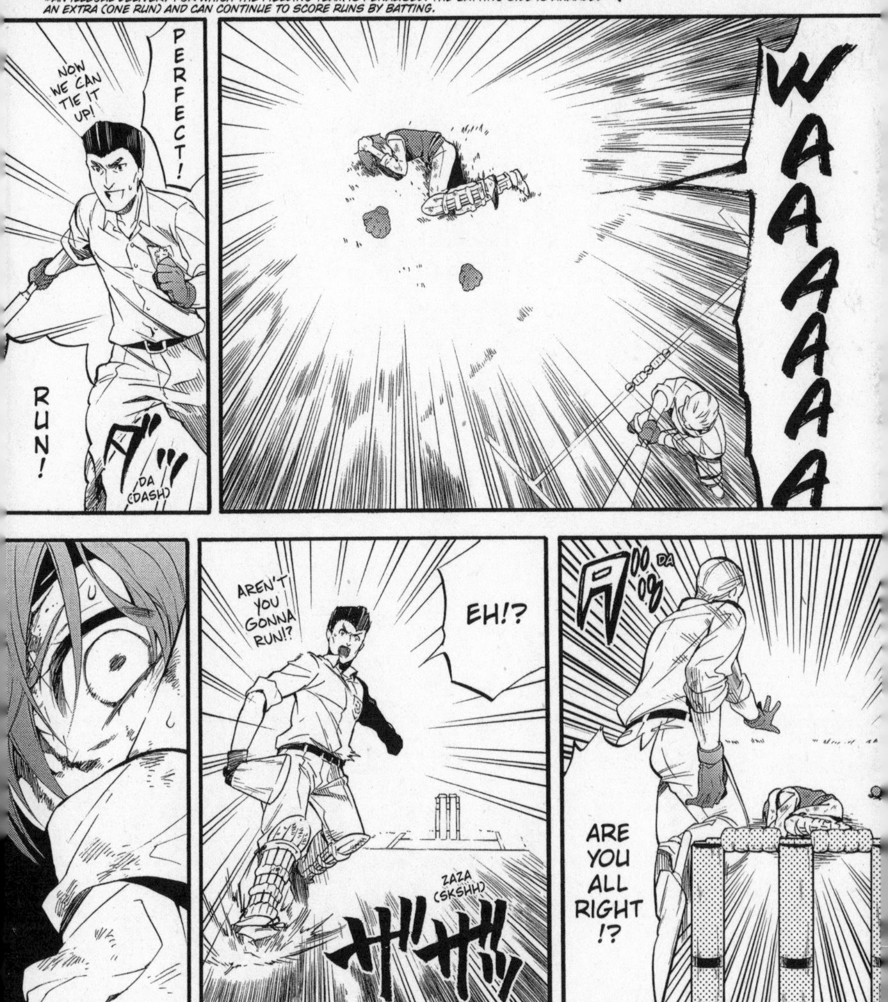
WAAAAAAA
PERFECT!
NOW WE CAN TIE IT UP!
RUN!
DA (DASH)
DA
ARE YOU ALL RIGHT!?
EH!?
AREN'T YOU GONNA RUN!?
ZAZA (SKSHH)

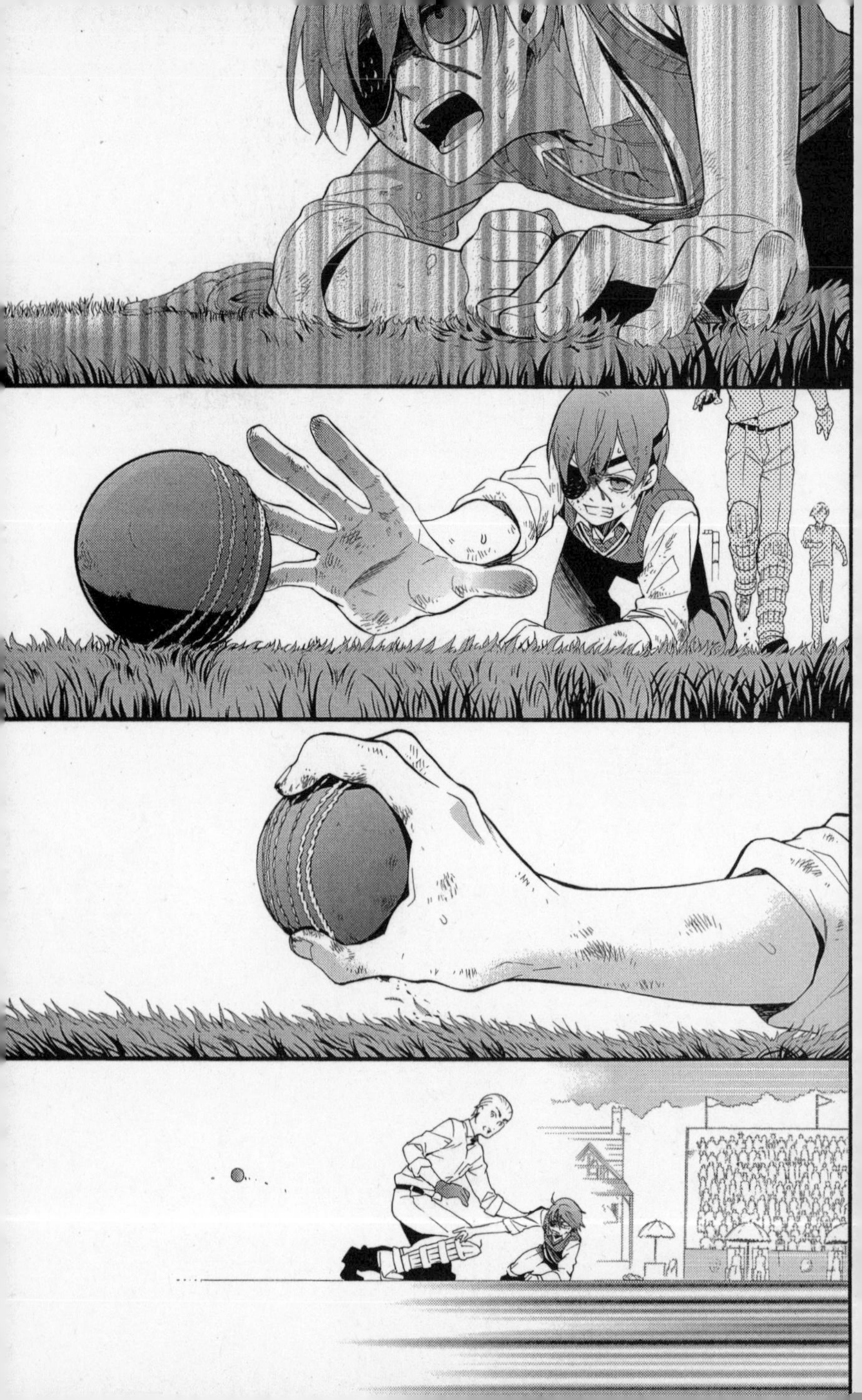

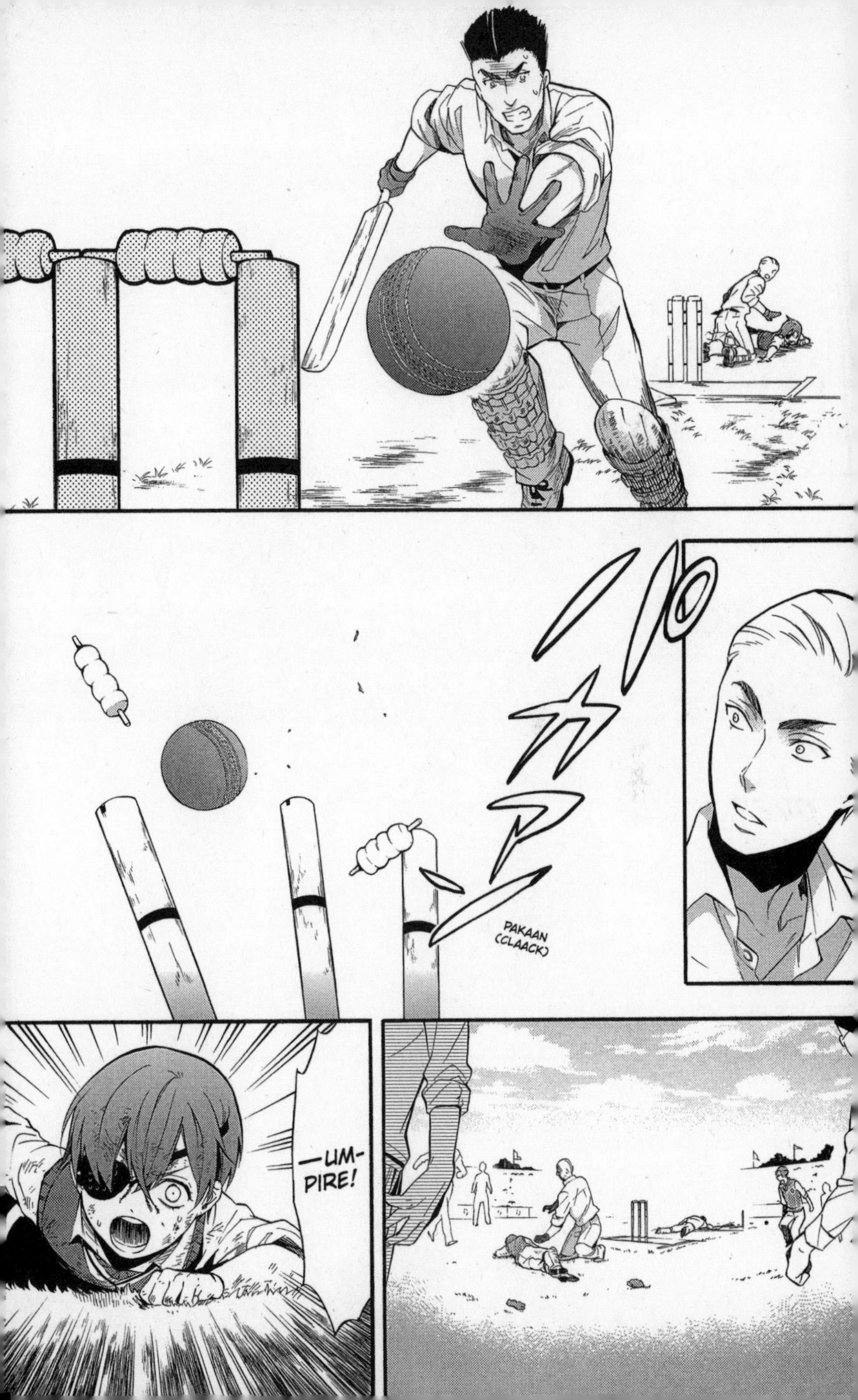
PAKAAN
(CLAACK)
—UM-
PIRE!

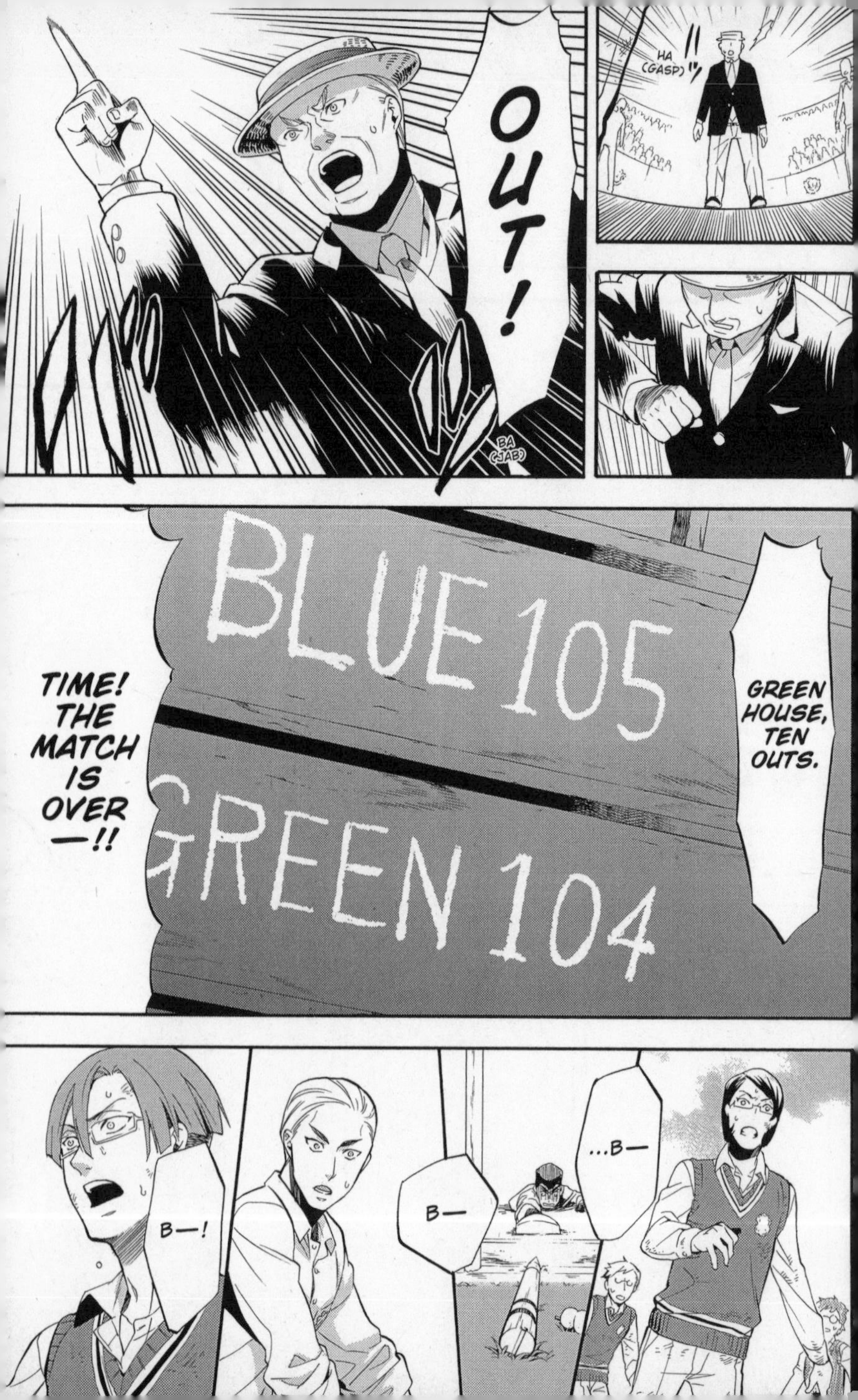
HA (GASP)
OUT!
BA (JAB)
GREEN HOUSE, TEN OUTS.
BLUE 105
GREEN 104
TIME! THE MATCH IS OVER—!!
...B—
B—
B—!

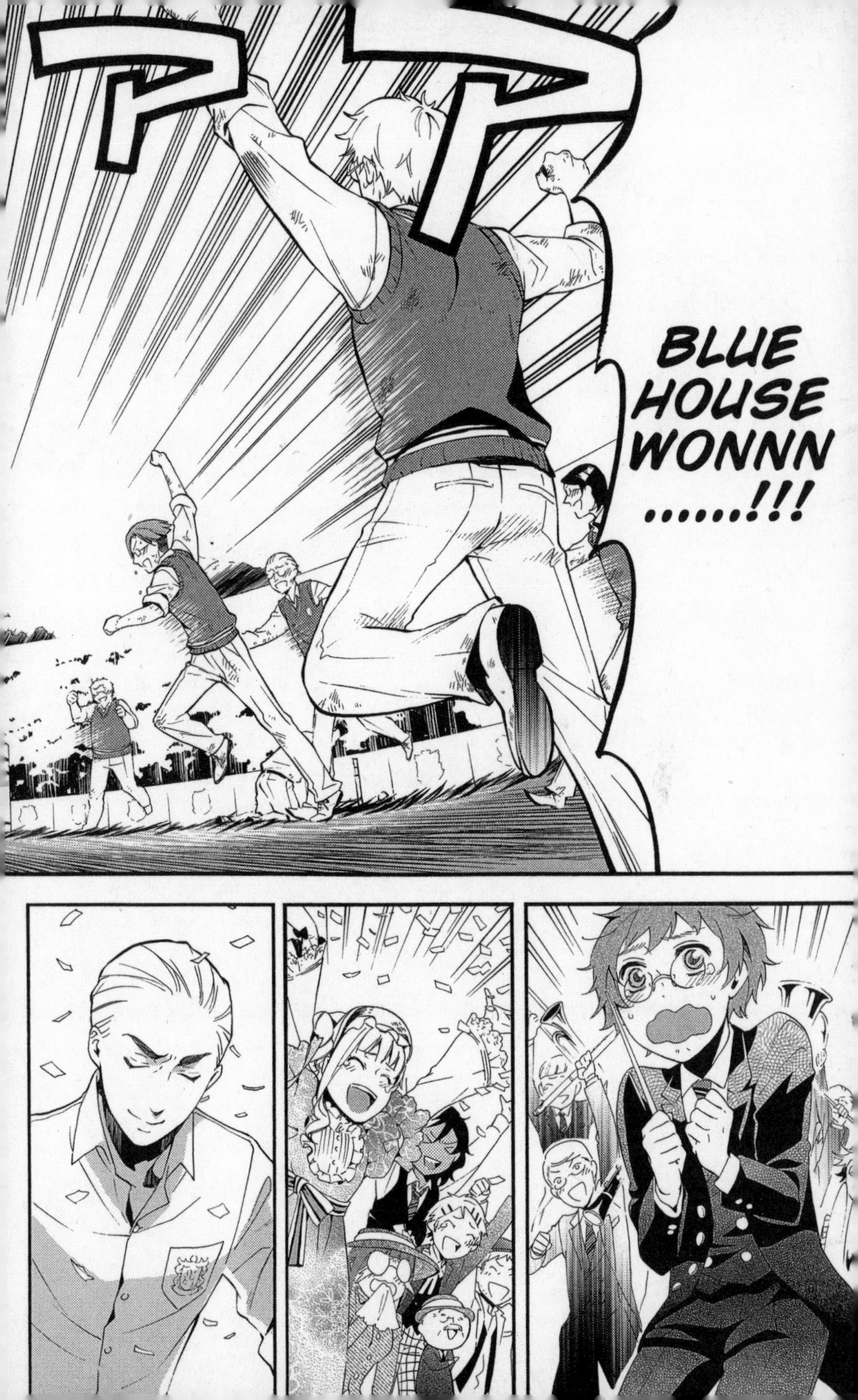

BLUE HOUSE WONNN ......!!!

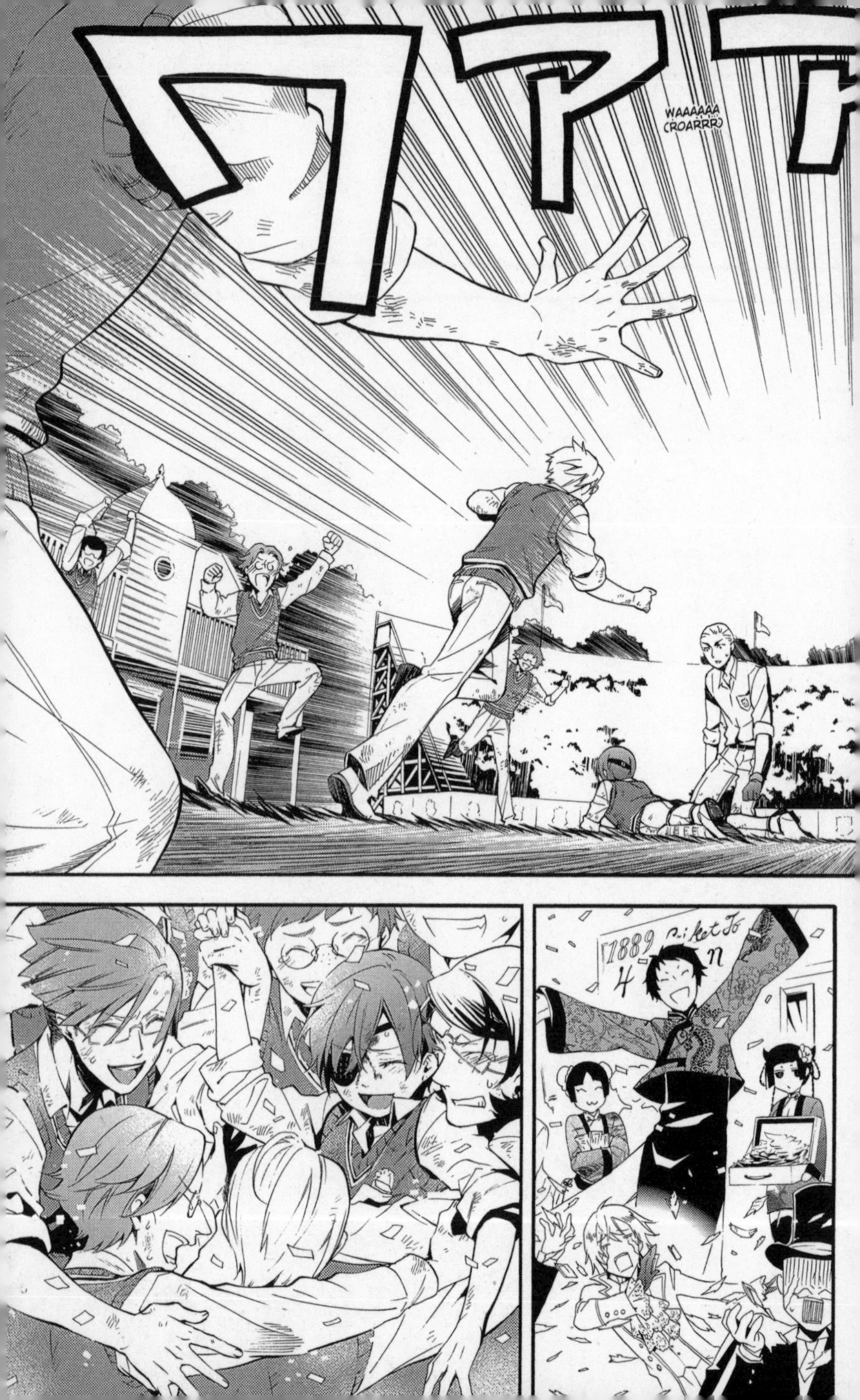
ワア
WAAAAAA
(ROARRR)
1889

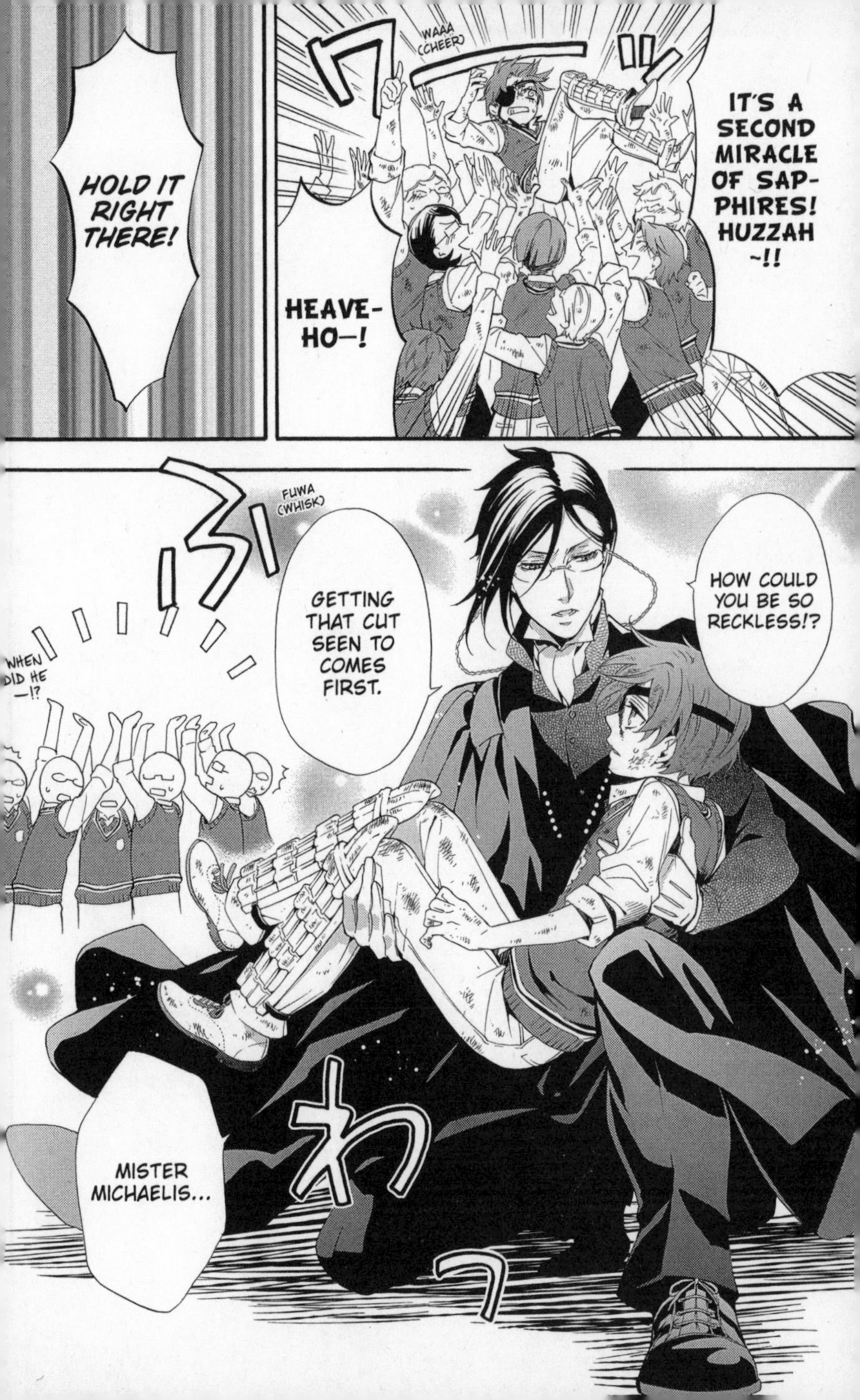
WAAA (CHEER)
IT'S A SECOND MIRACLE OF SAPPHIRES! HUZZAH~!!
HEAVE-HO—!
HOLD IT RIGHT THERE!
HOW COULD YOU BE SO RECKLESS!?
FUWA (WHISK)
GETTING THAT CUT SEEN TO COMES FIRST.
WHEN DID HE—!?
MISTER MICHAELIS...

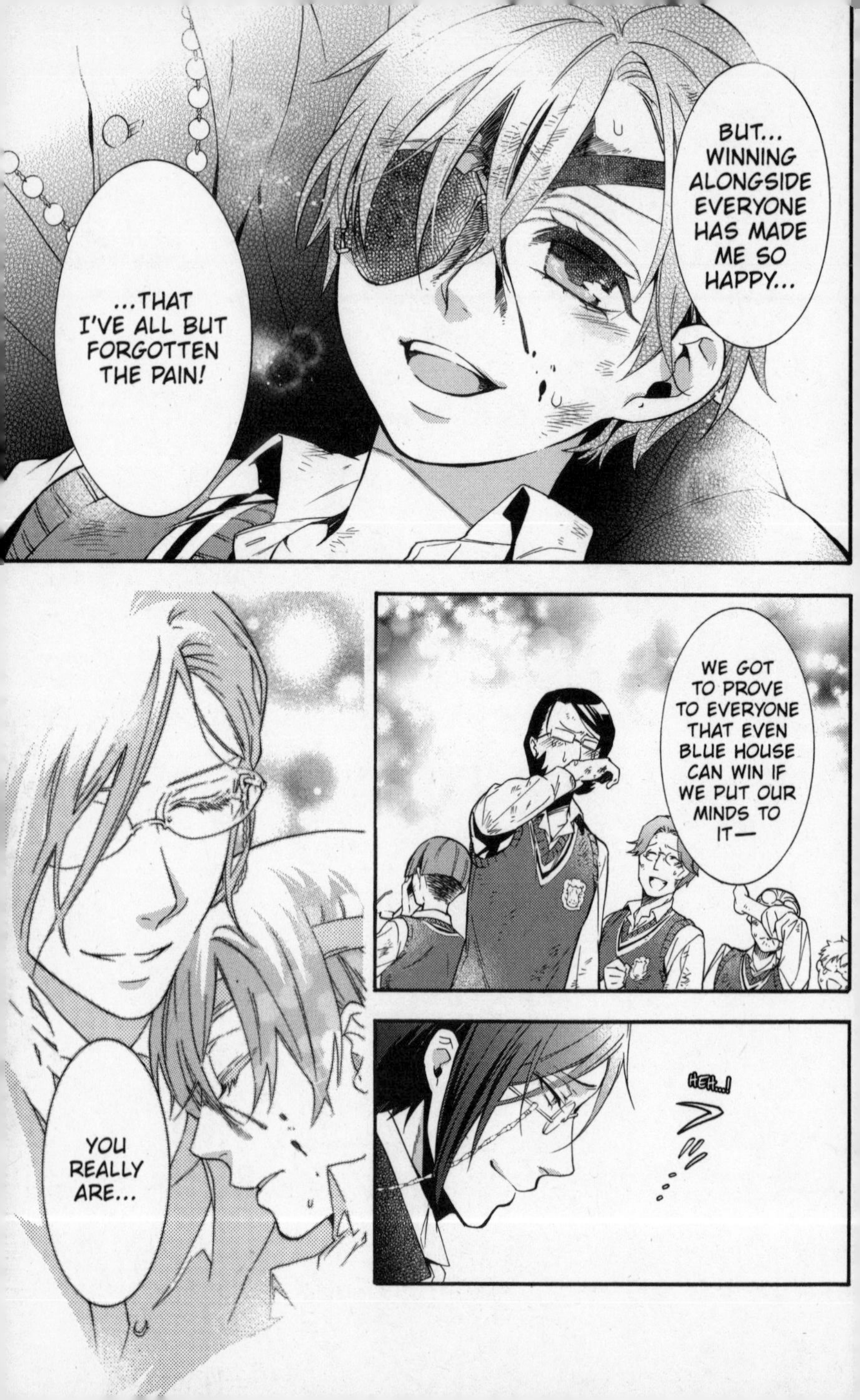
BUT... WINNING ALONGSIDE EVERYONE HAS MADE ME SO HAPPY...
...THAT I'VE ALL BUT FORGOTTEN THE PAIN!
WE GOT TO PROVE TO EVERYONE THAT EVEN BLUE HOUSE CAN WIN IF WE PUT OUR MINDS TO IT—
HEH...!
YOU REALLY ARE...

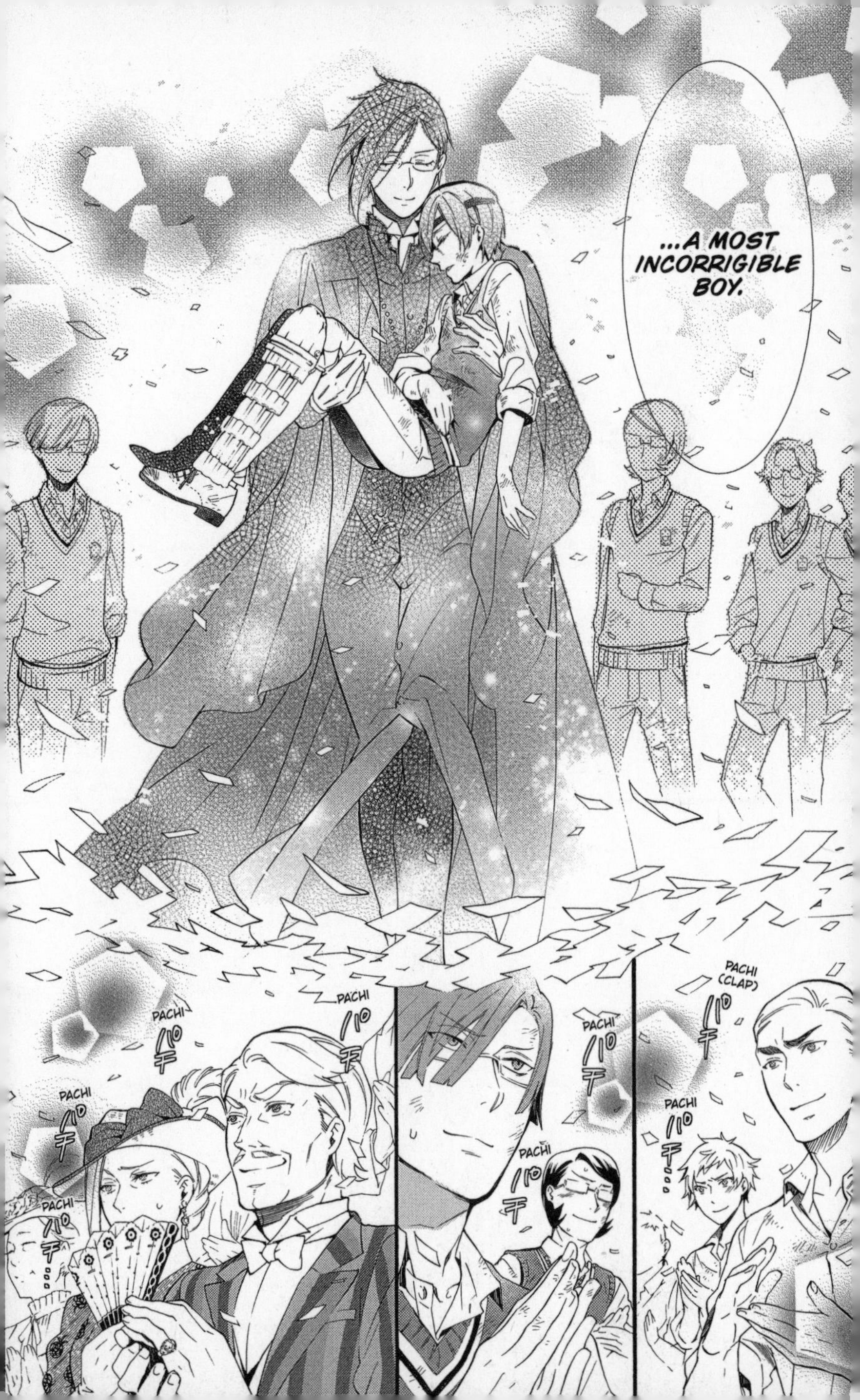
...A MOST INCORRIGIBLE BOY.
PACHI (CLAP)
パチ
PACHI
パチ...
PACHI
パチ
PACHI
パチ
PACHI
パチ
PACHI
パチ
PACHI
パチ...

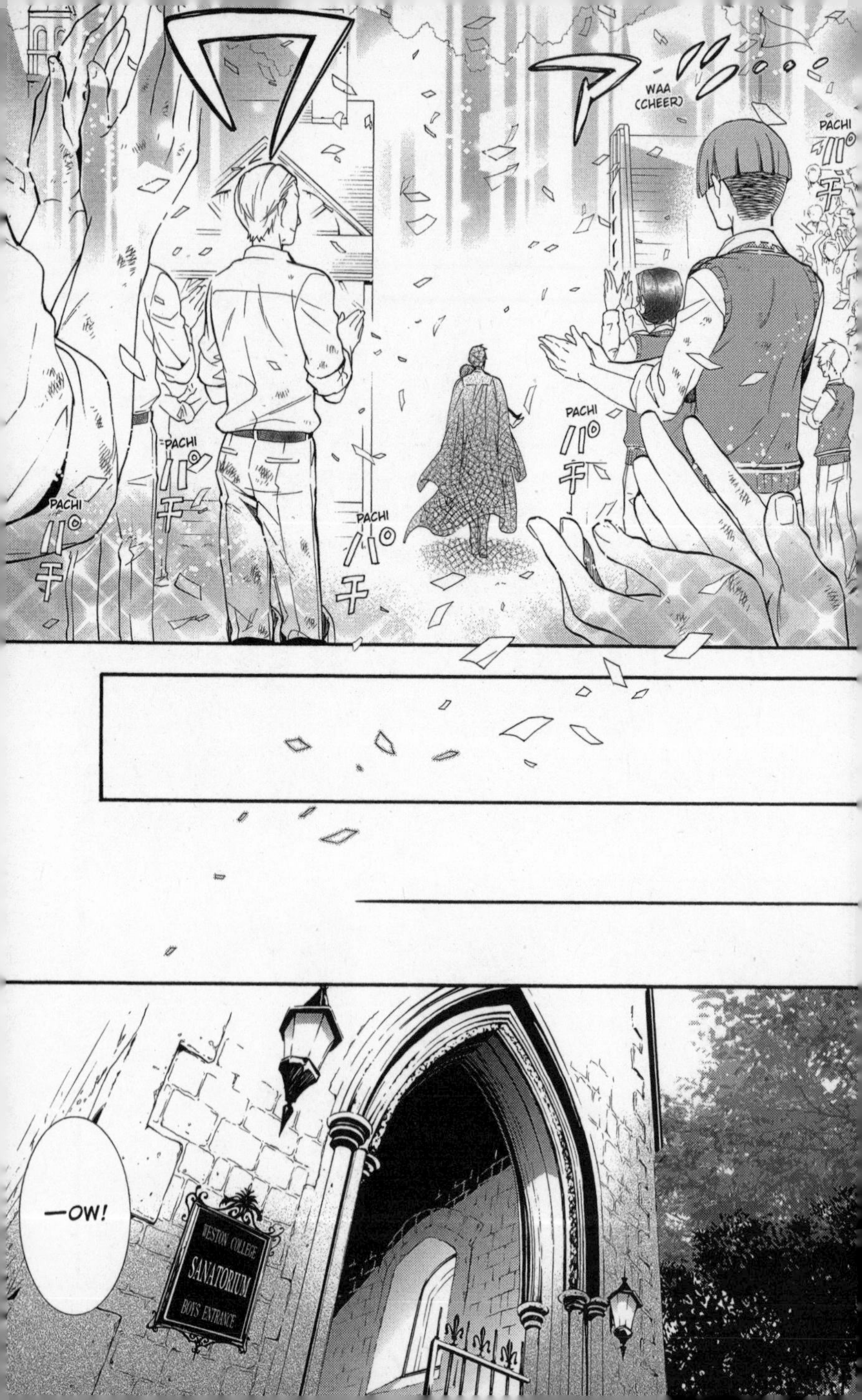
WAA (CHEER)
PACHI
PACHI
PACHI
PACHI
PACHI
WESTON COLLEGE SANATORIUM BOYS ENTRANCE
—OW!

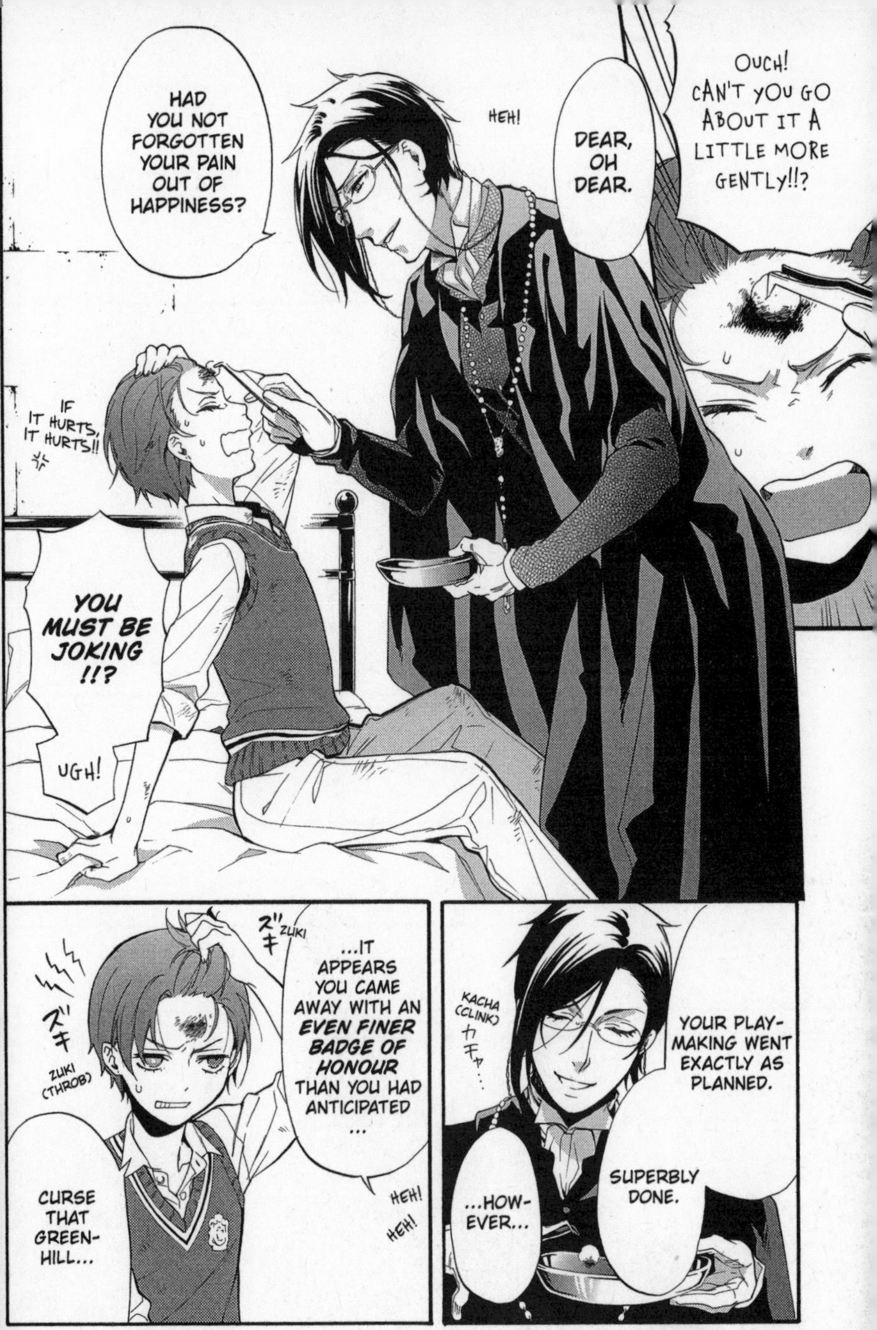
OUCH! CAN'T YOU GO ABOUT IT A LITTLE MORE GENTLY!!?
DEAR, OH DEAR.
HEH!
HAD YOU NOT FORGOTTEN YOUR PAIN OUT OF HAPPINESS?
IF IT HURTS, IT HURTS!!
YOU MUST BE JOKING!!?
UGH!
KACHA (CLINK)
カチャ…
YOUR PLAY-MAKING WENT EXACTLY AS PLANNED.
SUPERBLY DONE.
...HOW-EVER...
ズキ ZUKI
...IT APPEARS YOU CAME AWAY WITH AN ***EVEN FINER BADGE OF HONOUR*** THAN YOU HAD ANTICIPATED...
ズキ
ZUKI (THROB)
HEH! HEH!
CURSE THAT GREEN-HILL...

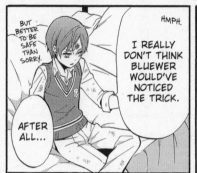

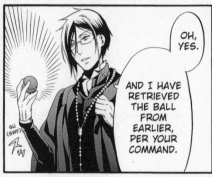

OH, YES.
AND I HAVE RETRIEVED THE BALL FROM EARLIER, PER YOUR COMMAND.
SU (SWF)
HMPH.
I REALLY DON'T THINK BLUEWER WOULD'VE NOTICED THE TRICK.
BUT BETTER TO BE SAFE THAN SORRY.
AFTER ALL...
TON (THP)
...THE WEIGHT OF THE BALL ONLY DIFFERS SLIGHTLY.
BUT THANKS TO THIS, WE WERE ABLE TO TAKE THE CHAMPIONSHIP ALL ACCORDING TO PLAN.
BLUEWER BOWLS THIS DOCTORED BALL LIKE USUAL.
THE SMALL DIFFERENCE IN WEIGHT ALTERS THE COURSE OF THE BALL GREATLY.

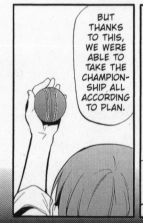

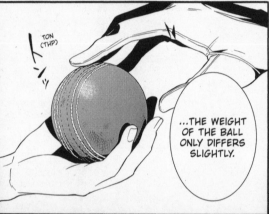

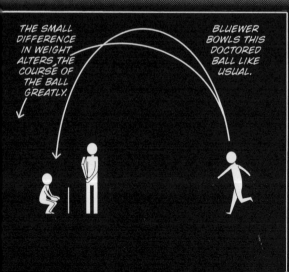

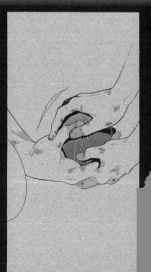

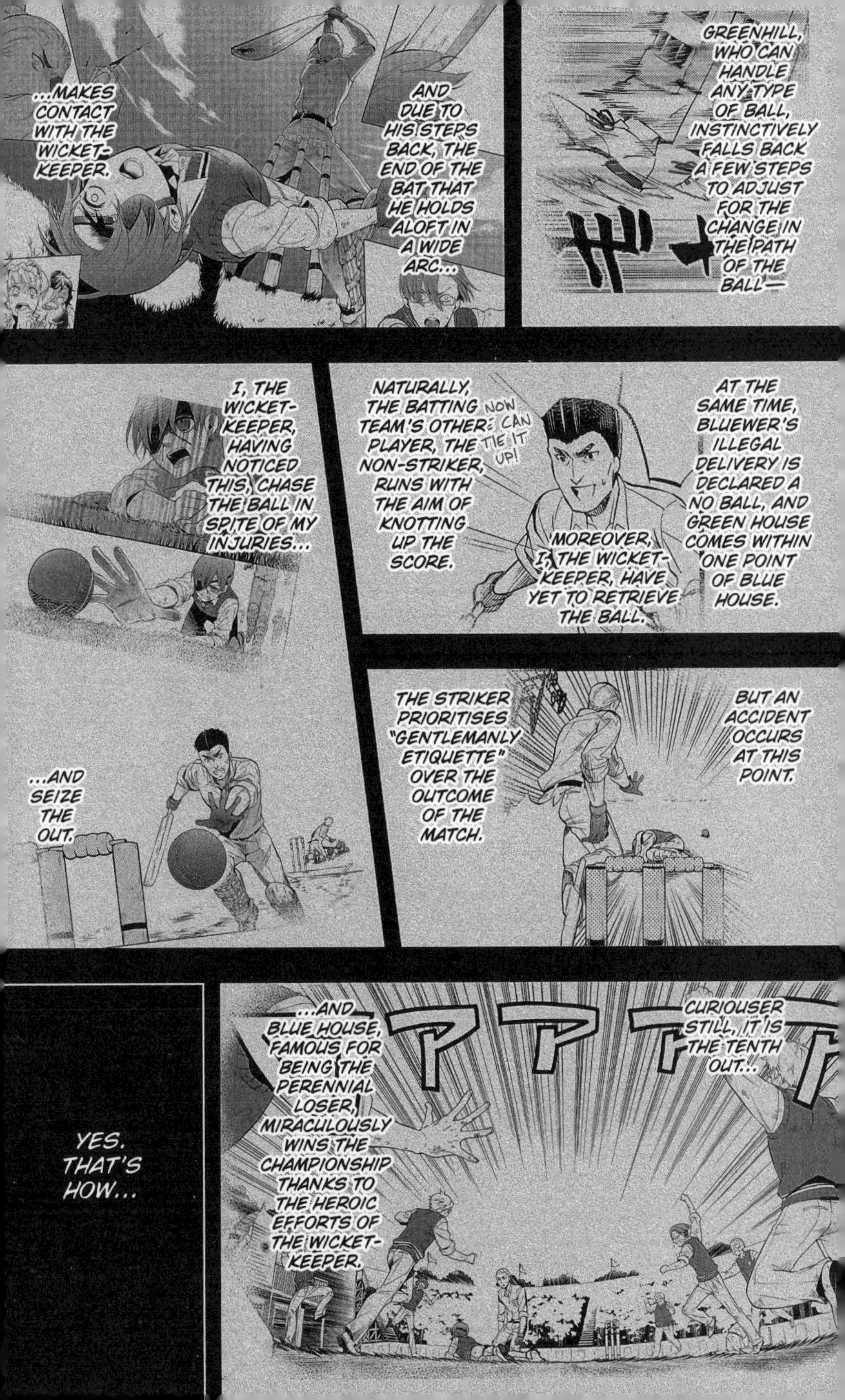

GREENHILL, WHO CAN HANDLE ANY TYPE OF BALL, INSTINCTIVELY FALLS BACK A FEW STEPS TO ADJUST FOR THE CHANGE IN THE PATH OF THE BALL—
AND DUE TO HIS STEPS BACK, THE END OF THE BAT THAT HE HOLDS ALOFT IN A WIDE ARC...
...MAKES CONTACT WITH THE WICKET-KEEPER.
AT THE SAME TIME, BLUEWER'S ILLEGAL DELIVERY IS DECLARED A NO BALL, AND GREEN HOUSE COMES WITHIN ONE POINT OF BLUE HOUSE.
NATURALLY, THE BATTING TEAM'S OTHER PLAYER, THE NON-STRIKER, RUNS WITH THE AIM OF KNOTTING UP THE SCORE.
NOW I CAN TIE IT UP!
MOREOVER, I, THE WICKET-KEEPER, HAVE YET TO RETRIEVE THE BALL.
BUT AN ACCIDENT OCCURS AT THIS POINT.
THE STRIKER PRIORITISES "GENTLEMANLY ETIQUETTE" OVER THE OUTCOME OF THE MATCH.
I, THE WICKET-KEEPER, HAVING NOTICED THIS, CHASE THE BALL IN SPITE OF MY INJURIES...
...AND SEIZE THE OUT.
CURIOUSER STILL, IT IS THE TENTH OUT...
...AND BLUE HOUSE, FAMOUS FOR BEING THE PERENNIAL LOSER, MIRACULOUSLY WINS THE CHAMPIONSHIP THANKS TO THE HEROIC EFFORTS OF THE WICKET-KEEPER.
YES. THAT'S HOW...

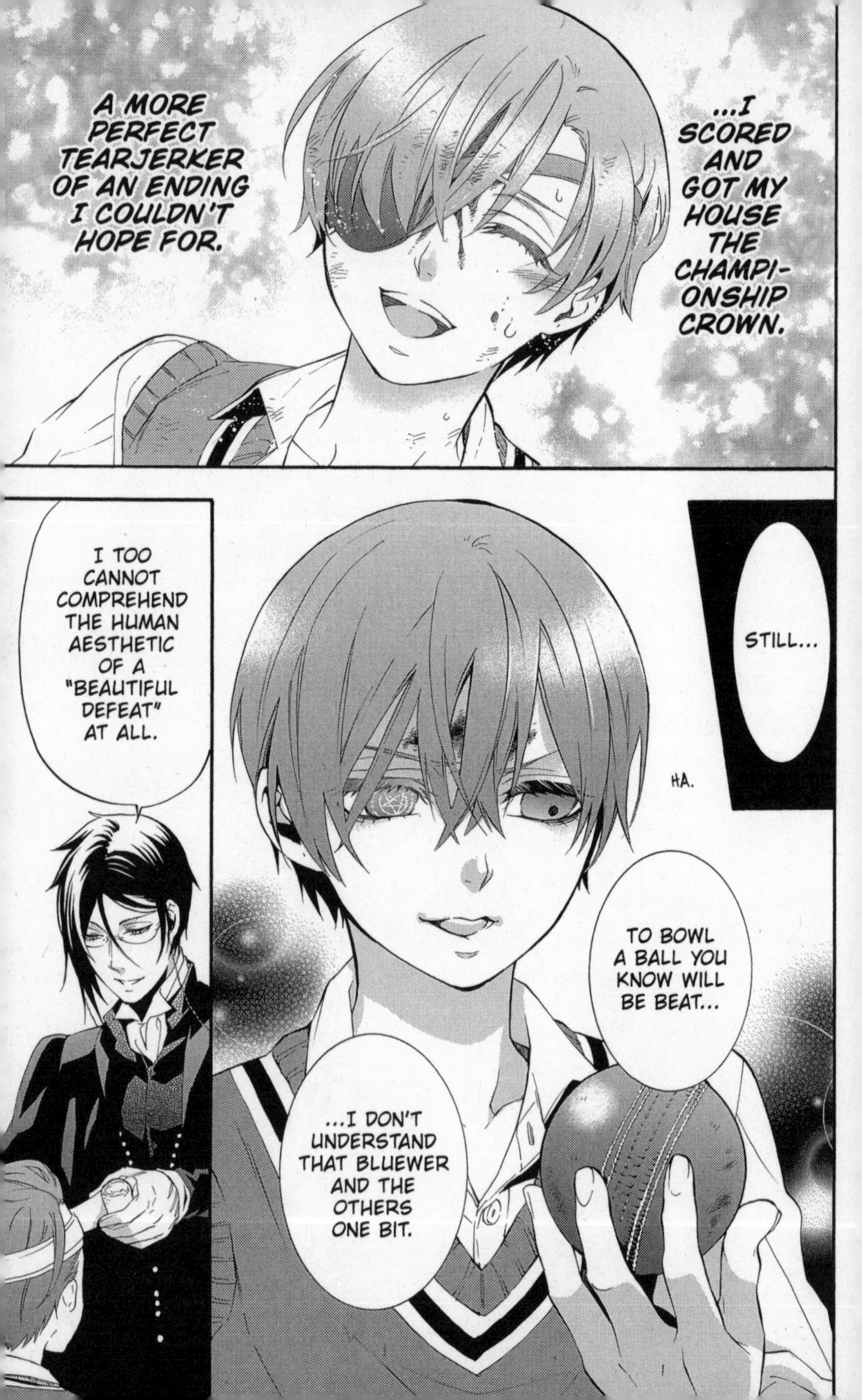
...I SCORED AND GOT MY HOUSE THE CHAMPIONSHIP CROWN.
A MORE PERFECT TEARJERKER OF AN ENDING I COULDN'T HOPE FOR.
STILL...
HA.
TO BOWL A BALL YOU KNOW WILL BE BEAT...
...I DON'T UNDERSTAND THAT BLUEWER AND THE OTHERS ONE BIT.
I TOO CANNOT COMPREHEND THE HUMAN AESTHETIC OF A "BEAUTIFUL DEFEAT" AT ALL.

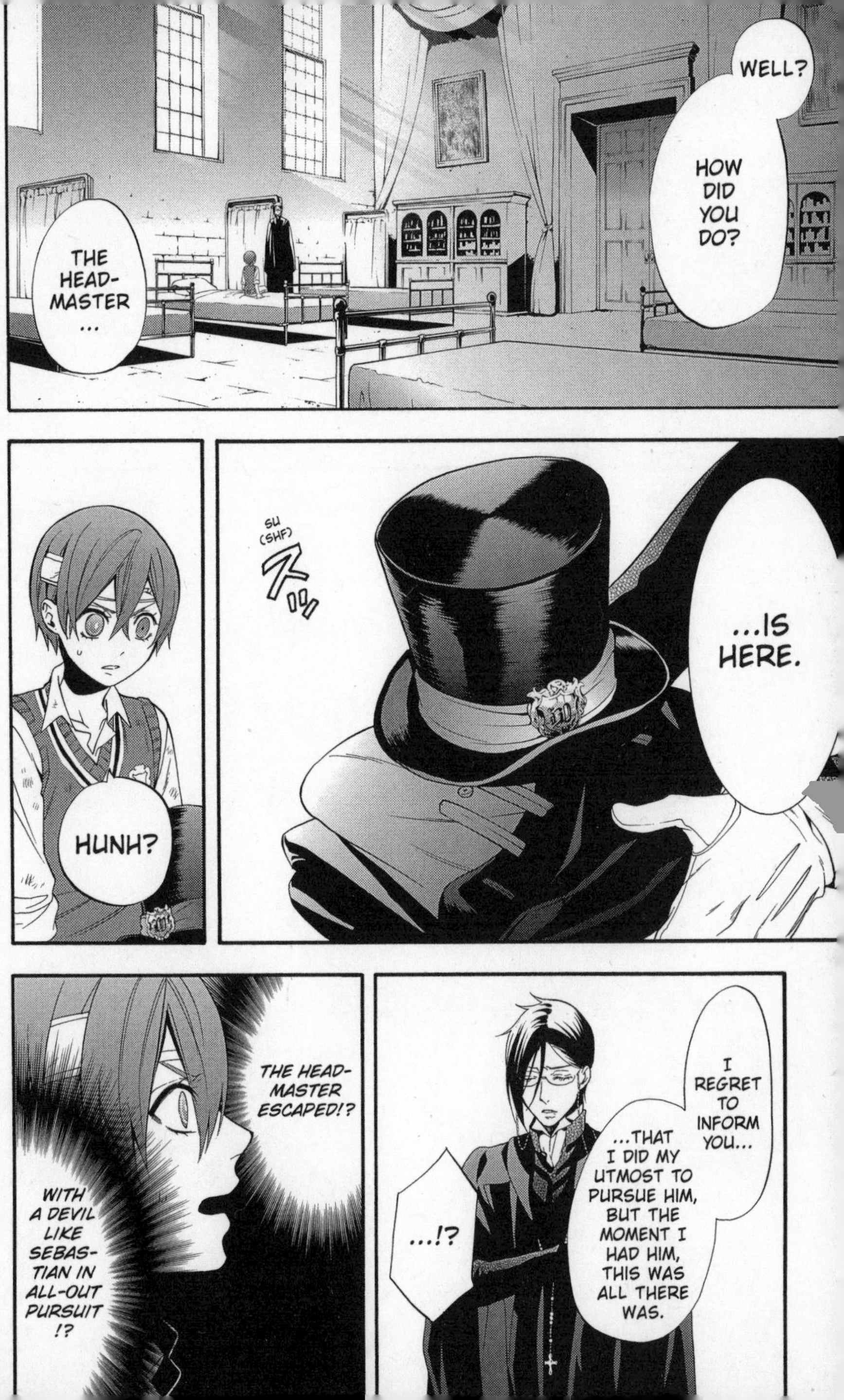
WELL?
HOW DID YOU DO?
THE HEADMASTER ...
...IS HERE.
SU (SHF)
HUNH?
I REGRET TO INFORM YOU...
...THAT I DID MY UTMOST TO PURSUE HIM, BUT THE MOMENT I HAD HIM, THIS WAS ALL THERE WAS.
...!?
THE HEADMASTER ESCAPED!?
WITH A DEVIL LIKE SEBASTIAN IN ALL-OUT PURSUIT!?

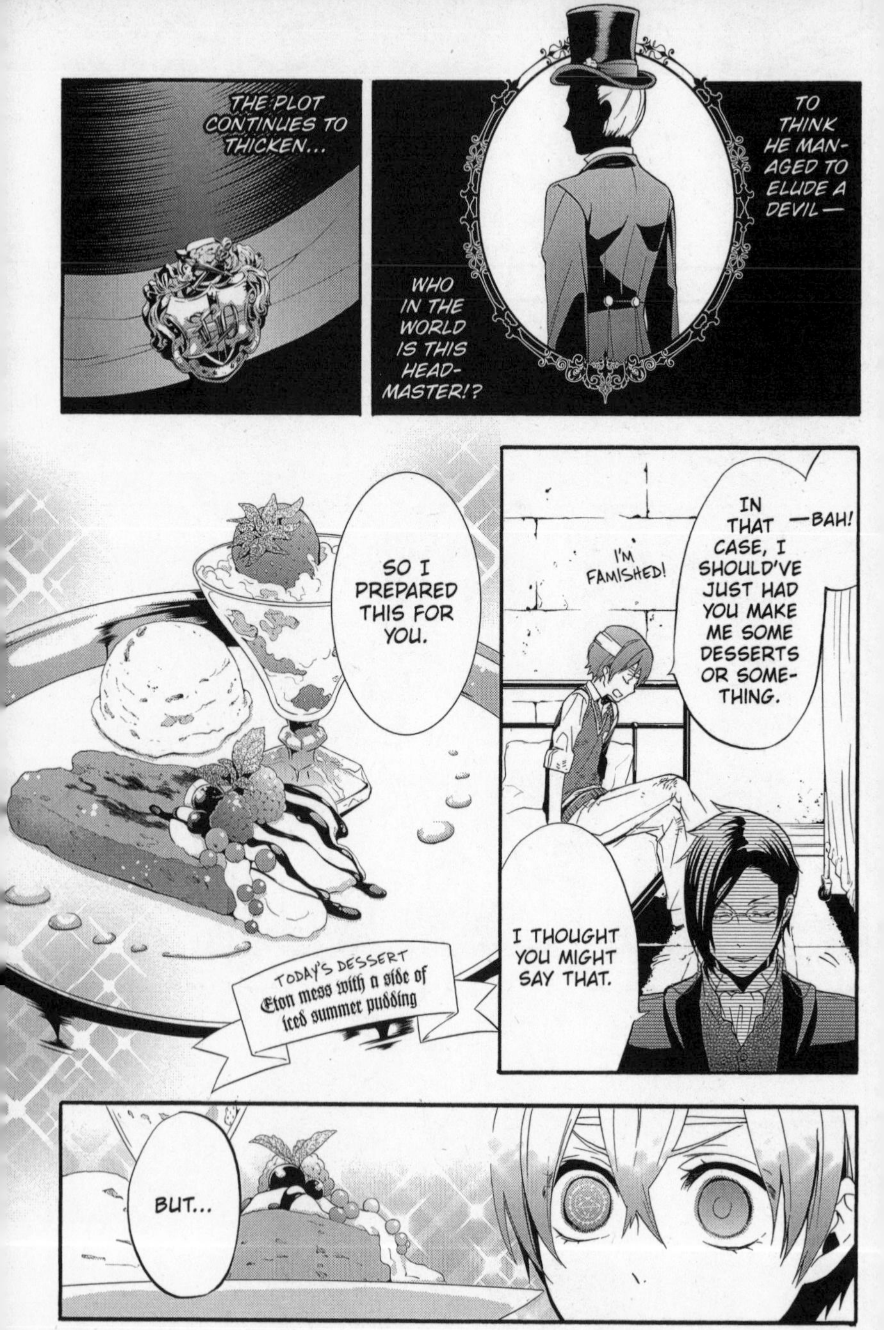
TO THINK HE MANAGED TO ELUDE A DEVIL—
WHO IN THE WORLD IS THIS HEADMASTER!?
THE PLOT CONTINUES TO THICKEN...
IN THAT CASE, I SHOULD'VE JUST HAD YOU MAKE ME SOME DESSERTS OR SOMETHING.
—BAH!
I'M FAMISHED!
I THOUGHT YOU MIGHT SAY THAT.
SO I PREPARED THIS FOR YOU.
TODAY'S DESSERT
Eton mess with a side of iced summer pudding
BUT...

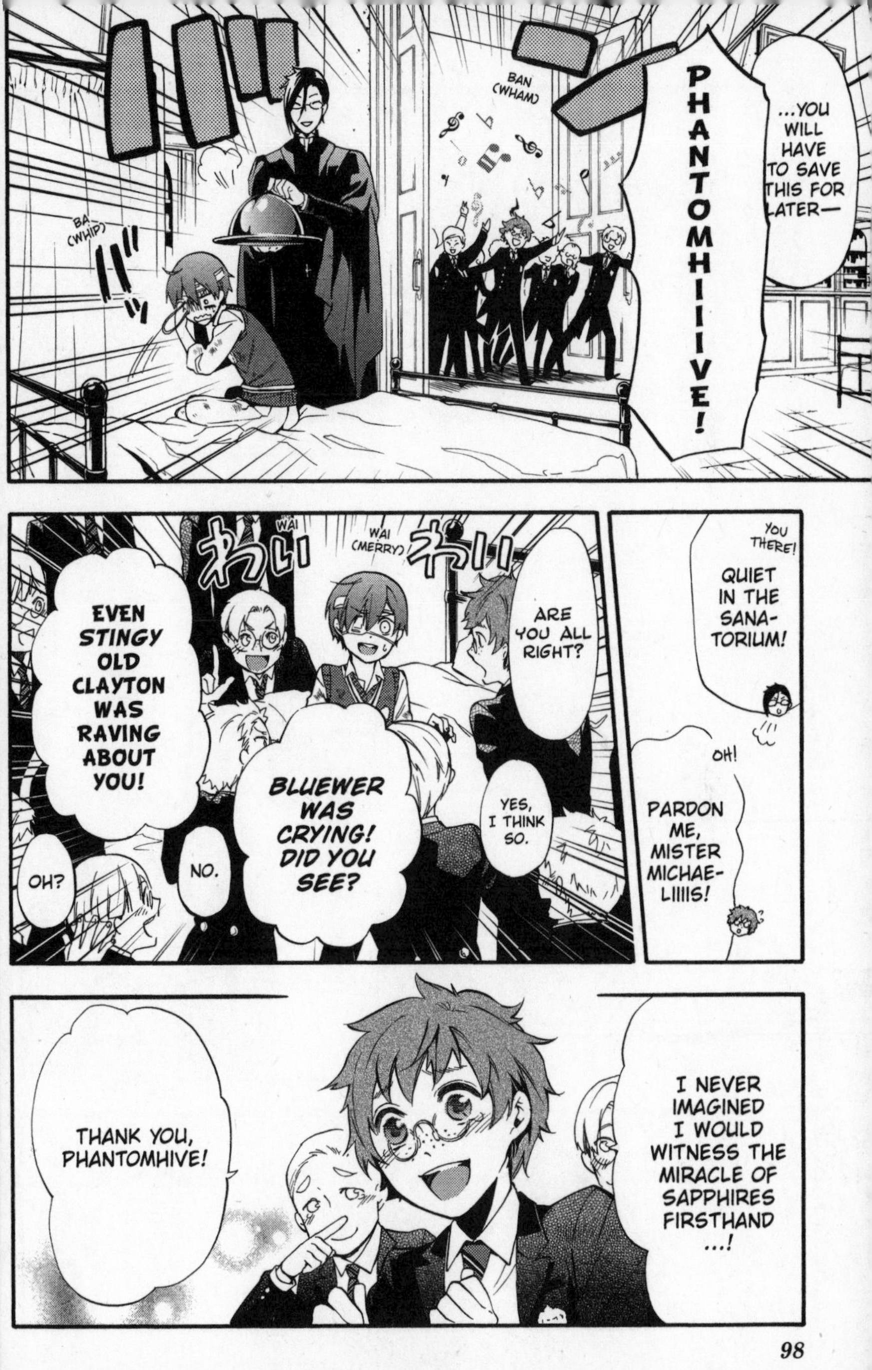
...YOU WILL HAVE TO SAVE THIS FOR LATER—
PHANTOMHIIIIVE!
BAN (WHAM)
BA (WHIP)
YOU THERE!
QUIET IN THE SANA-TORIUM!
OH!
PARDON ME, MISTER MICHAE-LIIIIS!
WAI (MERRY)
ARE YOU ALL RIGHT?
YES, I THINK SO.
BLUEWER WAS CRYING! DID YOU SEE?
NO.
EVEN STINGY OLD CLAYTON WAS RAVING ABOUT YOU!
OH?
I NEVER IMAGINED I WOULD WITNESS THE MIRACLE OF SAPPHIRES FIRSTHAND ...!
THANK YOU, PHANTOMHIVE!

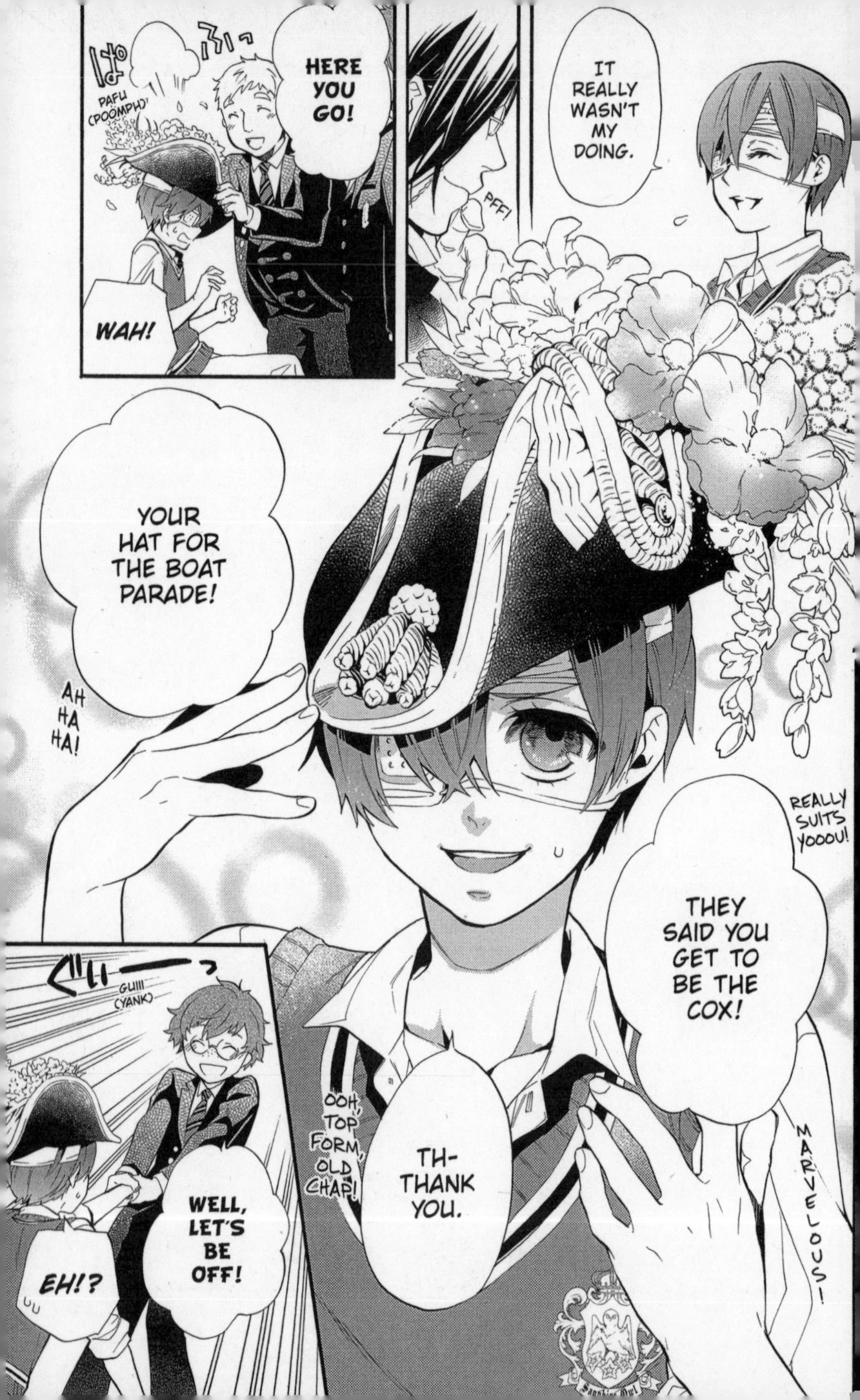
IT REALLY WASN'T MY DOING.
PFF!
ぱふっ
PAFU (POOMPH)
HERE YOU GO!
WAH!
THEY SAID YOU GET TO BE THE COX!
REALLY SUITS YOOOU!
YOUR HAT FOR THE BOAT PARADE!
AH HA HA!
MARVELOUS!
TH-THANK YOU.
OOH, TOP FORM, OLD CHAP!
ぐいーっ
GUIII (YANK)
WELL, LET'S BE OFF!
EH!?

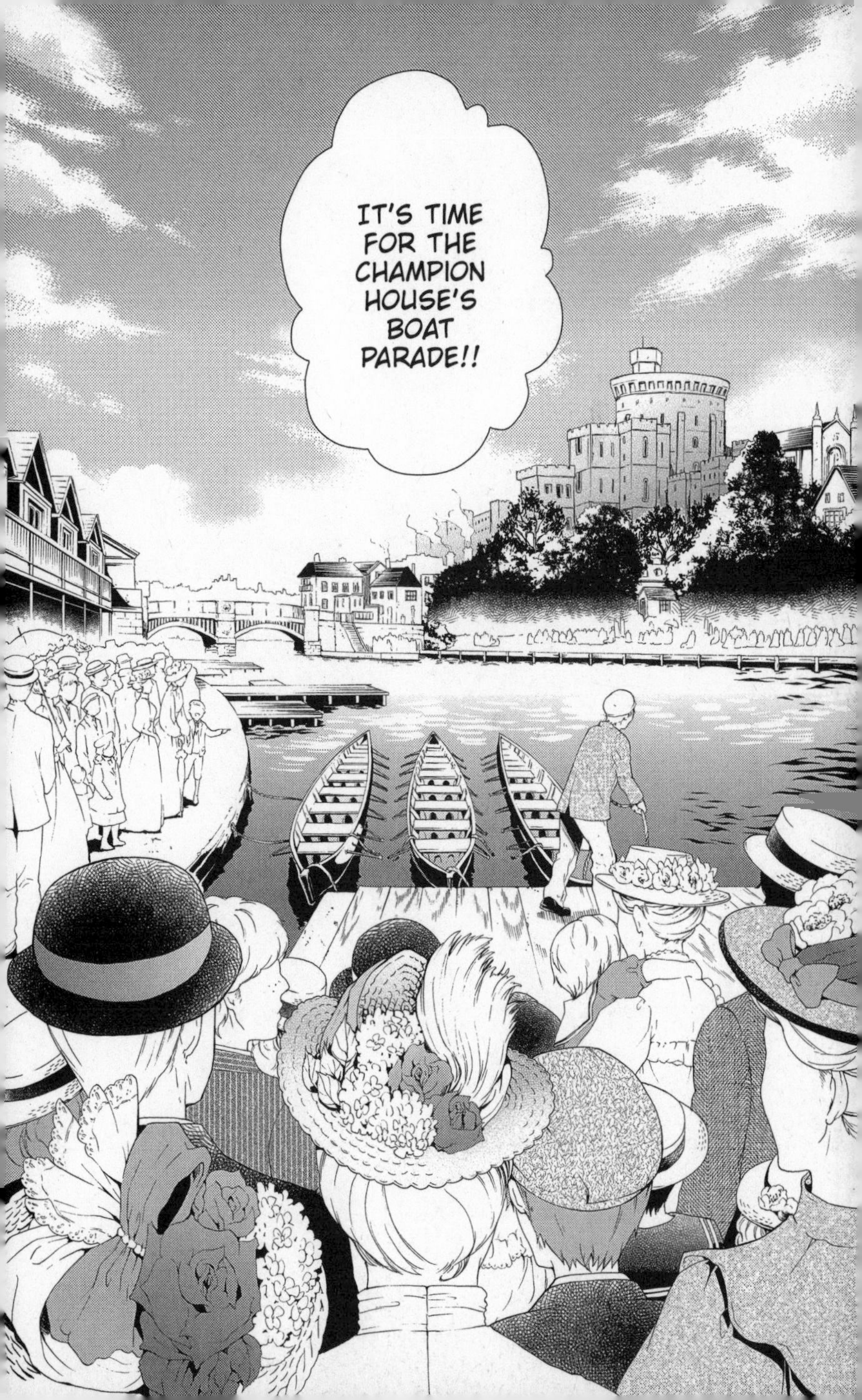
IT'S TIME FOR THE CHAMPION HOUSE'S BOAT PARADE!!

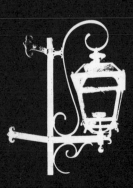

Black Butler

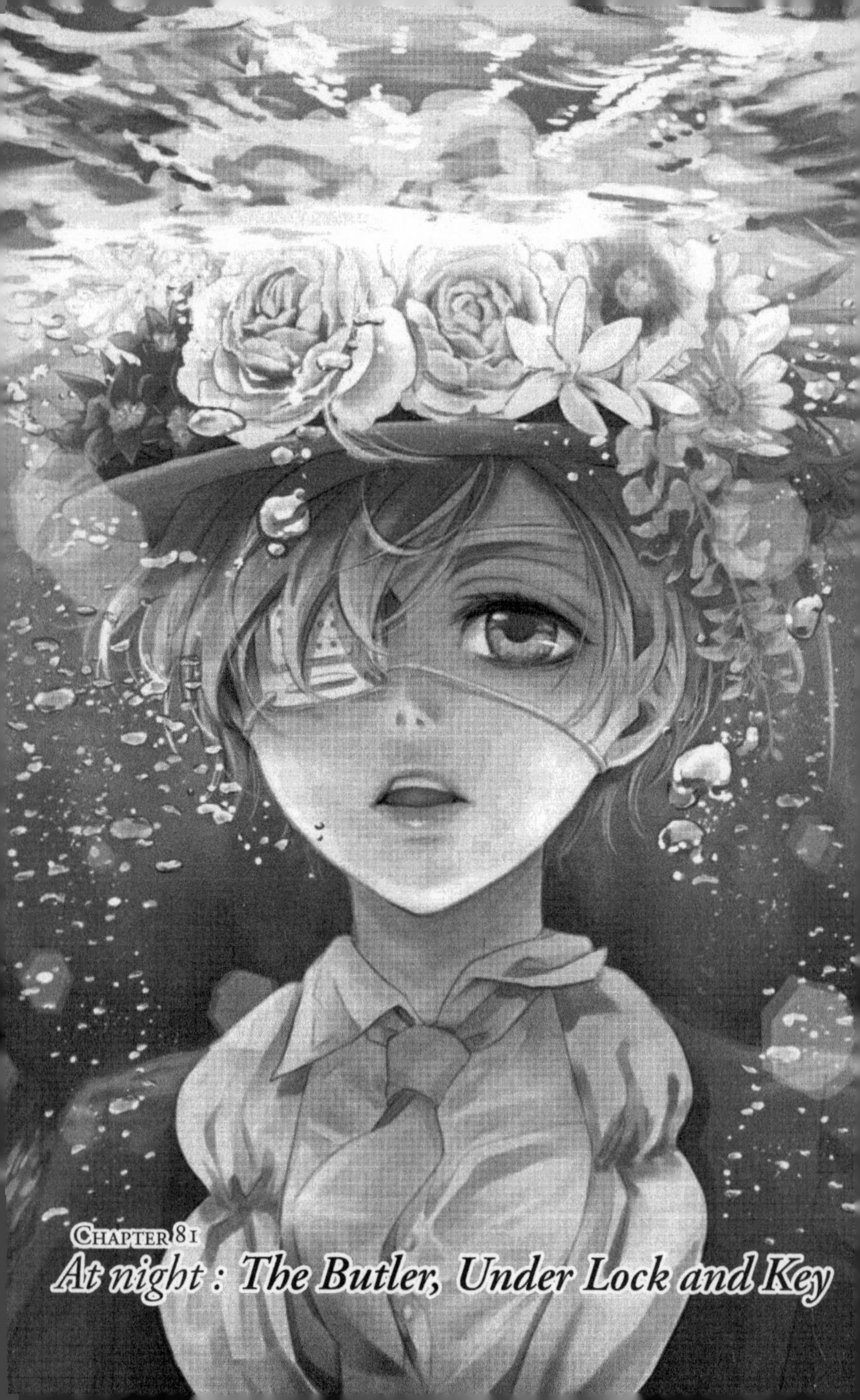

Chapter 81

At night : The Butler, Under Lock and Key

Black Butler

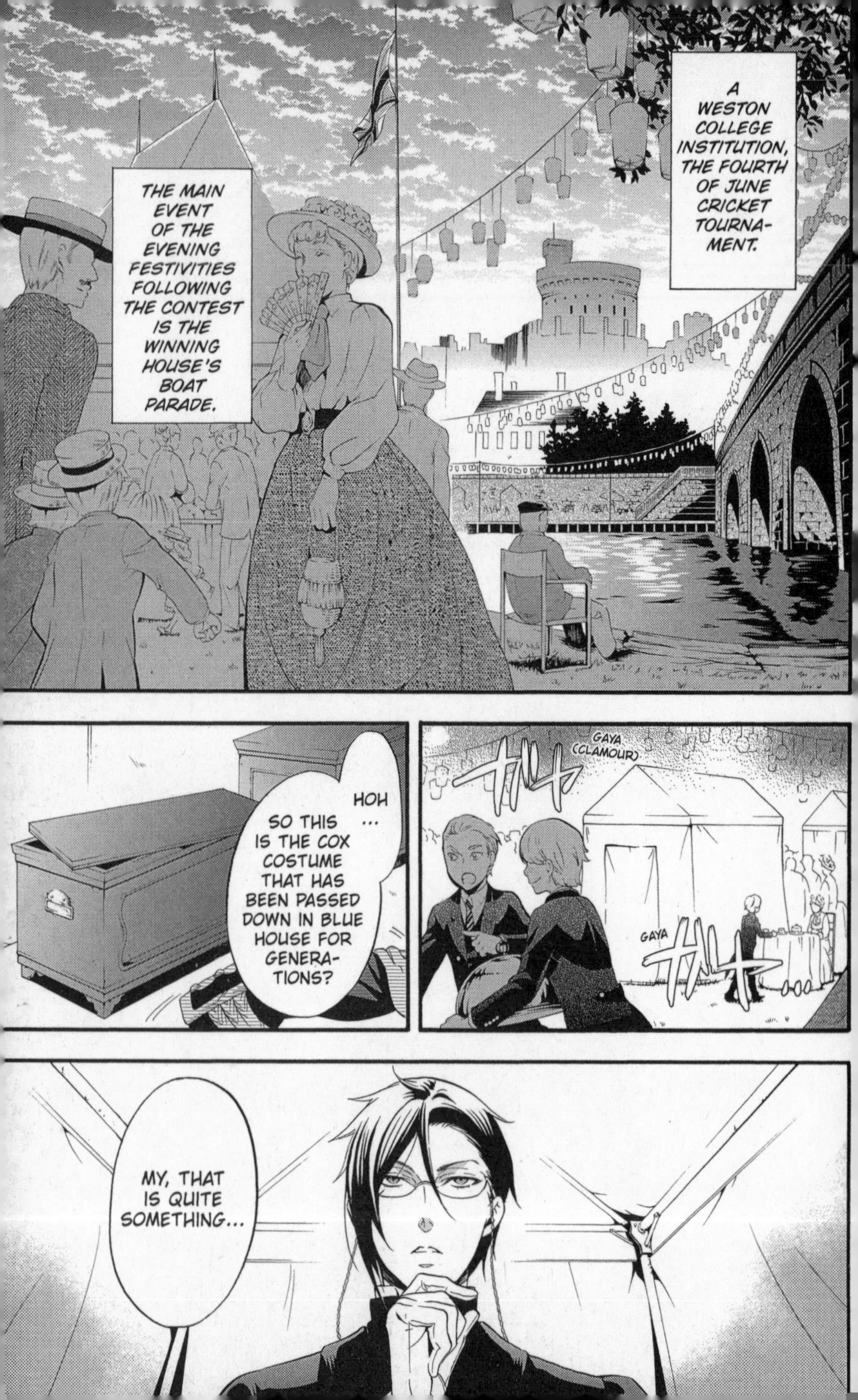
A WESTON COLLEGE INSTITUTION, THE FOURTH OF JUNE CRICKET TOURNAMENT.
THE MAIN EVENT OF THE EVENING FESTIVITIES FOLLOWING THE CONTEST IS THE WINNING HOUSE'S BOAT PARADE.
GAYA (CLAMOUR)
GAYA
HOH...
SO THIS IS THE COX COSTUME THAT HAS BEEN PASSED DOWN IN BLUE HOUSE FOR GENERATIONS?
MY, THAT IS QUITE SOMETHING...

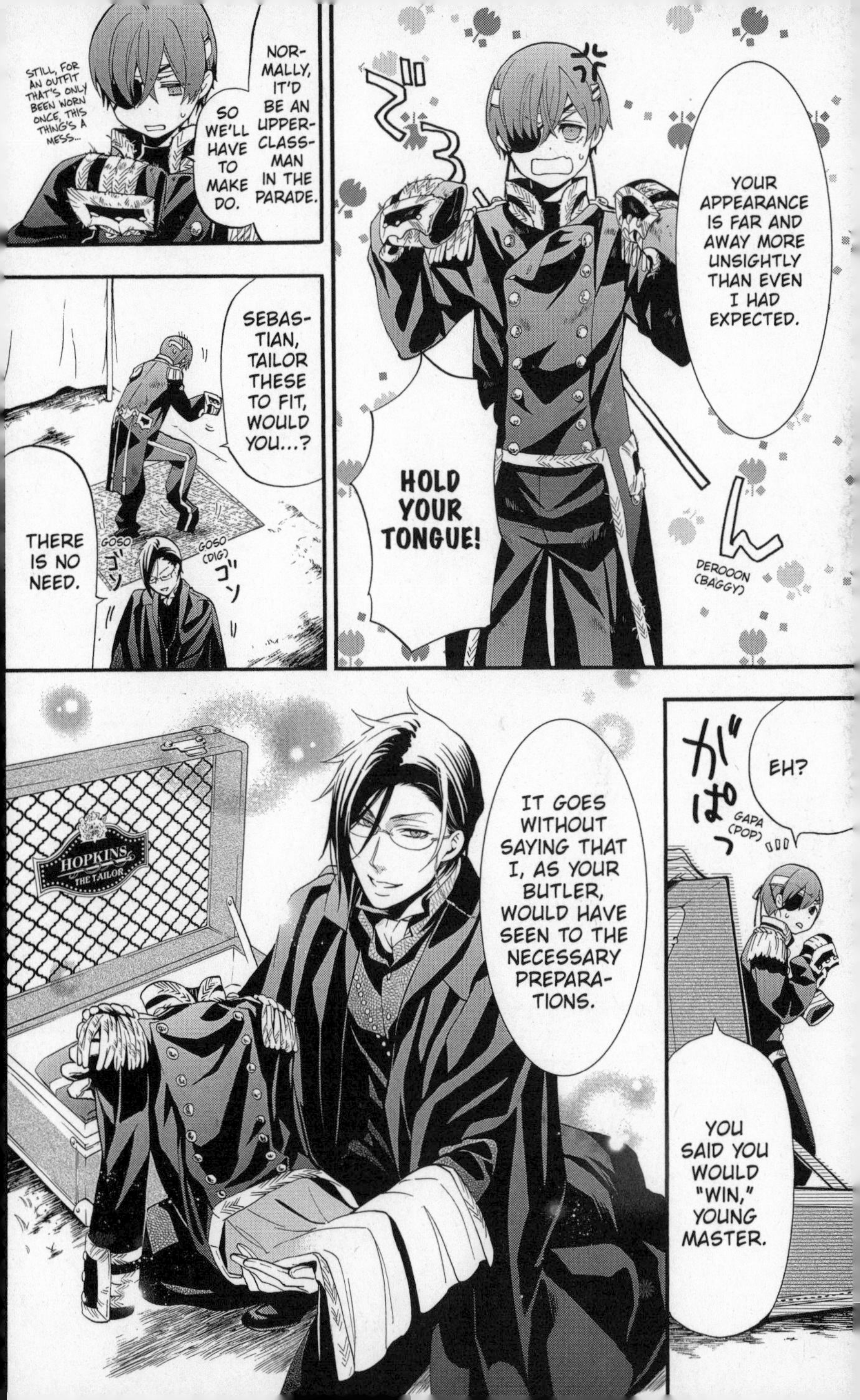
YOUR APPEARANCE IS FAR AND AWAY MORE UNSIGHTLY THAN EVEN I HAD EXPECTED.
DEROOON (BAGGY)
HOLD YOUR TONGUE!
NOR-MALLY, IT'D BE AN UPPER-CLASS-MAN IN THE PARADE.
SO WE'LL HAVE TO MAKE DO.
STILL, FOR AN OUTFIT THAT'S ONLY BEEN WORN ONCE, THIS THING'S A MESS...
SEBAS-TIAN, TAILOR THESE TO FIT, WOULD YOU...?
GOSO (DIG)
GOSO
THERE IS NO NEED.
EH?
GAPA (POP)
YOU SAID YOU WOULD "WIN," YOUNG MASTER.
IT GOES WITHOUT SAYING THAT I, AS YOUR BUTLER, WOULD HAVE SEEN TO THE NECESSARY PREPARA-TIONS.
HOPKINS THE TAILOR

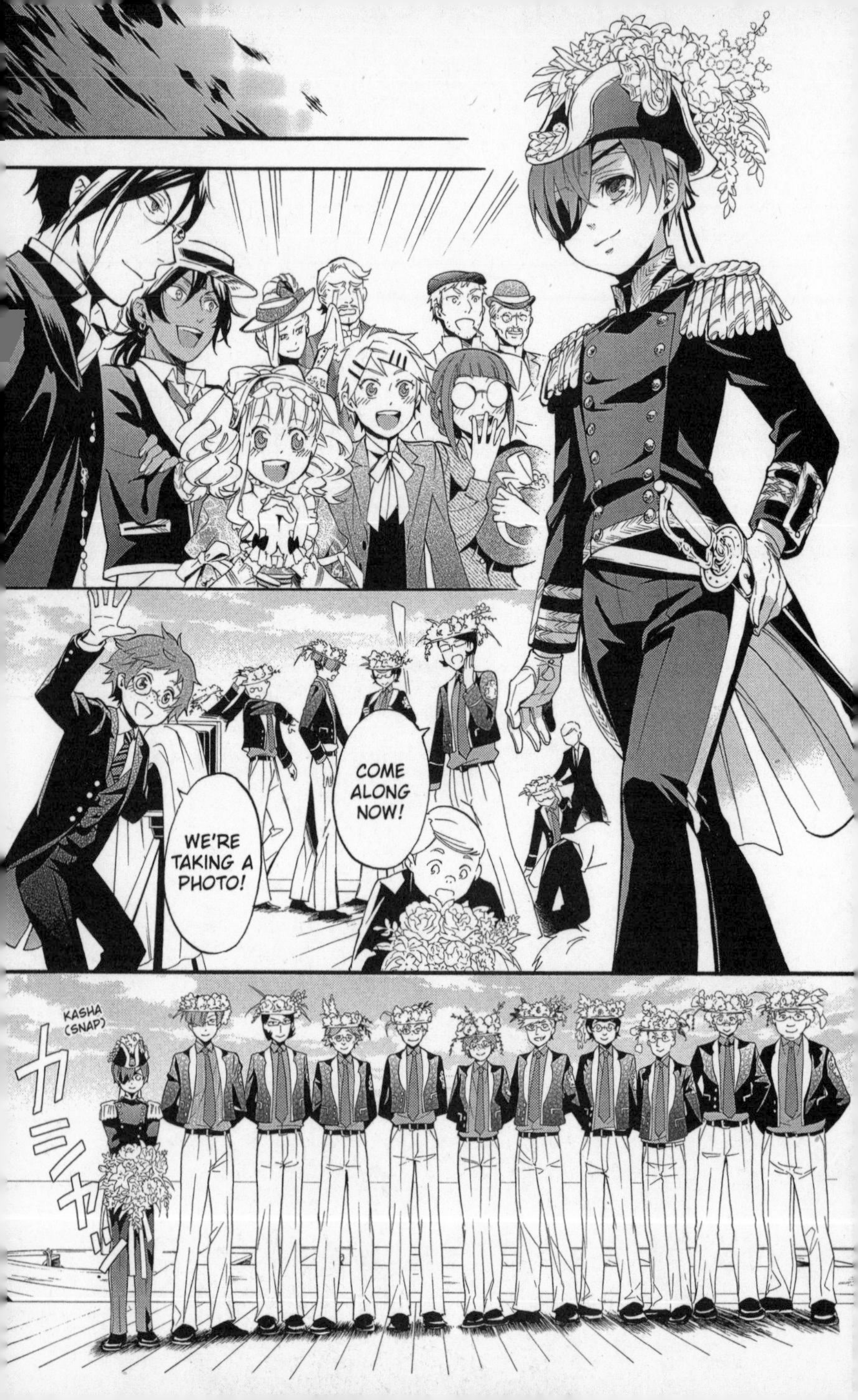
COME ALONG NOW!
WE'RE TAKING A PHOTO!
KASHA (SNAP)
カシャ

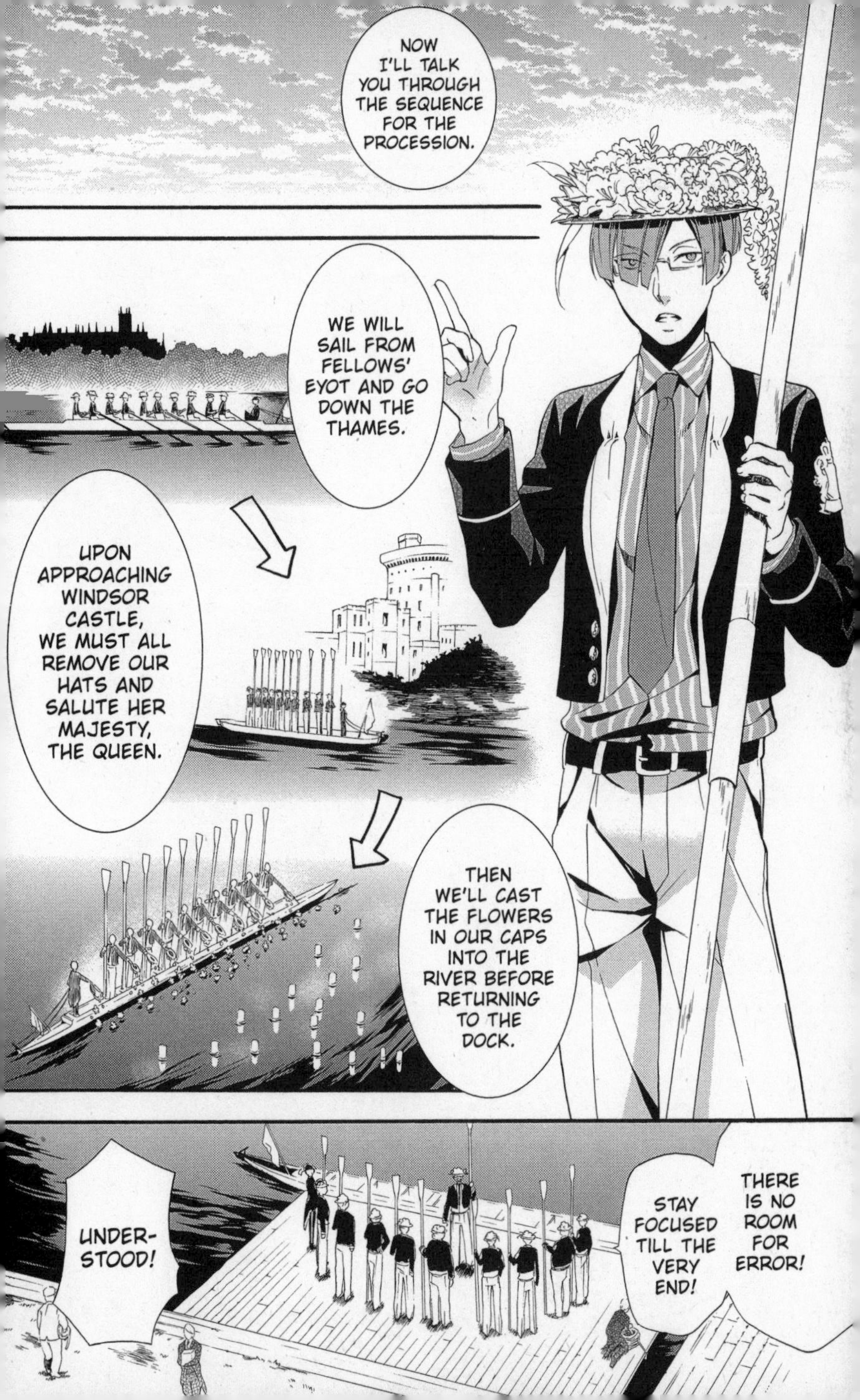
NOW I'LL TALK YOU THROUGH THE SEQUENCE FOR THE PROCESSION.
WE WILL SAIL FROM FELLOWS' EYOT AND GO DOWN THE THAMES.
UPON APPROACHING WINDSOR CASTLE, WE MUST ALL REMOVE OUR HATS AND SALUTE HER MAJESTY, THE QUEEN.
THEN WE'LL CAST THE FLOWERS IN OUR CAPS INTO THE RIVER BEFORE RETURNING TO THE DOCK.
THERE IS NO ROOM FOR ERROR!
STAY FOCUSED TILL THE VERY END!
UNDER-STOOD!

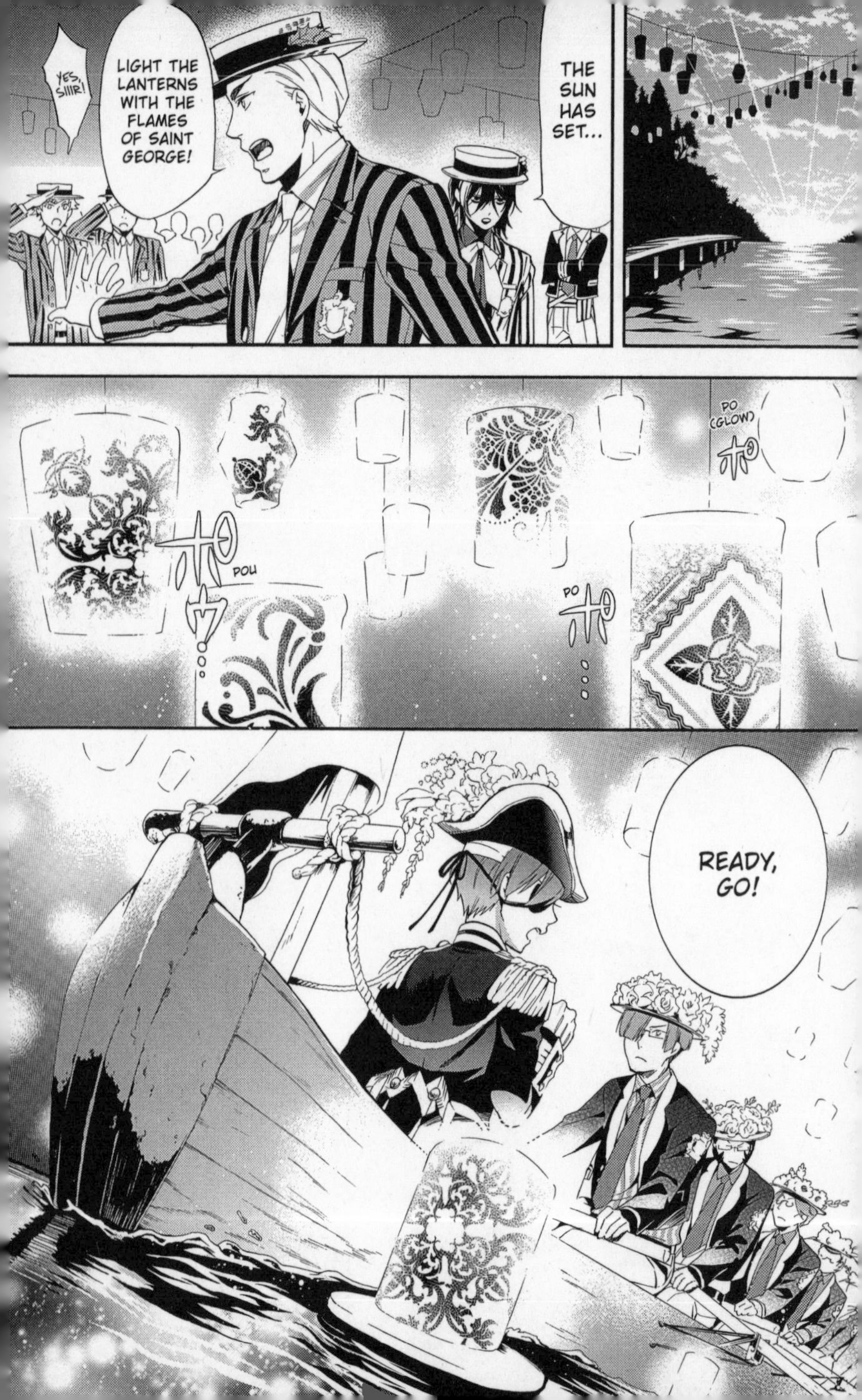
THE SUN HAS SET...
LIGHT THE LANTERNS WITH THE FLAMES OF SAINT GEORGE!
YES, SIIIR!
PO (GLOW)
PO
POU
READY, GO!

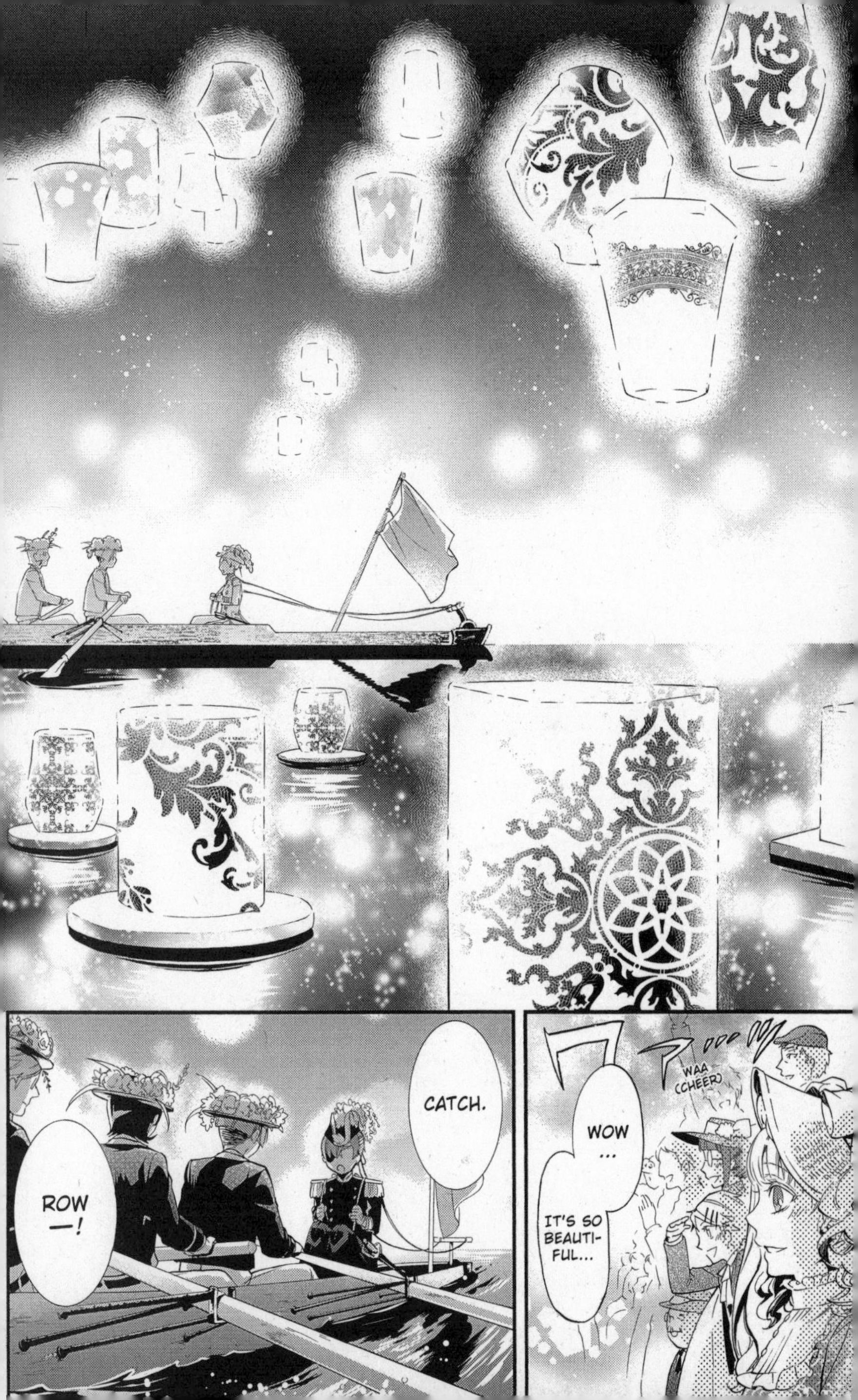
WAA (CHEER)
WOW...
IT'S SO BEAUTIFUL...
CATCH.
ROW—!

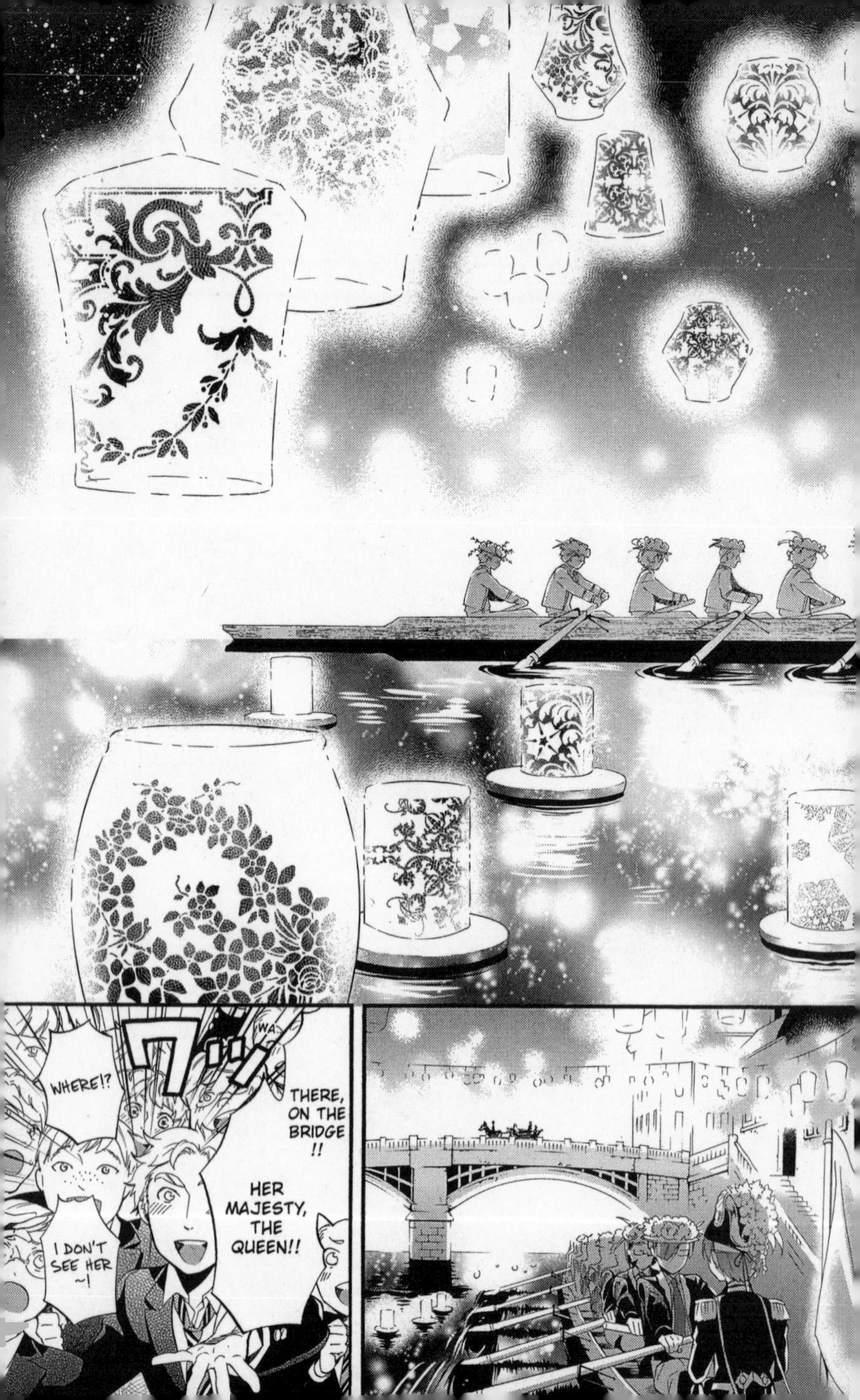
WA
THERE, ON THE BRIDGE!!
WHERE!?
HER MAJESTY, THE QUEEN!!
I DON'T SEE HER ~!

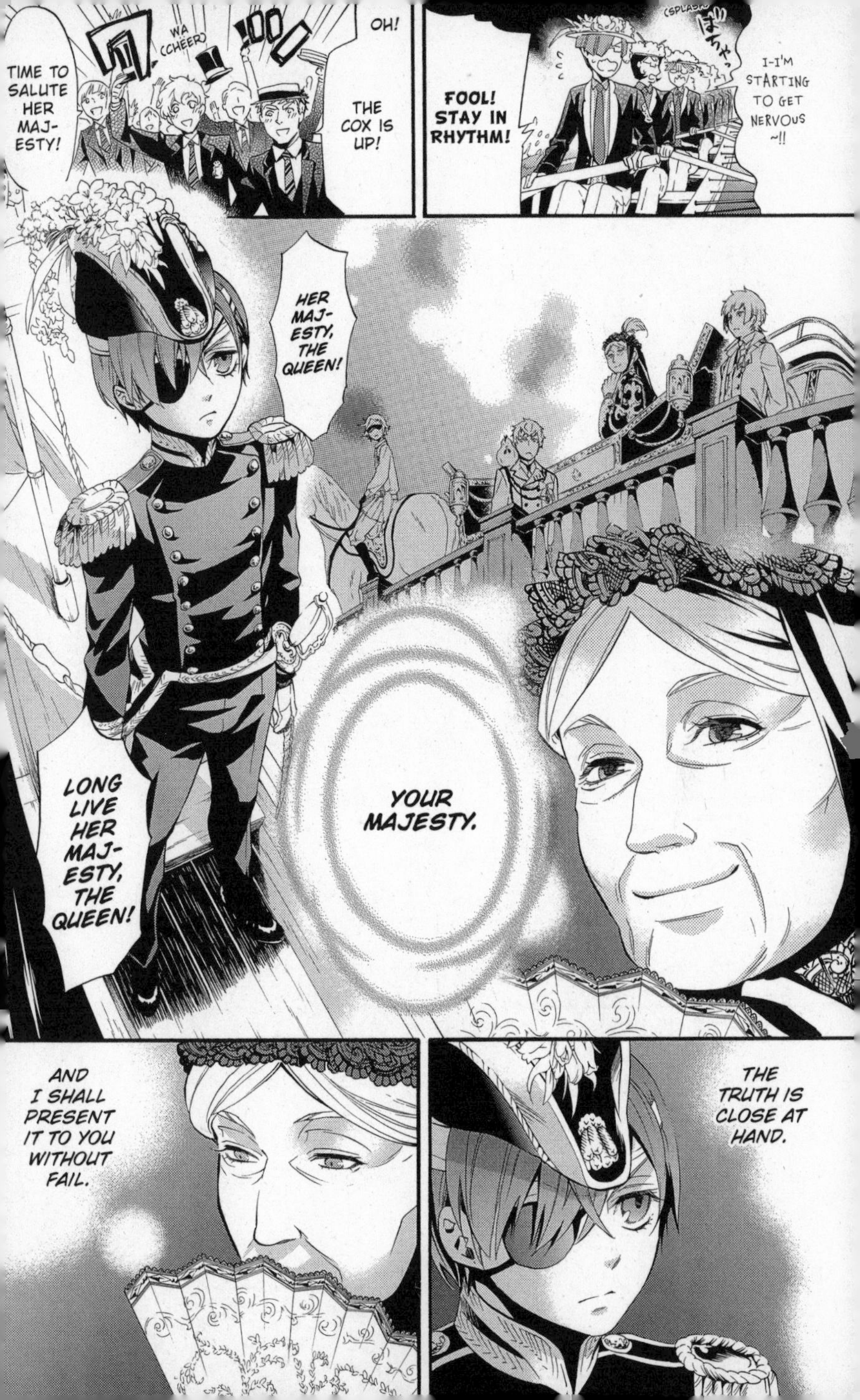
(SPLASH)
I-I'M STARTING TO GET NERVOUS ~!!
FOOL! STAY IN RHYTHM!
OH!
THE COX IS UP!
WA (CHEER)
TIME TO SALUTE HER MAJ-ESTY!
HER MAJ-ESTY, THE QUEEN!
YOUR MAJESTY.
LONG LIVE HER MAJ-ESTY, THE QUEEN!
THE TRUTH IS CLOSE AT HAND.
AND I SHALL PRESENT IT TO YOU WITHOUT FAIL.

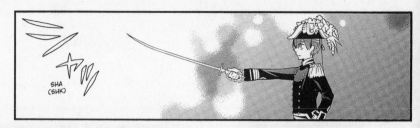

SHA
(SHK)
SALUTE HER MAJESTY, THE QUEEN!
WAA
PHANTOM-HIVE...
WE WON THIS TOURNAMENT THROUGH METICULOUS CALCULATION.
—HOWEVER...
...WE SEEM TO HAVE MADE ONE FATAL ERROR.
EH?

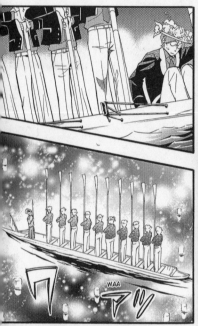

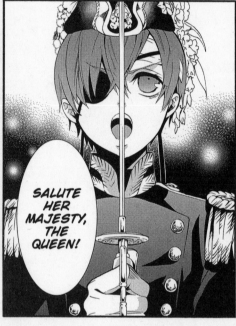

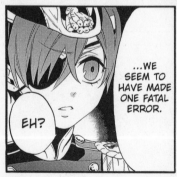

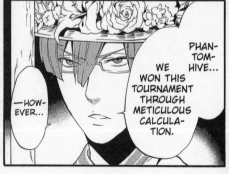

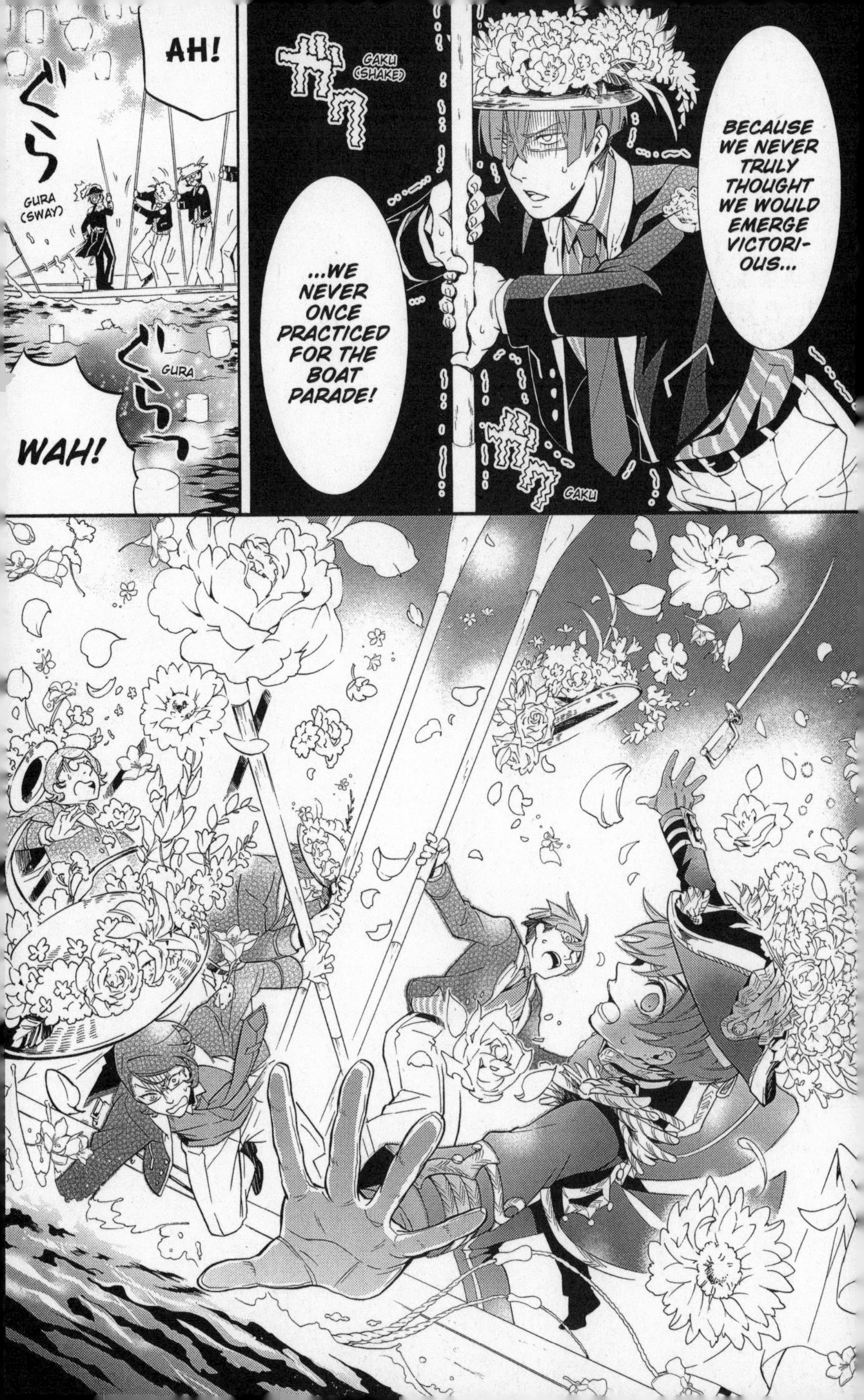
BECAUSE WE NEVER TRULY THOUGHT WE WOULD EMERGE VICTORI-OUS...
GAKU (SHAKE)
...WE NEVER ONCE PRACTICED FOR THE BOAT PARADE!
GAKU
AH!
GURA (SWAY)
GURA
WAH!

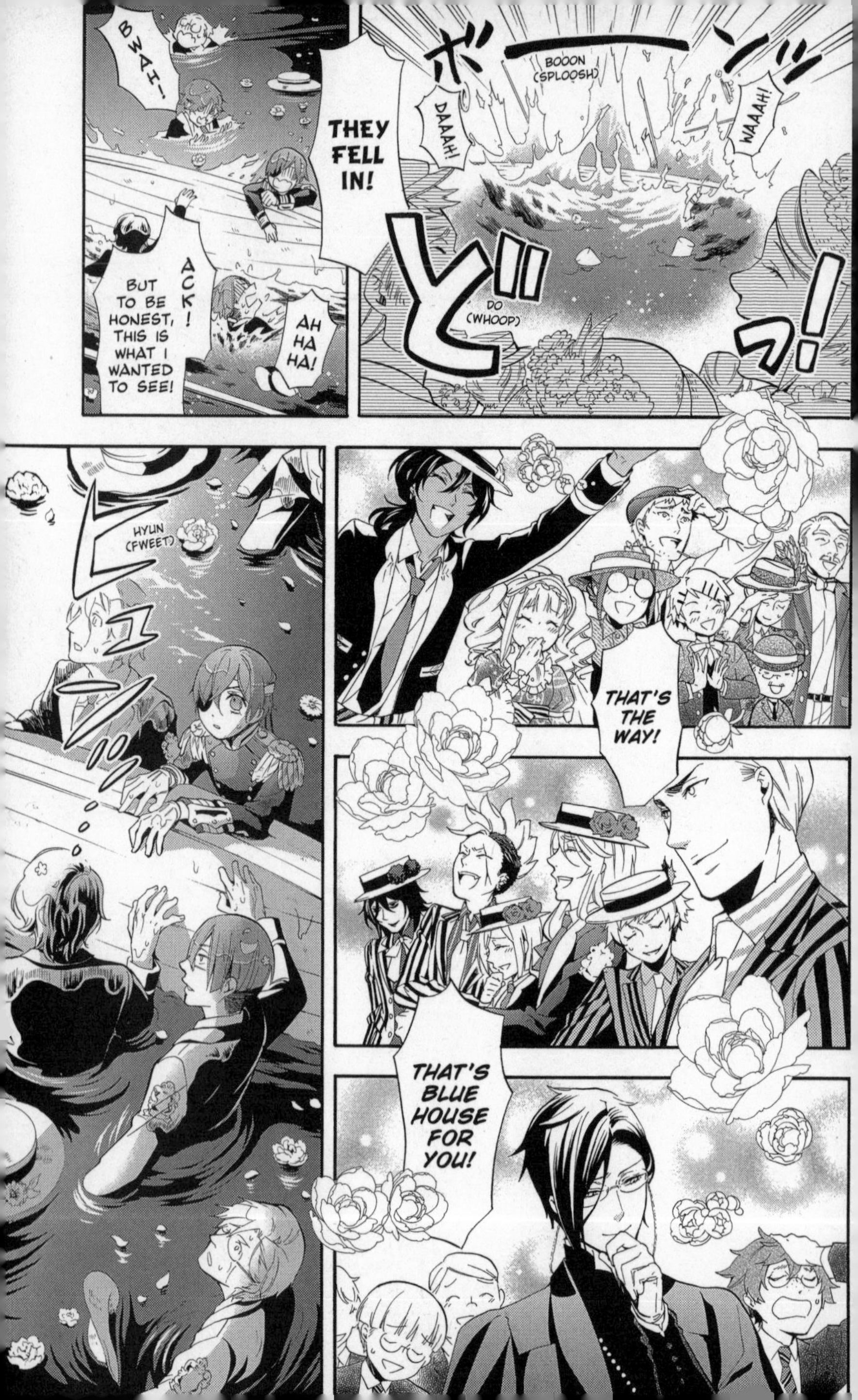
BOOON (SPLOOSH)
WAAAH!
DAAAH!
DO (WHOOP)
THEY FELL IN!
BWAH!
AH HA HA!
ACK!
BUT TO BE HONEST, THIS IS WHAT I WANTED TO SEE!
THAT'S THE WAY!
THAT'S BLUE HOUSE FOR YOU!
HYUN (FWEET)

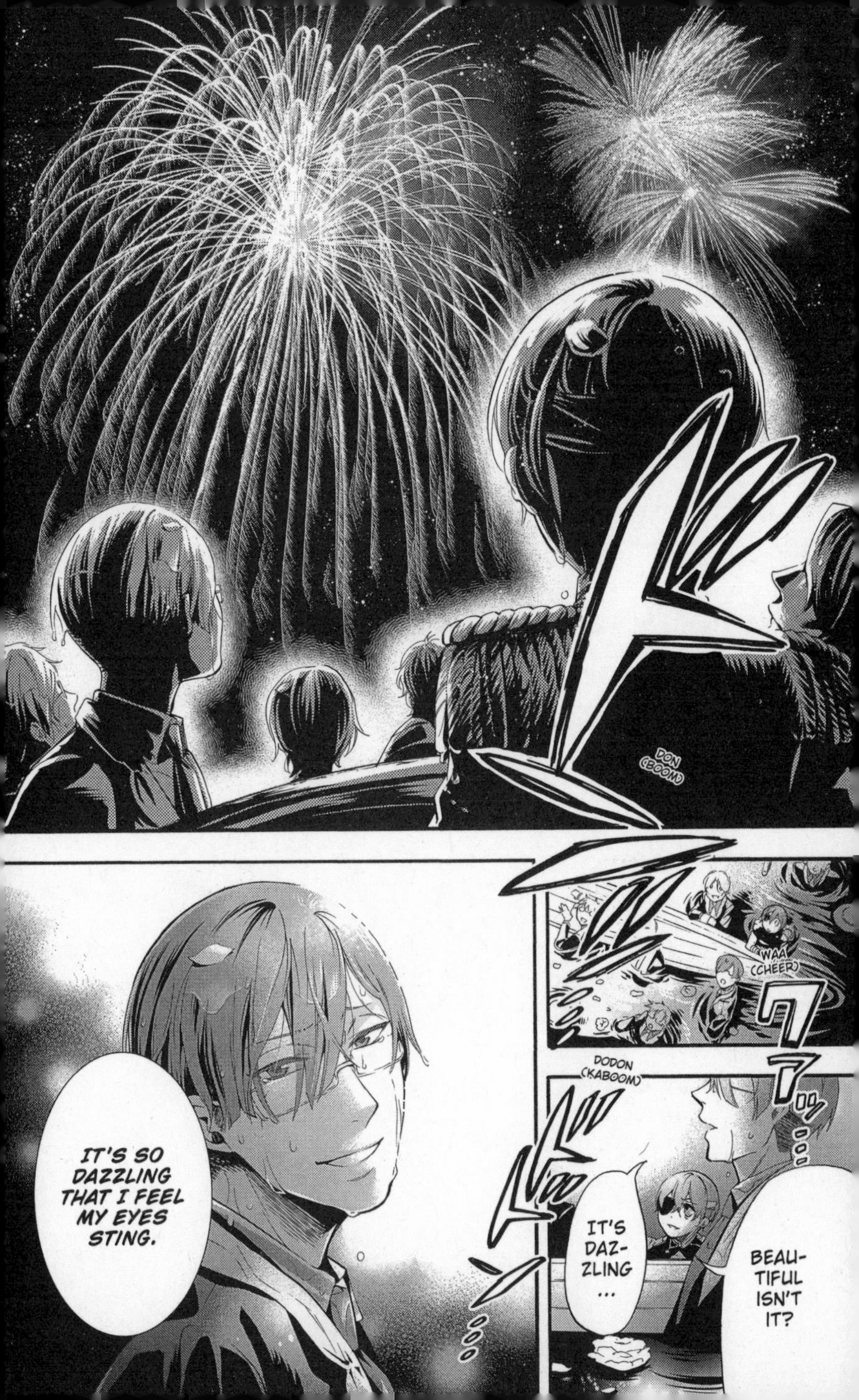
DON (BOOM)
WAA (CHEER)
DODON (KABOOM)
BEAU-TIFUL ISN'T IT?
IT'S DAZ-ZLING ...
IT'S SO DAZZLING THAT I FEEL MY EYES STING.

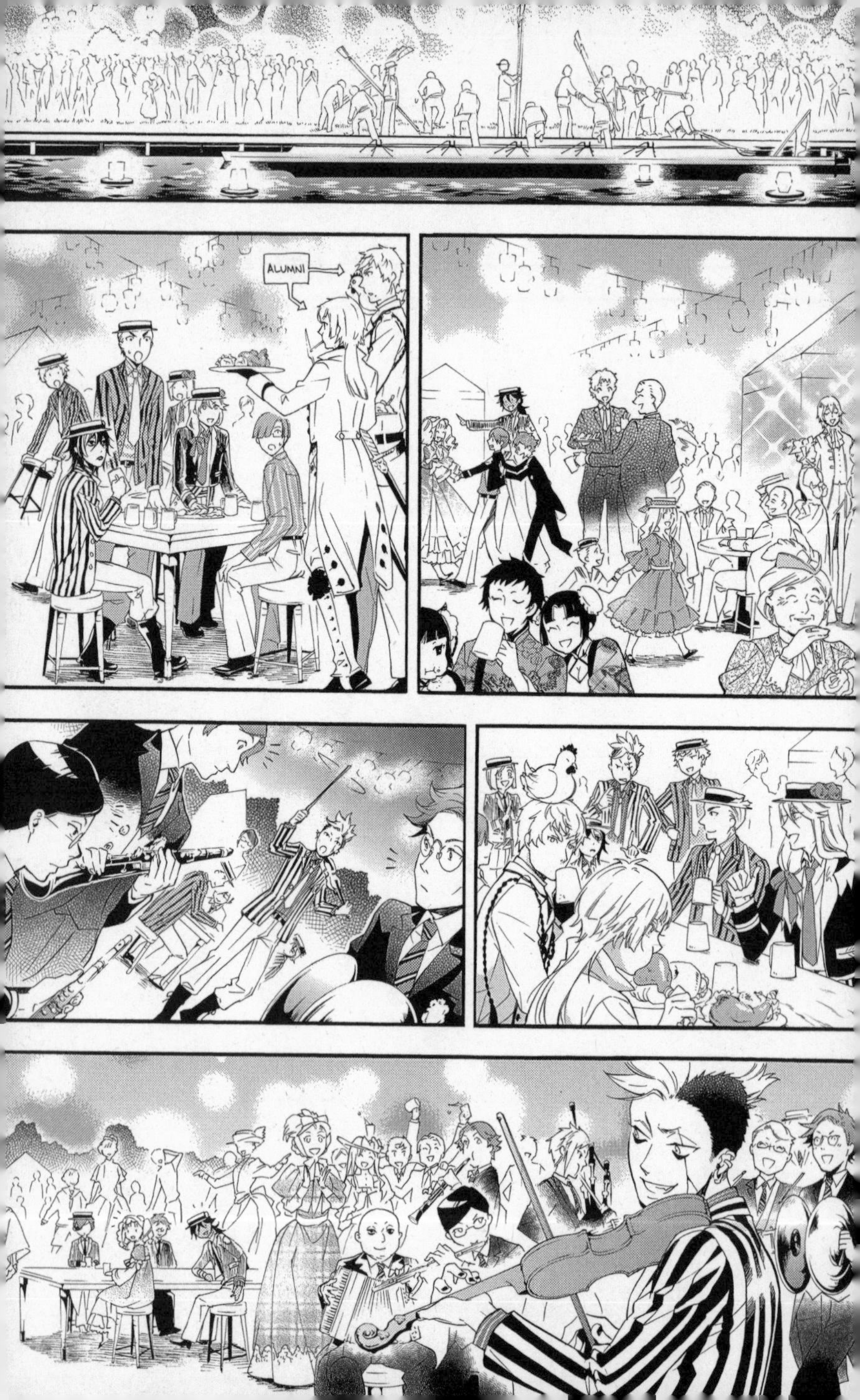
ALUMNI

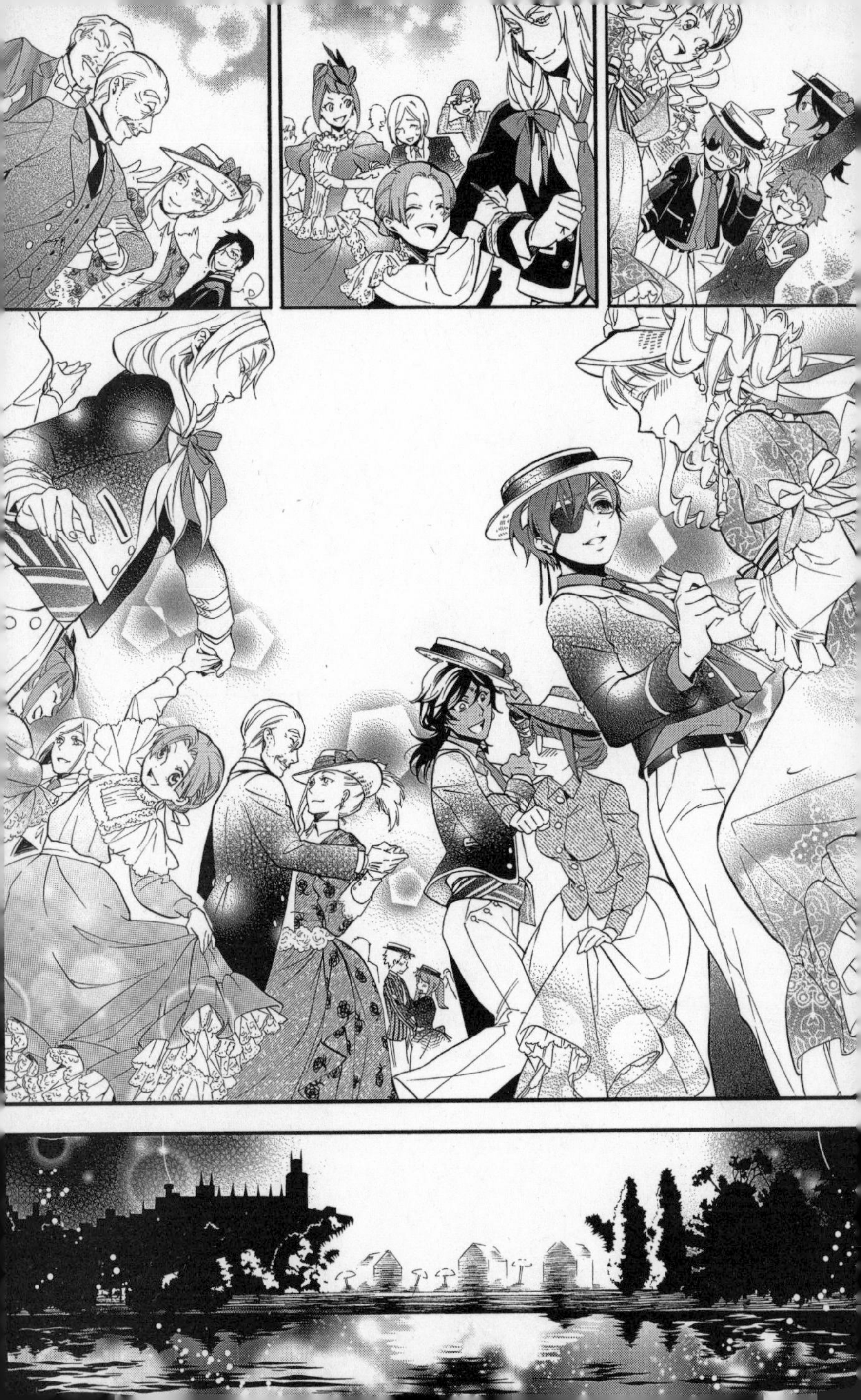

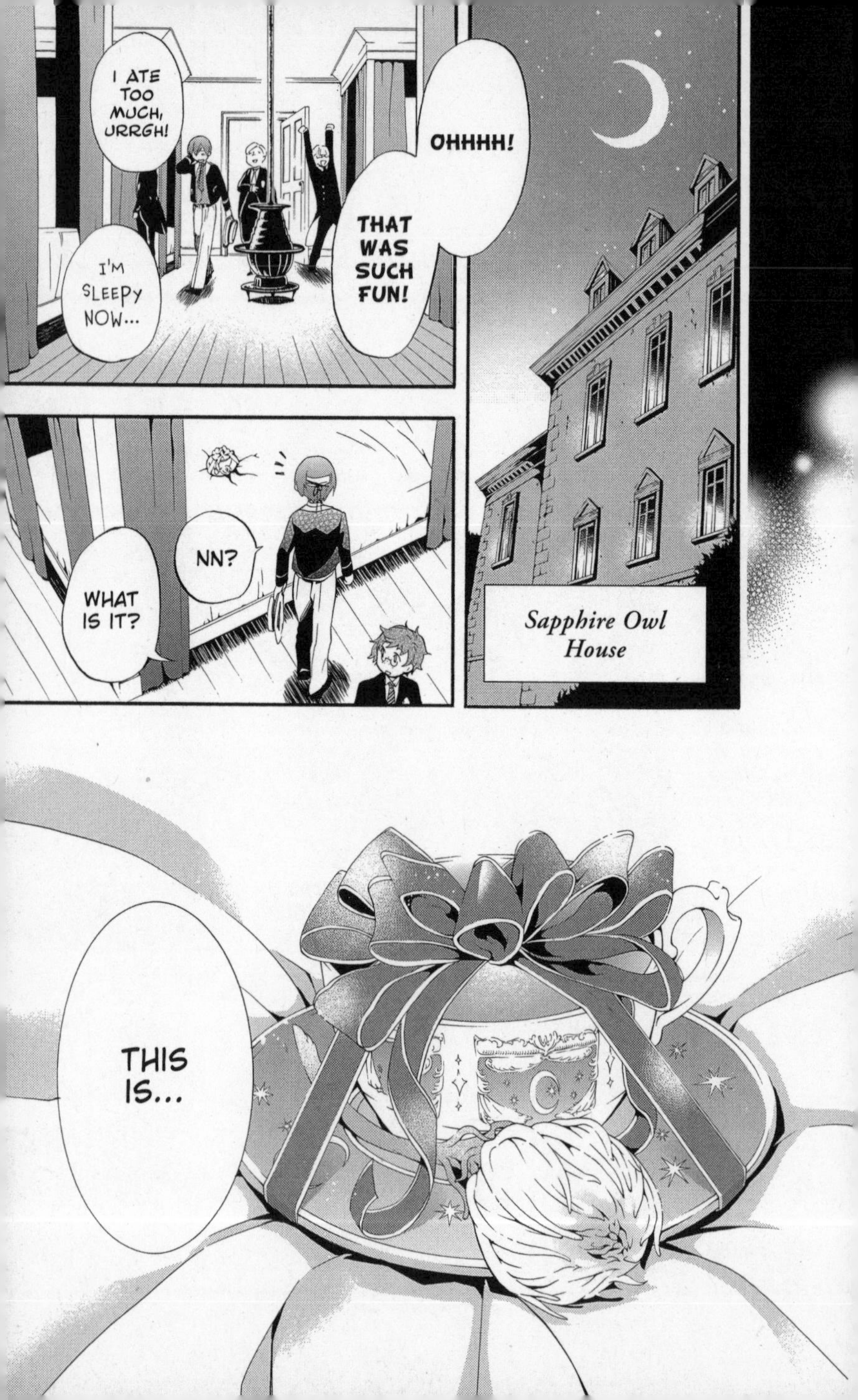
Sapphire Owl House
OHHHH!
THAT WAS SUCH FUN!
I ATE TOO MUCH, URRGH!
I'M SLEEPY NOW...
NN?
WHAT IS IT?
THIS IS...

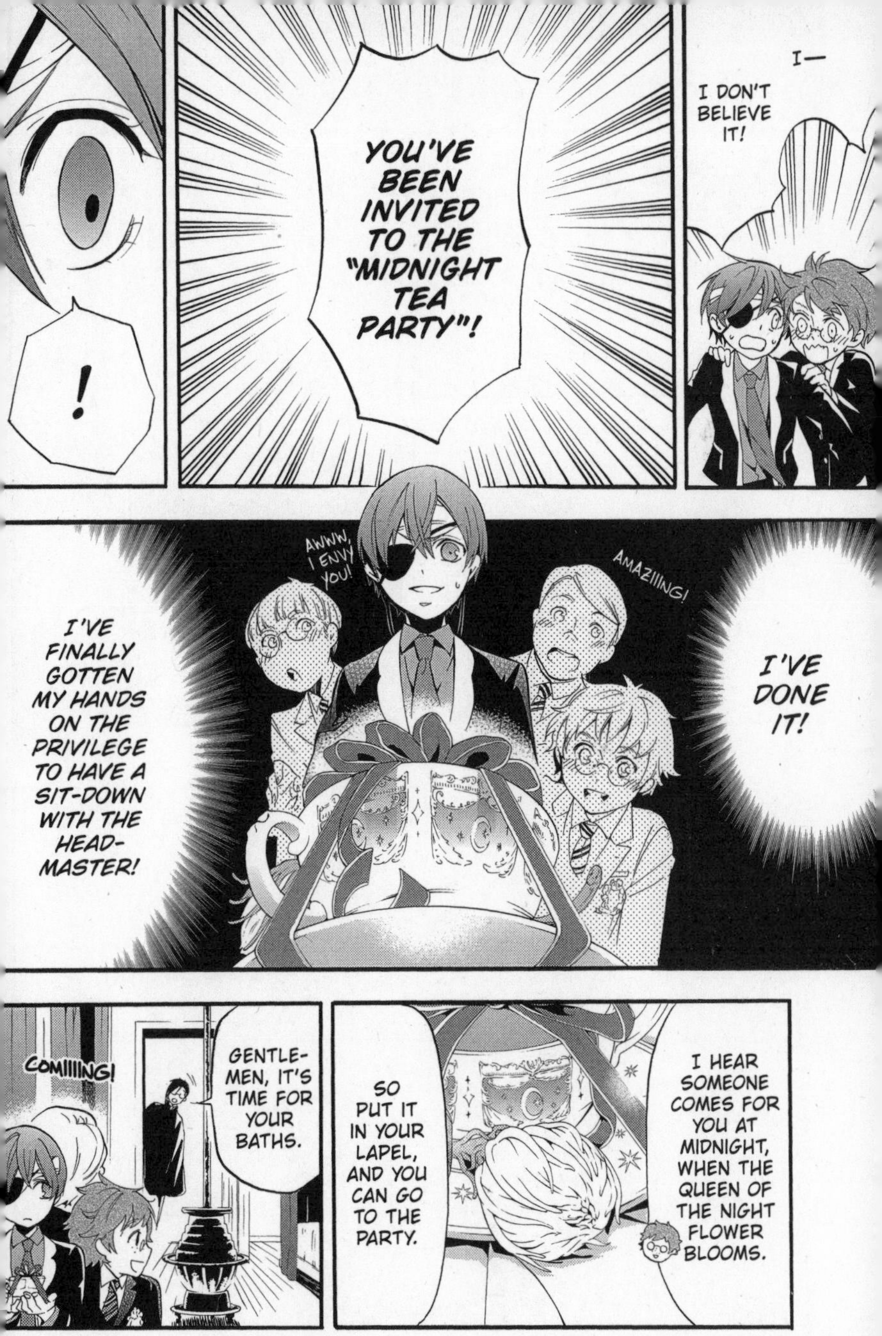
I—
I DON'T BELIEVE IT!
YOU'VE BEEN INVITED TO THE "MIDNIGHT TEA PARTY"!
!
AMAZIIING!
AWWW, I ENVY YOU!
I'VE DONE IT!
I'VE FINALLY GOTTEN MY HANDS ON THE PRIVILEGE TO HAVE A SIT-DOWN WITH THE HEAD-MASTER!
I HEAR SOMEONE COMES FOR YOU AT MIDNIGHT, WHEN THE QUEEN OF THE NIGHT FLOWER BLOOMS.
SO PUT IT IN YOUR LAPEL, AND YOU CAN GO TO THE PARTY.
GENTLE-MEN, IT'S TIME FOR YOUR BATHS.
COMIIIING!

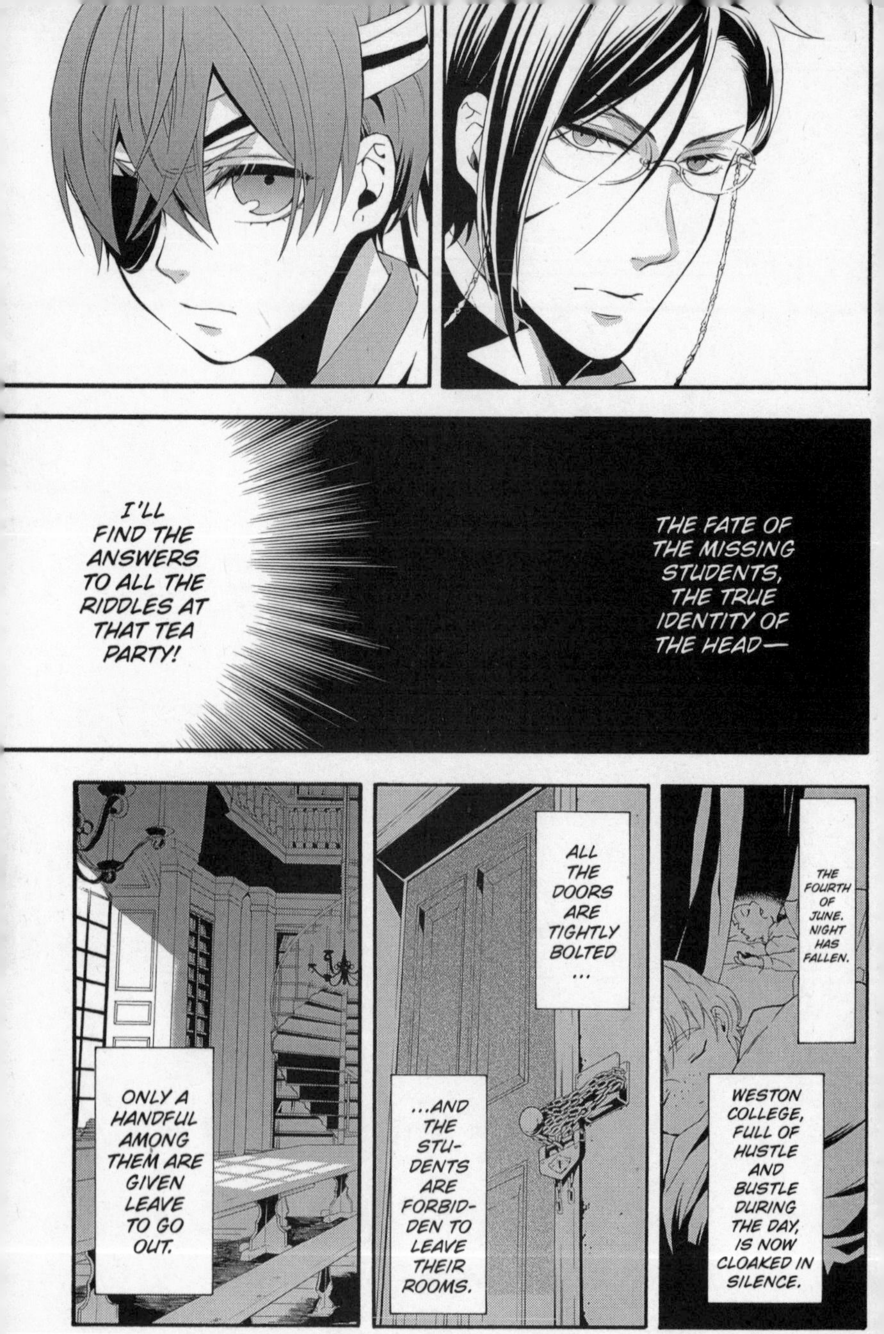
THE FATE OF THE MISSING STUDENTS, THE TRUE IDENTITY OF THE HEAD—
I'LL FIND THE ANSWERS TO ALL THE RIDDLES AT THAT TEA PARTY!
THE FOURTH OF JUNE. NIGHT HAS FALLEN.
WESTON COLLEGE, FULL OF HUSTLE AND BUSTLE DURING THE DAY, IS NOW CLOAKED IN SILENCE.
ALL THE DOORS ARE TIGHTLY BOLTED...
...AND THE STUDENTS ARE FORBIDDEN TO LEAVE THEIR ROOMS.
ONLY A HANDFUL AMONG THEM ARE GIVEN LEAVE TO GO OUT.

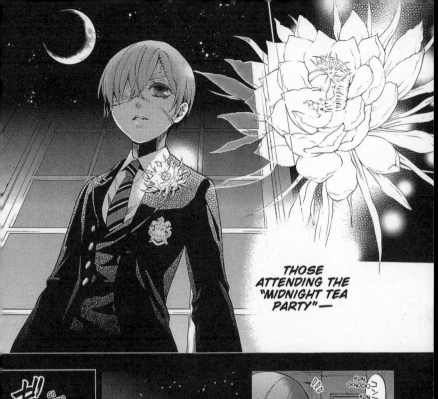

THOSE ATTENDING THE "MIDNIGHT TEA PARTY"—

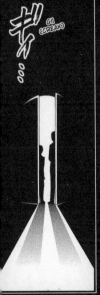

GII (CREAK)

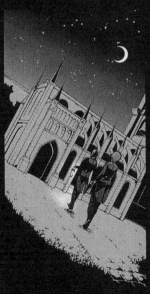

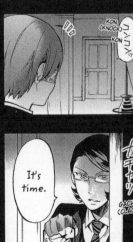

KON (KNOCK)
KON

It's time.

GACHA (CLACK)

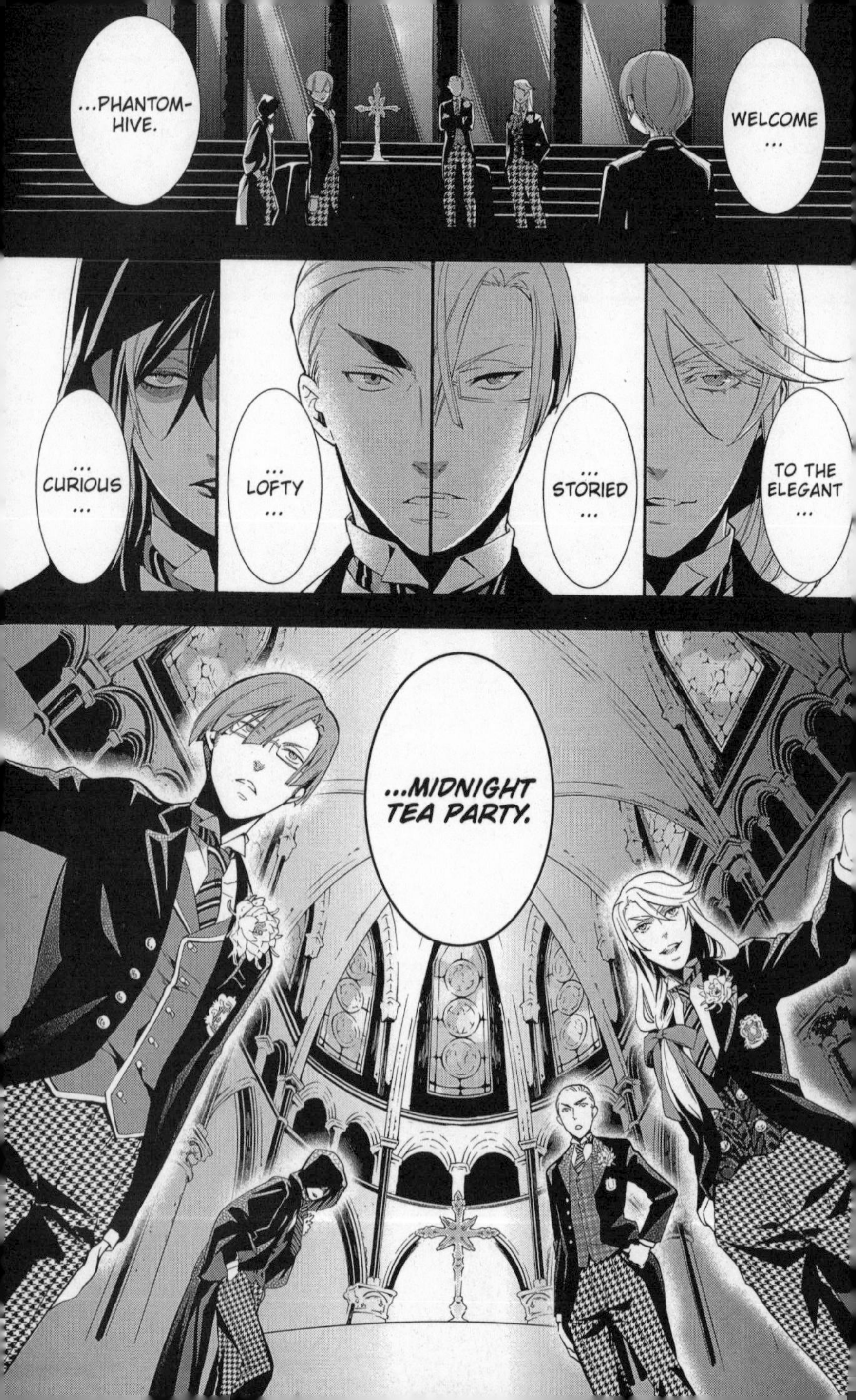
WELCOME ...
...PHANTOM-HIVE.
TO THE ELEGANT ...
... STORIED ...
... LOFTY ...
... CURIOUS ...
...MIDNIGHT TEA PARTY.

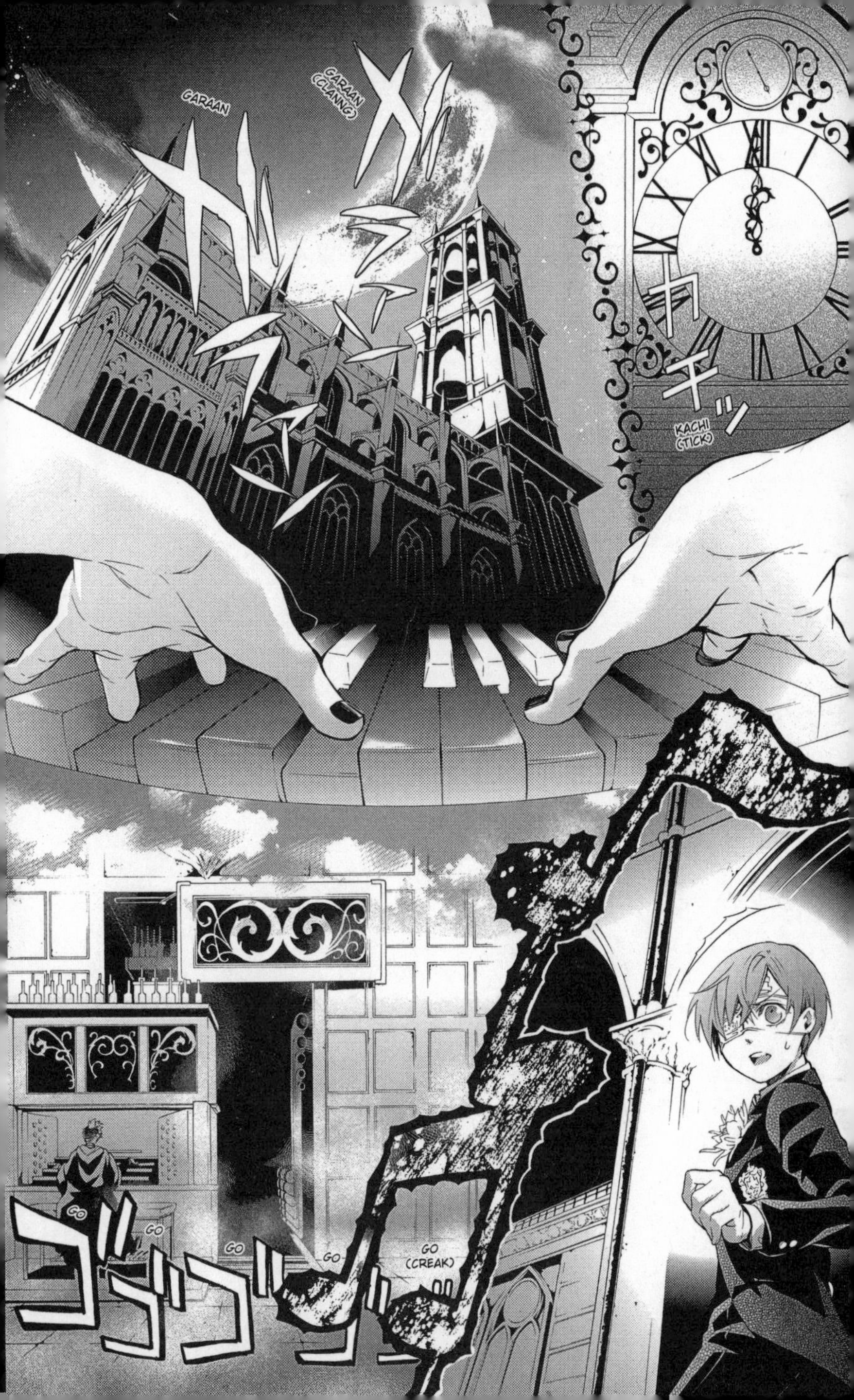
KACHI (TICK)
GARAAN (CLANNG)
GARAAN
GO GO GO GO GO (CREAK)

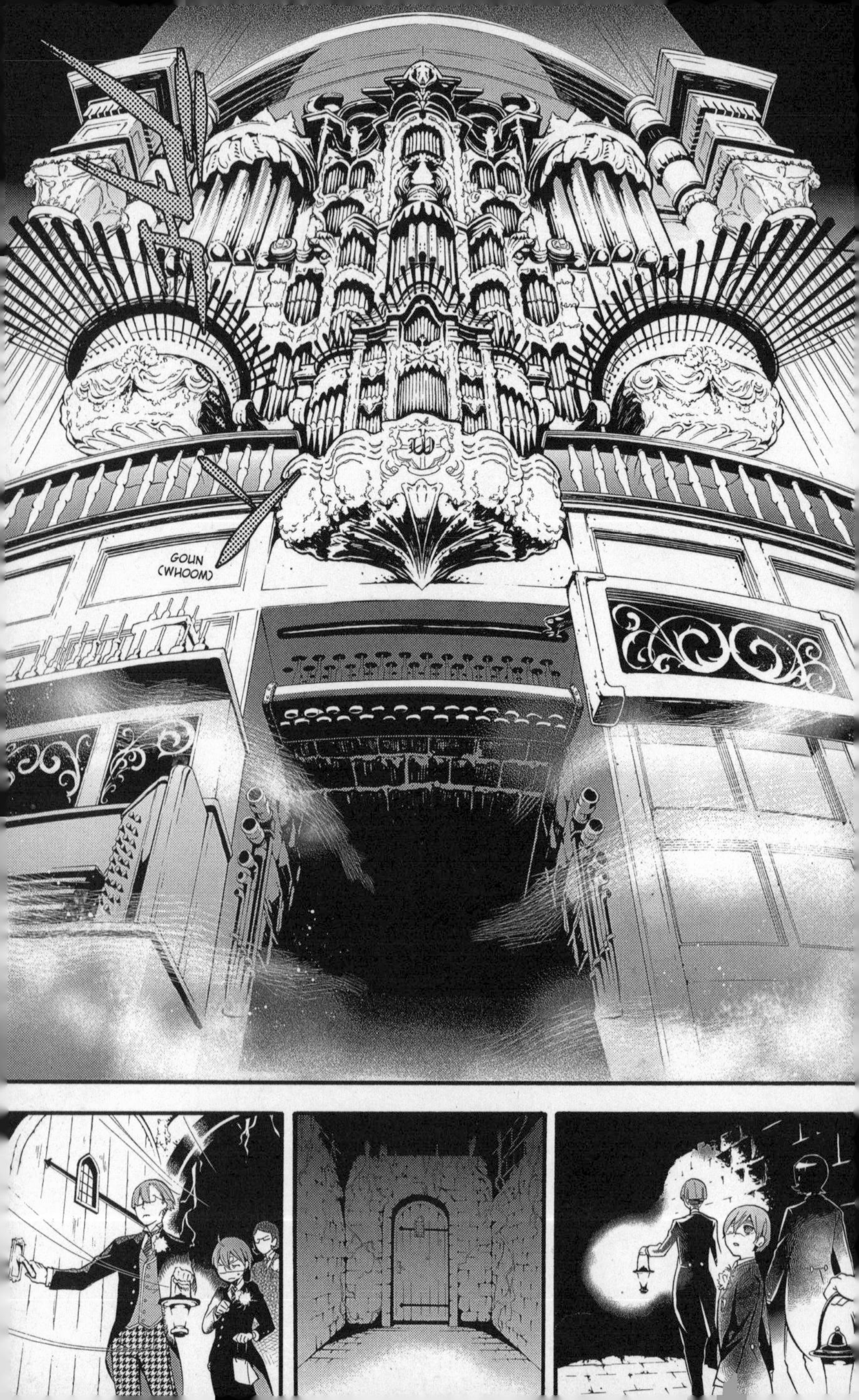
GOUN
(WHOOM)

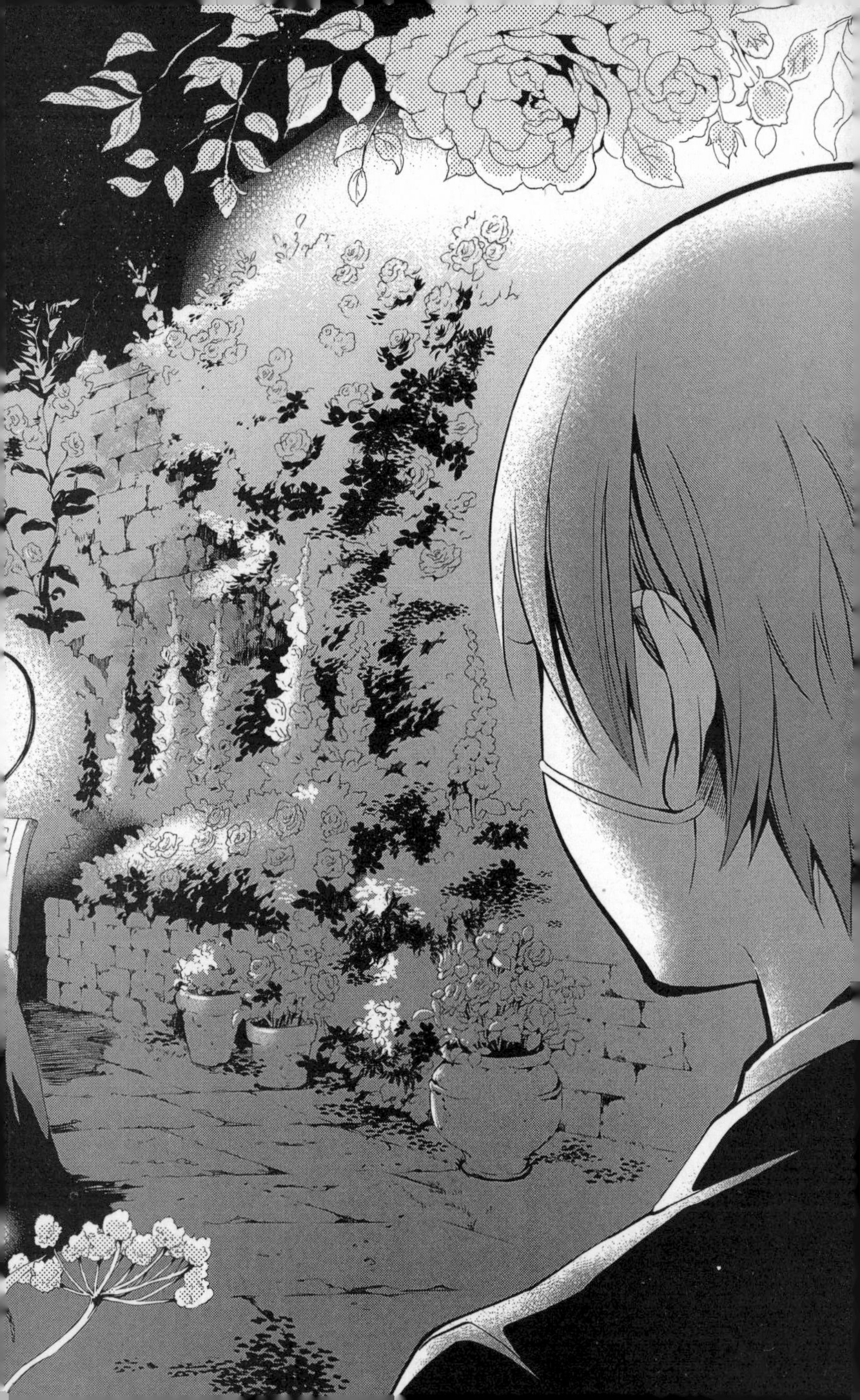

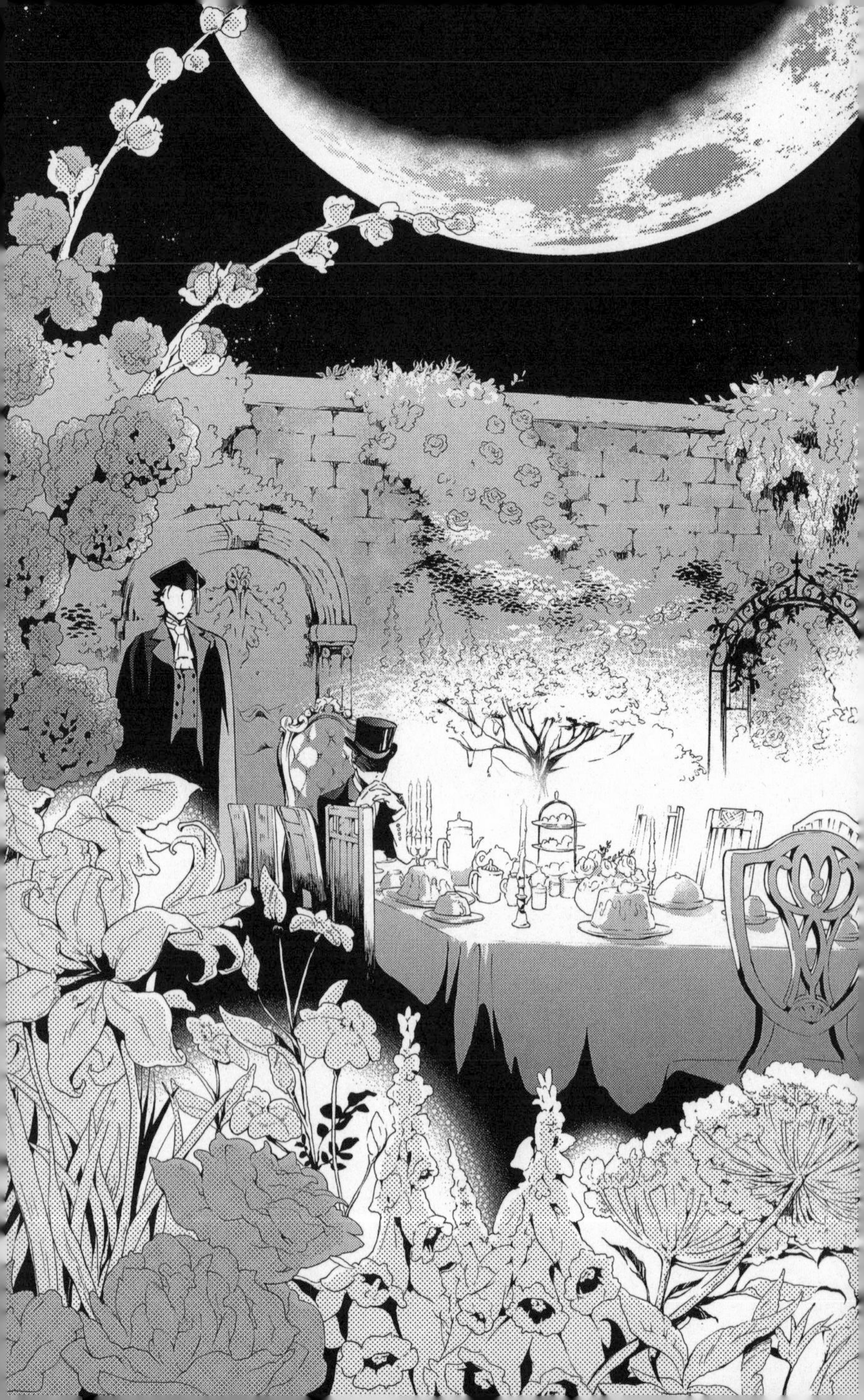

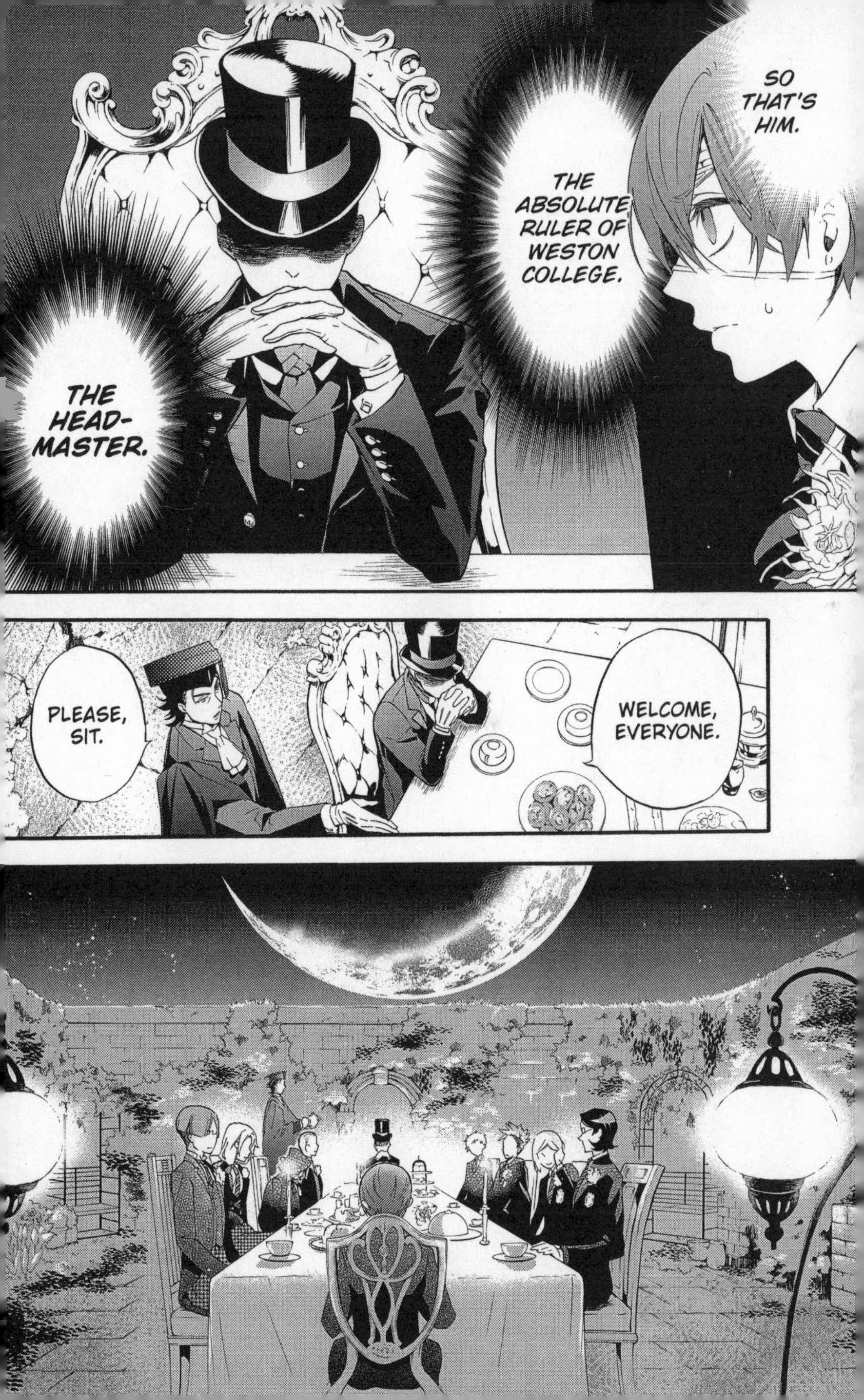
SO THAT'S HIM.
THE ABSOLUTE RULER OF WESTON COLLEGE.
THE HEAD-MASTER.
WELCOME, EVERYONE.
PLEASE, SIT.

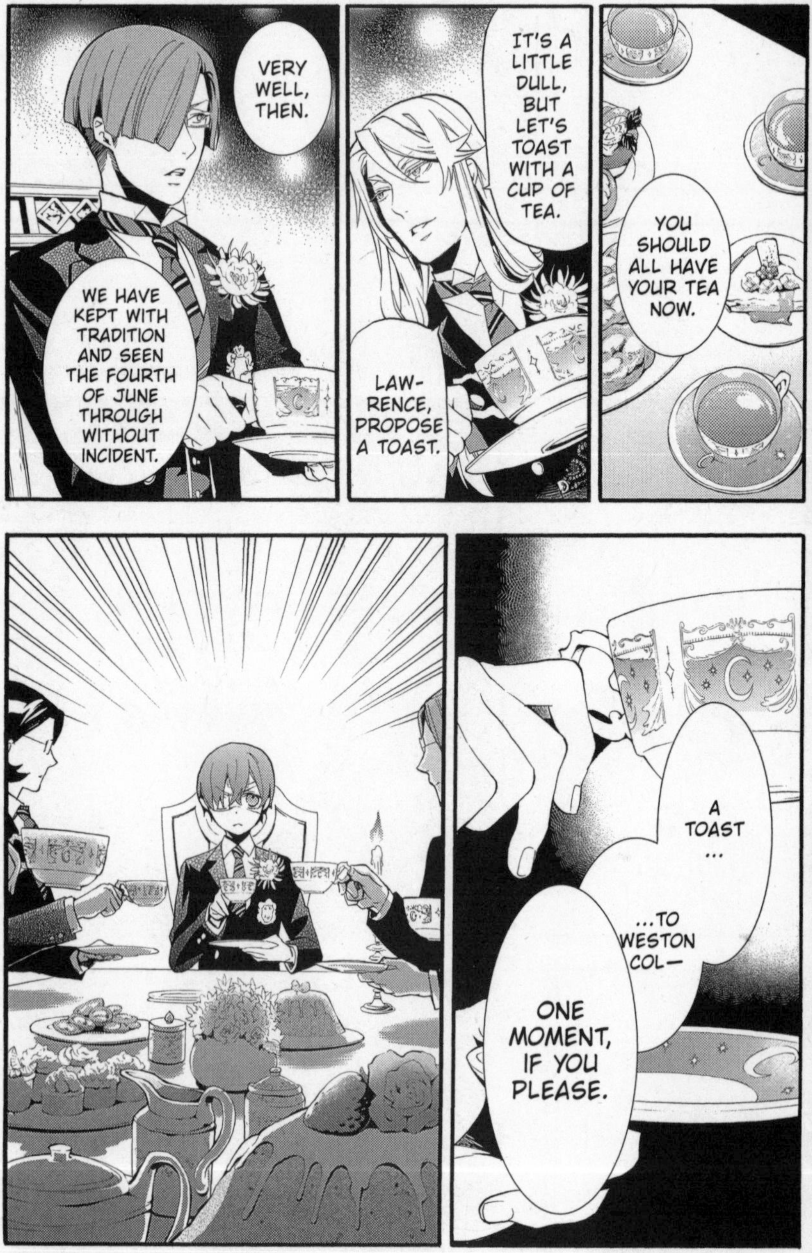
YOU SHOULD ALL HAVE YOUR TEA NOW.
IT'S A LITTLE DULL, BUT LET'S TOAST WITH A CUP OF TEA.
LAW-RENCE, PROPOSE A TOAST.
VERY WELL, THEN.
WE HAVE KEPT WITH TRADITION AND SEEN THE FOURTH OF JUNE THROUGH WITHOUT INCIDENT.
A TOAST ...
...TO WESTON COL—
ONE MOMENT, IF YOU PLEASE.

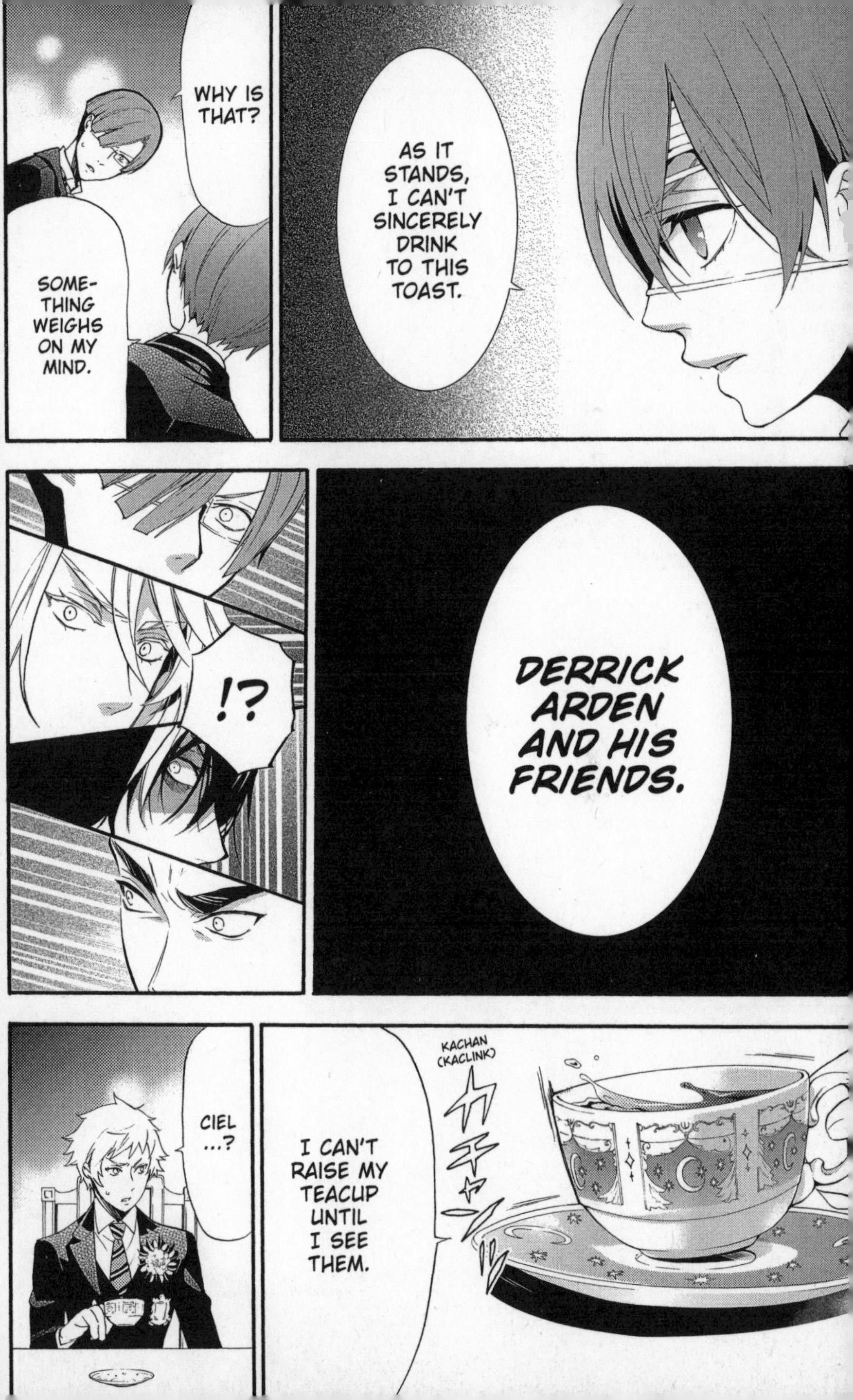
AS IT STANDS, I CAN'T SINCERELY DRINK TO THIS TOAST.
WHY IS THAT?
SOMETHING WEIGHS ON MY MIND.
DERRICK ARDEN AND HIS FRIENDS.
!?
KACHAN (KACLINK)
I CAN'T RAISE MY TEACUP UNTIL I SEE THEM.
CIEL ...?

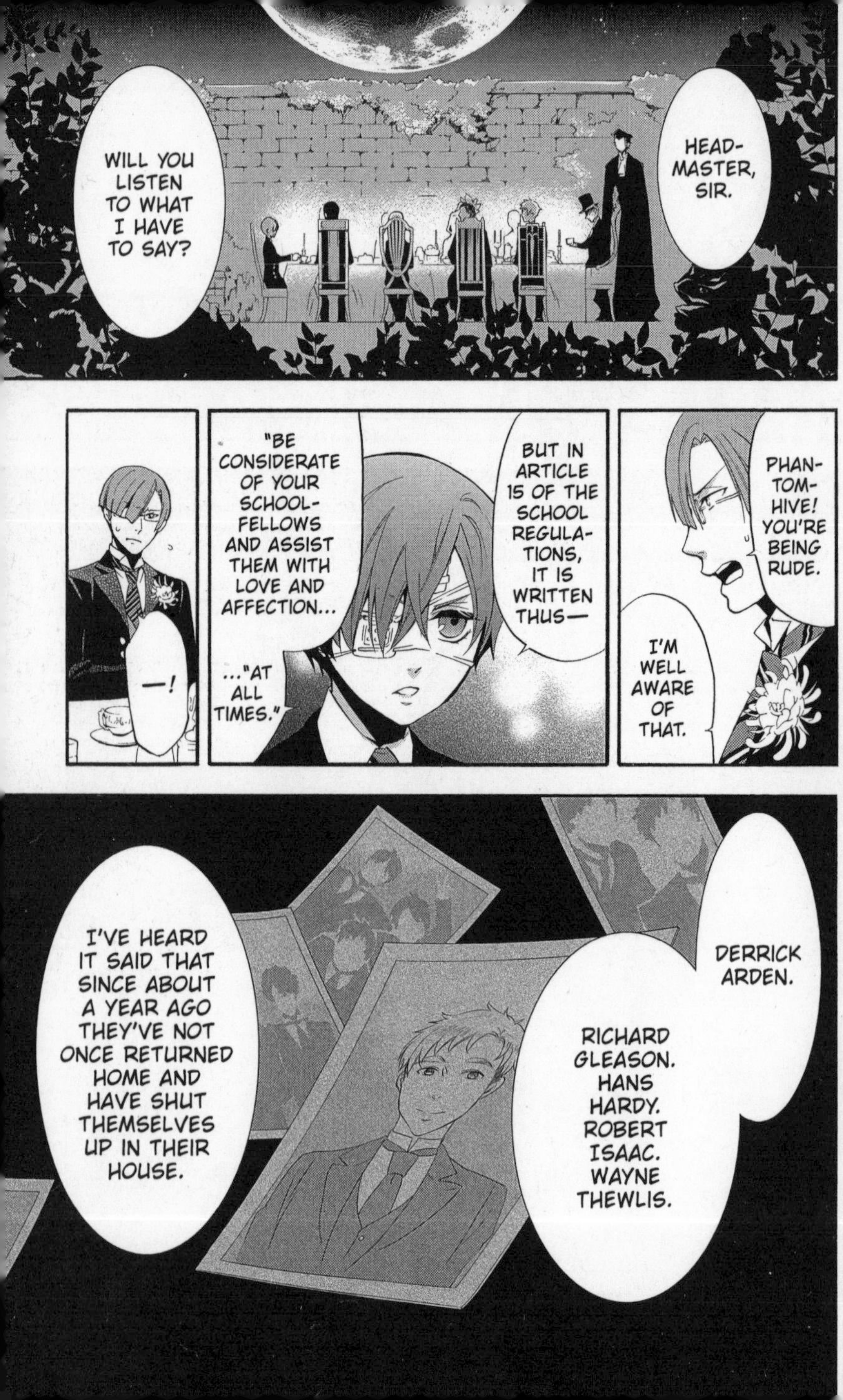
HEADMASTER, SIR.
WILL YOU LISTEN TO WHAT I HAVE TO SAY?
PHANTOMHIVE! YOU'RE BEING RUDE.
I'M WELL AWARE OF THAT.
BUT IN ARTICLE 15 OF THE SCHOOL REGULATIONS, IT IS WRITTEN THUS—
"BE CONSIDERATE OF YOUR SCHOOLFELLOWS AND ASSIST THEM WITH LOVE AND AFFECTION...
..."AT ALL TIMES."
—!
DERRICK ARDEN.
RICHARD GLEASON. HANS HARDY. ROBERT ISAAC. WAYNE THEWLIS.
I'VE HEARD IT SAID THAT SINCE ABOUT A YEAR AGO THEY'VE NOT ONCE RETURNED HOME AND HAVE SHUT THEMSELVES UP IN THEIR HOUSE.

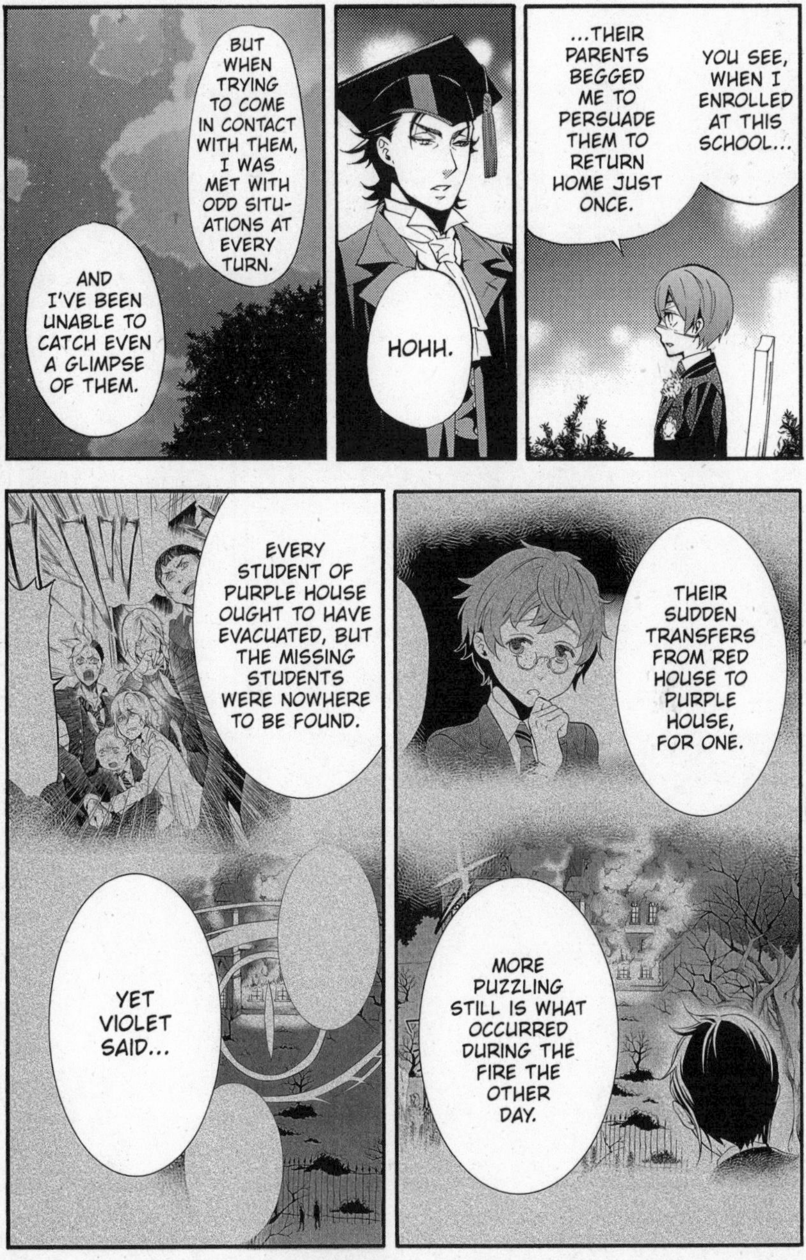
YOU SEE, WHEN I ENROLLED AT THIS SCHOOL...
...THEIR PARENTS BEGGED ME TO PERSUADE THEM TO RETURN HOME JUST ONCE.
HOHH.
BUT WHEN TRYING TO COME IN CONTACT WITH THEM, I WAS MET WITH ODD SITUATIONS AT EVERY TURN.
AND I'VE BEEN UNABLE TO CATCH EVEN A GLIMPSE OF THEM.
THEIR SUDDEN TRANSFERS FROM RED HOUSE TO PURPLE HOUSE, FOR ONE.
MORE PUZZLING STILL IS WHAT OCCURRED DURING THE FIRE THE OTHER DAY.
EVERY STUDENT OF PURPLE HOUSE OUGHT TO HAVE EVACUATED, BUT THE MISSING STUDENTS WERE NOWHERE TO BE FOUND.
YET VIOLET SAID...

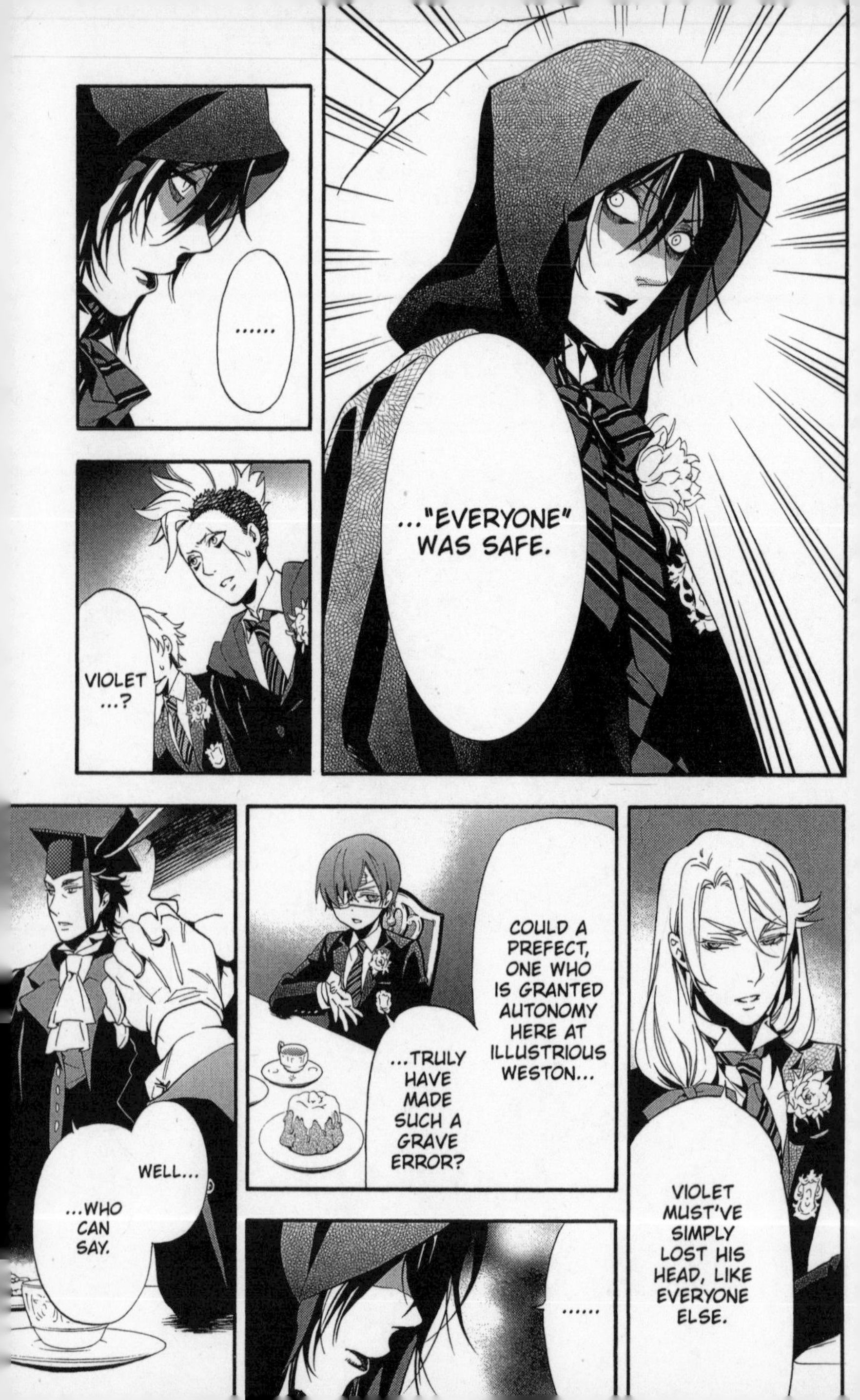
..."EVERYONE" WAS SAFE.
......
VIOLET ...?
VIOLET MUST'VE SIMPLY LOST HIS HEAD, LIKE EVERYONE ELSE.
COULD A PREFECT, ONE WHO IS GRANTED AUTONOMY HERE AT ILLUSTRIOUS WESTON...
...TRULY HAVE MADE SUCH A GRAVE ERROR?
......
WELL...
...WHO CAN SAY.

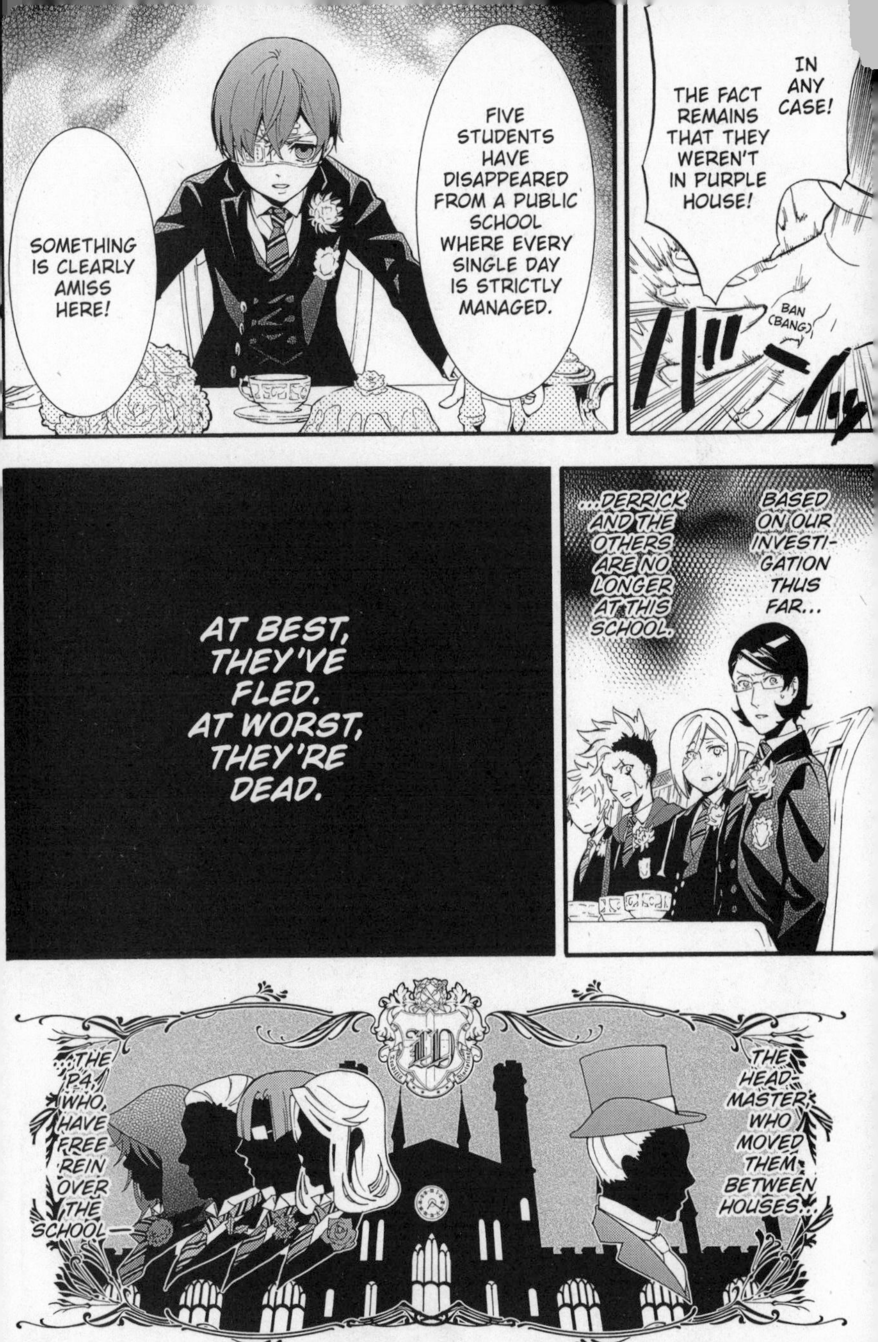
IN ANY CASE!
THE FACT REMAINS THAT THEY WEREN'T IN PURPLE HOUSE!
BAN (BANG)
FIVE STUDENTS HAVE DISAPPEARED FROM A PUBLIC SCHOOL WHERE EVERY SINGLE DAY IS STRICTLY MANAGED.
SOMETHING IS CLEARLY AMISS HERE!
BASED ON OUR INVESTI-GATION THUS FAR...
...DERRICK AND THE OTHERS ARE NO LONGER AT THIS SCHOOL.
AT BEST, THEY'VE FLED. AT WORST, THEY'RE DEAD.
THE HEAD-MASTER, WHO MOVED THEM BETWEEN HOUSES...
...THE P4, WHO HAVE FREE REIN OVER THE SCHOOL—

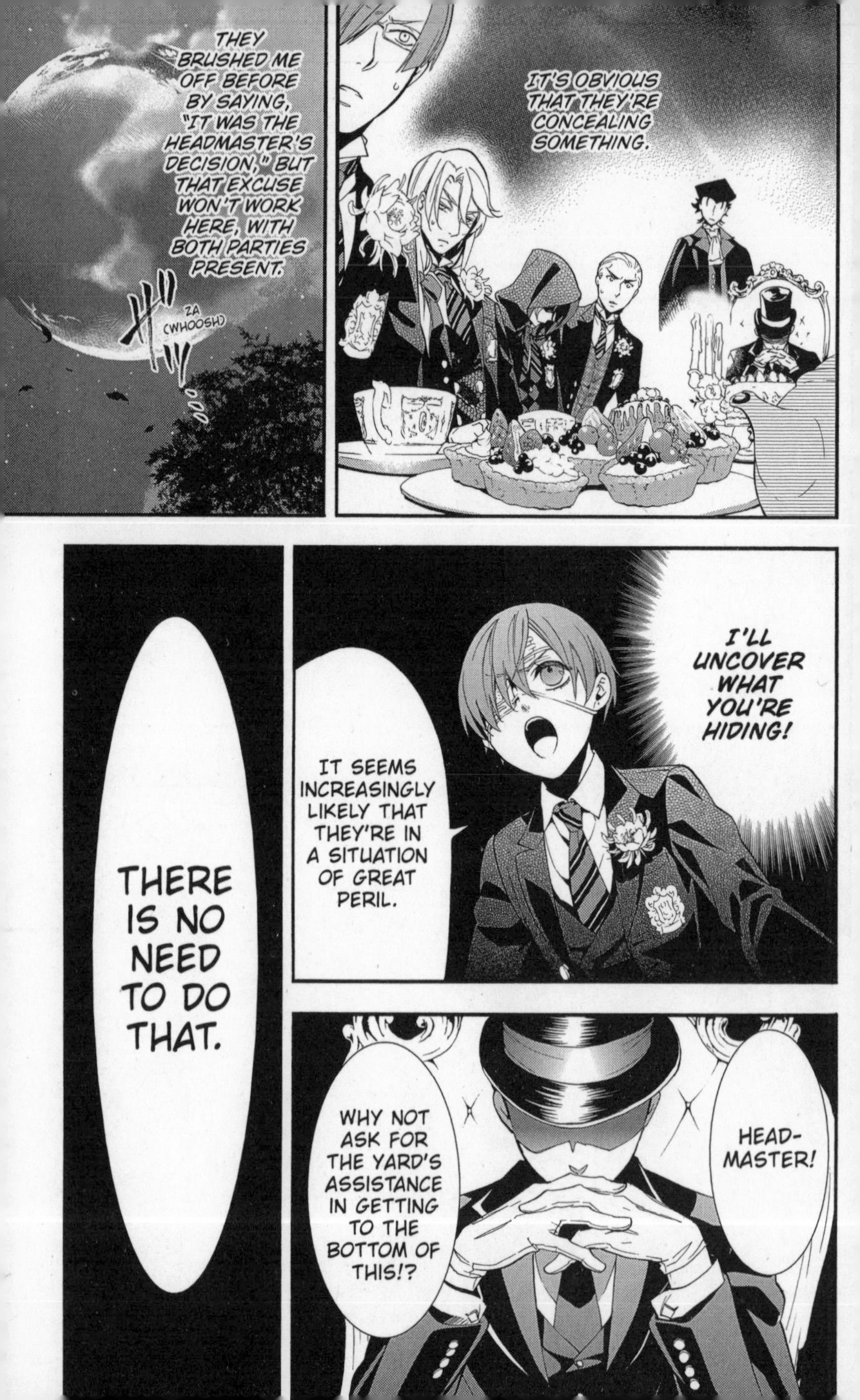
IT'S OBVIOUS THAT THEY'RE CONCEALING SOMETHING.
THEY BRUSHED ME OFF BEFORE BY SAYING, "IT WAS THE HEADMASTER'S DECISION," BUT THAT EXCUSE WON'T WORK HERE, WITH BOTH PARTIES PRESENT.
ZA (WHOOSH)
I'LL UNCOVER WHAT YOU'RE HIDING!
IT SEEMS INCREASINGLY LIKELY THAT THEY'RE IN A SITUATION OF GREAT PERIL.
HEAD-MASTER!
WHY NOT ASK FOR THE YARD'S ASSISTANCE IN GETTING TO THE BOTTOM OF THIS!?
THERE IS NO NEED TO DO THAT.

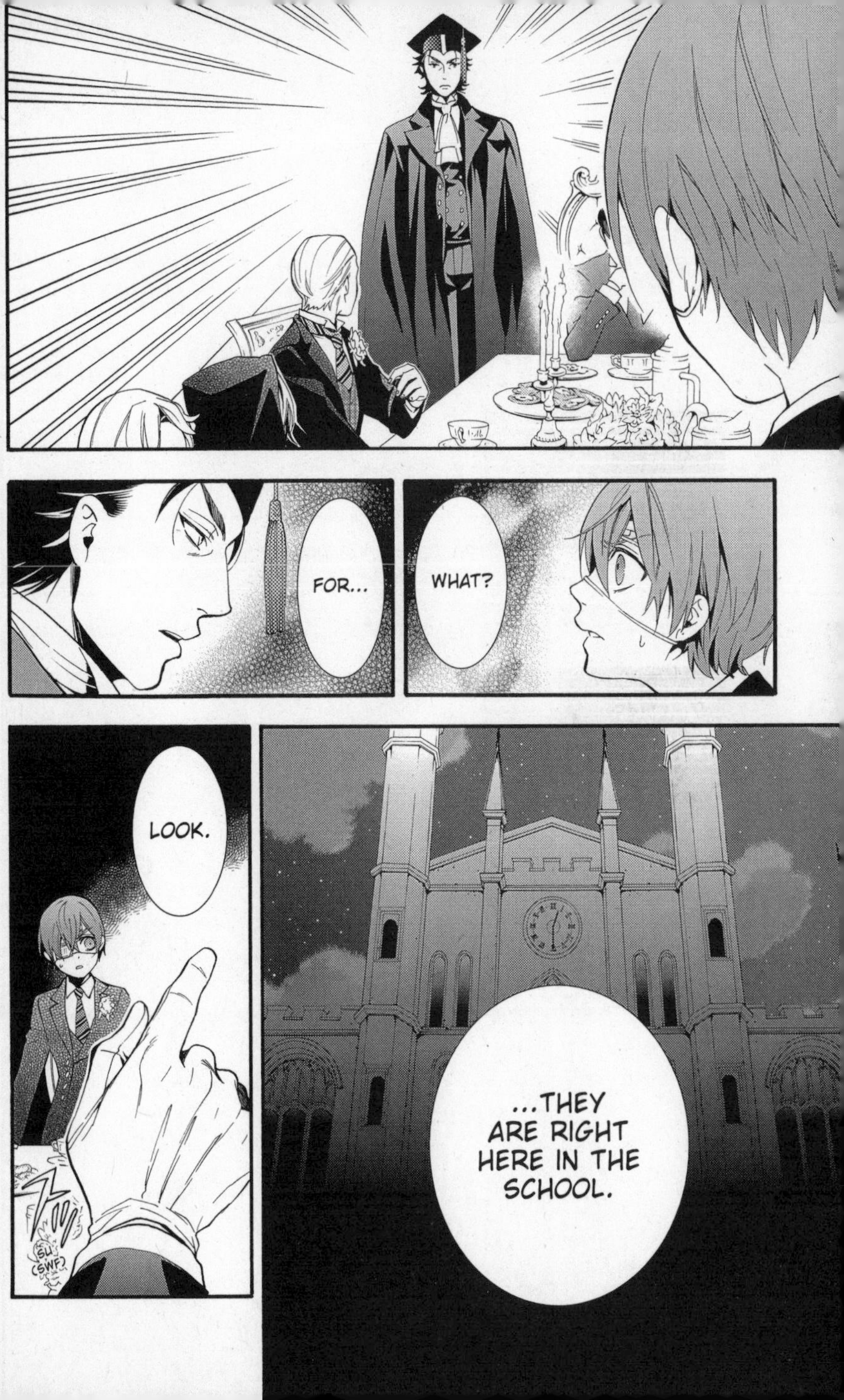
WHAT?
FOR...
...THEY ARE RIGHT HERE IN THE SCHOOL.
LOOK.
SU
(SWF)

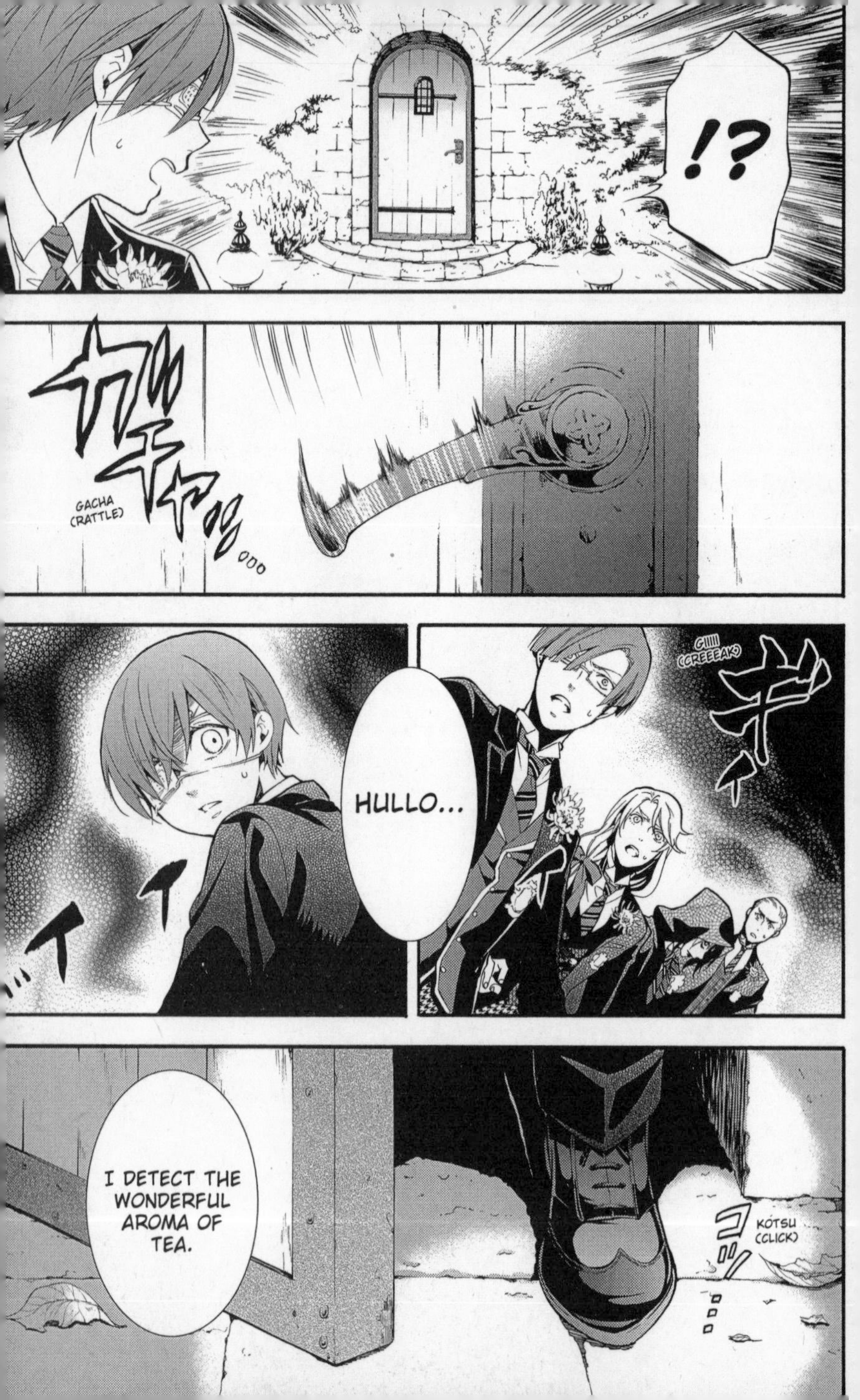
!?
GACHA (RATTLE)
GIIIII (CREEEAK)
HULLO...
I DETECT THE WONDERFUL AROMA OF TEA.
KOTSU (CLICK)

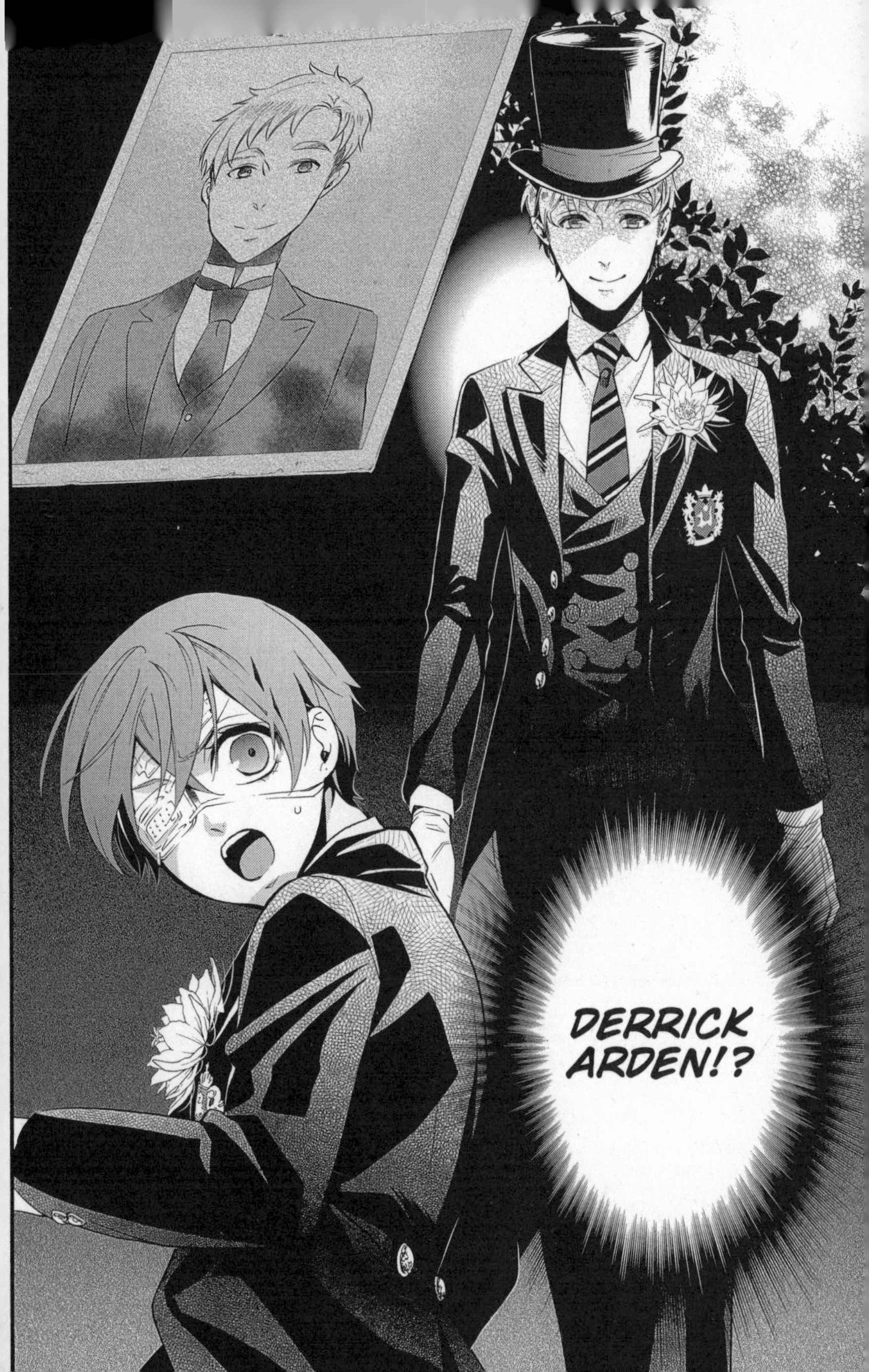
DERRICK ARDEN!?

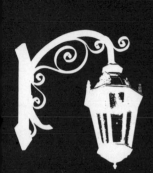

Black Butler

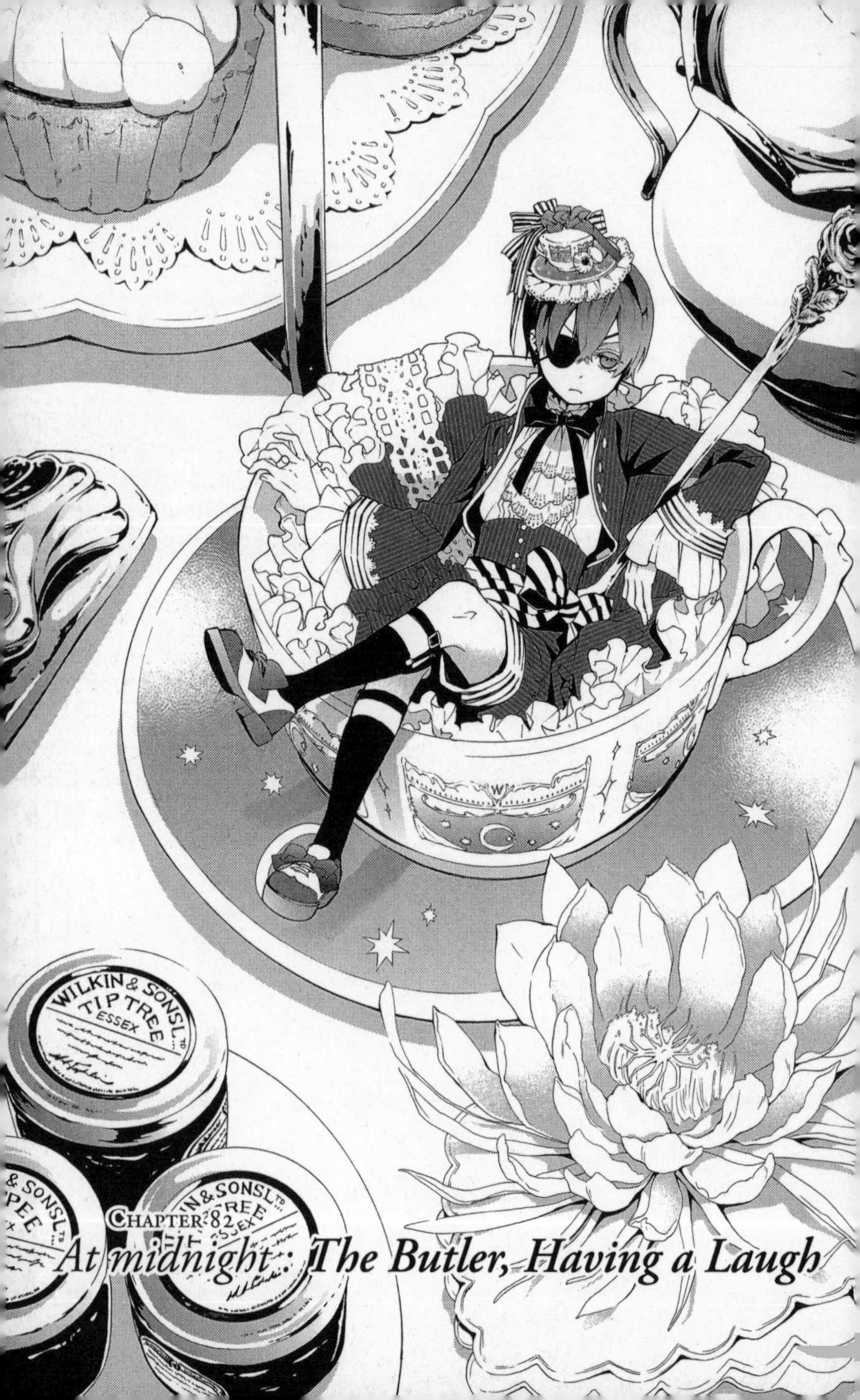
WILKIN & SONS LTD
TIP TREE
ESSEX

Chapter 82

At midnight: The Butler, Having a Laugh

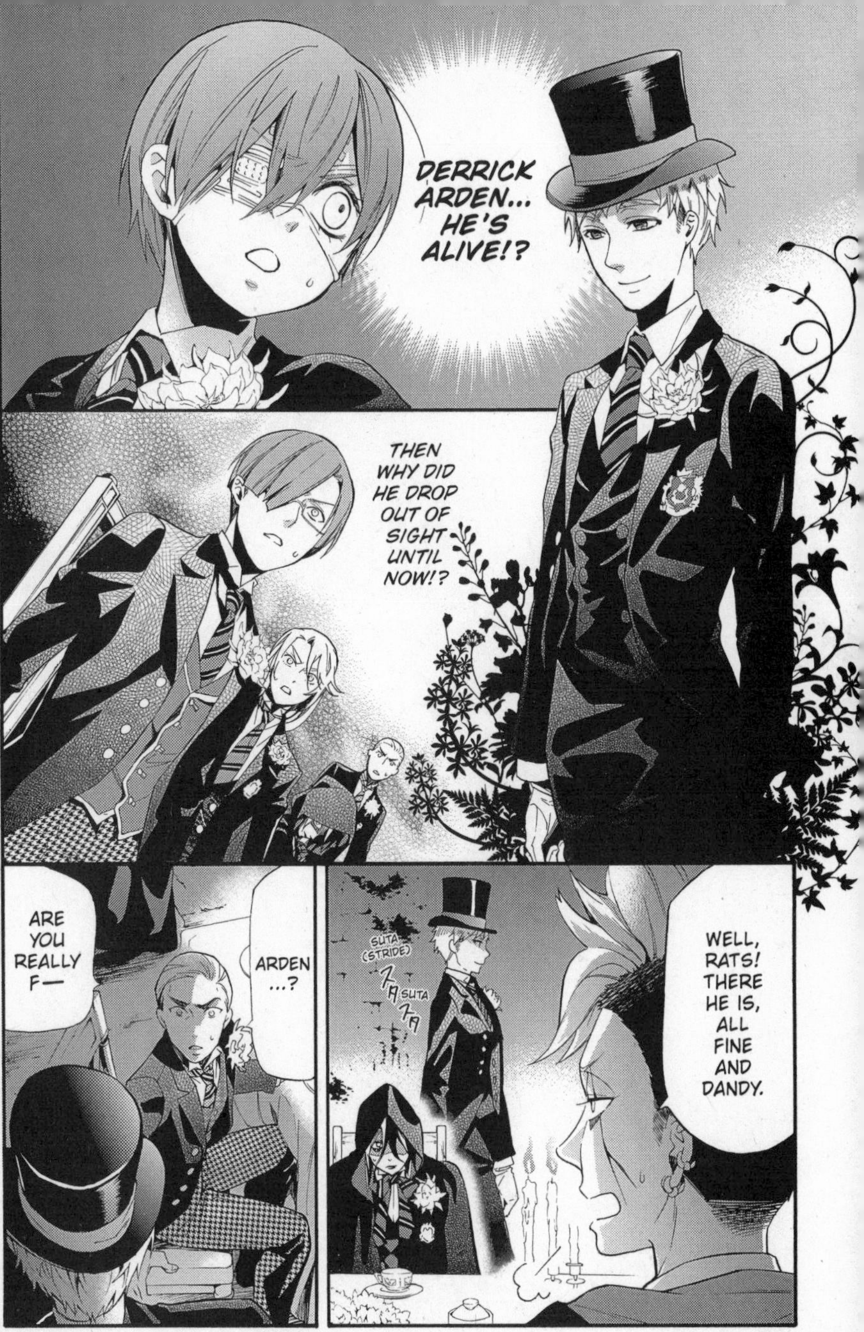
DERRICK ARDEN... HE'S ALIVE!?
THEN WHY DID HE DROP OUT OF SIGHT UNTIL NOW!?
SUTA (STRIDE)
SUTA
WELL, RATS! THERE HE IS, ALL FINE AND DANDY.
ARDEN ...?
ARE YOU REALLY F—

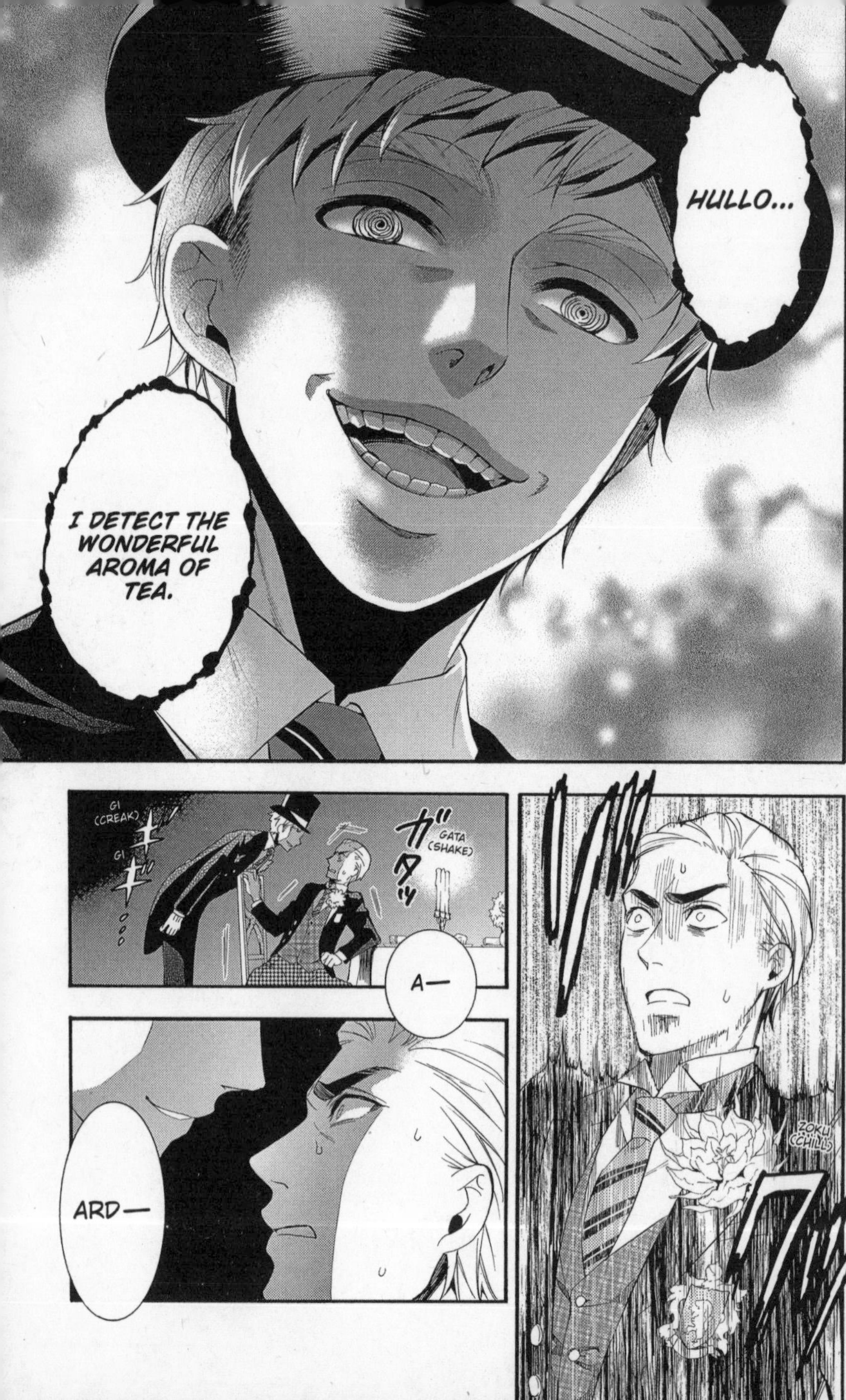
HULLO...
I DETECT THE WONDERFUL AROMA OF TEA.
ZOKU (CHILL)
GATA (SHAKE)
GI (CREAK) GI
A—
ARD—

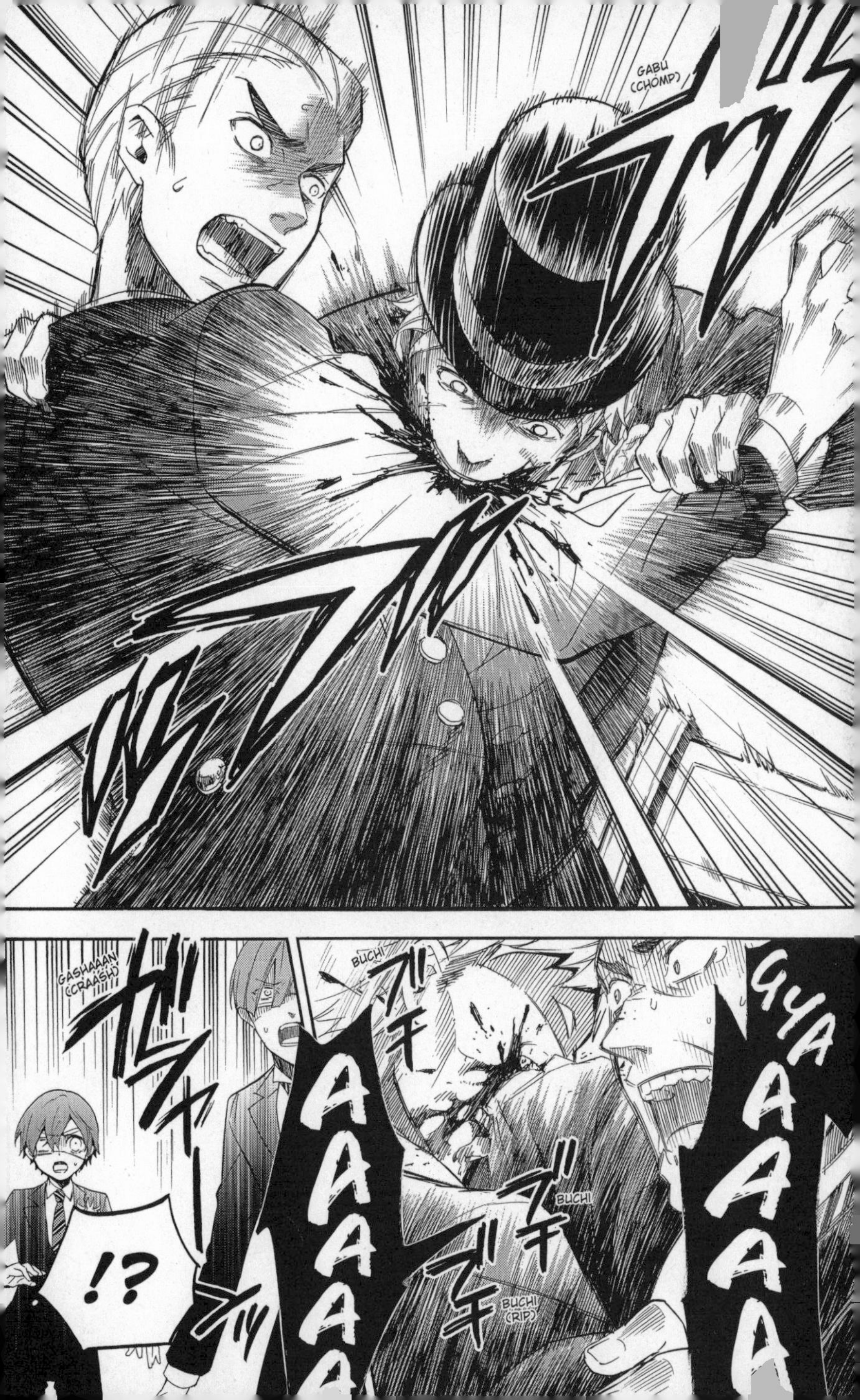
GABU (CHOMP)
GYAAAAAAA
BUCHI
BUCHI
BUCHI (RIP)
AAAAAAA
GASHAAAN (CRAASH)
!?

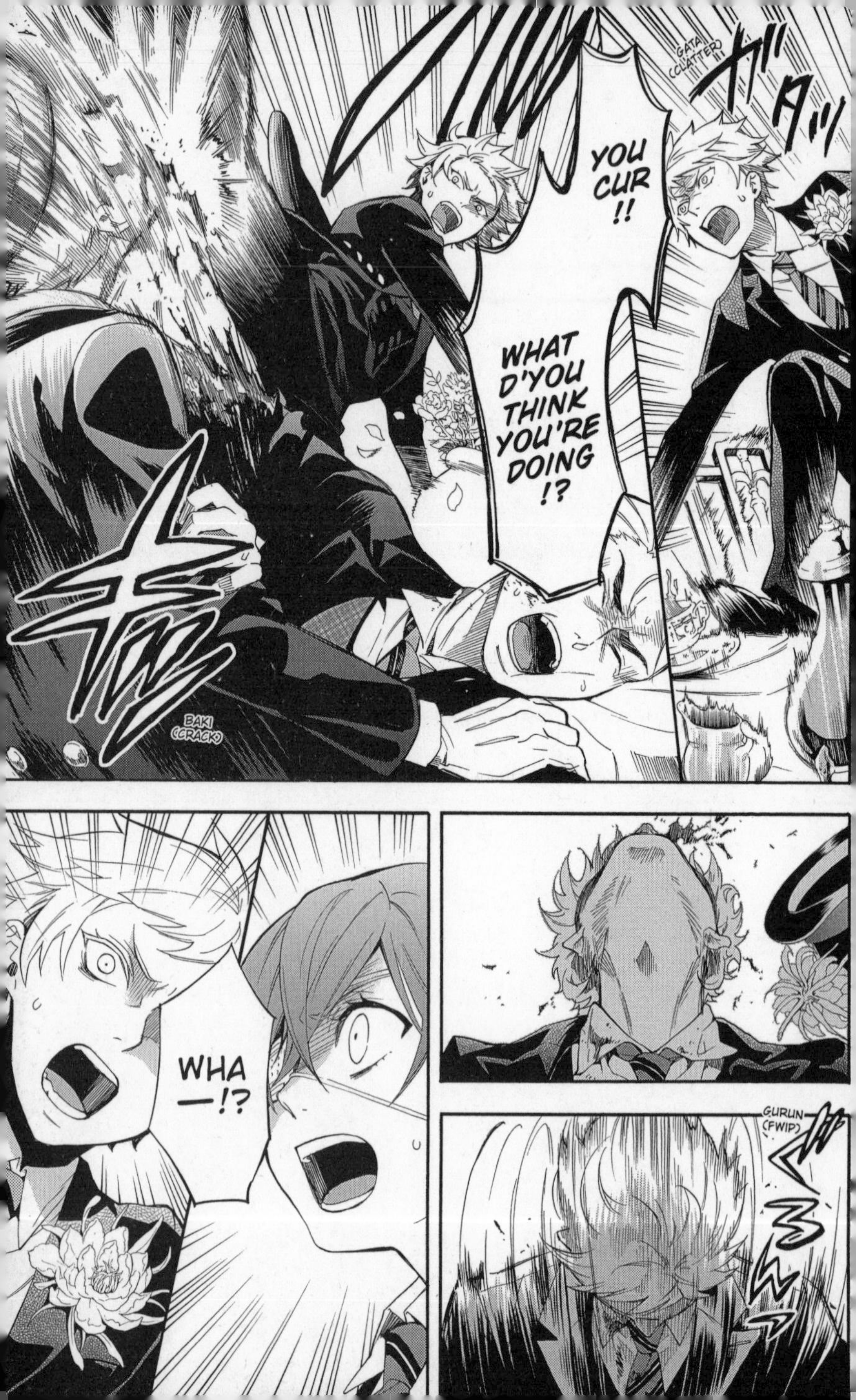

GATA (CLATTER)
YOU CUR !!
WHAT D'YOU THINK YOU'RE DOING !?
BAKI (CRACK)
WHA —!?
GURUN (FWIP)

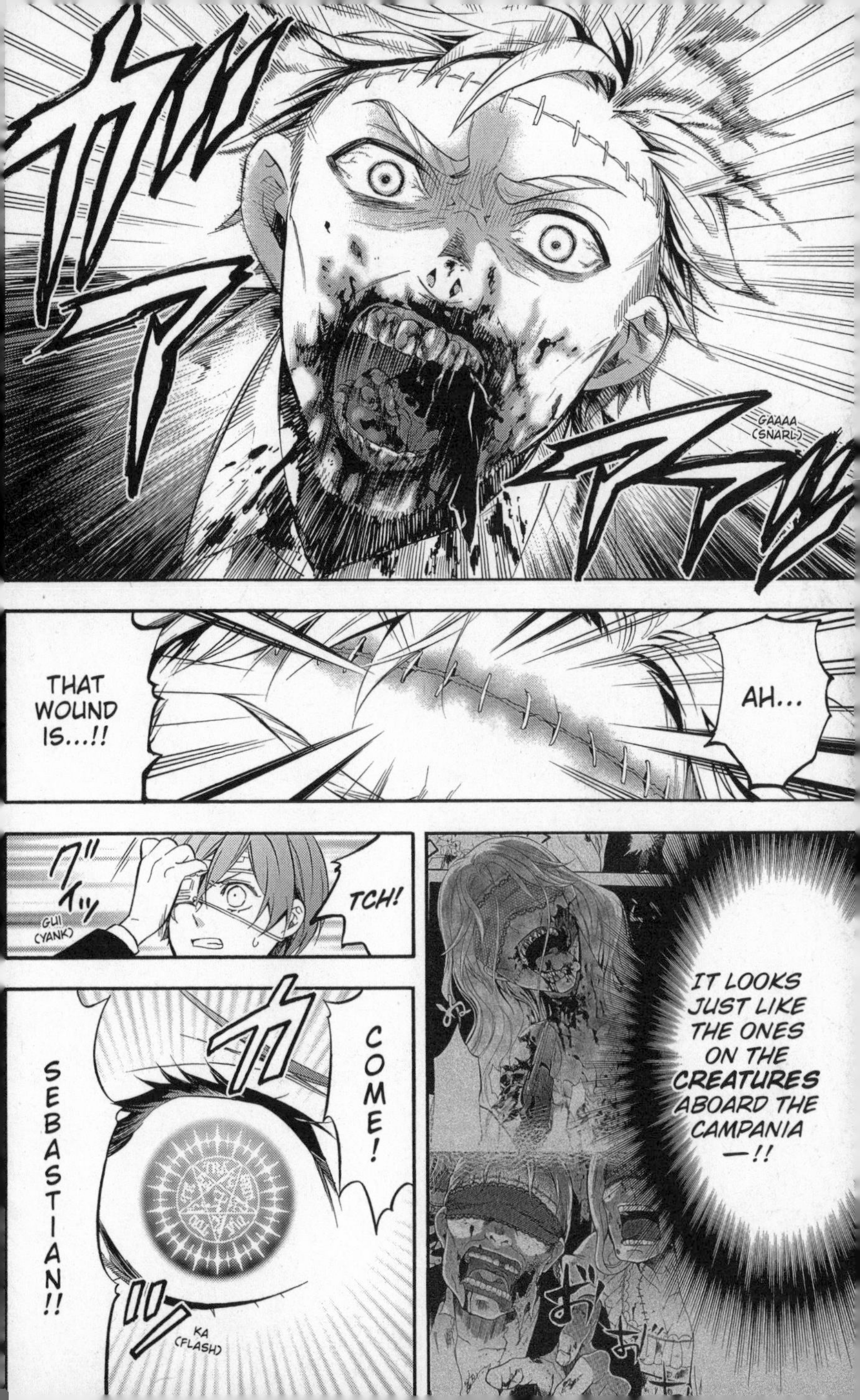
GAAAA (SNARL)
AH...
THAT WOUND IS...!!
IT LOOKS JUST LIKE THE ONES ON THE CREATURES ABOARD THE CAMPANIA—!!
GUI (YANK)
TCH!
COME!
SEBASTIAN!!
KA (FLASH)

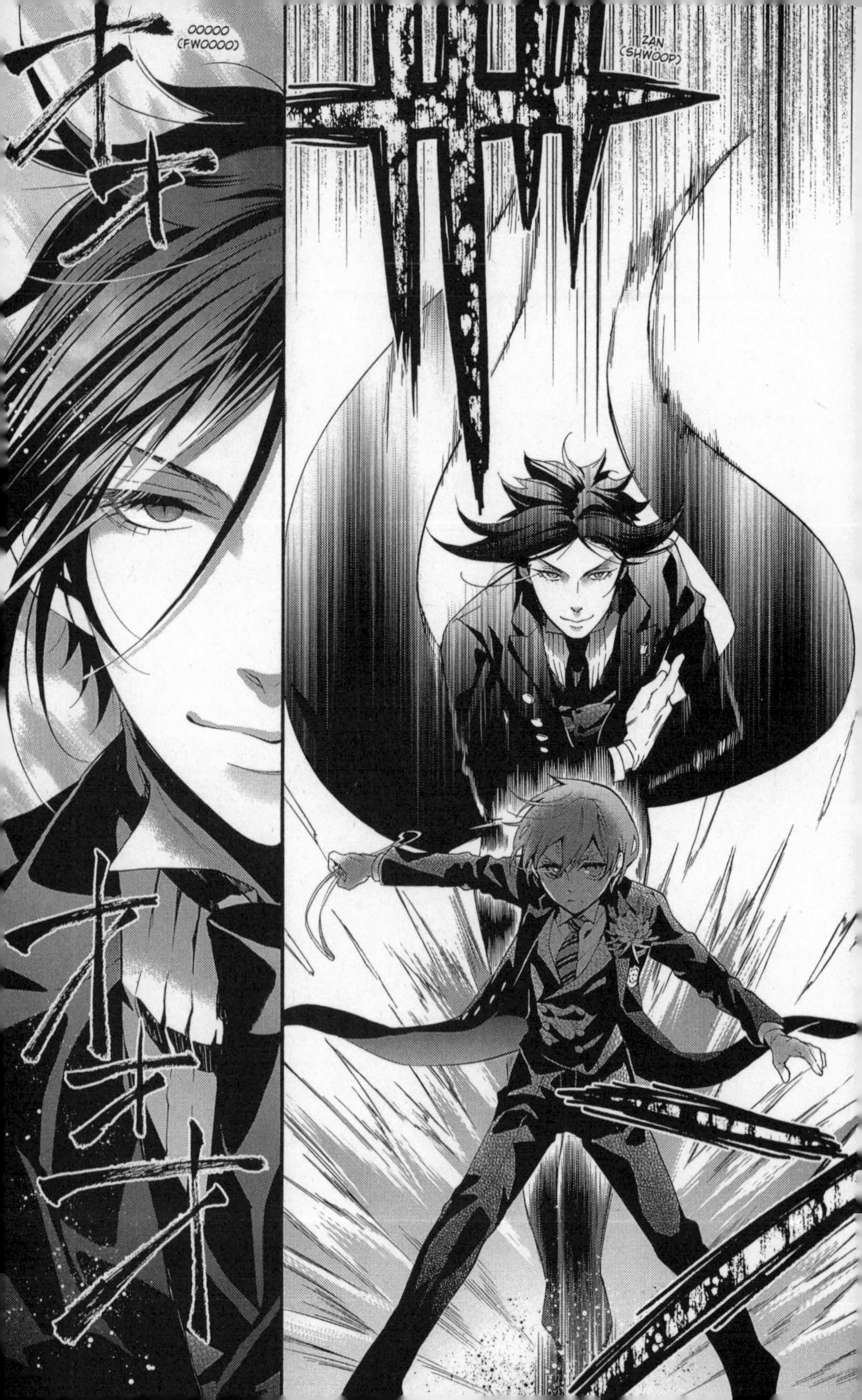
ZAN
(SHWOOP)
OOOOO
(FWOOOO)

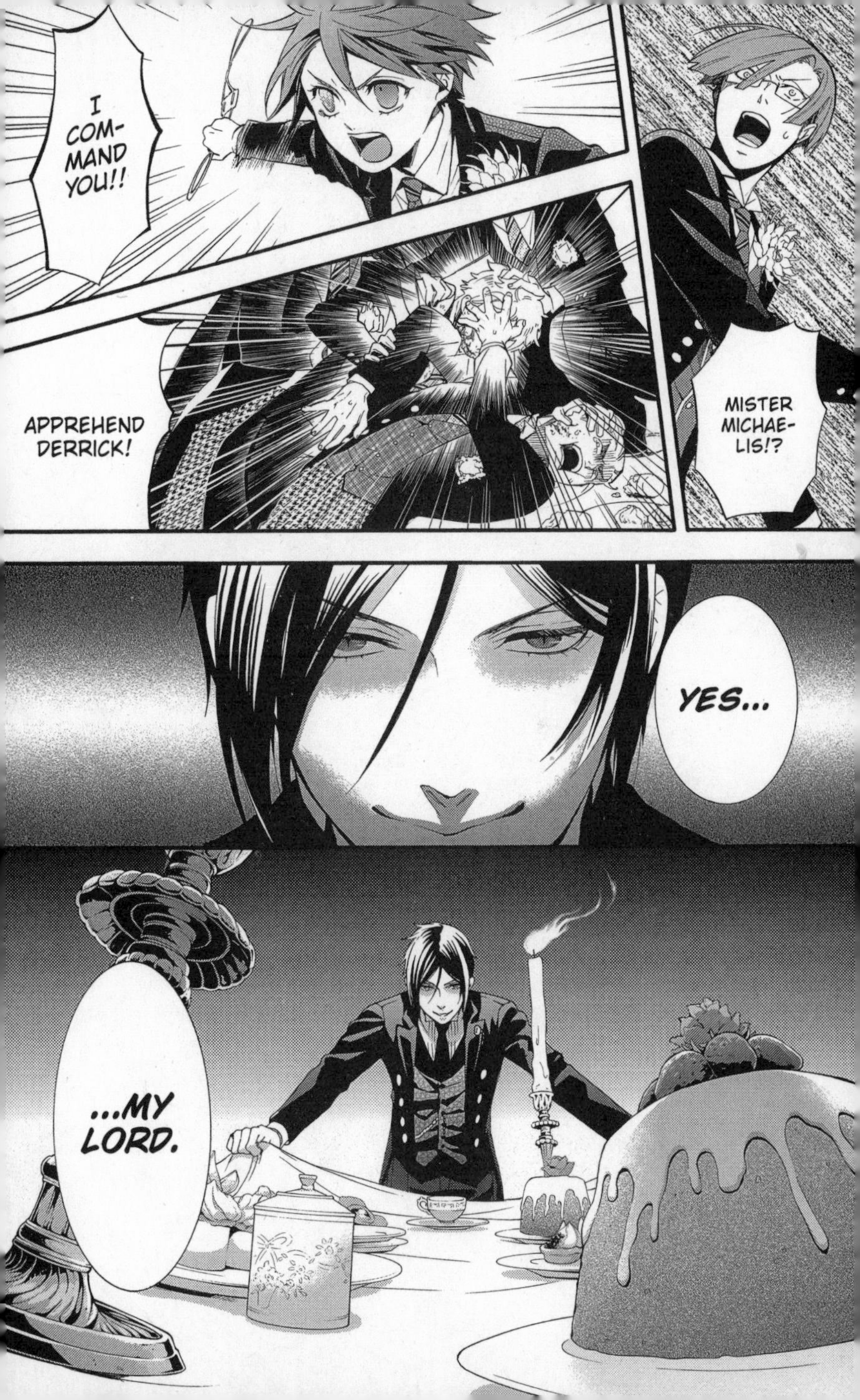
MISTER MICHAE-LIS!?
I COM-MAND YOU!!
APPREHEND DERRICK!
YES...
...MY LORD.

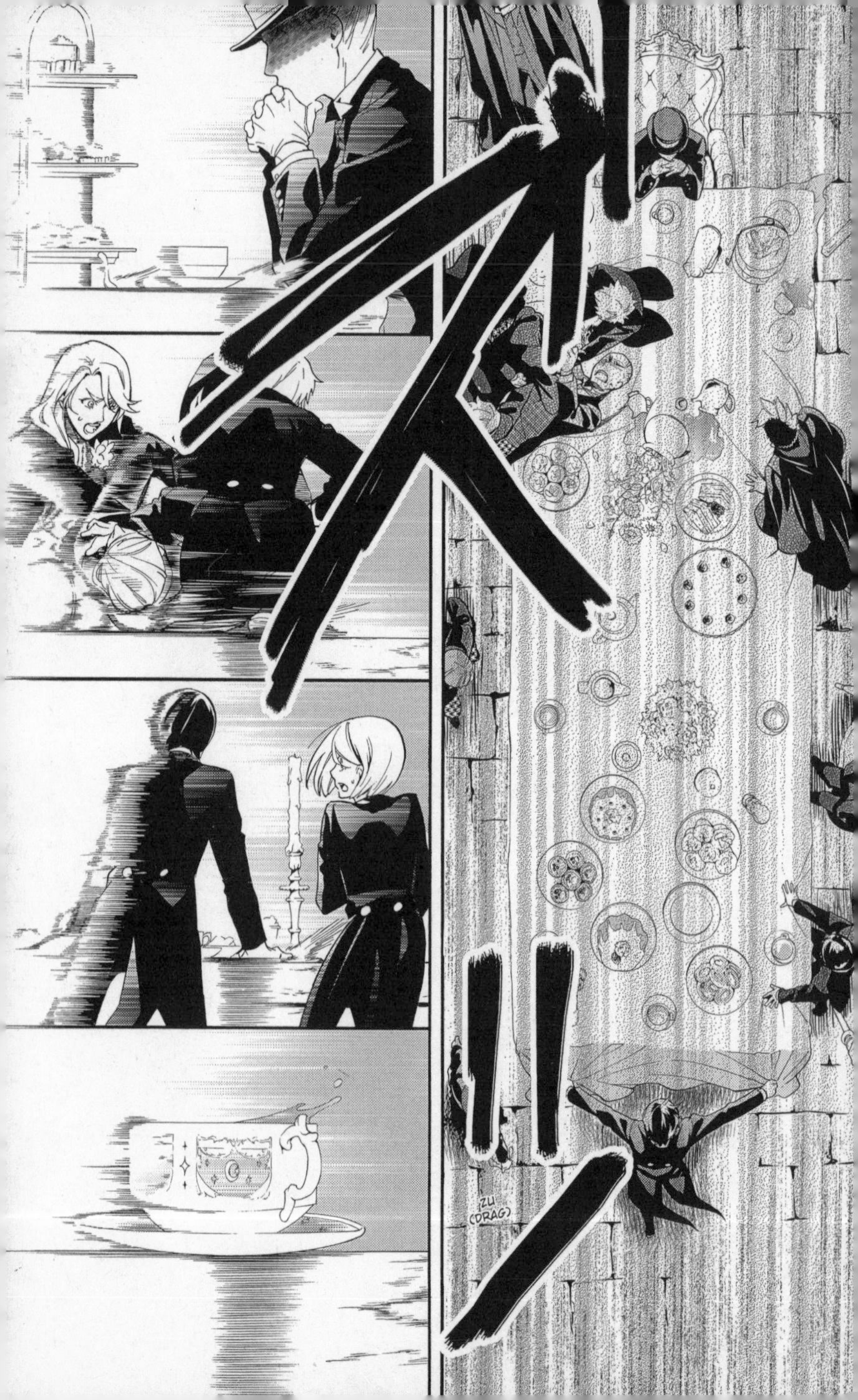
ZU
(DRAG)

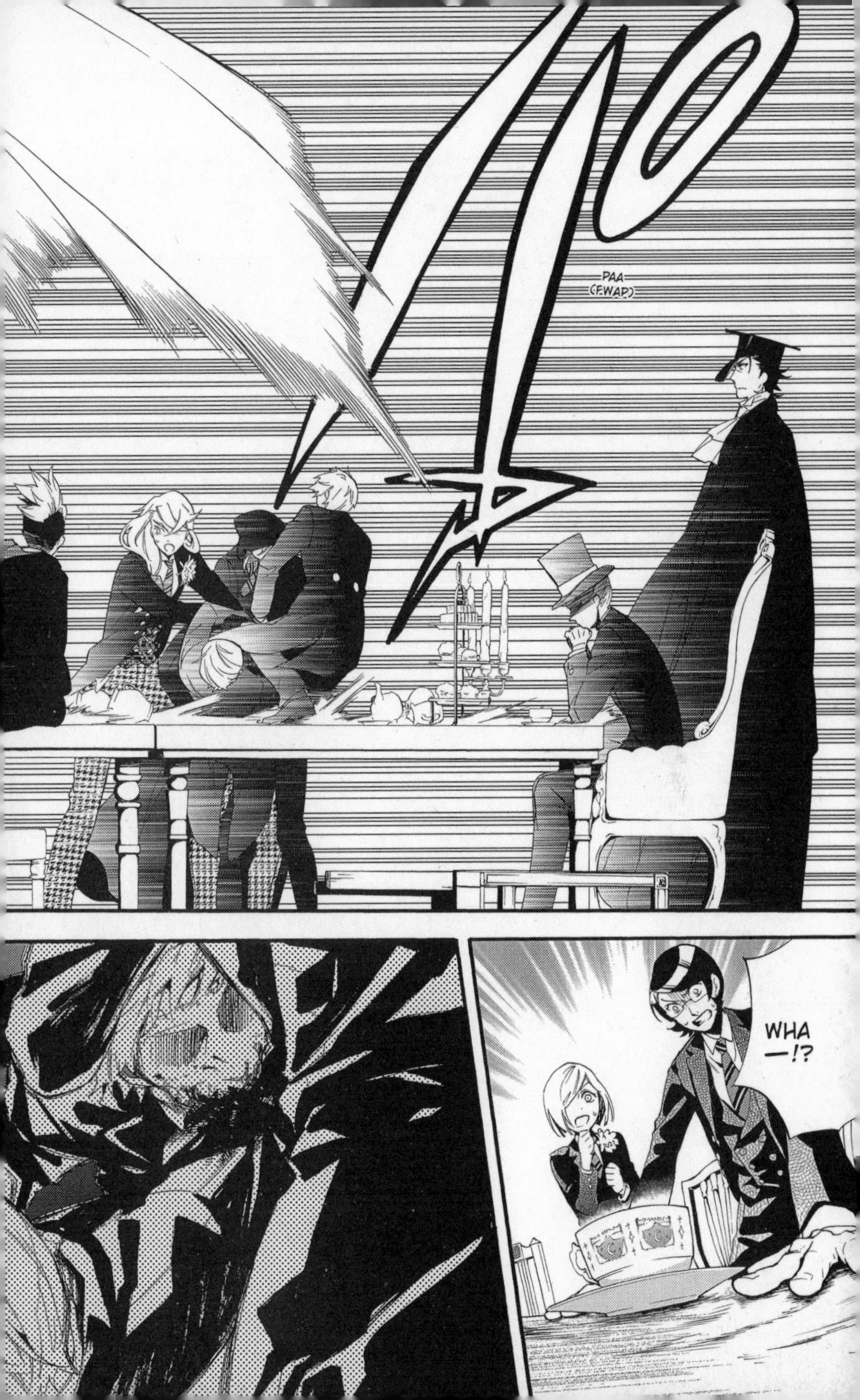
PAA
(FWAP)
WHA—!?

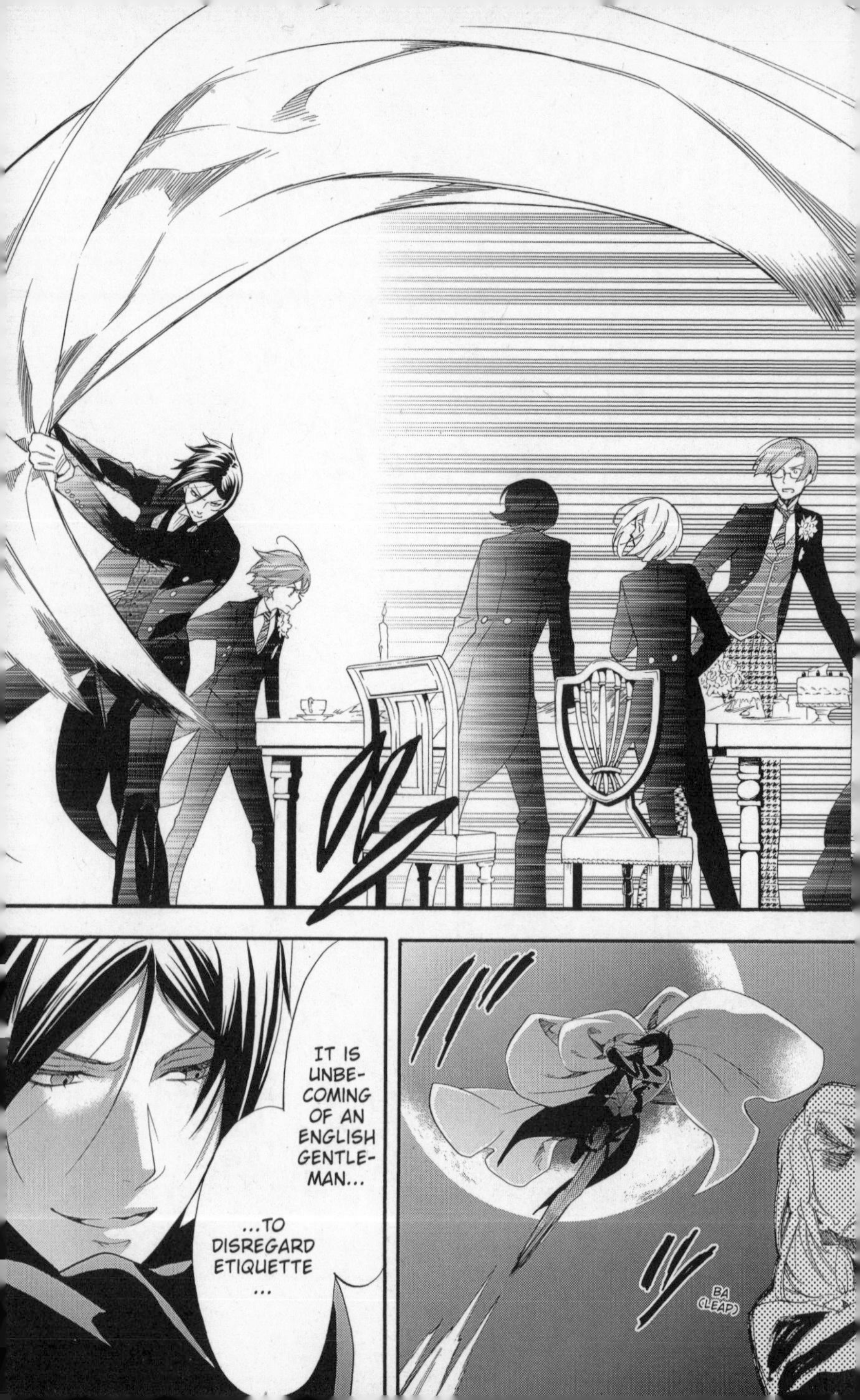
BA (LEAP)
IT IS UNBECOMING OF AN ENGLISH GENTLEMAN...
...TO DISREGARD ETIQUETTE ...

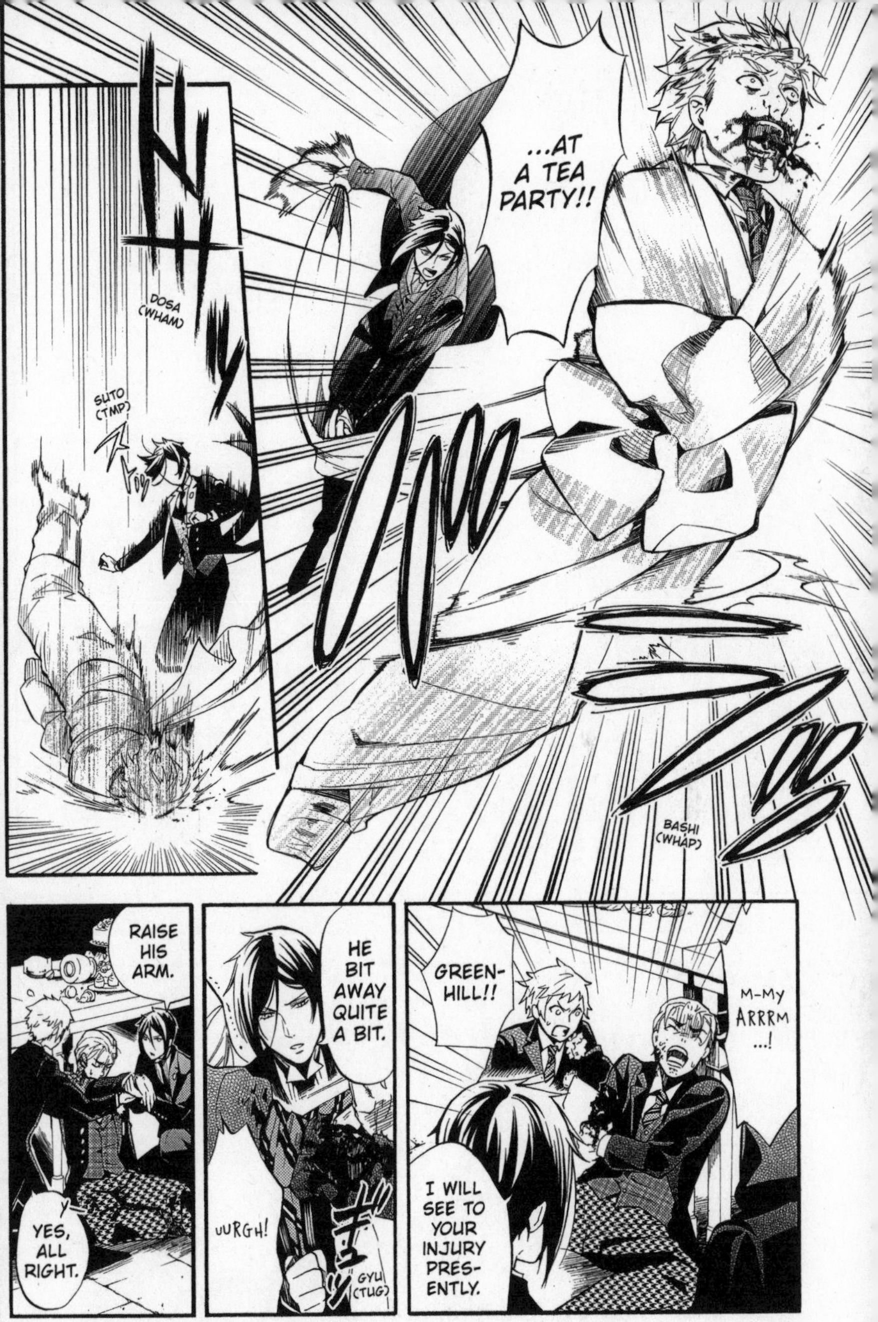

...AT A TEA PARTY!!
BASHI (WHAP)
DOSA (WHAM)
SUTO (TMP)
GREEN-HILL!!
M-MY ARRRM ...!
I WILL SEE TO YOUR INJURY PRESENTLY.
HE BIT AWAY QUITE A BIT.
UURGH!
GYU (TUG)
RAISE HIS ARM.
Y-YES, ALL RIGHT.

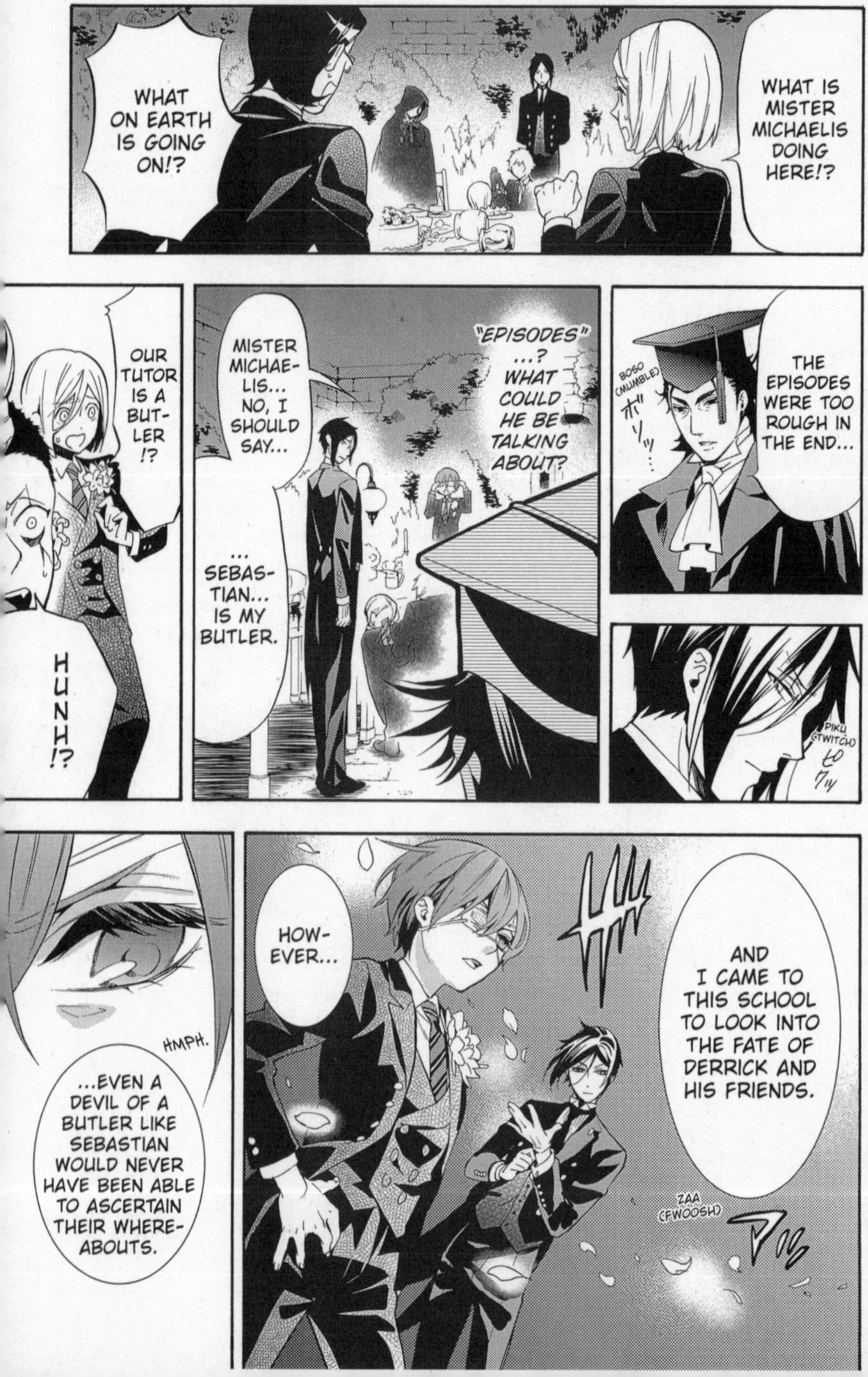
WHAT IS MISTER MICHAELIS DOING HERE!?
WHAT ON EARTH IS GOING ON!?
BOSO (MUMBLE)
THE EPISODES WERE TOO ROUGH IN THE END...
PIKU (TWITCH)
"EPISODES"...? WHAT COULD HE BE TALKING ABOUT?
MISTER MICHAE-LIS... NO, I SHOULD SAY...
... SEBAS-TIAN... IS MY BUTLER.
OUR TUTOR IS A BUT-LER !?
HUNH!?
AND I CAME TO THIS SCHOOL TO LOOK INTO THE FATE OF DERRICK AND HIS FRIENDS.
HOW-EVER...
ZAA (FWOOSH)
HMPH.
...EVEN A DEVIL OF A BUTLER LIKE SEBASTIAN WOULD NEVER HAVE BEEN ABLE TO ASCERTAIN THEIR WHERE-ABOUTS.

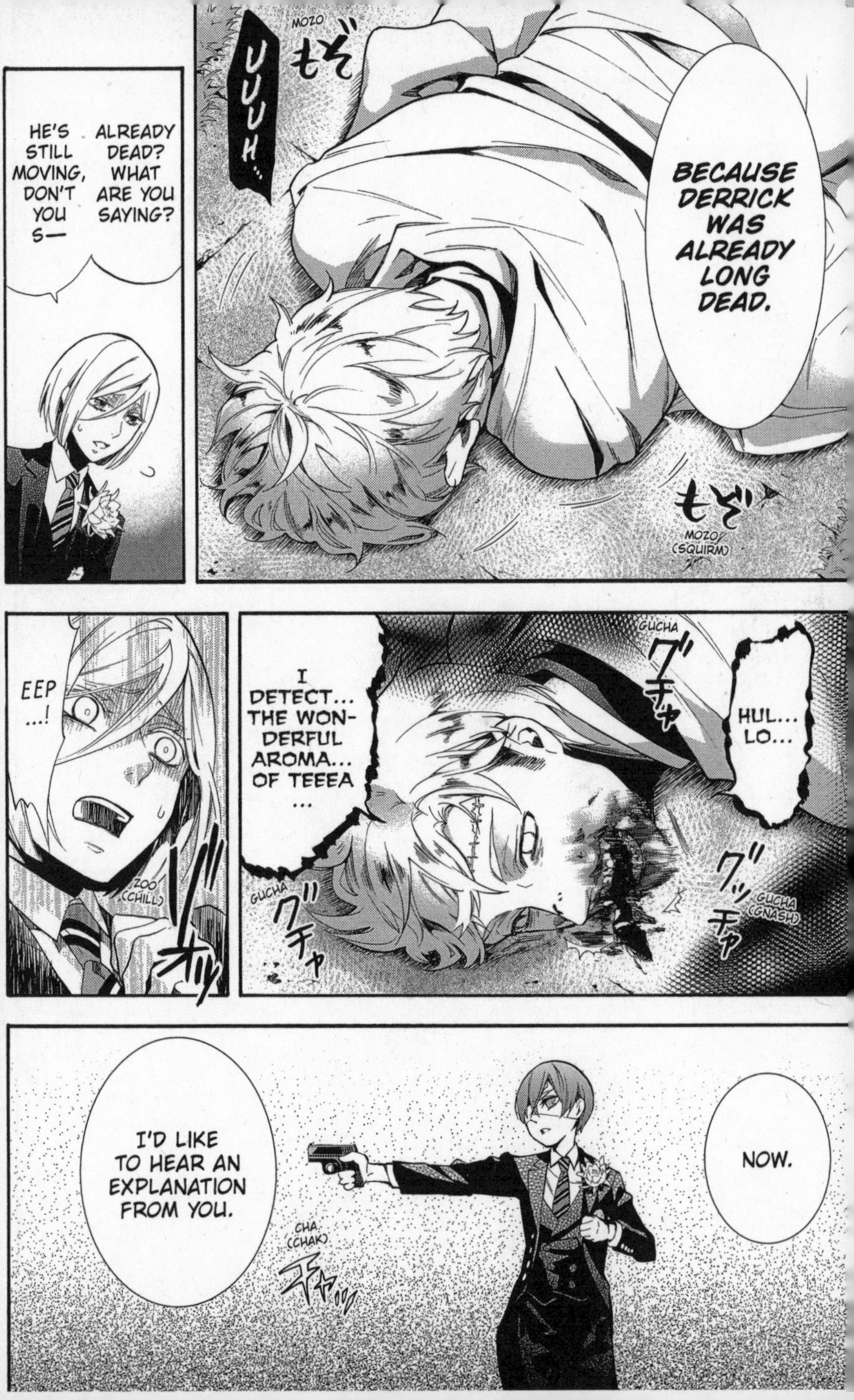
BECAUSE DERRICK WAS ALREADY LONG DEAD.
MOZO
もぞ
UUUH...
もぞ
MOZO (SQUIRM)
ALREADY DEAD? WHAT ARE YOU SAYING?
HE'S STILL MOVING, DON'T YOU S—
HUL... LO...
GUCHA
グチャ
I DETECT... THE WONDERFUL AROMA... OF TEEEA...
グッチャ
GUCHA (GNASH)
GUCHA
グチャ
EEP ...!
ZOO (CHILL)
I'D LIKE TO HEAR AN EXPLANATION FROM YOU.
NOW.
CHA (CHAK)

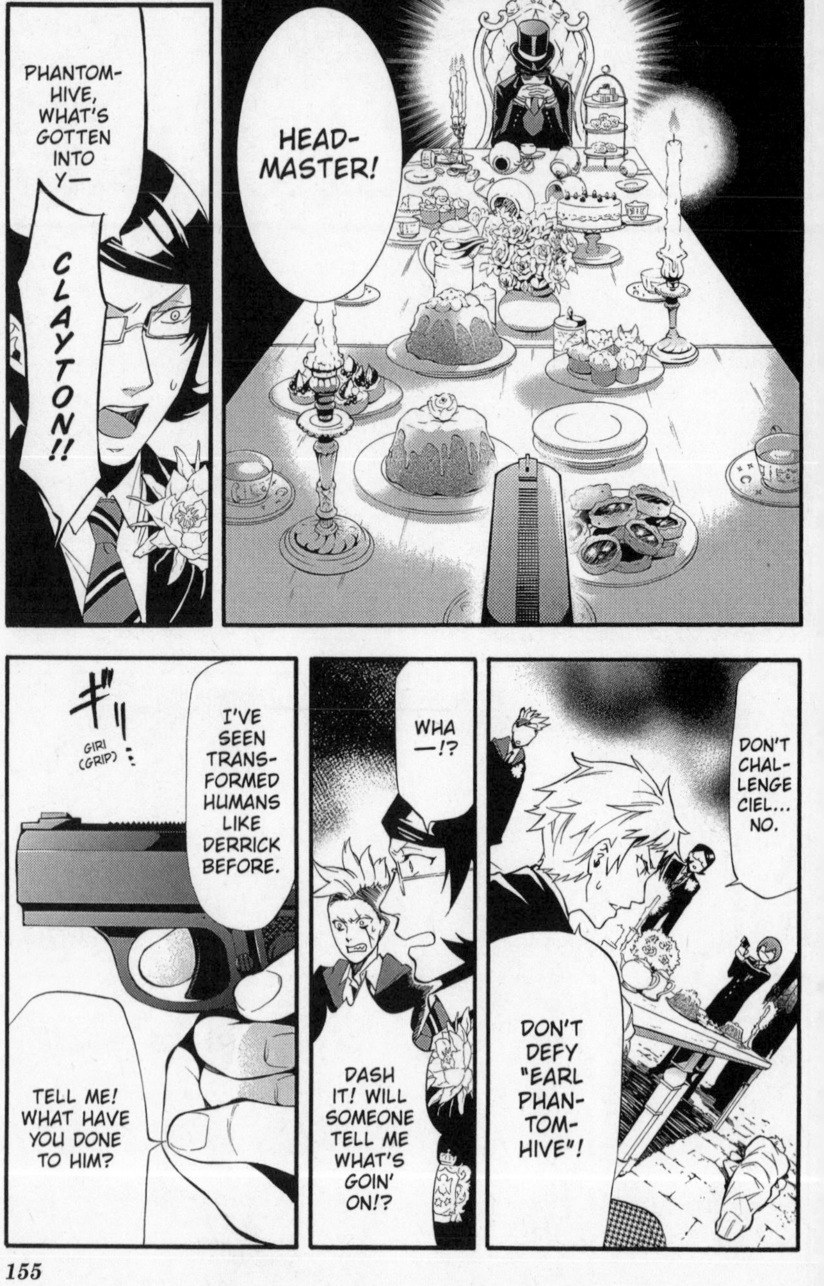
HEAD-MASTER!
PHANTOM-HIVE, WHAT'S GOTTEN INTO Y—
CLAYTON!!
DON'T CHAL-LENGE CIEL... NO.
DON'T DEFY "EARL PHAN-TOM-HIVE"!
WHA—!?
DASH IT! WILL SOMEONE TELL ME WHAT'S GOIN' ON!?
I'VE SEEN TRANS-FORMED HUMANS LIKE DERRICK BEFORE.
ギリ
GIRI (GRIP)
TELL ME! WHAT HAVE YOU DONE TO HIM?

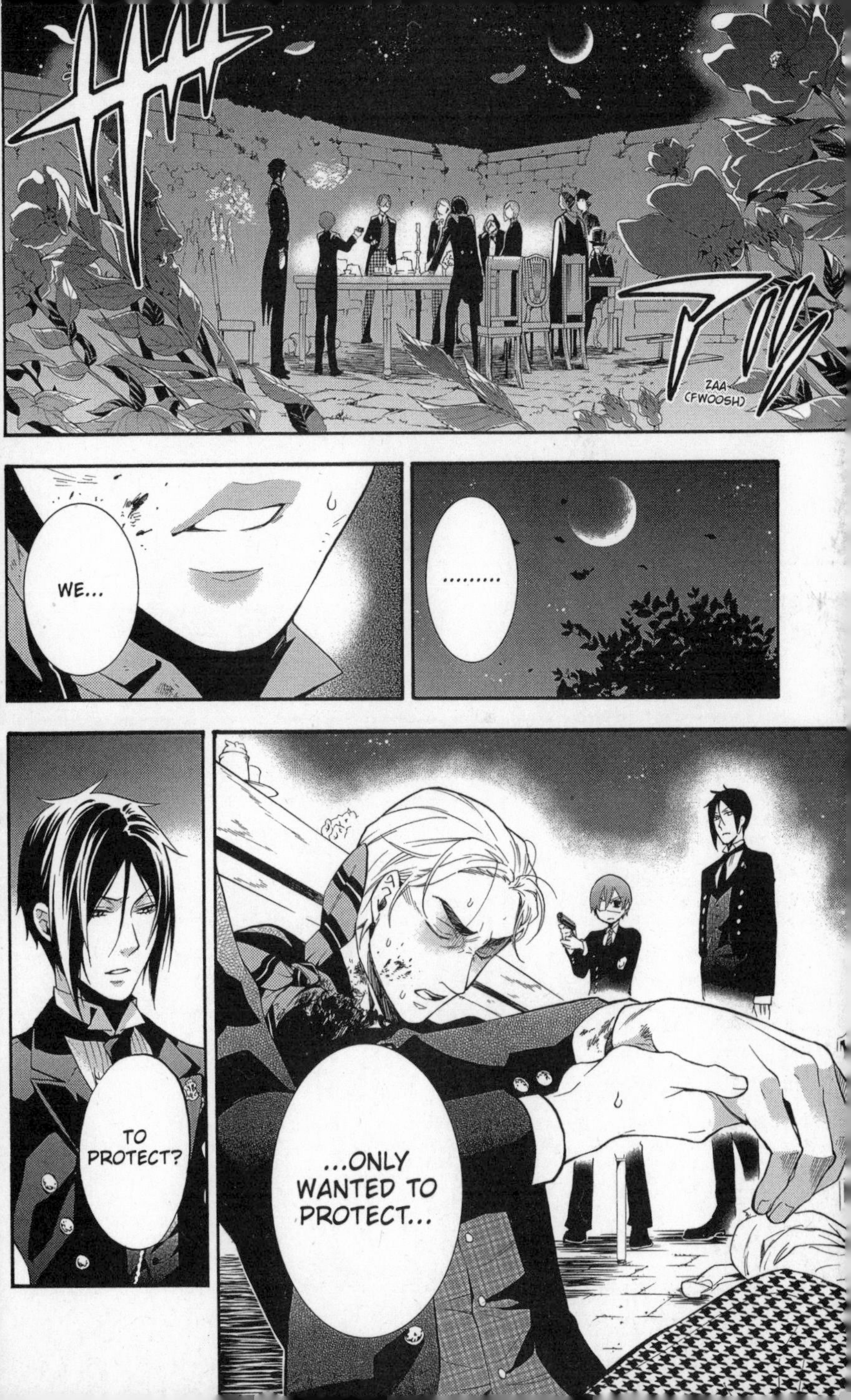
ZAA
(FWOOSH)
....
WE...
...ONLY WANTED TO PROTECT...
TO PROTECT?

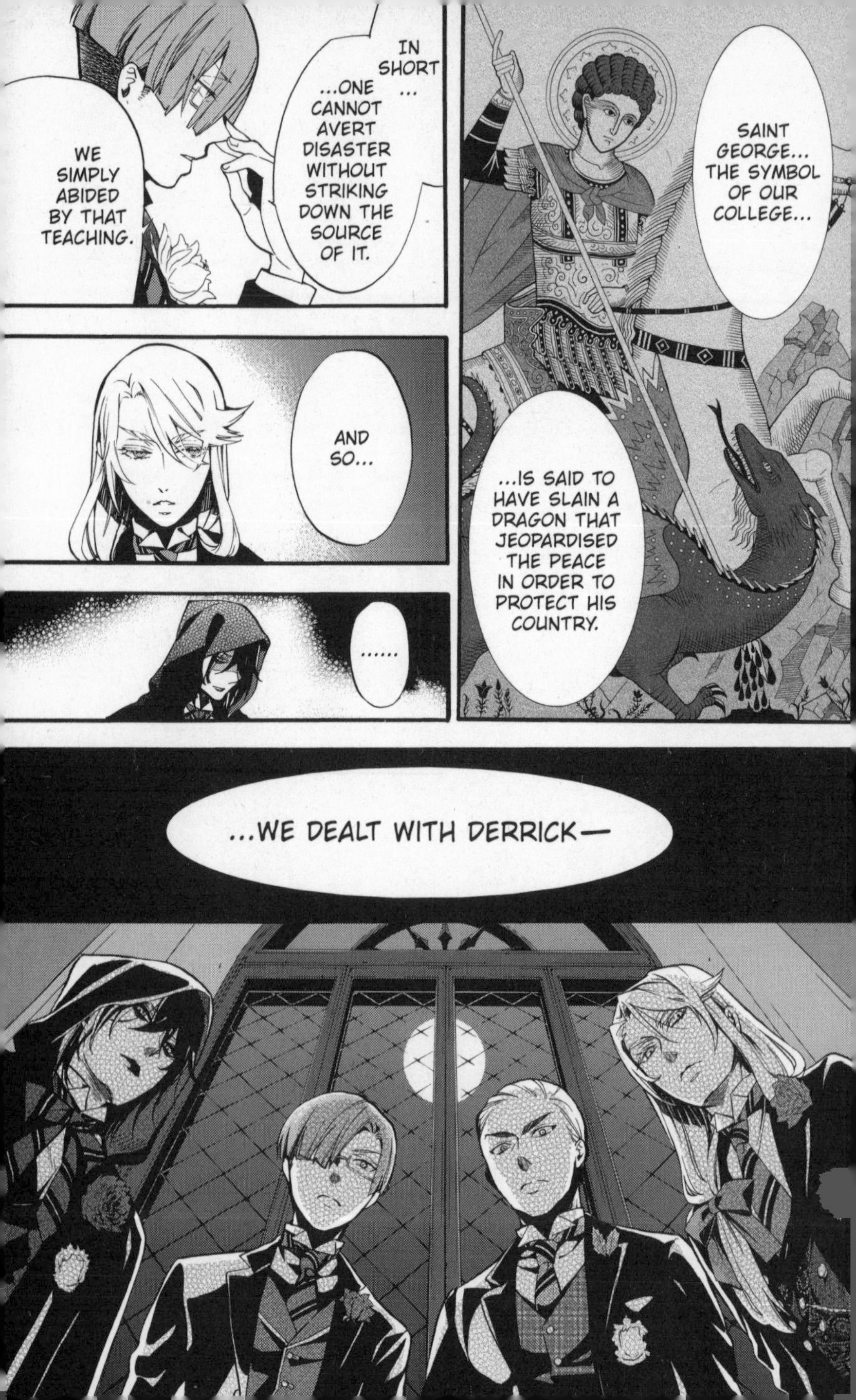
SAINT GEORGE... THE SYMBOL OF OUR COLLEGE...
...IS SAID TO HAVE SLAIN A DRAGON THAT JEOPARDISED THE PEACE IN ORDER TO PROTECT HIS COUNTRY.
IN SHORT ...
...ONE CANNOT AVERT DISASTER WITHOUT STRIKING DOWN THE SOURCE OF IT.
WE SIMPLY ABIDED BY THAT TEACHING.
AND SO...
......
...WE DEALT WITH DERRICK—

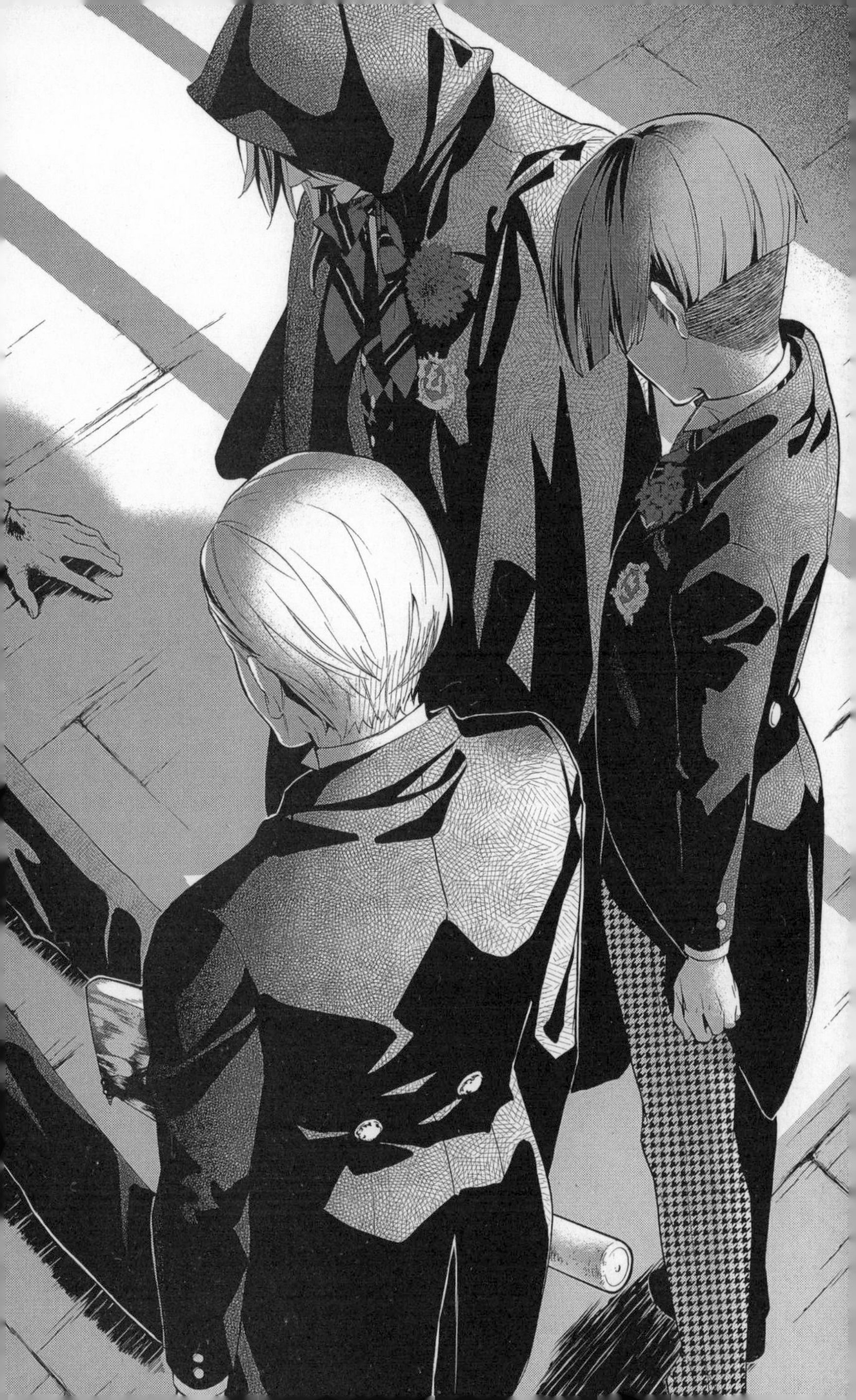

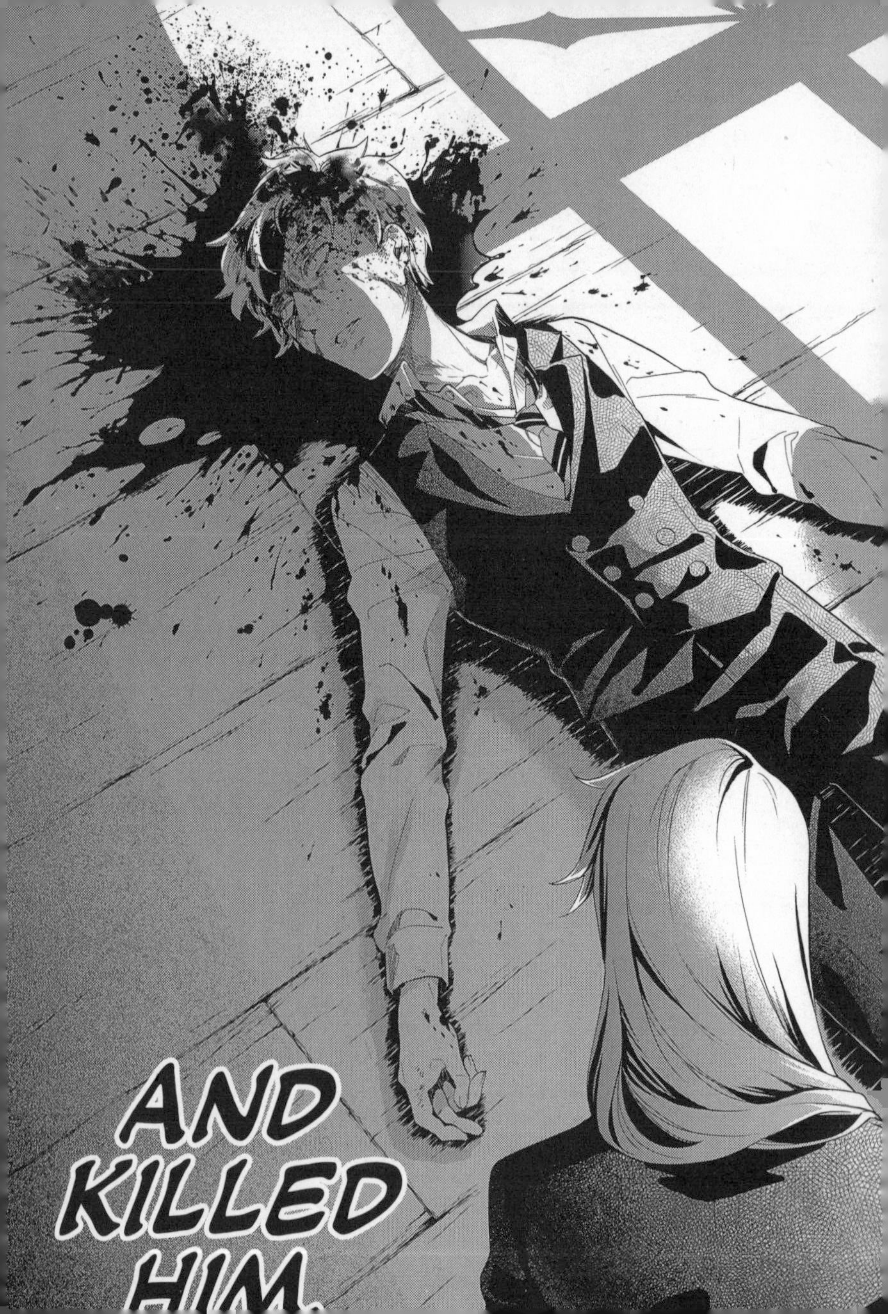
AND KILLED HIM.

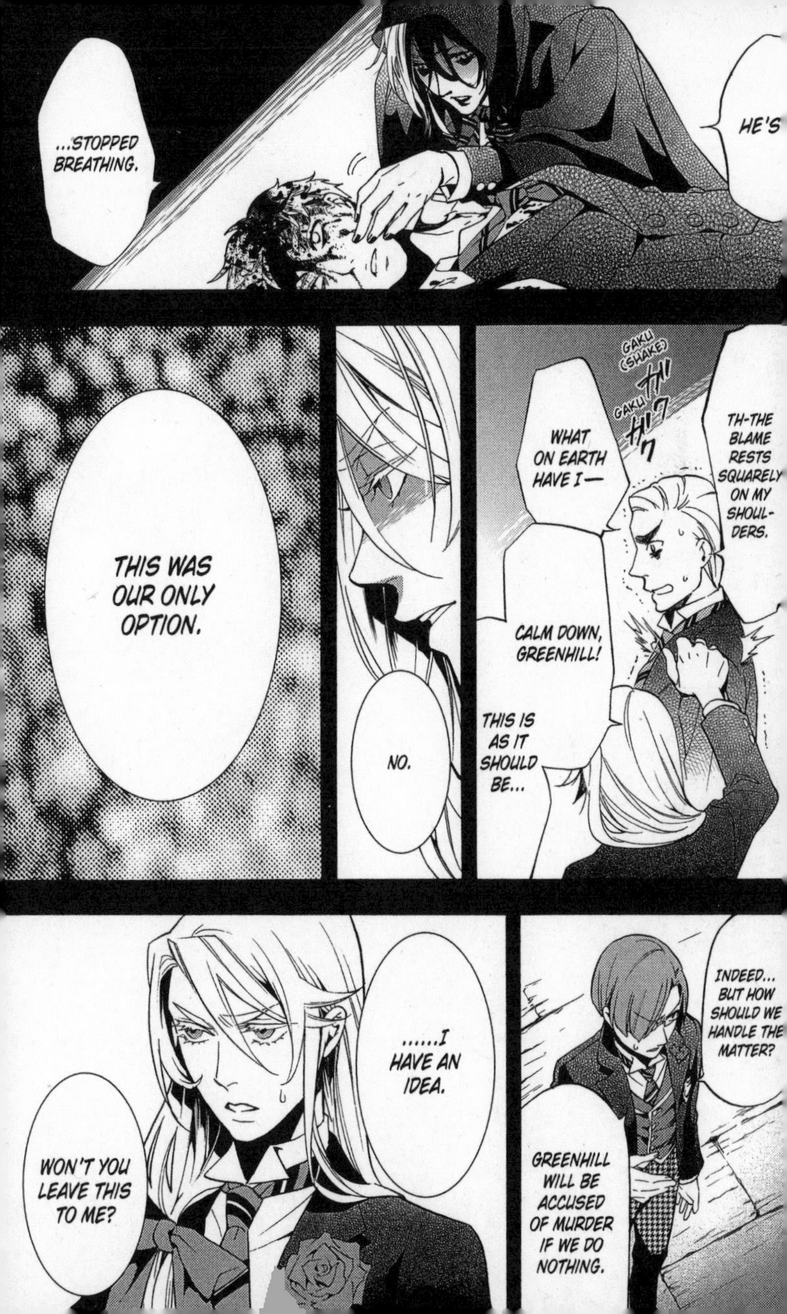
HE'S
...STOPPED BREATHING.
TH-THE BLAME RESTS SQUARELY ON MY SHOUL-DERS.
GAKU (SHAKE) GAKU
WHAT ON EARTH HAVE I—
CALM DOWN, GREENHILL!
THIS IS AS IT SHOULD BE...
NO.
THIS WAS OUR ONLY OPTION.
INDEED... BUT HOW SHOULD WE HANDLE THE MATTER?
GREENHILL WILL BE ACCUSED OF MURDER IF WE DO NOTHING.
......I HAVE AN IDEA.
WON'T YOU LEAVE THIS TO ME?

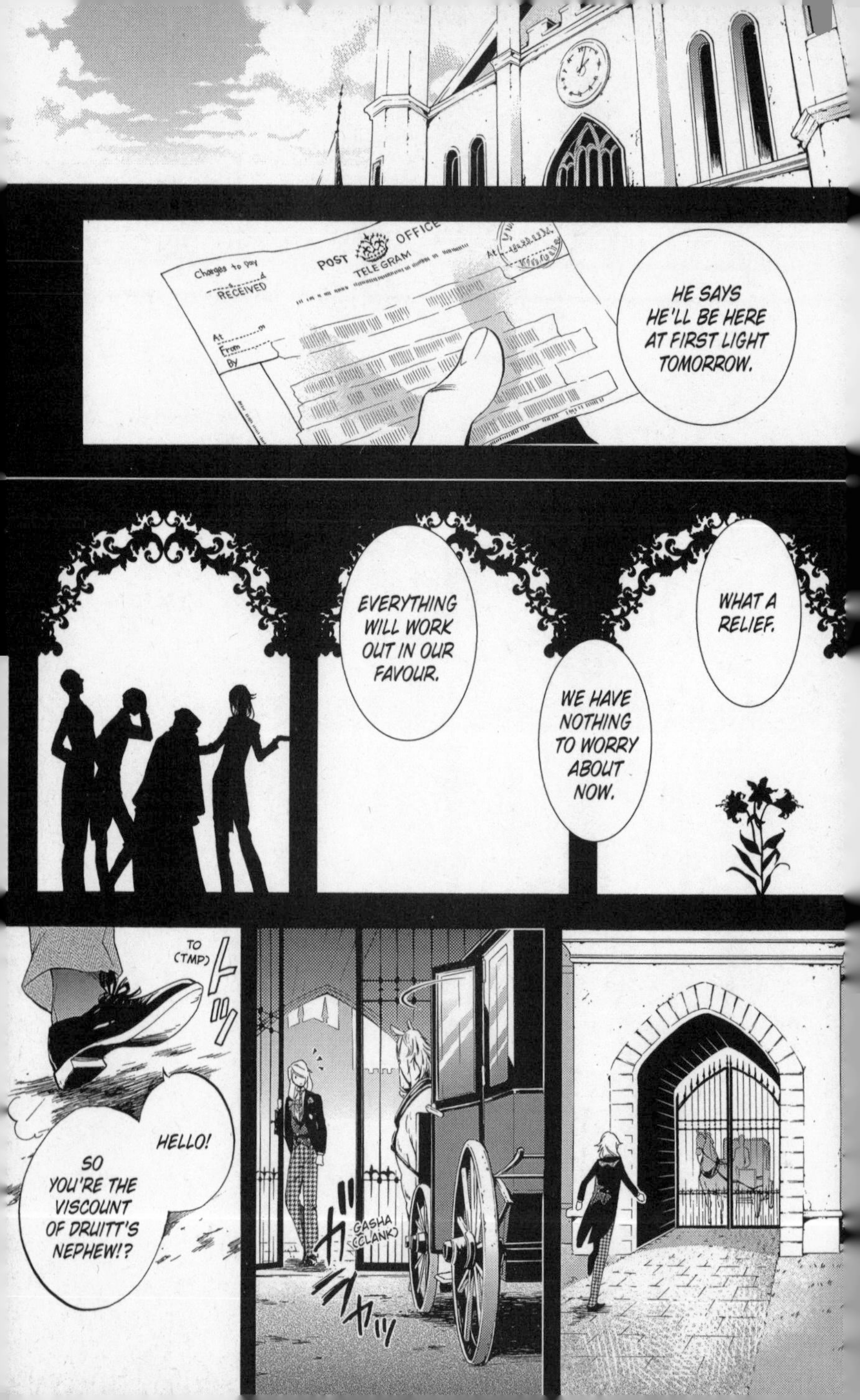
POST OFFICE
TELEGRAM
Charges to pay
RECEIVED
At
From
By
HE SAYS HE'LL BE HERE AT FIRST LIGHT TOMORROW.
WHAT A RELIEF.
WE HAVE NOTHING TO WORRY ABOUT NOW.
EVERYTHING WILL WORK OUT IN OUR FAVOUR.
GASHA (CLANK)
TO (TMP)
HELLO!
SO YOU'RE THE VISCOUNT OF DRUITT'S NEPHEW!?

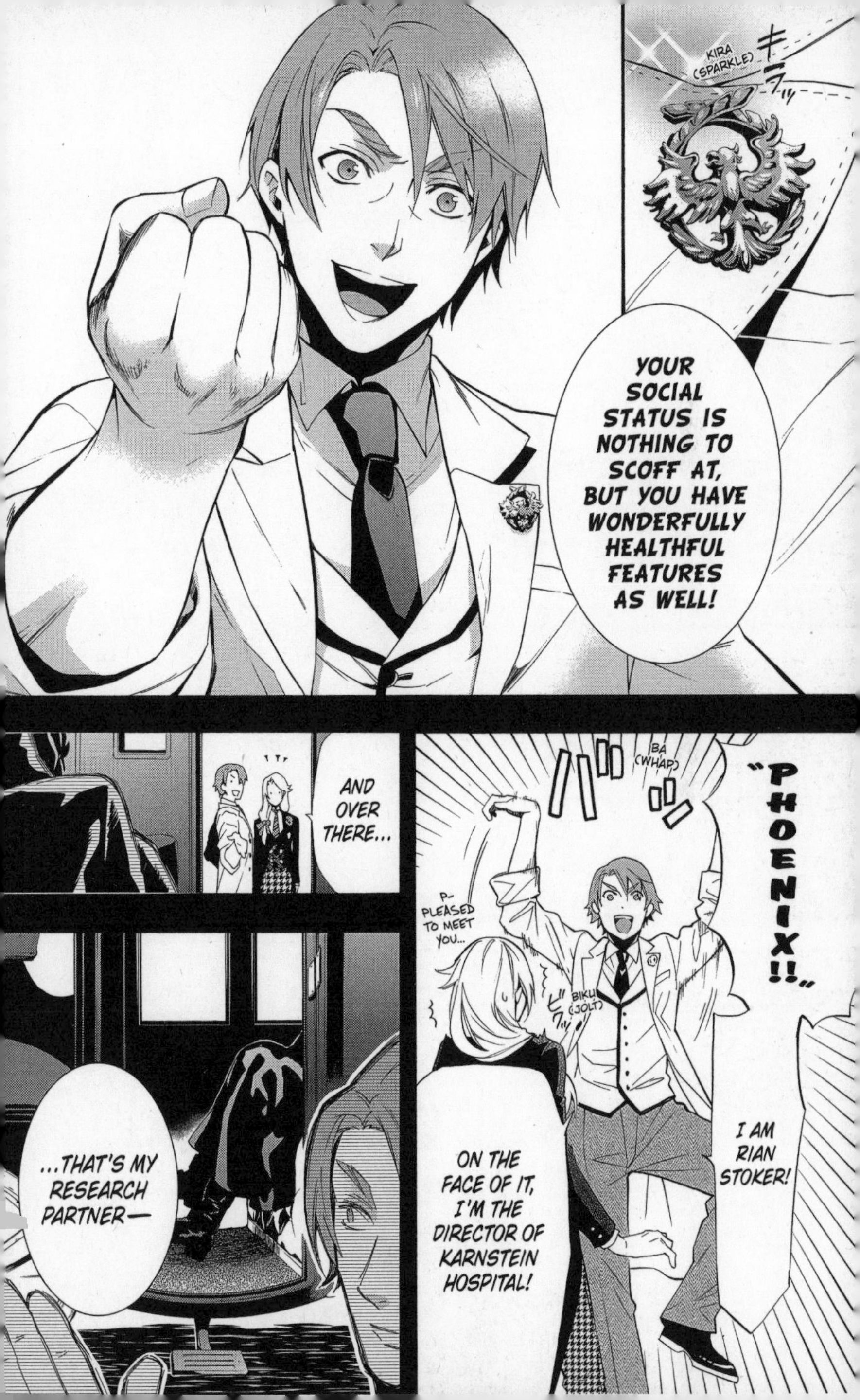
KIRA (SPARKLE)
YOUR SOCIAL STATUS IS NOTHING TO SCOFF AT, BUT YOU HAVE WONDERFULLY HEALTHFUL FEATURES AS WELL!
"PHOENIX!!"
BA (WHAP)
P-PLEASED TO MEET YOU...
BIKU (JOLT)
I AM RIAN STOKER!
ON THE FACE OF IT, I'M THE DIRECTOR OF KARNSTEIN HOSPITAL!
AND OVER THERE...
...THAT'S MY RESEARCH PARTNER—

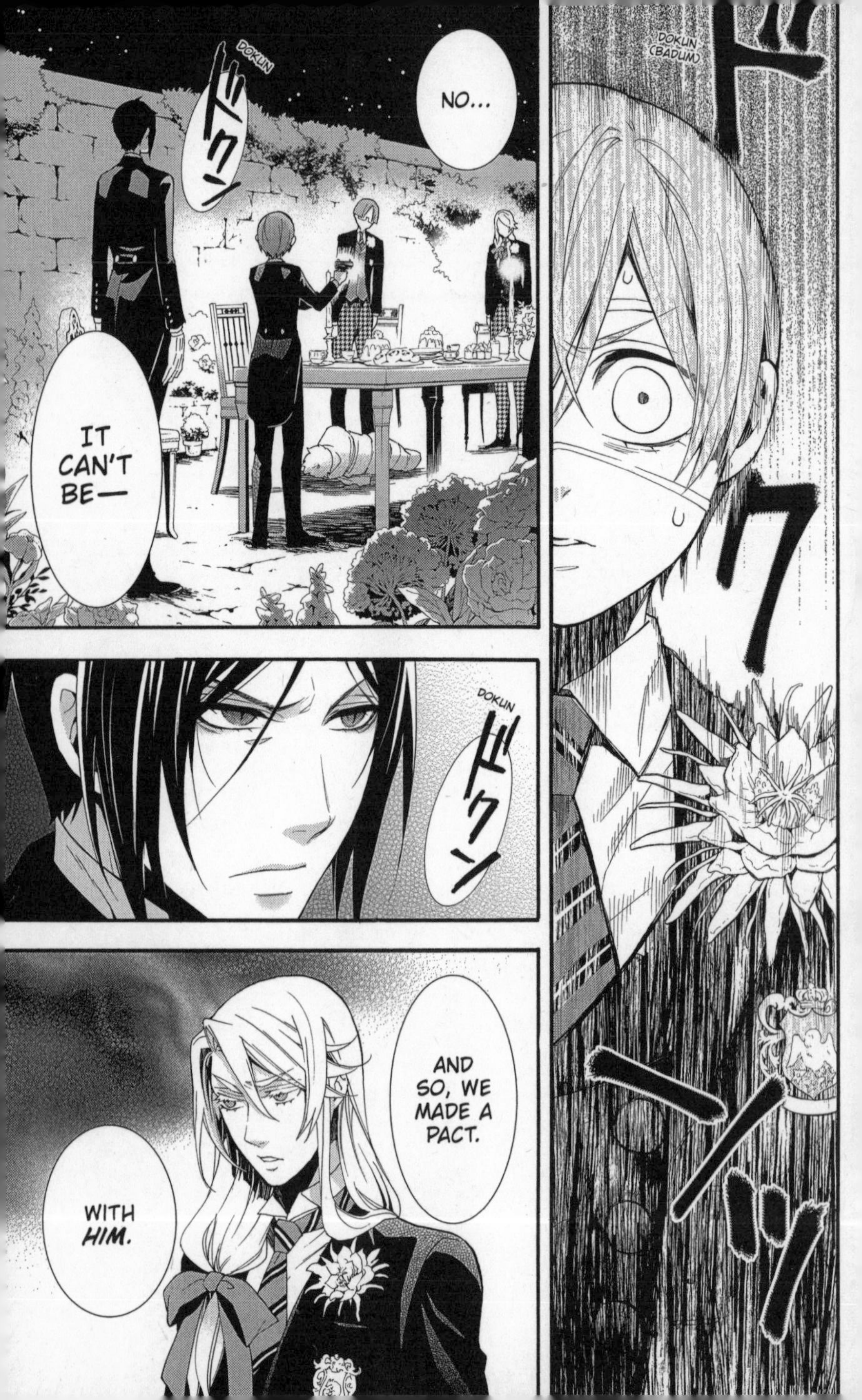
DOKUN (BADUM)
NO...
DOKUN
IT CAN'T BE—
DOKUN
AND SO, WE MADE A PACT.
WITH HIM.

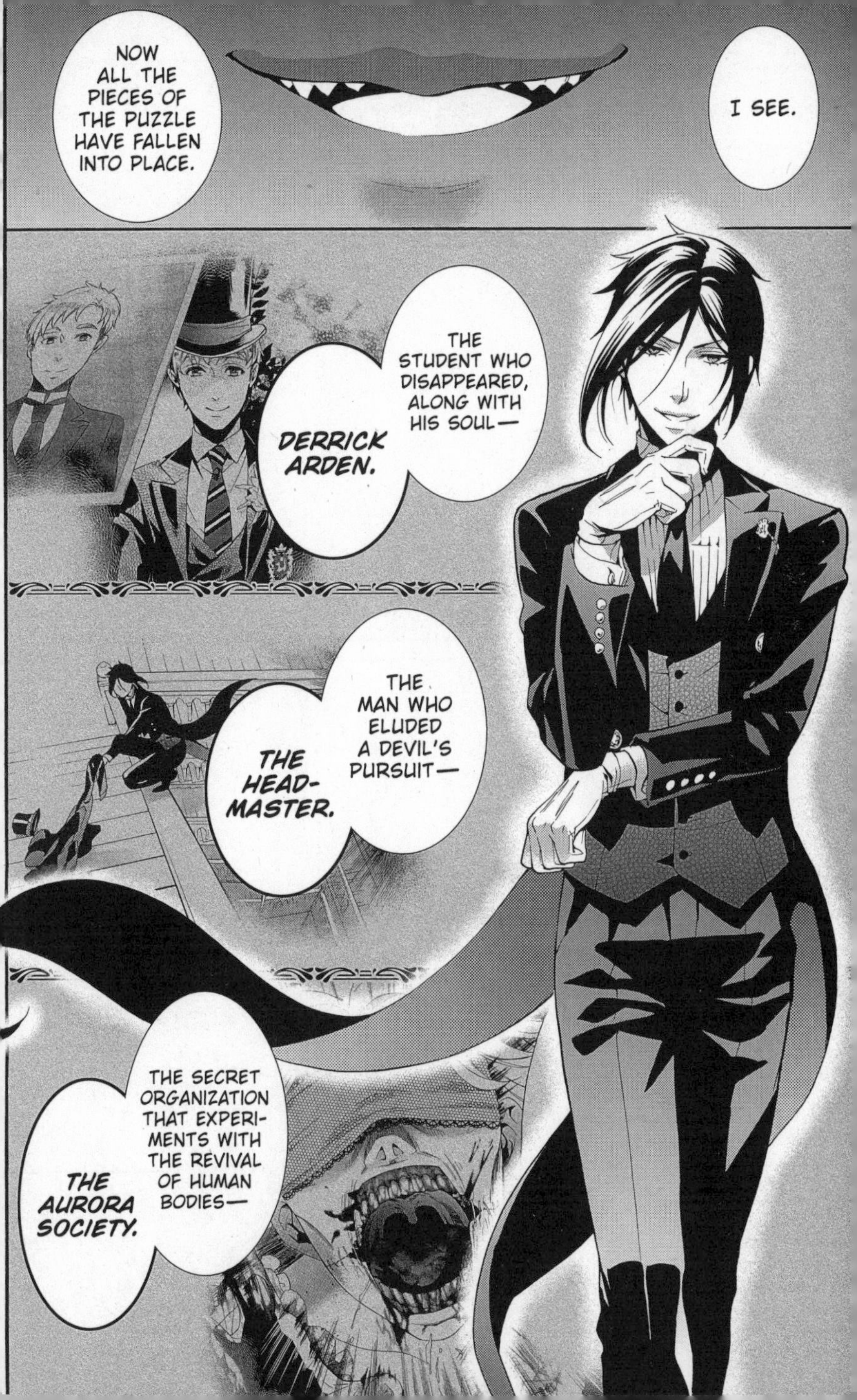
I SEE.
NOW ALL THE PIECES OF THE PUZZLE HAVE FALLEN INTO PLACE.
THE STUDENT WHO DISAPPEARED, ALONG WITH HIS SOUL—
DERRICK ARDEN.
THE MAN WHO ELUDED A DEVIL'S PURSUIT—
THE HEADMASTER.
THE SECRET ORGANIZATION THAT EXPERIMENTS WITH THE REVIVAL OF HUMAN BODIES—
THE AURORA SOCIETY.

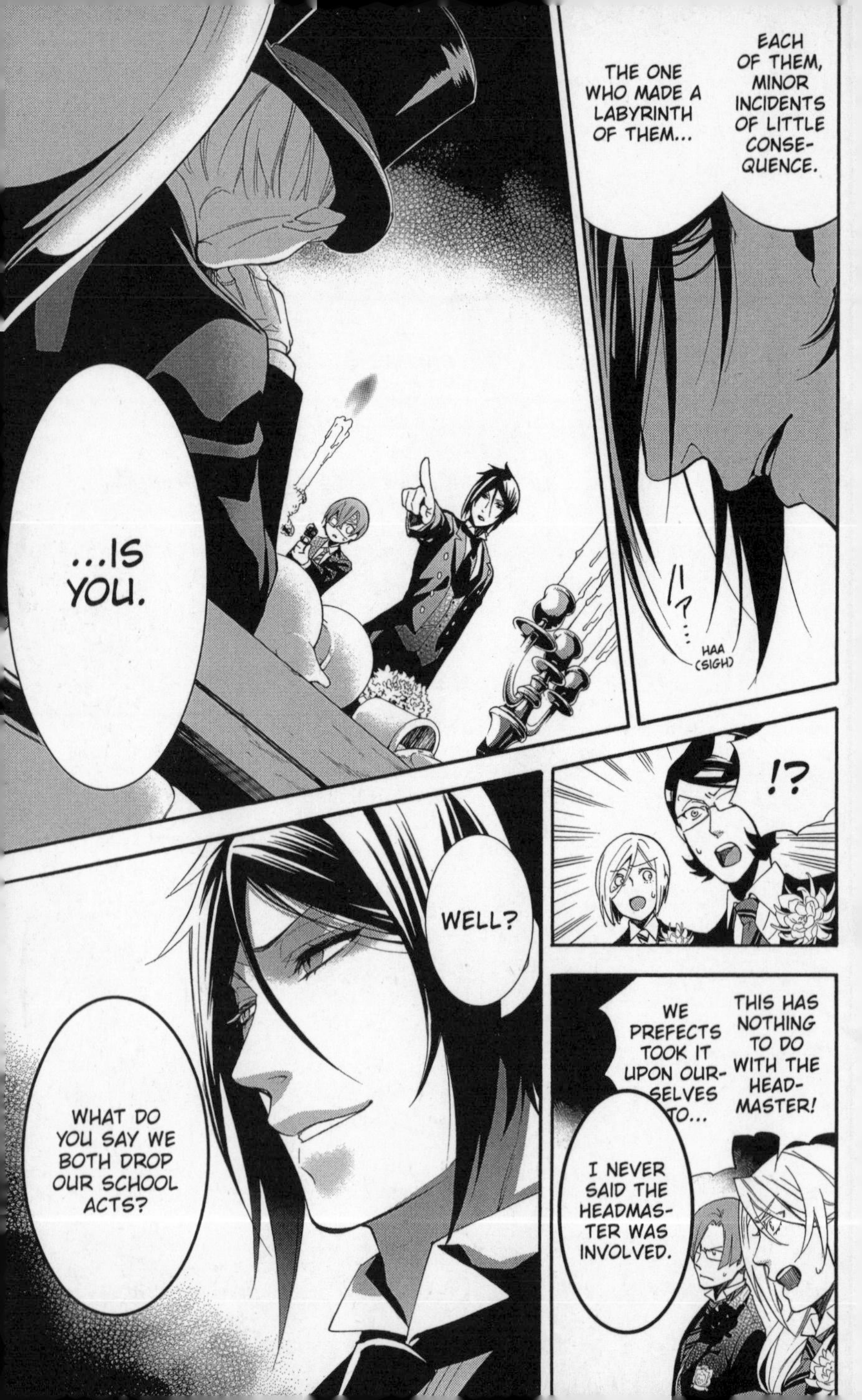
EACH OF THEM, MINOR INCIDENTS OF LITTLE CONSE-QUENCE.
THE ONE WHO MADE A LABYRINTH OF THEM...
HAA (SIGH)
...IS YOU.
!?
THIS HAS NOTHING TO DO WITH THE HEAD-MASTER!
WE PREFECTS TOOK IT UPON OUR-SELVES TO...
I NEVER SAID THE HEADMAS-TER WAS INVOLVED.
WELL?
WHAT DO YOU SAY WE BOTH DROP OUR SCHOOL ACTS?

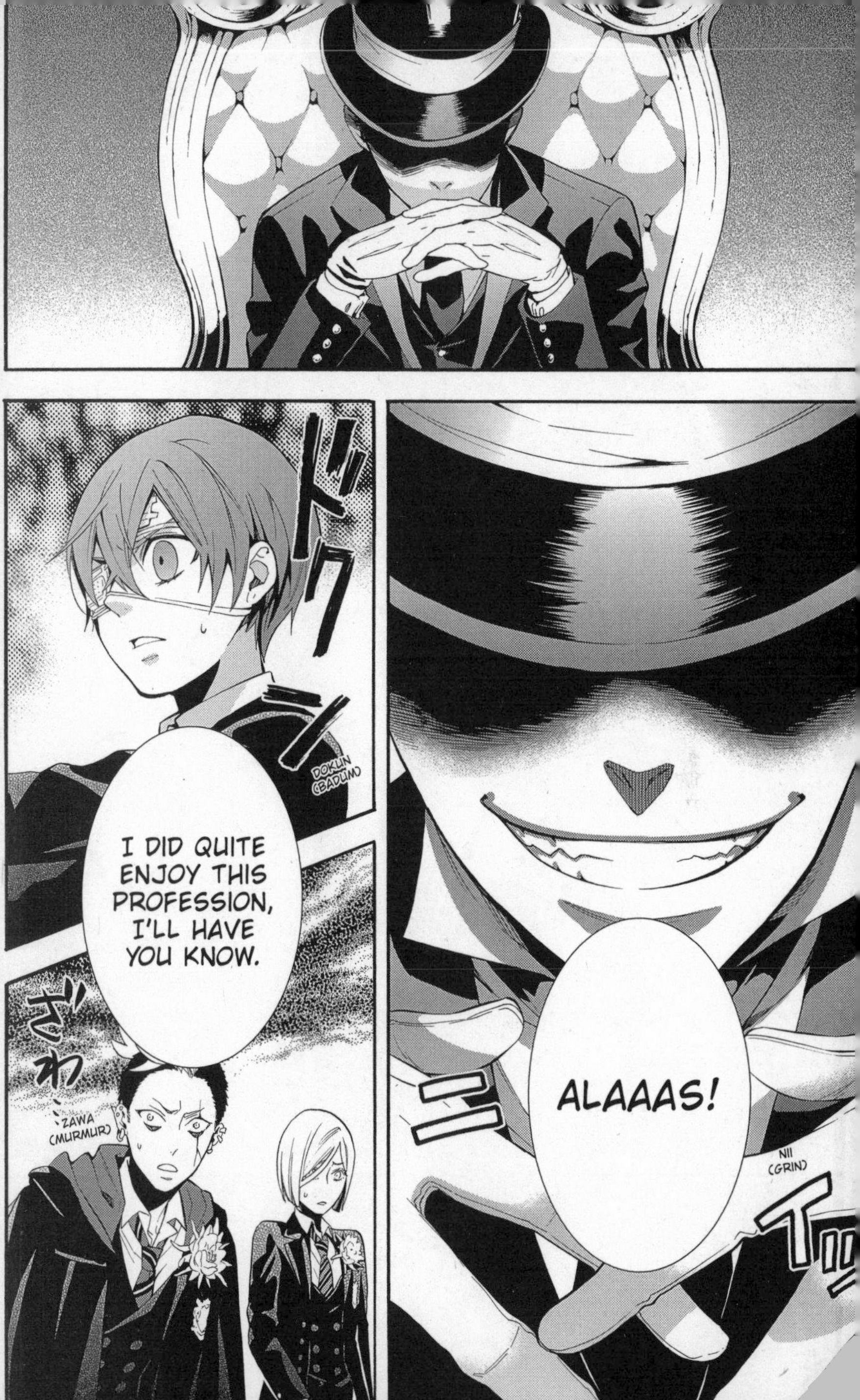
ALAAAS!
NII (GRIN)
DOKUN (BADUM)
I DID QUITE ENJOY THIS PROFESSION, I'LL HAVE YOU KNOW.
ZAWA (MURMUR)

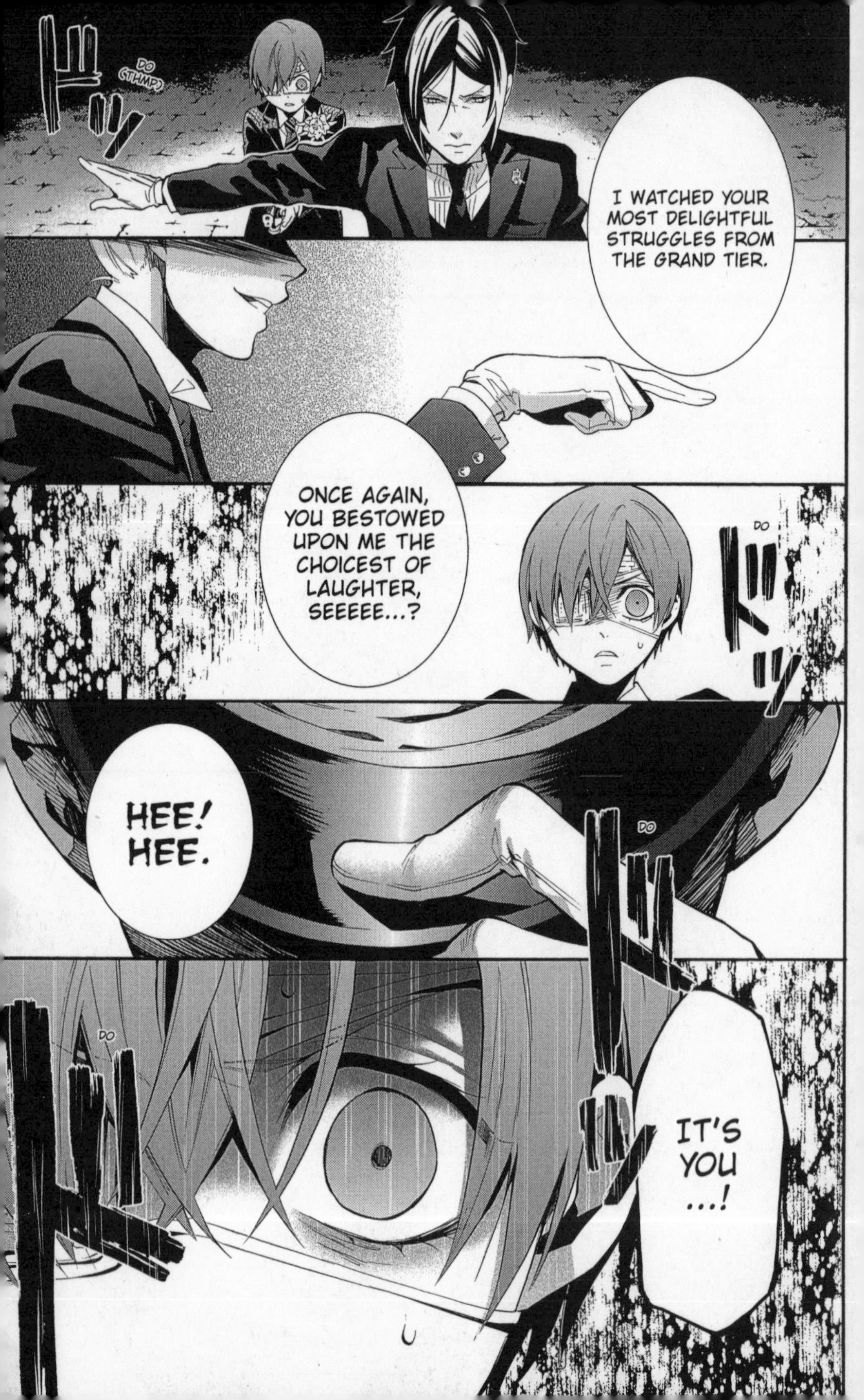
I WATCHED YOUR MOST DELIGHTFUL STRUGGLES FROM THE GRAND TIER.
DO (THMP)
DO
ONCE AGAIN, YOU BESTOWED UPON ME THE CHOICEST OF LAUGHTER, SEEEEE...?
DO
HEE! HEE.
IT'S YOU ...!
DO

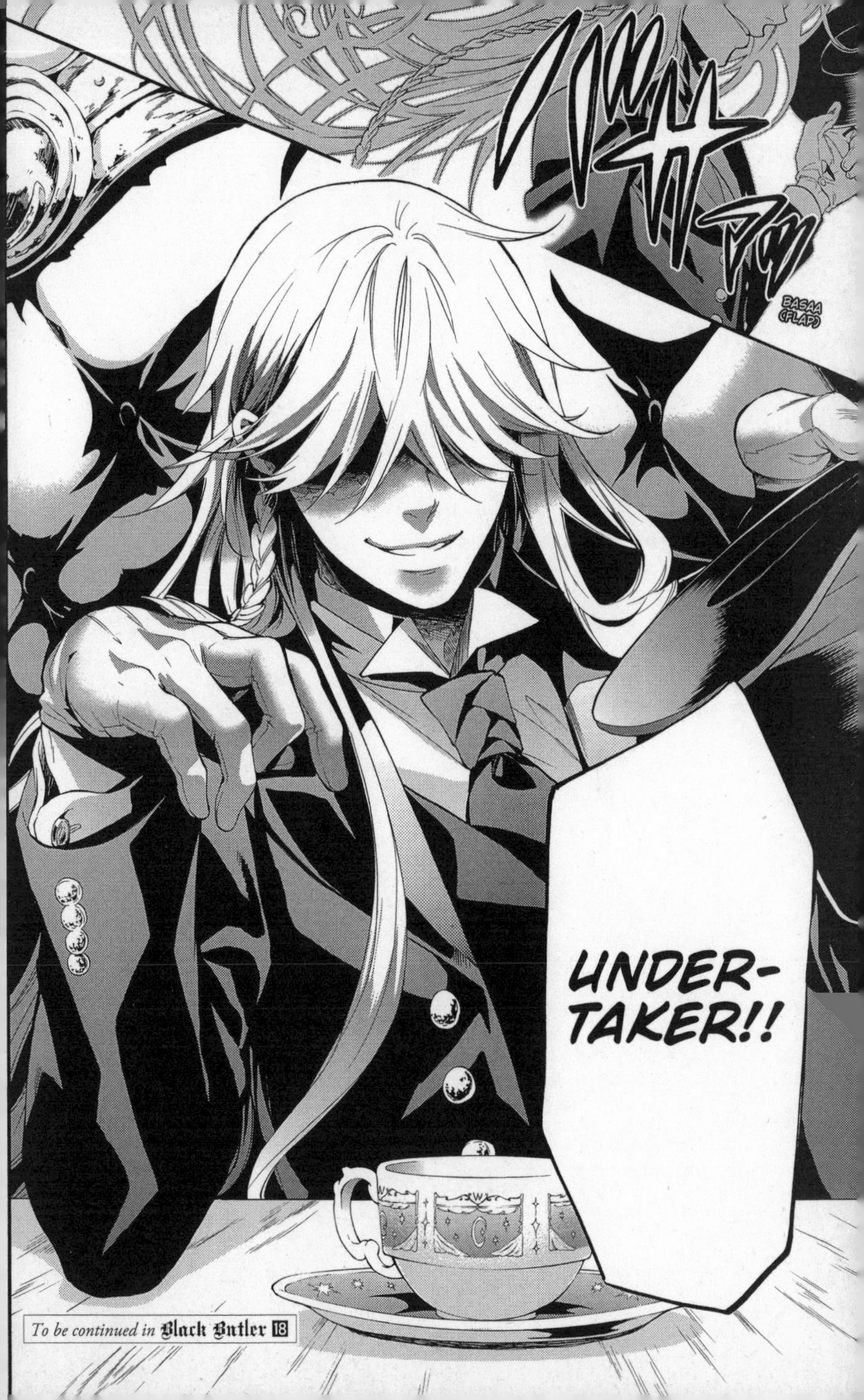
BASAA (FLAP)
UNDER-TAKER!!
To be continued in Black Butler 18

➤ Black Butler ◄
黒執事

❧

Downstairs

Wakana Haduki
7
Saito Torino
Tsuki Sorano
Chiaki Nagaoka
Asakura
*
Takeshi Kuma
*
Yana Toboso

❧

Adviser

Rico Murakami

Naoki Miyaji
(Japan Cricket Association)

Special thanks to You!

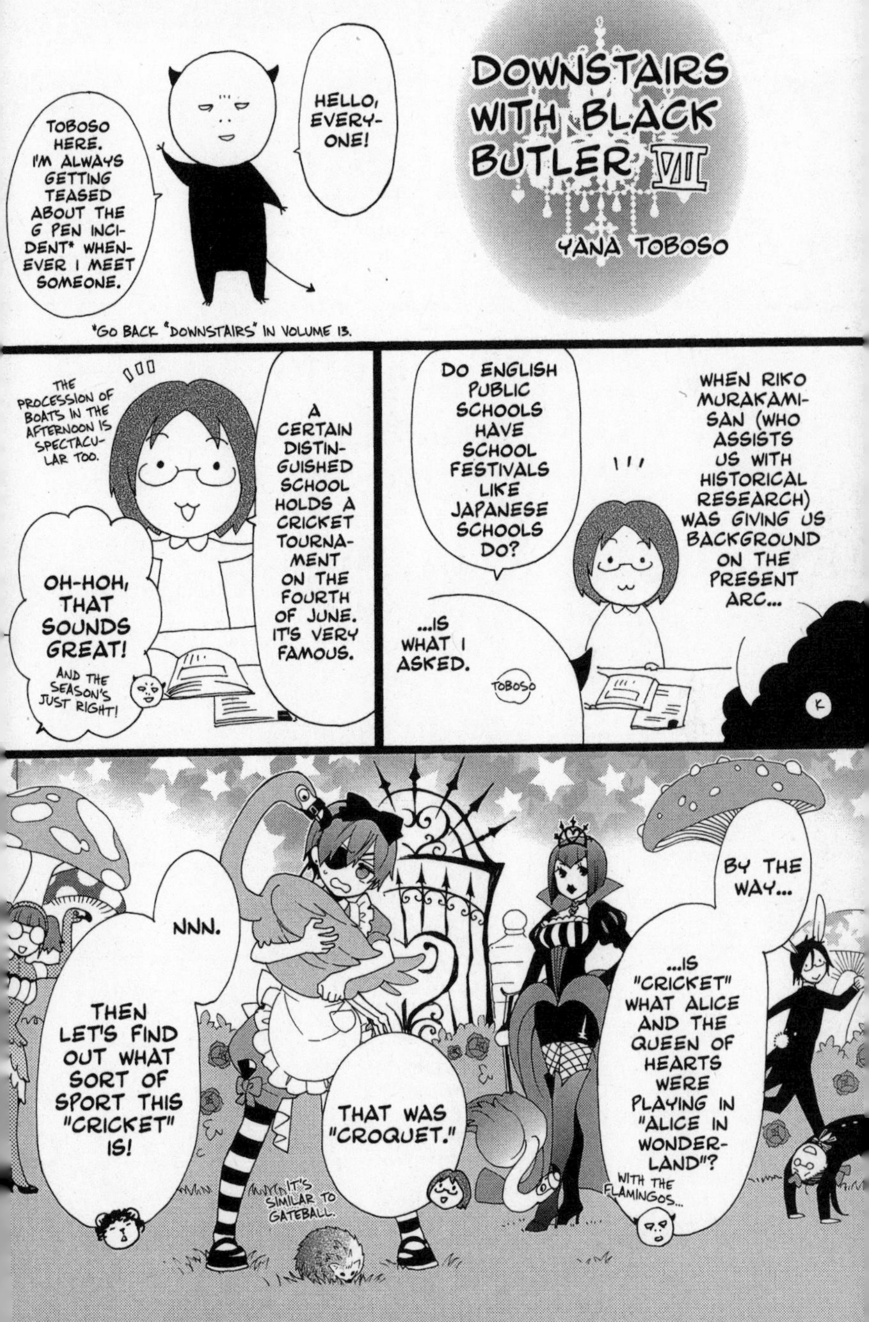
DOWNSTAIRS WITH BLACK BUTLER VII
YANA TOBOSO
HELLO, EVERYONE!
TOBOSO HERE. I'M ALWAYS GETTING TEASED ABOUT THE G PEN INCIDENT* WHENEVER I MEET SOMEONE.
*GO BACK "DOWNSTAIRS" IN VOLUME 13.
WHEN RIKO MURAKAMI-SAN (WHO ASSISTS US WITH HISTORICAL RESEARCH) WAS GIVING US BACKGROUND ON THE PRESENT ARC...
DO ENGLISH PUBLIC SCHOOLS HAVE SCHOOL FESTIVALS LIKE JAPANESE SCHOOLS DO?
...IS WHAT I ASKED.
TOBOSO
K
A CERTAIN DISTINGUISHED SCHOOL HOLDS A CRICKET TOURNAMENT ON THE FOURTH OF JUNE. IT'S VERY FAMOUS.
THE PROCESSION OF BOATS IN THE AFTERNOON IS SPECTACULAR TOO.
OH-HOH, THAT SOUNDS GREAT!
AND THE SEASON'S JUST RIGHT!
BY THE WAY...
...IS "CRICKET" WHAT ALICE AND THE QUEEN OF HEARTS WERE PLAYING IN "ALICE IN WONDERLAND"?
WITH THE FLAMINGOS...
THAT WAS "CROQUET."
IT'S SIMILAR TO GATEBALL.
NNN.
THEN LET'S FIND OUT WHAT SORT OF SPORT THIS "CRICKET" IS!

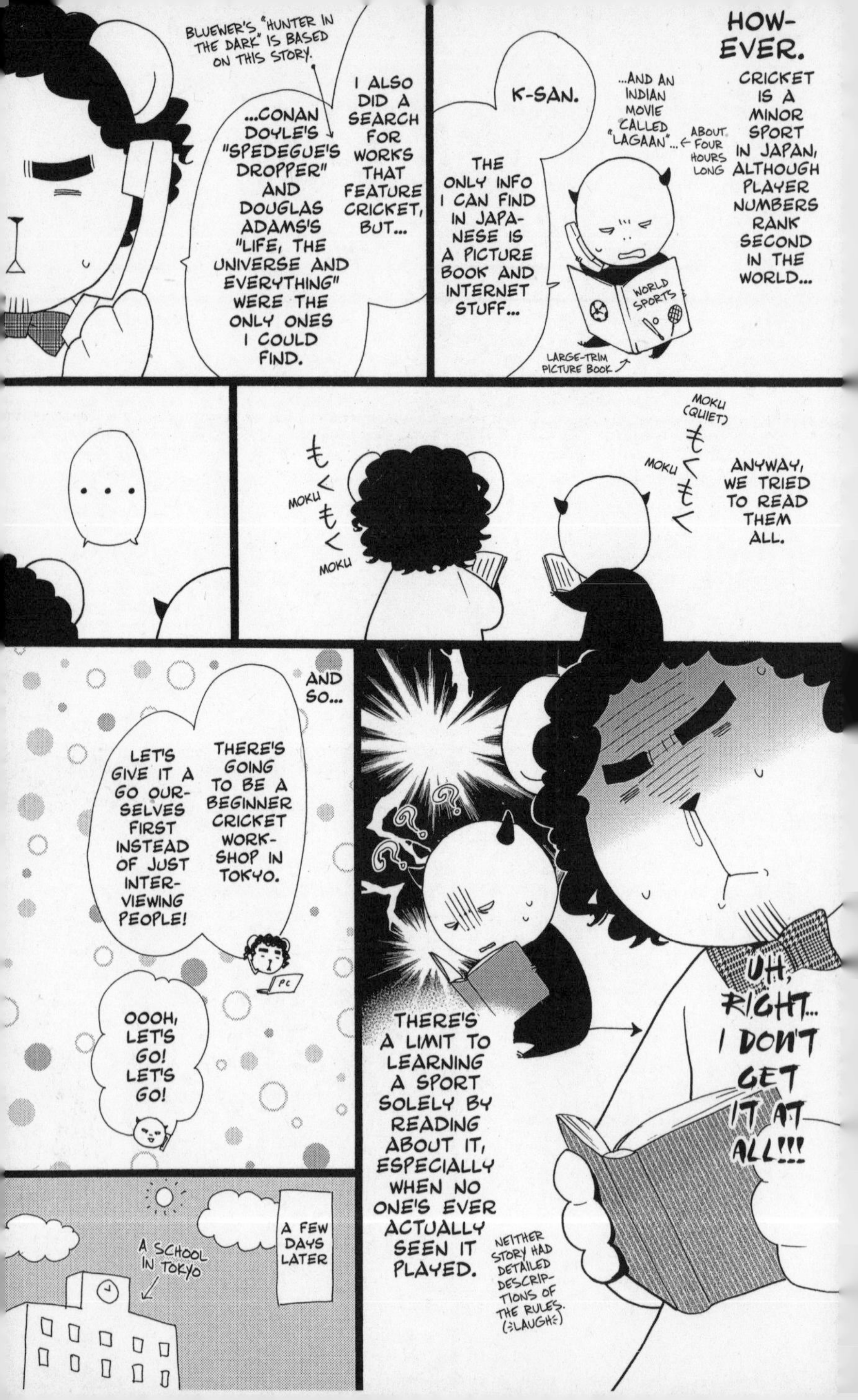
HOW-EVER.
CRICKET IS A MINOR SPORT IN JAPAN, ALTHOUGH PLAYER NUMBERS RANK SECOND IN THE WORLD...
ABOUT FOUR HOURS LONG
...AND AN INDIAN MOVIE CALLED "LAGAAN"...
K-SAN.
THE ONLY INFO I CAN FIND IN JAPANESE IS A PICTURE BOOK AND INTERNET STUFF...
WORLD SPORTS
LARGE-TRIM PICTURE BOOK
I ALSO DID A SEARCH FOR WORKS THAT FEATURE CRICKET, BUT...
BLUEWER'S "HUNTER IN THE DARK" IS BASED ON THIS STORY.
...CONAN DOYLE'S "SPEDEGUE'S DROPPER" AND DOUGLAS ADAMS'S "LIFE, THE UNIVERSE AND EVERYTHING" WERE THE ONLY ONES I COULD FIND.
ANYWAY, WE TRIED TO READ THEM ALL.
MOKU (QUIET)
もくもく
MOKU
もくもく
MOKU
MOKU
...
UH, RIGHT... I DON'T GET IT AT ALL!!!
THERE'S A LIMIT TO LEARNING A SPORT SOLELY BY READING ABOUT IT, ESPECIALLY WHEN NO ONE'S EVER ACTUALLY SEEN IT PLAYED.
NEITHER STORY HAD DETAILED DESCRIPTIONS OF THE RULES. (LAUGH)
AND SO...
THERE'S GOING TO BE A BEGINNER CRICKET WORKSHOP IN TOKYO.
LET'S GIVE IT A GO OURSELVES FIRST INSTEAD OF JUST INTERVIEWING PEOPLE!
PC
OOOH, LET'S GO! LET'S GO!
A FEW DAYS LATER
A SCHOOL IN TOKYO

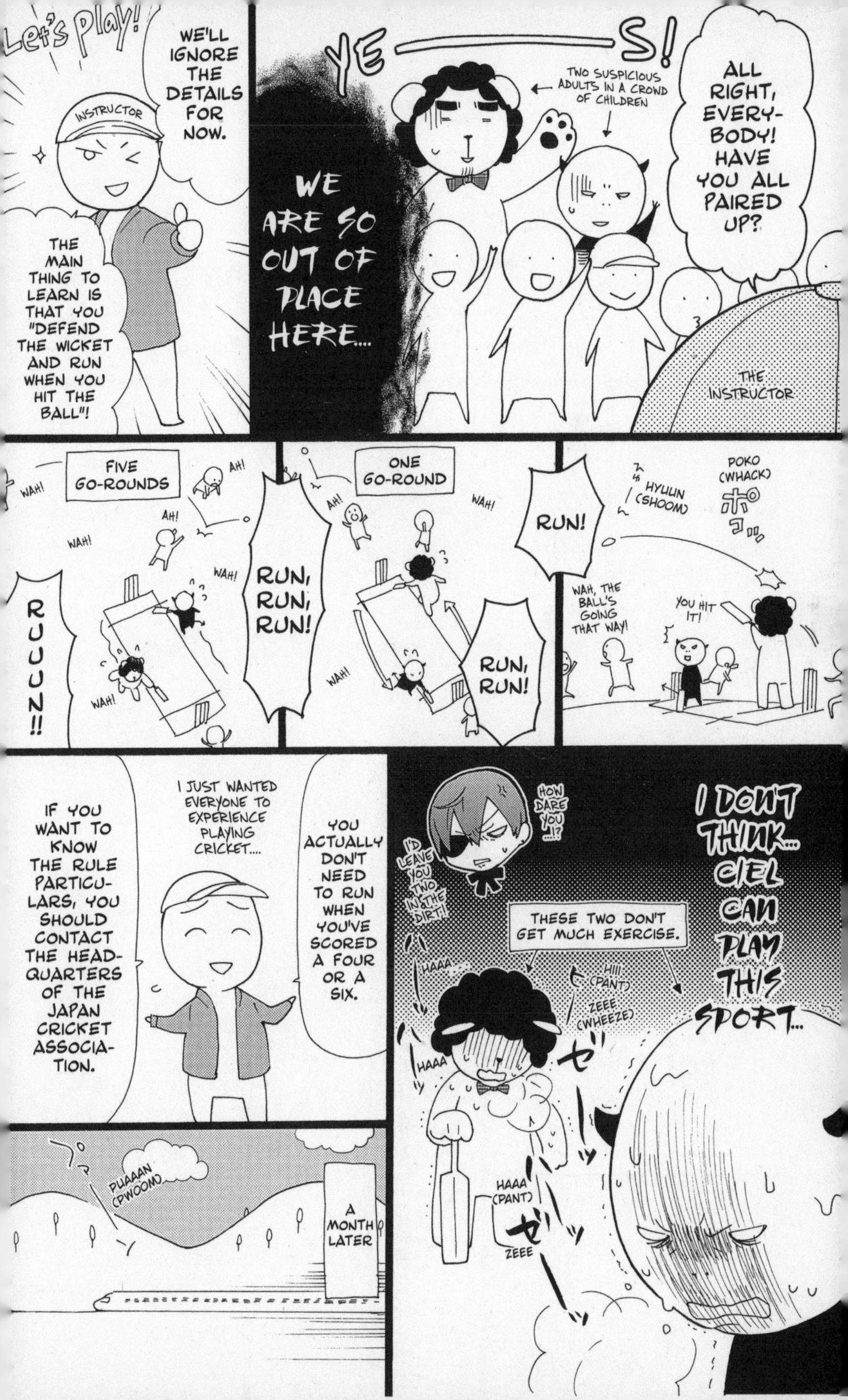
ALL RIGHT, EVERYBODY! HAVE YOU ALL PAIRED UP?
YE——S!
TWO SUSPICIOUS ADULTS IN A CROWD OF CHILDREN
WE ARE SO OUT OF PLACE HERE...
THE INSTRUCTOR
Let's play!
WE'LL IGNORE THE DETAILS FOR NOW.
INSTRUCTOR
THE MAIN THING TO LEARN IS THAT YOU "DEFEND THE WICKET AND RUN WHEN YOU HIT THE BALL"!
POKO (WHACK)
HYUUN (SHOOM)
RUN!
YOU HIT IT!
WAH, THE BALL'S GOING THAT WAY!
ONE GO-ROUND
WAH!
AH!
RUN, RUN, RUN!
RUN, RUN!
WAH!
FIVE GO-ROUNDS
AH!
WAH!
AH!
WAH!
WAH!
RUUUN!!
WAH!
I DON'T THINK... CIEL CAN PLAY THIS SPORT...
HOW DARE YOU...!?
I'D LEAVE YOU TWO IN THE DIRT!
THESE TWO DON'T GET MUCH EXERCISE.
HIII (PANT)
ZEEE (WHEEZE)
HAAA...
HAAA
HAAA (PANT)
ZEEE
YOU ACTUALLY DON'T NEED TO RUN WHEN YOU'VE SCORED A FOUR OR A SIX.
I JUST WANTED EVERYONE TO EXPERIENCE PLAYING CRICKET....
IF YOU WANT TO KNOW THE RULE PARTICULARS, YOU SHOULD CONTACT THE HEADQUARTERS OF THE JAPAN CRICKET ASSOCIATION.
A MONTH LATER
PUAAAN (PWOOM)

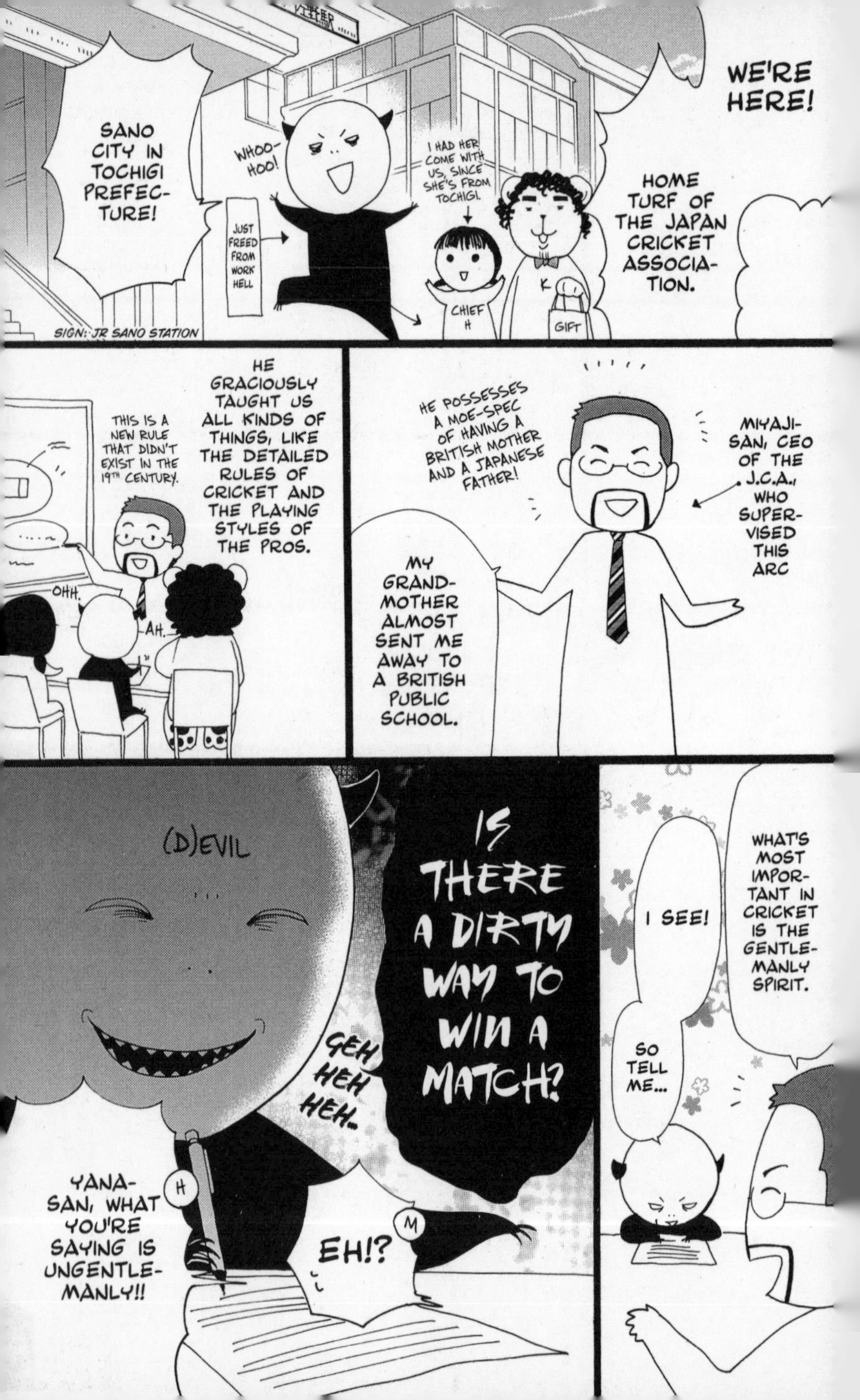

WE'RE HERE!
HOME TURF OF THE JAPAN CRICKET ASSOCIATION.
I HAD HER COME WITH US, SINCE SHE'S FROM TOCHIGI.
K
GIFT
CHIEF H
WHOO-HOO!
JUST FREED FROM WORK HELL
SANO CITY IN TOCHIGI PREFECTURE!
SIGN: JR SANO STATION
MIYAJI-SAN, CEO OF THE J.C.A., WHO SUPERVISED THIS ARC
HE POSSESSES A MOE-SPEC OF HAVING A BRITISH MOTHER AND A JAPANESE FATHER!
MY GRANDMOTHER ALMOST SENT ME AWAY TO A BRITISH PUBLIC SCHOOL.
HE GRACIOUSLY TAUGHT US ALL KINDS OF THINGS, LIKE THE DETAILED RULES OF CRICKET AND THE PLAYING STYLES OF THE PROS.
THIS IS A NEW RULE THAT DIDN'T EXIST IN THE 19TH CENTURY.
OHH.
AH.
WHAT'S MOST IMPORTANT IN CRICKET IS THE GENTLEMANLY SPIRIT.
I SEE!
SO TELL ME...
IS THERE A DIRTY WAY TO WIN A MATCH?
(D)EVIL
GEH HEH HEH..
M
EH!?
H
YANA-SAN, WHAT YOU'RE SAYING IS UNGENTLEMANLY!!

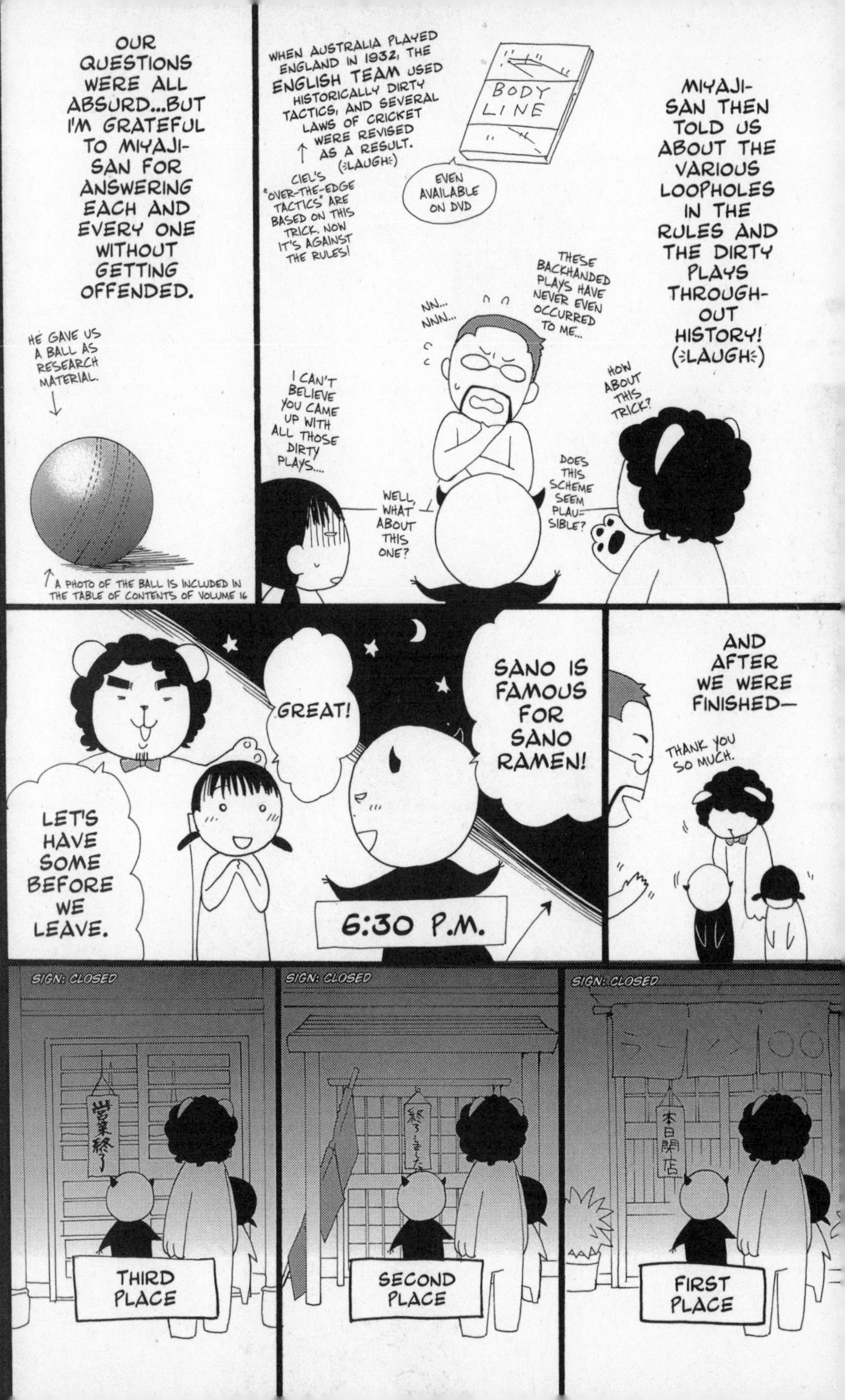
MIYAJI-SAN THEN TOLD US ABOUT THE VARIOUS LOOPHOLES IN THE RULES AND THE DIRTY PLAYS THROUGH-OUT HISTORY! (LAUGH)
WHEN AUSTRALIA PLAYED ENGLAND IN 1932, THE ENGLISH TEAM USED HISTORICALLY DIRTY TACTICS, AND SEVERAL LAWS OF CRICKET WERE REVISED AS A RESULT. (LAUGH)
BODY LINE
EVEN AVAILABLE ON DVD
CIEL'S "OVER-THE-EDGE TACTICS" ARE BASED ON THIS TRICK. NOW IT'S AGAINST THE RULES!
THESE BACKHANDED PLAYS HAVE NEVER EVEN OCCURRED TO ME...
NN... NNN...
HOW ABOUT THIS TRICK?
DOES THIS SCHEME SEEM PLAUSIBLE?
I CAN'T BELIEVE YOU CAME UP WITH ALL THOSE DIRTY PLAYS....
WELL, WHAT ABOUT THIS ONE?
OUR QUESTIONS WERE ALL ABSURD...BUT I'M GRATEFUL TO MIYAJI-SAN FOR ANSWERING EACH AND EVERY ONE WITHOUT GETTING OFFENDED.
HE GAVE US A BALL AS RESEARCH MATERIAL.
A PHOTO OF THE BALL IS INCLUDED IN THE TABLE OF CONTENTS OF VOLUME 16
AND AFTER WE WERE FINISHED—
THANK YOU SO MUCH.
SANO IS FAMOUS FOR SANO RAMEN!
GREAT!
6:30 P.M.
LET'S HAVE SOME BEFORE WE LEAVE.
SIGN: CLOSED
本日閉店
FIRST PLACE
SIGN: CLOSED
SECOND PLACE
SIGN: CLOSED
営業終了
THIRD PLACE

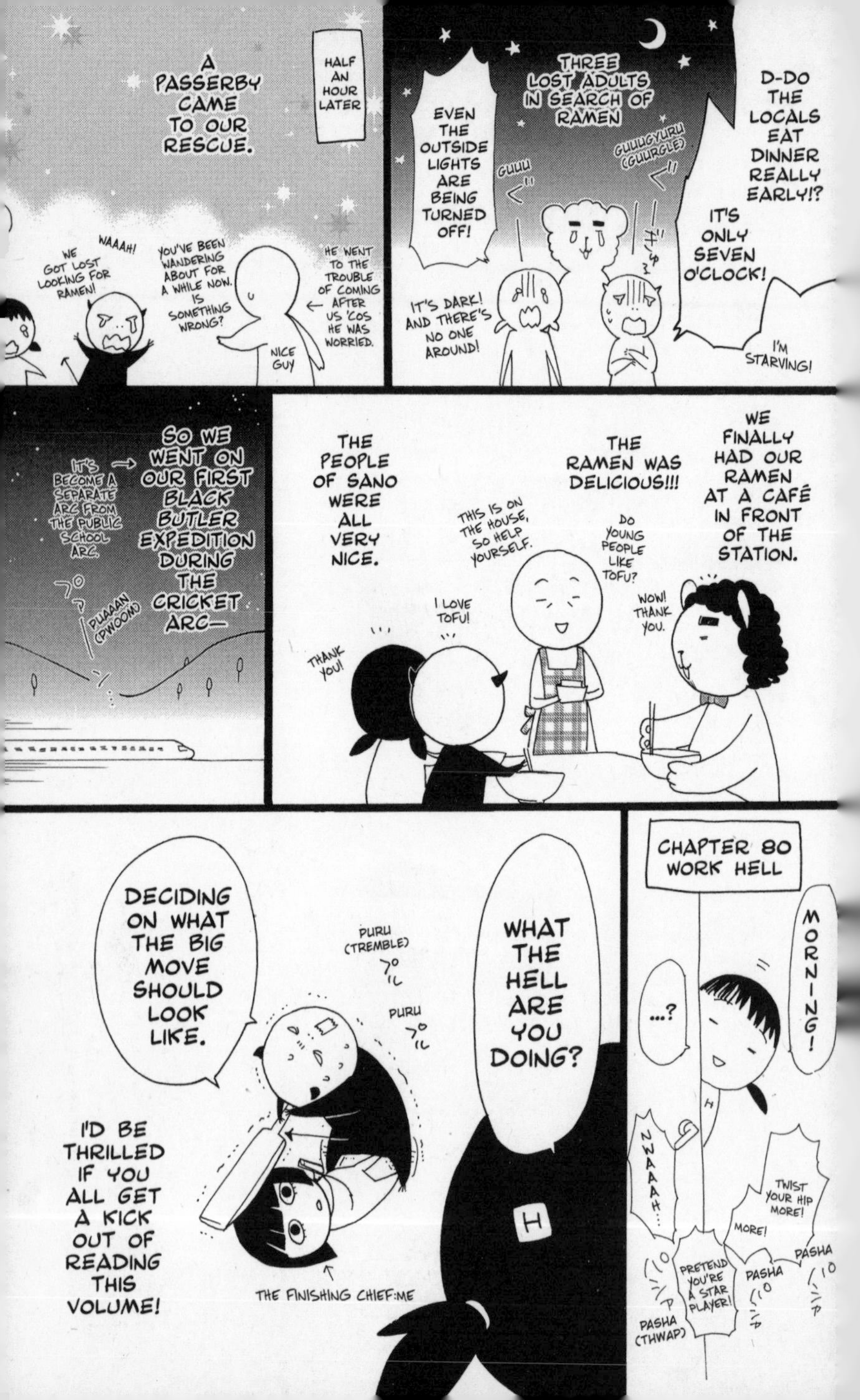

D-DO THE LOCALS EAT DINNER REALLY EARLY!?
IT'S ONLY SEVEN O'CLOCK!
THREE LOST ADULTS IN SEARCH OF RAMEN
GUUUGYURU (GUURGLE)
EVEN THE OUTSIDE LIGHTS ARE BEING TURNED OFF!
GUUU
I'M STARVING!
IT'S DARK! AND THERE'S NO ONE AROUND!
HALF AN HOUR LATER
A PASSERBY CAME TO OUR RESCUE.
HE WENT TO THE TROUBLE OF COMING AFTER US 'COS HE WAS WORRIED.
YOU'VE BEEN WANDERING ABOUT FOR A WHILE NOW. IS SOMETHING WRONG?
NICE GUY
WAAAH!
WE GOT LOST LOOKING FOR RAMEN!
WE FINALLY HAD OUR RAMEN AT A CAFÉ IN FRONT OF THE STATION.
THE RAMEN WAS DELICIOUS!!!
DO YOUNG PEOPLE LIKE TOFU?
THIS IS ON THE HOUSE, SO HELP YOURSELF.
THE PEOPLE OF SANO WERE ALL VERY NICE.
WOW! THANK YOU.
I LOVE TOFU!
THANK YOU!
SO WE WENT ON OUR FIRST BLACK BUTLER EXPEDITION DURING THE CRICKET ARC—
IT'S BECOME A SEPARATE ARC FROM THE PUBLIC SCHOOL ARC.
PUAAAN (PWOOM)
CHAPTER 80 WORK HELL
MORNING!
...?
NWAAAH...
TWIST YOUR HIP MORE!
MORE!
PASHA
PRETEND YOU'RE A STAR PLAYER!
PASHA
PASHA (THWAP)
WHAT THE HELL ARE YOU DOING?
PURU (TREMBLE)
PURU
DECIDING ON WHAT THE BIG MOVE SHOULD LOOK LIKE.
I'D BE THRILLED IF YOU ALL GET A KICK OUT OF READING THIS VOLUME!
THE FINISHING CHIEF: ME

Translation Notes

Inside Front and Back Covers
Segawa Express
The name of the despatch service is a parody of an actual Japanese parcel delivery service called Sagawa Express. The company's delivery people also wear striped shirts.

Summer gift
Ochuugen in Japanese, summer gifts, or Obon festival gifts, are given to express gratitude to the recipient, often work colleagues. The Obon festival is a Japanese national holiday held over three days every summer in thanks and remembrance of ancestors.

Page 50
Leg side vs. off side
Depending on whether the batsman is right- or left-handed, leg side, or on side, is the side of the cricket field to the rear of the batsman as he receives the ball. Off side is the side to which the batsman faces when receiving the ball.

Page 97
Eton Mess
This dessert takes its name from arguably the most famous English public school, Eton College, where it is served during the school's annual summer cricket match against Harrow School. The traditional English summer treat consists of strawberries, cream, and meringue.

Page 108
Fellows' Eyot
Fellows' Eyot is a field that runs along the River Thames and is a traditional spot from which to view the Procession of Boats at the famed Eton College.

Page 168
Fourth of June
Eton College has a huge gala on the Fourth of June, which includes the Procession of Boats. Like Weston, the school is opened to the students' family and friends during the celebrations.

Page 172
Gateball
A sport invented in Hokkaido, Japan in 1942, gateball is played in teams with mallets, much like croquet.

Page 176
Sano ramen
A unique fact about the ramen from Sano is that its noodles are prepared with green bamboo stalks instead of the standard rolling pins.

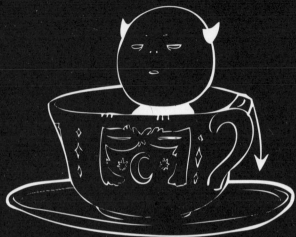

Yana Toboso

AUTHOR'S NOTE

Even if I were able to tell past me drawing Volume 1 that "*Black Butler* will some-day turn into a school manga," or "*Black Butler* will someday turn into a cricket manga," or "*Black Butler* will someday be made into a live-action movie," I'm pretty sure that past me will probably retort with "Nonsense!"

And that's the way with Volume 17.

BLACK BUTLER ⑰

YANA TOBOSO

Translation: Tomo Kimura • Lettering: Alexis Eckerman

KUROSHITSUJI Vol. 17 © 2013 Yana Toboso / SQUARE ENIX CO., LTD. All rights reserved. First published in Japan in 2013 by SQUARE ENIX CO., LTD. English translation rights arranged with SQUARE ENIX CO., LTD. and Yen Press, LLC through Tuttle-Mori Agency, Inc.

English translation © 2014 by SQUARE ENIX CO., LTD.

Yen Press
1290 Avenue of the Americas
New York, NY 10104

Visit us at yenpress.com
facebook.com/yenpress
twitter.com/yenpress
yenpress.tumblr.com
instagram.com/yenpress

First Yen Press Edition: July 2014

Yen Press is an imprint of Yen Press, LLC.
The Yen Press name and logo are trademarks of Yen Press, LLC.

ISBN: 978-0-316-37670-9

10 9 8 7

BVG

Printed in the United States of America

P9-ASL-799